WITHDRAWN

Borges and His Successors

Borges and His Successors

The Borgesian Impact on Literature and the Arts

Edited by *Edna Aizenberg*

University of Missouri Press

Columbia and London

Copyright © 1990 by
The Curators of the University of Missouri
University of Missouri Press, Columbia, Missouri 65211

Printed and bound in the United States of America

Library of Congress Cataloging-in-Publication Data

Borges and his successors : the Borgesian impact on literature and the arts /
edited by Edna Aizenberg.
    p. cm.
  Includes index.
  ISBN 0-8262-0712-X (alk. paper)
  1. Borges, Jorge Luis, 1899–1986—Criticism and interpretation. 2. Borges,
Jorge Luis, 1899–1986—Influence. 3. Literature—20th century—History and
criticism. I. Aizenberg, Edna.
PQ7797.B635Z63464   1989
868—dc20   89-4858
                                        CIP

♾™ This paper meets the requirements of the
American National Standard for Permanence of Paper
for Printed Library Materials, Z39.48, 1984.

Designer: Liz Fett
Typesetter: Connell-Zeko Type & Graphics
Printer: Thomson-Shore, Inc.
Binder: Thomson-Shore, Inc.
Type face: Garamond Light

5 4 3 2 1   94 93 92 91 90

Frontispiece: "Borges and Beppo" by Julie Méndez Ezcurra

Acompáñeme siempre su memoria;
Las otras cosas las dirá la gloria.

("Rafael Cansinos-Asséns")

Contents

Acknowledgments

Borges and His Successors is a collaborative effort, not only because it is a combination of essays written by colleagues as a labor of love, but also because many people gave of their time in numerous other ways. My colleagues Malva E. Filer, B. Bussell Thompson, and Christine de Lailhacar lent their ears, their advice, and their expertise; Christine also translated the essay by Françoise Collin. Suzanne Jill Levine helped me to obtain the piece by the late Emir Rodríguez Monegal. Lisa Block de Behar of *Revista Maldoror* in Montevideo gave me permission to translate and publish the piece, and Paul Budofsky assisted in the translation. Jorge Reiner of the Uruguayan Mission to the United Nations made room in the diplomatic pouch for correspondence to flow quickly between New York and Montevideo, facilitating our contacts.

Jacobo Kovadloff, former head of the Latin American Department at the Institute of Human Relations, American Jewish Committee, was responsible for the "discovery" of the Borges lectures on the Book of Job and Baruch Spinoza; the Instituto de Intercambio Cultural y Científico Argentino-Israelí in Buenos Aires through its Director of Culture, Inés Radunsky, gave me permission to translate and publish the material, which first appeared in their volume, *Conferencias*.

Jules Kirschenbaum and the Metropolitan Museum of Art in New York allowed me to reproduce *Dream of a Golem;* Richard Peña and The Film Center, School of the Art Institute of Chicago, made it possible for me to include the photos accompanying the article on Raúl Ruiz; *The CEA Critic* gave permission to include material previously published in the journal, in the article by Gerry O'Sullivan; and Cambridge University Press granted permission to reprint the article by Jaime Alazraki.

Pilar Martín, Rita Abelow, my parents, Zecharia and Rina Sitchin, and my sons, Salo and Gabriel Aizenberg, also deserve to be included in this list for their help; likewise Marymount Manhattan College for supporting my work and giving me the time to complete this project. Jane Lago, Pipp Letsky, and the staff at University of Missouri Press labored assiduously at my side in birthing this text.

As always, my husband, Joshua Aizenberg, did more than his share: to him and all the others, my sincerest thanks.

Abbreviations

References to frequently cited works by Borges are abbreviated as indicated below and are included parenthetically in the text.

AOS   *The Aleph and Other Stories 1933–1969.* Ed. and trans. Norman Thomas di Giovanni in collaboration with the author. New York: Dutton, 1970. Spanish edition used, *El Aleph.* 2d ed. Buenos Aires: Emecé, 1961.

BAR   *Borges, A Reader: A Selection from the Writings of Jorge Luis Borges.* Ed. Emir Rodríguez Monegal and Alastair Reid. New York: Dutton, 1981.

BEC   *Borges at Eighty: Conversations.* Ed. Willis Barnstone. Bloomington: Indiana University Press, 1982.

DBR   *Doctor Brodie's Report.* Trans. Norman Thomas di Giovanni in collaboration with the author. New York: Dutton, 1972.

Dt   *Dreamtigers.* Trans. Mildred Boyer and Harold Morland. Austin: University of Texas Press, 1964.

"Ep"   "Elementos de preceptiva." *Sur* 3:7 (1933): 158–61.

F   *Ficciones.* Ed. and intro. Anthony Kerrigan. New York: Grove, 1962.

F.S   *Ficciones.* Madrid: Alianza, 1978.

He   *Historia de la eternidad.* Buenos Aires: Emecé, 1953.

ia   *El idioma de los argentinos.* Buenos Aires: Gleizer, 1928.

L   *Labyrinths: Selected Stories and Other Writings.* Ed. Donald A. Yates and James E. Irby. Pref. André Maurois. New York: New Directions, 1964.

OC   *Obras completas.* Buenos Aires: Emecé, 1974.

OI   *Other Inquisitions 1937–1952.* Trans. Ruth L. C. Simms. Intro. James E. Irby. Austin: University of Texas Press, 1964. Spanish edition used, *Otras Inquisiciones (1937–1952).* Buenos Aires: Sur, 1952.

PA   *A Personal Anthology.* Ed. Anthony Kerrigan. New York: Grove, 1967.

SN   *Seven Nights*. Trans. Eliot Weinberger. Intro. Alastair Reid. New York: New Directions, 1984.

tme   *El tamaño de mi esperanza*. Buenos Aires: Proa, 1926.

UHI   *A Universal History of Infamy*. Trans. Norman Thomas di Giovanni. New York: Dutton, 1972. Spanish edition used, *Historia universal de la infamia*. Buenos Aires: Emecé, 1954.

Borges and His Successors

Edna Aizenberg ⸻

Introduction

A classic is that book which a nation, or a group of nations, or the passage of time has decided to read as if everything in its pages were deliberate, fated, profound as the cosmos, and open to endless interpretation. . . . Books like Job, the Divine Comedy, Macbeth *(and, for me, some of the Nordic sagas) contain the promise of long immortality—but we know nothing of the future, except that it will differ from the present.*

The episode belongs to a famous poem—that is to say, to a poem which has come to mean "all things to all men" (I Corinthians 9:22), since almost endless variations, versions, and perversions have been read into its pages.

I.

In these two quotations, one from his essay "Sobre los clásicos" (On the classics, *OC* 772–73), the other from "The Life of Tadeo Isidoro Cruz (1829–1874)" (published in *AOS*), Borges defines his sense of literary immortality. The essence of the definition is, in both contexts, the capacity for infinite interpretation. Reaching the status of a classic means being "all things to all men," that is, all things to all *readers.* Only what we can read as deliberate, fated, and profound, only what merits our rereading and rewriting, attains immortality; or rather, as Borges puts it in a characteristic vein, "contains the promise of *long* immortality," underlining in his comments the problematics of apprehending time; the transitoriness of our judgments, literary or otherwise; and the certainty of but one thing: change.

This volume is about some significant variations, versions, and perversions of Borges's work. These do not contain the pledge of eternal life for his writings; they do reveal a fervor and a loyalty on the part of multiple and diverse readers that may yet certify those works as classics. If we cannot foretell the future of Borges's books, we can say that he has already modified our literary past and present. For many, too, he is already a classic, "mentionable with the 'old masters' of twentieth-century fiction," perhaps with the old masters of fiction in general.[1] To

1. John Barth, "The Literature of Exhaustion," in *The Friday Book* (New York: Putnam's,

1

judge by the response to his inventions worldwide, by the impact of his "fragrant and delicate distillations"[2] on fictionmakers, critics, cineasts, and artists—in short, by his centrality to the contemporary imagination—Borges has quite possibly begun to meet the "test of time." The essays that follow attempt to outline how Borges's successors have initiated the process he sums up this way in "Sobre los clásicos": "The glory of a poet depends on the excitement or apathy of generations of anonymous men who put it to the test, in the solitude of their libraries" (*OC* 773).

In order to examine Borges's partial glory, the essential modes of his re-creation, the essays are grouped around registers important to Borges's successors. These registers are: Borges as a redefiner of national literatures; as a forerunner of a new critical idiom; as a dialogist with other writers; and as an inspirer of talents in the visual arts. The final section of the collection allows Borges to discuss two of his favorite precursors, in a circular movement appropriate to the author who has taught us the first principle of poetic influence—that each writer creates his own precursors.[3] In two little-known lectures, here translated into English for the first time, Borges expounds on the classic that heads his short list, the Book of Job, and its "uncertain, anonymous and immortal author" and on Baruch Spinoza, whose geometry of the divine, he claims, greatly influenced his literary artifices.

The intent of the volume, then, is to work toward a *global* idea of Borges's impact on the arts of our time, *global* being understood in its dual sense of "whole-earth" and "comprehensive." Total globalism is clearly impossible, but the endeavor has been to look at the international repercussions of Borges's oeuvre, and in connection with this to make known the insights of critics whose production is either unavailable or only partially available in English. The articles here have almost all been written or translated for this volume, so what the reader will find is not a collation of previously published pieces but, it is hoped, a combination of studies that expand the horizons of Borges's reception, either by taking up totally unexplored "successions" or by considering better known ones in a new light, through synthesis, updating, and revision. The aim of this *combinatoria* (some essays also fit into more than one register and could be moved around) is to provide a framework in which Borges's accomplishment is not fragmented by language or discipline, in which the spacious context facilitates a colloquy of

---

1984), 67. Throughout this essay, all translations from the Spanish are my own, unless otherwise noted.

   2. Peter Carey, letter to Robert Ross, October 22, 1986.

   3. Harold Bloom, *Yeats* (London: Oxford University Press, 1970), 4.

writing with writing: Borges with his successors, and his successors with each other.

II.

The opening essay by Ana María Barrenechea sets the tone for the collection by reassessing the interplay of the national and the universal in Borges's work. At a time when Argentines are engaged in a reevaluation of their national culture as part of the stocktaking of the postdictatorship years, Barrenechea revises the dichotomy between cosmopolitanism and localism that has been a hallmark of much criticism, especially Argentine criticism, on Borges—Borges, the simulacrum of an Argentine, the deracinated internationalist. Recalling that from his earliest days Borges advocated a "nativism conversant with the world and the I, with God and with death," she proceeds to outline some directions for an "investigation of Borges's achievement both in universalizing Argentine reality by giving it symbolic resonance and in making eternal, universal metaphors speak with a Latin American voice." Her focus becomes the manner in which Borges, through the transformational intricacies proper to his narrative practice—above all the strategy of repeating-with-variation paradigmatic events, situations, and images—forges a new idiom: an audacious cultural hybrid that can transfer the Crucifixion to an Argentine ranch, fuse Zeno's paradoxes with memories of the outlying neighborhoods of Buenos Aires, or incarnate God in gauchos and *guapos* (hoodlums). The forging of this idiom in an effort to meld "universal motifs with life on the periphery, in the far-off republics of the south," reflected Borges's program for national literary renewal, his search for means to produce "master works" worthy of Argentine reality. Shuttling between the abstract and the experiential, the "achronic" and the historical (Barrenechea notes how Borges subverts the European view of America as a continent without history), Borges in effect carried out his project; he created works whose innovative complexity not only belied any simple or simplistic polarizations but also served as models for successive writers.

This nuanced reading sets the tone for the volume, in its insistence on the universality of Borges's fiction and on framing this universality within a national setting. One of the registers in which Borges has been understood is in relation to his question: with what cultural materials does one reconstruct national literature? The next essay, by Marta Morello-Frosch, considers this problematics as it is taken up by the latest generation of Argentine authors—many still unfamiliar to English readers—whose "refashioning" of Borges, she argues, evinces the importance of his founding role in contemporary Argentine literary discourse. Dialoguing with their precursor, writers like Abelardo Castillo, Andrés Rivera, and Ricardo Piglia resort to his diction, metaphors, and language in an attempt to answer the question he posed half a century ago. Yet, as Morello-Frosch makes clear, their solutions—and political-ideological praxis—are quite different. Their emendation of the master is centered in historical contextualization, in not merely making the texts relevant to the latest, all-too-tragic phases of "life on the periphery" but in suggesting new events, situations, and images to define Argentine reality—for instance, the immigrant and proletarian in place of the gaucho and *guapo*. The philosophico-metaphysical speculations that Borges brought to Argentine literature are likewise historicized and presented as meditations on the country's past and future, on options for solutions to the hurts of the body politic.

Still, in reading Morello-Frosch along with Barrenechea, there is a sense that perhaps, to a greater extent than is readily visible, the ephebes recontextualize the contextualizer through tendencies already present in his literature. Barrenechea points out how, in his intricate weaving back and forth between the particular and the archetypal, Borges had—"long before Derrida"—deconstructed his own inclinations: keenly perceiving change and the eruption of the new (particularly on the American continent) despite his distrust of history, allowing an immigrant-narrator to demythologize one of his privileged myths, the myth of the neighborhood tough. This is not to deny the distance separating Borges's "Argentinizations" from those found in Rivera or Piglia; it is to reiterate what they and others perceive in him: the vastness of his texts, his continual challenging of accepted positions, and his lifelong interest in overcoming the "impoverishments" of the national milieu.

That Barrenechea converses easily with Morello-Frosch here is little wonder. What may be more astonishing is the facility with which her essay occupies common ground with Robert Ross's discussion of Borges and Australia's Peter Carey. It is no understatement to affirm that comparative studies of Australian and Argentine literature are practically nonexistent, though the two countries share more than the initial letters of their names and the use of *Austral* as a mark of identity. (Argentina's currency is called the *austral*.) In fact, their common latitude in the southern hemisphere, which gave—and gives—each of them analogous status as the ultima Thule of a European center, makes for significant parallels. One of these, in Ross's words, is the endeavor to find "the faraway continent's distinctive literary voice." Until recently, in Australia this endeavor has by and large resulted in stock accounts "of such seasoned matter as life in the bush, family struggles on a sheep or cattle station, mateship, pioneering, and the labor movement." Anyone who suggested a "metaphysical handling of Australian materials," who attempted to give universal-philosophical resonance to Australian themes, was dubbed "international," a label with generally the same connotations as the "cosmopolitanism" imputed to Borges. But it was precisely the Borgesian model (whose impact, in Carey's Borgesian turn of phrase, "cannot *not* be there") that helped young writers like himself break the mold of journalistic realism (as Borges did in Argentina). In so doing, their aim is not to elude their Australianness but to complicate and ironize it, to utilize the artistry of their prose and the pleasure of storytelling—another Borgesian lesson—as instruments for probing their environment: the problem of ideals that turn materialistic, or of existence as a lottery in a perpetual "Client State." These fictions are grounded in Australian reality, yet they engage perplexities unbound by geographical locales.

The homologies between Australia and Argentina, between the need to reconform a "peripheral" national literature along lines that avoid the extremes of conversational localism and exaggerated refinement, led to a fruitful "Australianization" of Borges. In the European metropolis, however, even in a country with an urgent need for cultural *aggiornamento,* different conditions resulted in an inimical reception for his work.

In "Borges in Germany," Rafael Gutiérrez Girardot recounts how the "complex political history of the German Federal Republic and the deep-seated prejudices against the New World" blocked a "balanced reception" and an "enriching Germanization" of Borges's writing. Among the factors he details is the paradoxical provincialism of those renewers of postwar German literature, who sought to break out of the isolation imposed by the Nazis' Teutonic nationalism, but who did so either by encouraging a Eurocentrism that had no room for "inferior," "exotic" literatures such as the Latin American or by promoting a kind of rustic German nativism that could tolerate Borgesian fabulations even less. Since they relegated the Latin American to the status of the barbaric and the natural (as opposed to the European and the historical), Germans could not accept that the continent had a fiction at once unique and universal. Consequently, Borges was accused of "adventurism"—an accusation he had fought in his own milieu when he took to task those "nationalists" who wanted to "limit the poetic exercise of . . . [the Argentine] mind to a few impoverished local themes" ("The Argentine Writer and Tradition," *L* 182).

Other aspects of West Germany's political situation and approach to Hispanic letters also obstructed Borges's Germanization. In a pointed analysis, Gutiérrez Girardot outlines how the blinders of both the left and the right forced an unproductive reading of Borges. For example, leftist intellectuals "conveniently forgot" that Borges had been pro-Jewish and anti-Nazi long before Germany's postwar antifascists and that, while he had taken actions favorable to the right, he had not hesitated to criticize it. Conservative thinkers such as Curtius, on the other hand, interested in presenting a European face and therefore positing such neophilological tenets as a European continuity based on unchanging characteristics and topoi, transformed Borges into a latter-day Góngora repeating the gestures of the seventeenth-century Spanish Baroque. As a result of these and attendant limitations, the critical response to Borges did not prepare the ground for him to "speak German"—to be assimilated in the land whose culture he so admired and to have an impact in Germany as he did elsewhere.

Though Gutiérrez Girardot's "negative" essay highlights how, in one European setting, Borges encountered multiple difficulties (which were not all strictly European), the following article by Françoise Collin illustrates quite another reaction on the Continent. In Germany the historical circumstances and the consequent strategies for reconstructing the national culture prevented Borges from becoming a useful contributor to the process of renewal. To the contrary, in France, Borges found propitious soil, with moves already present within French literature and criticism that would convert him into a crucial pivot in the turn to modernity.

Collin's piece synthesizes the French interest in Borges—with important implications beyond France—even as she calls for a fuller understanding of his oeuvre. Terming his work a "wellspring of reference" for France, she concentrates on one of his earliest and most attentive commentators, Maurice Blanchot, as the "revealing criterion" for the fact and mode of his reception and influence. Blanchot, Collin recalls, was among the eminent articulators of the crisis in literature's claim to figure reality, a crisis related to the developing critique of the West's metaphysics of representation. His "acclimatizing" of Borges—for example, his well-known text on Borges and the literary infinite—flowed from the affinities between Borges and his own thought: "Priority of the book or of language over the real . . . ; totality disintegrating into the infinite; beginning that absorbs itself in the rebeginning; collapse of the subject into the neuter." With Blanchot's and others' acclimatizations, Borges's fictional handling of these themes, his giving of narrative substance to the metaphysical, served as a stimulus for the *new* in France—*la nouvelle critique, le nouveau roman, la nouvelle vague,* and beyond.

But Collin's piece does more than review how Borges was instrumental in reorienting French letters; it proposes a renewed French reading of his writing, in a move that takes us back to Barrenechea's essay.

Collin's reorientation is, in effect, directed toward the Orient, taken as a metaphor for everything in Borges that "produces a lush efflorescence of images and sensations" and "focuses on the dazzling power of the finite, sole carrier of the infinite." French readers, she argues, have reduced Borges by ignoring the joyous eruption of the concrete and banal in his work, since his literature must be apprehended in a double register: the insurmountable tension of book and life, the interminable and the specific, soul and body. May we suggest that Collin's reinsertion of the tangible and corporal into the "French" Borges and her uncovering of the "grand and simple lover" within the "skeptical intellectual" constitute a feminist revision of the acceptation of his writing?

III.

Collin's study amplifies into another significant register of Borges's impact: his role in the constitution of a new critical idiom. The second group of essays investigates this register, which in the past has been looked at in a "preliminary" way.[4] In "Borges's Modernism and the New Critical Idiom," Jaime Alazraki reintroduces the Borgesian strategy of repetition-with-variants (the "diverse intonation of a few metaphors") as the linchpin of the most modern approaches to literary theory. Though he rejected modernity, Borges achieved it through his insistence that literature is a *syntactical* event in which images are not created but *reelaborated*. In positing—from the twenties and from distant Argentina—that the storyteller's craft lay in retelling essential stories in a style marked by "total efficiency and total invisibility," Borges reached conclusions similar to those of Russian Formalism (texts seen as evolving from other texts; change seen as change in form); he prefigured structuralism (literature as system; writing degree zero) and inspired intertextuality, the palimpsestic approach that Genette and others have made a center of poststructuralist criticism.

The end of Alazraki's overview becomes the beginning of Gerry O'Sullivan's essay on intertextuality in Borges and Foucault, whose *Les Mots et les choses* (we know from a direct and well-known admission) arose intertextually from a passage in "The Analytical Language of John Wilkins." The impossibility of classifying or representing the universe suggested by the passage (and by all Borges's writing) leads into Foucault's "heterotopia," the realm where tropes such as the library or archive undermine all "centrisms": "seamless canons; isolate and individual works of genius; linear chronologies; . . . ends and origins; . . .

4. Martin Stabb, "Introduction: Borges and His Critics," in *Jorge Luis Borges: An Annotated Primary and Secondary Bibliography,* ed. David William Foster (New York: Garland, 1984), xiii-xxxvi.

authoritative, authorial voices." The library/archive in Borges and
Foucault is not the place for stabilizing ingathering but for destabilizing
intertextual dispersion, where mimesis gives way to exteriority—books
dreaming other books, the enunciative domain referring to its own
surface. (The mirror, O'Sullivan reminds us, is another such Borgesian-
Foucauldian trope.)

The relationship that Alazraki and O'Sullivan draw between Borges
and the latest trends in European criticism should not, however, keep us
from remembering that Borges was also a key for the formation of a
new critical idiom on his own continent. Suzanne Jill Levine, in her
essay on Borges and Emir Rodríguez Monegal, pays tribute to one of
Borges's most persistent and perspicacious critics. Monegal was among
Borges's early readers, and the discovery was cataclysmic: Monegal
rejected the "old-fashioned" approaches characteristic of Spanish-language criticism and followed the writer he called the "wild man" on a
journey that postulated literature as a broad and "joyous epiphany"
centered in the linguistic act, a journey that short-circuited authors and
epochs; connected past and future in the interaction of writer and
reader, fiction and life; and prepared a space for the acceptance of an
innovative Latin American literature about to "boom."

But even as Borges "created" Monegal, the critic-son, Monegal "created" his mentor-father. Levine explains how Monegal used the rhetoric
of Borges's own Pierre Menard, the rhetoric of reading as writing,
to fashion a different (and not uncontroversial) Borges, whose readerly mask hid the violence with which he supplanted his father and became a writer. (This is developed most fully in Monegal's biography of
Borges.)[5]

Significantly, Monegal's final essay, published in English for the first
time in this volume, returns to this thematics even as it illustrates the
encyclopedism and contemporaneity of his criticism. Here, we see
Borges's biographer in a Borgesian mood: bringing together Borges
and Derrida, denying that Derrida influenced his reading of Borges,
peppering his analysis with personal anecdotes and humor, and leaving
us with an idiosyncratic but important updating of his pioneering survey of Borges and the new French criticism.[6] Making use of interlinear
reading—the operative principle of deconstruction—he pursues the
Borgesian markings that Derrida disperses in "La Pharmacie de Platon"
and other writings to seek the coincidences between the two "apothe-

5. Emir Rodríguez Monegal, *Jorge Luis Borges: A Literary Biography* (New York: Dutton, 1978).

6. Emir Rodríguez Monegal, "Borges and La Nouvelle Critique," *Diacritics* 2:2 (1972):
27–34.

caries," for whom the *pharmakon* of writing is both remedy and poison. In this "anachronistic" reading, Derrida and Plato—Derrida's reading of Plato's *Phaedrus*—are approached through Borges, as Monegal finds that the French philosopher produced the same "model": writing as symbolic parricide. Of course, Monegal himself was a practitioner of the subversive art, at once killing and immortalizing Borges, his mentor-father, through his rewritings—rewritings, let us not forget, that are masked as readings.

In the dialogue that Monegal establishes among himself, Derrida, and Borges, there appears another interlocutor, Paul de Man. Derrida's fellow in the deconstructive endeavor, de Man was among the first North American critics to comment on Borges in his influential article "A Modern Master." There he concluded that Borges's "stories are about the style in which they are written" and noted that this style (like the universe) is both binding and chaotic, continuous and infinite—"the ordering but dissolving act" that transforms the unity of the experience into the sum of its parts.[7]

Herman Rapaport's piece builds on this insight from the perspective of the later de Man, whose deconstruction of reading, like Borges's narratives, demonstrates the resistance to interpretive closure and readerly identification in rigorously systematic texts. Toward the end of his discussion Rapaport, deconstructively blending description with praxis, applies this resistance to the closure that claims to separate criticism from literature. If writing is inherently a critical deconstruction that capsizes all unities, then "such a deconstruction itself is always already literature." Borges's fictions and de Man's allegories of reading thus broach another moment of identification, but it is a moment that resists synthesis and stasis, that is itself realized as a limit: the undecidability that both de Man and Borges articulate.

The various strands that compose the register of Borges as forerunner of a new critical idiom come together in Christine de Lailhacar's examination of Umberto Eco's *The Name of the Rose* and its Borgesian codes. On the pages of Eco's book theory is infused, in a Borgesian way, with the drama of detective fiction as Eco's Lönnrot, William of Baskerville, faces his Scharlach, the blind librarian Jorge de Burgos, in a "semiotic showdown" not unrelated to the search for "the Name" in "Death and the Compass." In the inverted mirror of the novel—an inversion that is both parody and homage—de Burgos is the standard-bearer of dogma and monoreferential meaning, the enemy of the laugh-

---

7. Paul de Man, "A Modern Master," *New York Review of Books,* November 19, 1964, pp. 8–10 (9; 10). For more on this concept, see Barrenechea's and Collin's essays.

ter that dissolves all codes. (Compare here the birth of Foucault's heterotopia in the laughter produced by Borges's dissolving passage.) Baskerville, on the other hand, stands, in a Borgesian way, for the open
spirit (and the open work); for language as betrayal of meaning, as
confusion, explosion, dissemination; for one code leading to another,
as in an encyclopedia; for mirrors that do not reflect but disperse; for
treacherous books that are *pharmaka,* at once venom and cure.

IV.

The arbitrariness of all systematization suggested by the work of
Borges and his successors should not dissuade us from elaborat-
ing classifications. Eco as novelist cannot be separated from Eco as
semiotician, but here it is his function as a novelist that serves as the
link to an examination of Borges's dialogue with contemporary fictionmakers on three continents. They are: Italo Calvino in Italy; innovative North American writers such as John Barth, Robert Coover, and
others; and in Latin America Salvador Elizondo and Severo Sarduy. In
this section Borges is primarily elaborated as a precursor of what has
come to be known as postmodern fiction. The previous section was
essentially about Borges the forerunner of postmodern criticism. His
ficciones and *artificios* are read as seminal examples of the kind of
narrative writing that rejects representation as impossible and flaunts
itself as an artifice rehearsing that impossibility. Central characteristics of postmodern fiction—self-referential, intertextual writing;
parody of textual and epistemological conventions; the end of the
unified subject, which leads to the blurring of distinctions between
fact and fiction; the world seen as a hermeneutical realm of textual
meaning—are "recognized" in Borges, whose voice is echoed in a
variety of texts.

Thus Jerry Varsava, in his consideration of Calvino and Borges,
engages both as classicists who contest the notion of the "new" and find
their strength in revitalizing old problems (see also Alazraki's essay).
Their answer to the problem of creative limits is irony and parasitism,
but irony and parasitism that—ironically—revitalize the host. (J. Hillis
Miller's formulations lurk in the background.)[8]

Similar ideas are developed by Geoffrey Green, whose meditation
on reading Borges opens onto a panorama of Borgesian "images" found
in current North American authors—the instability of generic conventions (Barth's "used-upness of forms"), the inability of texts to embody
meaning, and the confusion of dream and reality. He discusses not only

8. J. Hillis Miller, "The Critic as Host," in Harold Bloom et al., *Deconstruction and Criticism* (New York: Seabury, 1979), 217–53.

Borges's most celebrated successors, those who in the sixties inaugurated what Morris Dickstein called the "Borgesian phase" of North American fiction, but also more recent creators: R. M. Koster, Edmond Whittemore, Celia Gittelson, Rebecca Goldstein. At a time when fiction in the United States has entered a period of synthesis, when the lessons learned from experimentalist patriarchs like Borges are being meshed with a renewed concern with reality, Green finds the master's voice "ingrained within," so much a part of contemporary fiction that we find him everywhere.[9]

From Europe and North America, the examination of Borges, the experimentalist guru, moves back to Latin America, where Malva Filer examines Borges as the father of the modern Spanish American novel. Carlos Fuentes, in *La nueva novela hispanoamericana,* had characterized "the final meaning of Borges's prose" as the constitution of a "new Latin American language which . . . reveals the lie, the submission, and the deceit of what traditionally was taken for 'language' among us."[10] Filer's study expands on Fuentes's characterization, as she looks at the Mexican Salvador Elizondo and the Cuban Severo Sarduy, in whom Borges's "postulation of a nonreferential and self-reflective writing" and "concept of writing as the deconstruction of the repertoire of universal philosophy and culture" are taken to their ultimate consequences. Her contribution paints a portrait of the artist as constituted by the Boom writers of the sixties. For Fuentes, Cortázar, García Márquez, Elizondo, Sarduy, and others, what mattered was what García Márquez termed Borges's verbal "violin," since their hallmark was formal innovation, and more than one of them found Borges's Americanist concerns nonexistent or sorely lacking. It is interesting that in post-Boom literature, where national-historical preoccupations have intensified and language is seen less as a doubling back on language, Borges has been reread in a national vein. (Barrenechea's and Morello-Frosch's essays attest to that.) Oddly, as Morello-Frosch remarks, it is Borges as the proposer of national literary renovation who has become the cultural ancestor of younger writers in Argentina, rather than Cortázar, who is closer to them ideologically. What has changed is not

9. Significantly, Barth used Borges to give impetus to the "Borgesian phase" of North American fiction—the way to overcome the exhaustion of literary forms is to rehearse these forms in a Pierre Menardian way ("The Literature of Exhaustion," in *The Friday Book,* 62–76). More recently, Barth has cited Borges in his argument for the synthetic approach: literature can never be exhausted because it is read and written differently in different ages, and this period calls for a different reading—the "transcension" of present and past, irrealism and realism ("The Literature of Replenishment," in *The Friday Book,* 193–206).

10. Carlos Fuentes, *La nueva novela hispanoamericana* (Mexico: Joaquín Mortiz, 1969), 26.

Borges, but the necessities of Borges's successors: each writer *creates* his own precursors.

V.

While Borges has served as the forerunner mostly of writers and critics, other arts have also felt his impact. One is the cinema. Richard Peña writes that Borges was a "rare example of a major Latin American intellectual figure working before 1960 who showed any real interest" in the new medium, producing a significant film criticism and claiming cinematic influence on his writing. His stories, in turn, have been considered sources of inspiration for European filmmakers, particularly in the French New Wave, with films such as *L'Année dernière à Marienbad, Paris nous appartient,* and *Alphaville* "quoting" Borgesian texts and motifs. More in-depth work remains to be done in this field, however, for Borges's relation to recent Latin American filmmakers who are aware of his concerns has scarcely been explored. Peña undertakes to show how Raúl Ruiz, a Chilean exiled in France and one of the most important cineasts working today, approaches certain problems of cinematic narration and representation that Borges reflected upon in the thirties and forties—how stories are told, the relationship of the characters to the narrative process, and the role of the viewer. Such (postmodern) Borgesian issues as the difficulty of telling a story (since images are infinitely meaningful) or the instability of all ordering principles (artist, narrator) are engaged by Ruiz, whose encyclopedism and skepticism bring to the screen what Borges brought to literature.

Affinities with the world Borges creates are similarly found in the work of the North American painter Jules Kirschenbaum. His *Dream of a Golem* (1980–1981), part of the collection of twentieth-century art at the Metropolitan Museum of Art in New York, is a version of "The Circular Ruins." It invokes the artist's or golem-maker's (vain) craving for the transcendental power of creative invention while it also attempts to fashion an autonomous, carefully shaped imaginative world. The painting shows "Kirschenbaum" standing near a still-life filled with *vanitas* objects—bones, skulls, a mirror—and holding a bottle beside the words *en-sof* (Hebrew for *infinite*), a cabalistic term referring to God as the source of creation. To the upper left is a phylactery (worn by Jews on the forehead and arm during prayer) that is inscribed with *emeth* (Hebrew for *truth*), and the same inscription is placed on the forehead of the clay golem figure in order to give it life. The center of the picture contains a quotation from Borges's fiction, another contemporary interpretation of the legend of the golem, which in the Cabala

represented the human desire to penetrate or emulate the divine mysteries of creation.[11]

Kirschenbaum's remarks about himself and his art have a decidedly
Borgesian ring:

> I don't really have much to say about how I see myself in the contemporary
> art scene. I don't seem to fit anywhere in particular. Some sort of realism, I
> suppose. I consciously avoid making marks or forms that would connect
> me to any modern style, and I almost never go to contemporary exhibi-
> tions. My interests are in older art. There is everything to learn from early
> painting. Unamuno says somewhere that "we all lead into the future even if
> we walk backwards." You can't avoid being contemporary no matter what
> you do. He also says that "the only reactionaries are those who find them-
> selves at home in the present." By these standards I'm no reactionary.[12]

Like Borges, Kirschenbaum turns away from the pursuit of the moment
and achieves contemporaneity—the complex and problematic "realism" today seen as a significant alternative to abstraction—by looking
to the past. His paintings cite this past in a variety of ways, from the
medium in which many are executed (egg tempera, an older type of
paint); to the literary quotations they incorporate (as in *Dream of a
Golem*); to their connections with the religious iconography of late
Medieval and Renaissance art, alchemy, and the Cabala. The result of
such "parasitism" is hardly a "realism" in the mimetic sense: Kirschenbaum is opposed to the notion of "illustrating" anything, and his studio, an intellectual realm much in the mold of Borges's library/archive,
is a predominant theme in his work. Rather, Kirschenbaum uses fragments of the real world, including objects created by the imagination, as
a catalyst for the evocation of the inward world of fantasy, metaphysics,
and religion. In a Borgesian manner, he explores the *artistic* possibilities of premodern and irrational transcendentalisms less for their
claims to truth than for their power for "immanent revelation" and their
allusion to a spiritual-ethical dimension. For Kirschenbaum as for
Borges, the creative process, when undertaken as what Valéry terms a
"resistance to the facile," becomes an exemplary destiny, where virtue
can be manifested and the mundane and transitory can be overcome—
at least temporarily.[13]

---

11. Edna Aizenberg, *The Aleph Weaver: Biblical, Kabbalistic and Judaic Elements in
Borges* (Potomac, Md.: Scripta Humanistica, 1984), and Neal Benezra, "Beyond Realism: The
Work of Jules Kirschenbaum," *Jules Kirschenbaum: Painting Survey, 1950–1983* (Des
Moines: Des Moines Art Center, 1983).

12. Jules Kirschenbaum, letter to author, August 8, 1987.

13. The reference to Valéry is found in Kirschenbaum's painting *Meditations on Death:
Paul Valéry,* 1972. Borges's homage to the writer is the essay "Valéry as Symbol" (*L* 197–98).

VI.

In creating Borges as his "cabalistic" precursor, Kirschenbaum recognizes the importance of "the archaic mysteries of the Cabala" for Borges's innovativeness. Indeed, Borges's vindication of Jewish mysticism, particularly of the mystics' hermeneutic techniques in approaching the language of Scripture, served as a touchstone not only for his writing but also for some of the latest trends in literary theory. My piece on Borges and the Hebraism of Derrida, Hartman, and Bloom comments on this development, studying how his secularization of such sacred notions as the deification of the Writ, the Torah as a text completed by *midrash* (Hebrew for *commentary*), and tradition as a mask for revisionism helped prepare the text milieu in which these critics operate. The article precedes Borges's two Hebraist lectures, introduced separately, whose content likewise points to a chief axis of his literature: the aesthetic use of religious and philosophical ideas. In this way the volume about Borges and his successors does not end but is absorbed by the sources, those sources that can be "all things to all men," as in some measure can Borges's literature.

I
Redefining National Literatures

Ana María Barrenechea

On the Diverse (South American) Intonation of Some (Universal) Metaphors

Borges's earliest essay collections, *Inquisiciones* (Inquisitions, 1925) and *El tamaño de mi esperanza* (The measure of my hope, 1926), set forth a program that was, as he put it, a "profession of literary faith" for his generation. In these books—despite occasional fluctuations, restrictions, or exclusions—Borges recognized that certain men (Rosas, Irigoyen) and certain genres or texts (the tango, *Martín Fierro*) had become enduring symbols of Argentina.[1] Still, he noted, Argentines had not as yet produced masterworks worthy of the reality they had to live.

For Borges, the measure of a writer's greatness lay in his ability to create enduring symbols; but it also lay in his capacity to shape lifelike characters. To put it succinctly: it lay in the writer's ability to create paper beings that were lifelike yet could symbolize destinies. An admirer of Quevedo, Borges argued in the introduction to an anthology of his work (later included in *Other Inquisitions*) that this writer's "partial glory," his inability to become an author of universal fame, was due to the fact that "he had not found a symbol that captures the popular imagination" (*OI* 36).

In his youth, at a time when he had grandiose visions for himself and his generation, Borges was content with nothing less than the power of the "demi-god, the angel whose works could change the world" in order to give poetic expression to Buenos Aires.[2] In *El tamaño de mi esperanza,* he asserted that the pampa was the "most appropriate (*llevadero*) symbol" for the countryside, and he spoke of the gaucho as the "human expression" of this "consummate symbol" (*tme* 21). He also spoke of a symbol that was still taking shape, a "half-baked symbol," as he called it: the *orilla* or suburb, the outlying, marginal neighborhood. The language Borges uses in the essay "La pampa y el subur-

---

1. Rosas ruled Argentina for most of the period between 1829 and 1852; Irigoyen was president from 1916 to 1922 and from 1928 to 1930. *Martín Fierro* by José Hernández, published in 1872, is the masterwork of the gauchesque genre, poetry written about the gaucho in forms that attempted to reproduce his language and traditions.

2. Jorge Luis Borges, *Inquisiciones* (Buenos Aires: Proa, 1925), 28.

bio son dioses" (The pampa and the suburb are gods), from which I have been quoting, is revealing: "The suburb and the pampa . . . two presences of God, two *realities*. . . . Both already have their *legend*. . . . I would like to write each with a capital letter to better underline its *archetypal quality,* the quality of something *not subject to the vagaries of time*" (*tme* 18, my emphasis). This is a paradoxical text, where reality is transformed into literature, and earthly objects become platonic archetypes.

Simultaneously, however, Borges vindicates another characteristic of poetry, which is in apparent contradiction to its symbolic function: the power to insinuate "souls . . . idiosyncrasies . . . destinies" (*tme* 147). This power explains poetry's hold on us, despite its frequent awkwardness and inevitable tentativeness. Although he begins his essay "Profesión de fe literaria" (A profession of literary faith) by affirming that "all literature is autobiographical," he makes clear that what is expressed may not be a direct revelation of the writer's soul (*tme* 146). The autobiographical may remain hidden, "like a heart that beats from the depths," only to blossom forth *indirectly,* through those things that "are poetic merely by implying destinies: the map of a city, a rosary, the names of two sisters" (*tme* 149, 150). We see here a form of thinking typical of Borges, an oblique mode in which what is lost is recouped and what is effaced is made to reappear; a mode lived in the shuttle space between the concrete and the abstract, the abstract and the experiential; a mode that inverts these terms, manipulating their intermediate stages—for example, iconic signs like maps or names—weaving a dense web, rich in allusions.

"El tamaño de mi esperanza," the leading essay in the collection by the same name, ends with a declaration of extreme poverty:

> This land has not produced a single mystic or metaphysician nor engendered a single person who can feel or understand life! . . . There are no legends in this land, and not a single ghost haunts our streets. . . . Our lived reality is great and our mental reality impoverished. No idea has been born here that can compare with my Buenos Aires. . . . For Buenos Aires is already more a country than a city, and one must find the poetry and music and painting and religion and metaphysics suited to its greatness. (*tme* 7–9)

Thus, from his earliest days, Borges advocated a "nativism conversant with the world and the I, with God and with death" (*tme* 10).

Despite this posture, the aggressive style of Borges's formative years could neither overcome the tension between conversational localism and exaggerated refinement nor serve as a medium for the creation of stories that effectively melded universal motifs with life on the periphery, in the far-off republics of the south. Only at a later stage was Borges able to impose his personal vision on his material, showing his readers that a "wild, mulatto" version of God could be incarnated in smugglers, hoodlums, or gauchos, as in "Funes the Memorious" (published in *L*) and "The Dead Man" (in *AOS*); that Zeno's paradoxes could be fused with his memories of the desolate outlying neighborhoods of Buenos Aires, the skyscrapers that dominate the estuary of the River Plate, and the Adrogue Hotel of his childhood summers to create the nameless city of "Death and the Compass" (*L*); or that Pier Damiani's theologico-philosophical speculations could be justified by an obscure farmhand's battle charge at Masoller, in an obscure factional war, in the obscure republic of Uruguay, in "The Other Death" (*AOS*).

My intent here is not to produce an exhaustive study of the subject under consideration. Borges's closing remark in "Pascal's Sphere" (which reiterates the essay's opening sentence with only minor variation) is pertinent in this regard: "Perhaps universal history is the history of the *diverse intonation* of a few metaphors" (*OI* 9, my emphasis). If Borges's texts are essential metaphors, repeated in poems, stories, and essays, as are, by his own account, Odysseus's journeys and the Crucifixion, then it is clear that he has expressed them in ways that have renewed contemporary literature: in Borges we read these metaphors as if we were reading them for the first time.[3]

What I want to do, then, is outline some possible directions for an investigation of Borges's achievement both in universalizing Argentine reality by giving it symbolic resonance and in making eternal, universal metaphors speak with a Latin American voice. Such an investigation would entail an analysis of the ways in which these metaphors are simultaneously handled on a number of levels. One is language, a topic I have dealt with elsewhere.[4] In this essay, I would like to focus on

3. The reference to these metaphors appears not in one of Borges's essays but in the story "The Gospel According to Mark," in *Doctor Brodie's Report*. There Borges says of the protagonist, Espinosa: "It also occurred to him that the generations of men, throughout recorded time, have always told and retold two stories—that of a lost ship which searches the Mediterranean seas for a dearly beloved island, and that of a god who is crucified on Golgotha" (*DBR* 19). The fiction gives narrative substance to a concern found repeatedly in Borges's essays: the importance of eternal legends, metaphors, or symbols. Here, however, this concern is expressed through the mind of the protagonist who ambiguously combines the imitation of Christ with the lessons in elocution learned at "the English school in Ramos Mejía" (*DBR* 15).

4. For Borges's ideas on language, see my essay "Borges y el lenguaje," *Nueva Revista de Filología Hispánica* 7 (1953): 551-65. The final part of this essay is included in chap. 3 of my *La expresión de la irrealidad en la obra de Jorge Luis Borges* (Mexico City: El Colegio de México, 1957; 2d ed., Buenos Aires: Paidós, 1967; expanded ed., Buenos Aires: Centro Editor de América Latina, 1984), as well as in chap. 4 of my *Borges the Labyrinth Maker*, trans. and ed. Robert Lima (New York: New York University Press, 1965). The first part of this essay appears as an appendix, "Borges y el idioma de los argentinos," in the second and expanded editions of *La expresión de la irrealidad*.

other areas, starting with Borges's characteristic repetition of events, situations, and actions occurring in different places and times to different people.

There are occasions when this type of repetition can be found in a single text. In "Story of the Warrior and the Captive" (*L*) for example, the birth of a new Italian culture that is neither barbarian nor Roman is the inverted mirror image of the birth of another new culture on the southern frontier of the South American continent.[5] The single story contained in the two apparently opposed narrations is the mechanism through which the universal and the American are harmonized. Other fictions achieve a similar effect by the insertion of a narrative cell that miniaturizes, *en abîme,* the overall structure of the story. Still other texts create this unity through the use of sinuous, interwoven lines, as in the poem "The Cyclical Night" (*BAR*).

But in many instances the repetition of certain events, whether inverted or not, is found in different texts and can only be perceived within the macrostructure of Borges's entire oeuvre by those familiar with his work. One example that comes to mind is the old man who witnesses the final judgment in "The Man on the Threshold" (*AOS*), a figure repeated in the old gaucho who hands the knife to Dahlmann, the protagonist of "The South" (*F*). In the first story Borges gives the following description of this character:

> At my feet, motionless as an object, an old, old man squatted on the threshold. I'll tell what he was like, for he is an essential part of the story. His many years had worn him down and polished him as smooth as water polishes a stone, or as the generations of men polish a sentence. . . . I felt, on speaking these words, the pointlessness of questioning this old man for whom the present was hardly more than a dim rumor. (*AOS* 131–32)

The description is repeated almost verbatim in "The South": "On the floor, and hanging on to the bar, squatted an old man, immobile as an object. His years had reduced and polished him as water does a stone or the generations of man do a sentence. He was dark, dried up, diminutive, and seemed outside time, situated in eternity" (*F* 172). What is modified is the locale—from a house in India (which, Borges confesses, is itself a transformation of "the sudden and recurring glimpse into a deep set of corridors and patios of a tenement house around the corner from Paraná Street, in Buenos Aires" [*AOS* 274]) to the Argentine pampa. What is also varied is the man's clothing—a ragged tunic and turban in the first case; a kerchief, poncho, *chiripá,* and colt boots in the

---

5. Arturo Echavarría, " 'Historia del guerrero y de la cautiva' de Borges: tentativa de co-dificación de un lenguaje 'americano,' " *Actas del VI Congreso Internacional de Hispanistas* (Toronto: Department of Spanish and Portuguese, University of Toronto, 1980), 222–24.

second. (This gaucho dress is intentionally archaic or anachronistic, that is, *a-chronic*.) But what is invariable is the comparison to a stone or a sentence, a comparison coined by Borges to underline the man's legendary old age.

In the Indian setting, the old man, a symbol of the divinity or of destiny, is untouched by the vicissitudes of life. This changes when he is placed in a Latin American environment. He still views humanity *sub specie aeternitatis,* but he is now touched by something we find in many of Borges's texts: the sense that we have hidden destinies blind as the blood we inherit. To quote from "The South": "From a corner of the room, the old ecstatic gaucho—in whom Dahlmann saw a summary and cipher of the South (his South)—threw him a naked dagger, which landed at his feet. It was as if the South had resolved that Dahlmann should accept the duel" (*F* 174). And the resolution is—paradoxically—both blindly obeyed and freely elected.

In Borges's writings the same story, the story of a traitor, for example, can appear in different times, places, and circumstances, with different characters: in revolutionary Ireland in "The Shape of the Sword" (*L*); in ancient Palestine in "Three Versions of Judas" (*L*); or in the slums of Buenos Aires, where a Jewish adolescent betrays the neighborhood hero whom he admires in "The Unworthy Friend" (*DBR*). The same motif—the voice of an invisible bird—can likewise find repeated expression: in the essay "The Nightingale of Keats" (*OI*); in Borges's discussions of diverse versions of the motif found in world folklore; and in "The Life of Tadeo Isidoro Cruz (1829–1874)" (*AOS*), where the motif is adapted to the story's Argentine setting as the cry of a *chajá,* a wading bird native to the region.[6] Such repetition-with-variants is often vague and circumstantial, yet this fact may make it all the more revealing of Borges's transformational modus operandi.

Another line of investigation might concentrate on Borges's mode of narration. To mention but one example, in the story "The End" (*F*) he gives universal resonance to a local subject. (The project Borges undertakes in this fiction—to continue Hernández's *Martín Fierro* from the perspective of a twentieth-century writer—seems impossible from the very outset.) There are many things that could be said about the story; I would like to note just one: Borges narrates the story "laterally," from the perspective of Recabarren, the Spanish shopkeeper who gazes out on the infinite plain (a circle that symbolizes the divinity), motionless,

---

6. For the references to the motif in world folklore, see my *Borges the Labyrinth Maker,* 104–6. In the essay devoted to Keats, Borges also mentions Schopenhauer's cat, another version of the motif that appears in his work, for example in the poem "The Golem" (*BAR*) and in the movie script of *Invasión* (Argentina, 1968–1969). In real life the cat was materialized as his pet, Beppo.

immobilized by paralysis. This gives him the characteristics and vision of a god who contemplates events outside time, under the aspect of eternity.

Still another line of investigation, to which I have already alluded, is Borges's use of remote and often interchangeable geographic settings: Ireland; a vague Orient, variously incarnated as India, China, or Persia; the Anglo-Saxon world of the sagas; Mexico at the time of the Spanish conquest. Such distancing infuses his tales with a paradigmatic quality, transforming them into archetypal fables. At the same time, there are Borges's South American spaces—the frontier south of Buenos Aires and the border areas of Brazil and Uruguay, which he has converted into mythic symbols, and the outlying neighborhoods of Buenos Aires—metamorphosed in his poetry into a personal, lyric image, an image also tending toward archetype. Like the foreign settings, these American locales are forms of estrangement (*extrañamiento, ostranenie*), but they differ from the foreign settings in that they also aim to be forms of penetration and vehicles for the in-depth exploration of the self (*entrañamiento*).

It is interesting that Borges, an author who tends to dehistoricize his stories (using archetypes, essential metaphors, or motifs like the Eternal Return) and who distrusts history along with any other linguistic, philosophic, or theological attempts to systematize the universe, can astonish his readers with his keen perception of the new.[7] In his texts there is a frequent irruption of the nonrepetitive, of that specificity characteristic of every minute of lived history. To cite a few examples:

1. Borges likes to fix those circumstances and dates that mark moments of radical change, even in texts that seem to focus on the timelessness of symbolic forms. We find this in essays like "From Allegories to Novels," "The Modesty of History," and "On the Cult of Books" (all in *OI*). It is of little consequence that some of the moments he selects seem arbitrary to us—as when he fixes the passage from the allegory to the novel on "that day" when Chaucer translated a line from Boccaccio (*OI* 157)—while others appear more plausible—for instance, his underlining of the importance of Aeschylus's invention of the theater in the history of world culture. (Borges recalls that he came upon this event in an English book on Greek literature, when his interest was aroused by the following "somewhat enigmatic" sentence in the text: "He brought in a second actor" [*OI,* 167–68].) What is important is the way Borges manages to win over the reader; and this is achieved less through the

---

7. For more on this, see chap. 3 of my *Borges the Labyrinth Maker;* Carlyle's views, cited by Borges in "About William Beckford's *Vathek*" (*OI*); and Borges's rejection of the concept of history at the end of "From Someone to Nobody" (*OI* 148).

strength of his documentation than through the peculiarly Borgesian manner—a blend of the marvelous, the fantastic, and the detective—in which he presents the experience of discovery. There are times, however, when he fascinates us with a discovery that constitutes a true turning point. This is the case with his description of the scene in which Saint Augustine discovers his master Saint Ambrose "removed from the tumult of business," reading silently, without "moving his tongue," a scene that establishes the instant when the transition from oral to written culture began (*OI* 117). Needless to say, whether Borges "invented" these "historical" facts or whether he was just citing what others had already unearthed is a moot question.

2. Borges has also observed that a fact or an object added to the universe can change not only the past but also the future—that is, it can modify our reading of history. In "Kafka and His Precursors" he confesses that he took this idea from T. S. Eliot (*OI* 108).

3. From a very early stage, Borges reversed the terms of the time-honored opposition between the nations of Europe (considered to possess long, established traditions) and the peoples of America (described as young nations, without a history). In his view, the American continent had a much greater sense of the historical past and a much keener awareness of the changes wrought by time. Thus, in his well-known essay on eternity, "New Refutation of Time" (*L*), he includes a vignette entitled "Sentirse en muerte" (Feeling in death), based on what he calls a "portentous and pathetic" experience he had on the streets of Buenos Aires, when he felt that time had stopped.[8] He says, "'This is the same as it was thirty years ago.' I guessed at the date: a recent time in other countries, but already remote in this changing part of the world" (*OI* 179–80).

In one of his stories, "The Unworthy Friend," Borges likewise affirms: "Our image of the city is always slightly out of date. Cafes have degenerated into barrooms; old arched entranceways with their grilled inner gates, once giving us a glimpse of patios and of overhanging grapevines, are now dingy corridors that lead abruptly to an elevator" (*DBR* 25). Here Borges completely inverts the archetypal, almost platonic, vision of a legendary Buenos Aires that he had cultivated in his poetry, in some of his narrations, and in the essays on Evaristo Carriego. Instead, he underlines the contrast between tradition as preserved by memory and the vertiginous transformation of reality. This change in vision is appropriate to a fiction that sets out to demythologize the

8. The piece was first published in his books *El idioma de los argentinos* (Buenos Aires: Gleizer, 1928) and *Historia de la eternidad* (Buenos Aires: Viau y Zona, 1936), and later reprinted in the booklet *Nueva refutación del tiempo* (Buenos Aires: Oportet & Haereses, 1947) as well as in *Otras inquisiciones* (Buenos Aires: Sur, 1952).

romantic image of the *compadrito* (urban tough). This demythologiz-
ing is carried out by a narrator—the son of Jewish immigrants—who
recounts his betrayal of the "heroic" figure without any remorse, since
the neighborhood hero and the old neighborhood that harbored him
are, like old Buenos Aires, expressions of a part-real, part-literary past
that is no more.[9]

Borges's audacity allowed him to reread, relive, rewrite, and even
continue a classic work of Argentine literature, *Martín Fierro*. (I could
mention "Pierre Menard, Author of the *Quixote*" here, but that would
take me far afield.) Later, he also dared to transfer the crucifixion on
Golgotha, the central act of Christianity, to an Argentine ranch, thus
boldly rewriting an eternal and untouchable book. The very title of his
story, "The Gospel According to Mark" (*DBR*), proclaims this intent.

It is true that in order to carry out his project Borges needed to
invoke the South—a place already mythologized in his literature—and
to flood it with the waters of the Salado River, thereby separating it from
the world and alluding to another Deluge. He further had to surround
his protagonist with the savage Gutre family, whose forebears, the
Guthries of Inverness, are also introduced into the story, but with a
typically Borgesian twist that challenges Hispanic literary tradition.
The Gutres, descendants of Bible readers, have become barbarians;
they have lost the ability to read, write, and speak English, and even
Spanish gives them trouble. Still, two traditions survive "in their blood,
like faint tracks": though they lack any faith, in them can be found "the
rigid fanaticism of the Calvinist and the superstitions of the pampa

9. In his "A Note on Carriego," Borges observes that Carriego's poetry was influenced by
the real suburb and by the suburb as portrayed in popular Argentine music; in turn, Carriego's
literary vision of the suburb changed reality, or the way *we* view the "suburban locale" (*OI*
31). It would be interesting to study the stories in *Doctor Brodie's Report* as a macrostructure
in order to determine how Borges developed the theme of the neighborhood tough (*orillero*)
and his legendary bravery, particularly in knife duels. Such a study would also throw light on
the evolution of this figure in Borges's writing and help clarify his role within the corpus of
Borges's work. Six of the stories in *DBR* deal with the world of the toughs. Borges calls them
"realistic"; despite his considerable irony, one can at least say that they purport to present an
"objective" view of the *orillero*'s world as seen and interpreted by an outsider. (In two of the
stories the narrative voice belongs to the protagonist.) Generally speaking, the stories
demythologize the tough, but two of them, "The Meeting" and "Juan Muraña" (which,
Borges admits, "hold the same fantastic key"), retain something of the epic tradition's exalta-
tion of an individual's fighting courage. For the image of Buenos Aires in Borges's early writing, see Sylvia Molloy, "*Flâneries* textuales: Borges, Benjamin y Baudelaire," in *Homenaje a
Ana María Barrenechea*, ed. Lía Schwartz Lerner and Isaías Lerner (Madrid: Castalia, 1984),
487–96; Enrique Pezzoni, "*Fervor de Buenos Aires:* autobiografía y autorretrato," *Filología*
20:2 (1985): 235–60; reprinted in Enrique Pezzoni, *El texto y sus voces* (Buenos Aires:
Sudamericana, 1986), 67–96; and Enrique Pezzoni, "*Fervor de Buenos Aires:* vaciamiento y
saturación," *Vuelta Sudamericana* 1:4 (1986): 27–31.

Indian" (*DBR* 19). Their reddish hair and Indian features attest to this blending of races.

Before the Gutres rises the God-hero, Espinosa, whose name captures the essence of what the Jewish tradition (in its Hispanic-Sephardic line) signifies for Borges: the intellectual exercise of the mind, philosophical and theological speculation. But Borges also endows Espinosa with autobiographical touches, for instance the freethinking father and the Catholic mother who asks him to say the Lord's Prayer every night.

Through its transformation of the archetypal story, Borges's narration itself becomes a cultural hybrid, a literary expression of the plural ethnicity inherent in its characters. Barbarizing the Gospel is as valid an enterprise as reading the original text; for it vindicates not only the eternity of the symbol in its South American form but also the writer's inevitable task, which is to repeat, re-create, and translate eternal metaphors into his own language. The mere undertaking of this task already forges a new idiom, a "language of dawn," as Borges called the language of the Nordic sagas.

To recapitulate: Borges's narrative practice can be described as a gesture that continually establishes distinctions, undoes them, and then reverts to them anew with greater, more disturbing complexity. Long before Derrida, his deconstructions were the masterful result of an endless process of dispersal, a dispersal resolved into a dazzling unity through following new, untrodden paths: it is a gesture of erasure that retains in filigree not only the marks of what has been effaced but also deeper and more hurtful wounds.

Translated by Edna Aizenberg

Marta Morello-Frosch _____

Borges and Contemporary Argentine Writers

Continuity and Change

It was one of Borges's chief concerns to establish a literary lineage for himself, a task he carried out by tracing cultural ancestors and by identifying predecessors of his own choosing—more often than not giving them an apocryphal paternity. Conversely, if we identify the Borgesian markers left in more recent texts, we could compose a considerable list.[1] What I will try to do here is both more difficult and more rewarding: to explore and analyze the text that the Borgesian influence elicits from new Argentine writers who are his opposites in ideological and literary aims. What I want to do is trace the continuity and change of literary influence and identify differences in the manifestly influenced text. This means that I will not consider Borges's antagonists, a group that has already been well studied.[2] Furthermore, I will analyze difference as a relational concept, as Fredric Jameson has suggested, rather than as an inventory of divergences.[3] We must also remember that the texts under analysis here are intimately related to their time of production, precisely through their corrections, emendations, variances, and ultimately through their open questioning of their literary paradigms. To work against and with a Borges text, to historicize it, to modify it, to contextualize it, is for the younger writers a form of mediation with the past, a way of making out of this past a literary future that transgresses

1. I could add to those analyzed in this essay the names of Pedro Orgambide, Marco Denevi, Isidoro Blastein, Amalia Jamilis, and Elvira Orphée. Unless otherwise noted, all translations from the Spanish are my own.

2. See Emir Rodríguez Monegal, *El juicio de los parricidas* (Buenos Aires: Deucalión, 1956). For an analysis of criticism on Borges, consult Maria Luisa Bastos, *Borges ante la crítica argentina, 1923–1960* (Buenos Aires: Hispamérica, 1974). For oppositional criticism of Borges, see Adolfo Prieto, *Borges y la nueva generación* (Buenos Aires: Letras Universitarias, 1954). A more recent book on the same topic is Juan Fló, ed., *Contra Borges* (Buenos Aires: Galerna, 1978).

3. Fredric Jameson, *The Political Unconscious: Narrative as a Socially Symbolic Act* (Ithaca: Cornell University Press, 1981), 41.

not only the self-imposed limits of Borges's work but his literary program as well.

The younger literary figures I will consider belong to the cultural debate of the post-Peronist period, and two of them, through their literary production, also represent alternatives to the official story forged by the political process that ended in 1983. The decade of the sixties and the beginning of the seventies saw a cultural revisionism practiced publicly in forums and publications of various kinds—a revisionism that centered on a reevaluation of the role to be played by intellectuals in the reconstitution of culture. During the early seventies, these debates concentrated mainly on the redefinition of culture that had occurred in the first Peronist period (1946–1955). Discussions focused specifically on the negative role played by most intellectuals during that time. Intellectuals now found their antagonistic attitude wanting, since their opposition to Peronist cultural policies did not lead to the elaboration of viable alternatives. Belatedly, they recognized that they had been blind to the social changes, the new alliances, and the regroupings of citizens that had taken place during Perón's postwar reign. They realized they had missed the opportunity to serve as mediators with new and enriching third positions in the cultural arena, standing neither for nor against Peronism but salvaging what was useful from the populist movement. Thus, during the sixties and seventies, the main focus of intellectual discourse was to search for ways to insert culture within a political praxis by creating new forms of cultural mediation— new symbolic constructs that could bridge the distance between national cultural projects and the people at large. The writers of the period saw this task as very urgent, particularly in light of their negative assessment of the Peronists' cultural project, which, in retrospect, they found to have been ineffectual in its efforts to broaden the concept of culture to include larger sectors of the population.[4] In this respect, the Peronist programs appeared to them to be not very different from the educational agendas devised in the previous century by Domingo Faustino Sarmiento and Juan Bautista Alberdi—two founders of Argentina's nationalist discourse—since the Peronists wanted to widen the cultural public while maintaining nearly without change the concept of culture that had prevailed since the 1850s.

The young generation of writers had some specific aims in mind. These authors abandoned the convention of the totalizing text, which had dominated the preceding generation of writers. We need only recall *Megafón o la guerra* (Megaphone or the war, 1970) by Leopoldo

4. Andrés Avellaneda, *El habla de la ideología* (Buenos Aires: Sudamericana, 1983).

Marechal and *Abaddón el exterminador* (Abaddon the destroyer, 1974) by Ernesto Sábato. While these works had a loose structure and included a variety of cultural components, they also revealed an organizing point of view that assigned specific discursive functions and spaces to the voice of the "others." These "others" were designated, nominated, and ultimately controlled by the authorial voice, which included them but did not allow them to act or speak freely.[5] In these works, the marginal voices were present and audible, but there was no new cultural proposal put forth through their limited discourse. Now, on the other hand, cultural discourse was to be extended to include a larger number of voices and to account for dissidence, alterity, and marginality—all forms of difference that had been proscribed for a long time. The new generation made its project the production of texts with multitudes of narrators and equally numerous points of view. It was not a matter of vindicating relativism; on the contrary, the aim was to account for the presence and value of "otherness": not only other voices but also other views, attitudes, and interests. This effort often resulted in texts that seemed to be deliberately fashioned out of fragments, or remnants, of other discourses, texts that achieved an effect of bricolage by including components of varied natures and origins.

I shall consider here the works of one author from the sixties, Abelardo Castillo, and two from the late seventies, Ricardo Piglia and Andrés Rivera. They provide what could be called a rereading of Borges, an example of the use and abuse of their literary predecessor; or, to borrow from Harold Bloom, they carry out deliberate misreadings and deviant interpretations of their literary forerunner.[6] There is little idealization of the Borges text, which the younger writers appropriate as a cultural artifact to be resemanticized in new and surprising ways. At the same time and in another literary register, they reveal the stylistic markers of their precursor in their own text. Borges is refashioned and his function redefined; his personal diction, his metaphors, his language are borrowed but put to use with different aims.

As they turn to Borges, these writers try to answer the question: with what cultural materials does one reconstruct national literature? Obviously, Borges becomes a basic foundation in this enterprise, the starting point—together with Roberto Arlt—of modern Argentine literature.[7] It

5. Beatriz Sarlo, "Literatura y política," *Punto de vista* (Buenos Aires) 19 (1983): 8–11.

6. Harold Bloom, *The Anxiety of Influence: A Theory of Poetry* (London: Oxford University Press, 1979).

7. Arlt, a contemporary of Borges (1900–1942), was the chronicler of the frustrated hopes of urban, immigrant Argentina, above all in the city of Buenos Aires. His was an underworld of delinquents, outcasts, and madmen portrayed through a grotesque optic that belied organic development both in life and in the novel.

is important to clarify that the young writers turn to Borges as their ancestor despite their considerable difference in ideology and cultural politics. Like Borges, they fashion an apocryphal lineage for themselves, but one made up of analogies as well as differences with the master. In fact, difference is the starting point of their approach to Borges, for they recognize in him his own "otherness," what turned him into an original, often dissident, and always heterodox figure in the national sphere.[8] While Borges remained steadily independent of the prevailing literary fashions even though he belonged to some influential literary groups and magazines, his successors try to redefine this attitude, bridging the spaces that separate them from "the others."[9] Borges is never a lonely figure in their new texts. The relations between *his* text and those of the new writers is never mere mental play, for these relations point to long-range cultural projects needing to be carried out within a specific political framework. We encounter a new fiction of origins that justifies the presence of the predecessor in the here and now. But, contrary to Borges's stance, the new interpretation of Argentine culture is not a paradigm of personal preferences or subjective, cherished myths; nor is it an ancestry of glorious warriors.[10] In the new fiction, the genealogy is made up of indigent immigrants and intellectuals, who arrived in Argentina without a language to articulate their own discourse. The new texts do not eliminate the ethnic and class contradictions in the national culture, nor do they, like Borges, provide a literary space where these contradictions can be resolved. Instead, the contradictions are seen in the new texts as the result of a historical process closely wedded to social practice: the violence of life on the periphery as well as the violence exercised in the seats of power by those who control the cultural patrimony and defend it against the disenfranchised and the uneducated. The new texts, in sum, do not maintain the dichotomy between civilization and barbarism that Borges upheld in his works. They show how the biography of the newly arrived did not become a parallel of the *grande histoire,* for these groups were left without history, without even a footnote in the official narrative of the national project. The younger writers now write these *parallel* lives.

Another Borgesian trait that his successors preserve is the use of the text as an undefined discursive zone: a mixture of fiction, confession, testimony, archival file, oral report, quotes from nonexistent works, or

8. On opposition and difference, see the introduction to Richard Terdiman, *Discourse/ Counter-Discourse: The Theory and Practice of Symbolic Resistance in Nineteenth-Century France* (Ithaca: Cornell University Press, 1985).

9. Enrique Pezzoni, *El texto y sus voces* (Buenos Aires: Sudamericana, 1986), 77.

10. Ricardo Piglia, "Ideología y ficción en Borges," *Punto de vista* 5 (1979): 3–6.

adjudication of apocryphal quotes to historical figures. This deliberate use of the text as an open area requires a new type of reader who has abandoned the old interpretive practices. The younger authors declare that their own function is not only to be writers of new texts but reader-receivers as well, a double role that Borges had favored in his own works.[11] I should add, finally, that Borges's own predilection for the marginal and the heterodox, in the form of things remote, things removed in space and common knowledge, is modified in the new texts by a predilection for the marginal *within* the national—for the socially, historically, and culturally devalued, which is then made visible and set at the center of the fictions.

The first example of this appears in *Cuentos crueles* (Cruel stories) by Abelardo Castillo.[12] The story entitled "Réquiem para Marcial Palma" (Requiem for Marcial Palma) is an example of what could be called a historicized reading of Borges's "Streetcorner Man." Castillo cancels out the earlier fiction with his own version of the duel, foregrounding the fact that the protagonist—as well as the previous rendition of the story—has been killed by history. There is neither knifing nor shooting in this peculiar encounter, just blows administered to Palma's body and pride by a newcomer who represents the outsiders. Even the scene of the duel has changed. The locale has become a trivial riverside bar, full of Coca Cola ads and the sounds of tarantella, possibly a reminder of the outsider's not-so-remote Italian origins. Marcial's lover, Valeria, is present too, and she tries to ally herself with the victorious outsider, only to be rejected by him. As the newcomer leaves the scene, without bothering with what goes on behind him, the defeated Palma ineffectually wields a knife that has now become irreversibly obsolete.

This is the updated version of the Borges story. But Castillo introduces another element by making the narrator an old man who reminisces about the naval encounter at Obligado—a battle that took place between the Argentine confederate forces and the British during Rosas's government (1835–1852) to defend free access to the port of Buenos Aires along the River Plate. In the sixties, this act was often mentioned as an example of the preservation of national sovereignty before the foreign aggressor. The old narrator, through his comments, relates the action at Obligado to Palma's defeat by history. And the voice of Valeria, now old, wonders about Palma's defeat by the outsider. Castillo's narrative—unlike Borges's—is precisely that: the grotesque account of a defeat, of the canceling out of a myth no longer viable or historically

11. Marta Morello-Frosch, "Ficción e historia en *Respiración artificial* de Ricardo Piglia," *Discurso literario* 1:2 (1983): 243–55.

12. Abelardo Castillo, *Cuentos crueles* (Buenos Aires: Jorge Alvarez, 1966).

relevant. That is why the fight is described in terms of an almost comic western bar brawl, in a counterreading of the cult of courage Palma had represented both in literature and in history. The new text cancels any value this myth may have had for any new discourse pertinent to the national situation.

The narrative similarly foregrounds the obvious changes that have taken place in the last three decades: the presence of the outsider, the stranger, the immigrant from the interior or from abroad; the new forms of fighting and settling accounts that these newcomers brought with them; the new proletariat. And these changes are placed in a definite sociogeographic site: the periphery of the city, where the new-comers lived and where they left an imprint quite different from that of the knife-wielding *guapo* privileged by Borges.[13] These newcomers produce a new cult of courage very unlike the epic renditions of their predecessor. Both the modernization of Borges's story and the allusion to the encounter at Obligado call into question the historical relevance of certain myths and underline the need to reexamine and update them.[14] The canceling out of an epic of primitive courage and violence, and the rereading of an encounter that perhaps did not defend any sovereignty but accommodated both parties, exemplifies the revi-sionist attitude of the younger writer. Furthermore, in Castillo's story the reconstruction of the mythical duel is made to appear like "a pho-tograph in a yellowing newspaper," thus emphasizing its semidocu-mentary nature as old data. But there is also the presence of the two narrating voices: the old man and old Valeria, witnesses who have themselves experienced the changes of history. The story becomes not the account of a single mythologizing voice—as in Borges—but obser-vations from historical subjects who comment on deeds that are not always clear to them. The dramatic tension of the story lies precisely here, in the contamination that these narrators bring to the tale, as they contrast their own expectations—which are colored by the power of myth—with the actual results of the events that were both experienced and observed. The duel/battle is also a literary one, as Castillo deliber-ately leaves all sorts of Borgesian markings in his narrative, creating the illusion that we are rereading the old master. But the conjectural dis-course so dear to Borges—the portrayal of characters who attempt to infer meaning from the flux of lived experience—is canceled out by the

13. On the topic of the suburbs, see Pezzoni, *El texto y sus voces,* and Beatriz Sarlo, "Sobre la vanguardia, Borges y el criollismo," *Punto de vista* 11 (1981): 3–8.

14. It is well known that the blockade did not prevent access to the port of Buenos Aires and that both sides exerted selective interference in this naval encounter. On the subject, see Tulio Halperin Donghi, *Historia argentina: De la revolución de independencia a la con-federación rosista* (Buenos Aires: Paidós, 1972).

ending of Castillo's story, in which all the characters return to the place of their desire and failed hopes: Marcial Palma looking at his victorious enemy while he holds a useless knife in his hand; Valeria, the rejected lover, with eyes downcast; the old narrator seeking to return to the river bend where he dreams of fighting the old foes from Obligado.

Castillo's story forecloses one of Borges's most recurrent themes: man's choice of destiny at the time of a duel. But most important perhaps is the story's questioning of social and literary myths: epic violence, knife duels, Obligado. Castillo sounds like Borges, yet he produces a fiction that becomes a total inversion of Borges's stance. At the same time that he invokes the voice of his literary predecessor, he re-creates Borges's form if not his aim; he declares Borges worthy not only of recovery but also of correction, of remembrance, of salvaging.

In another narrative, "Triste le ville" from *Las panteras y el templo* (The panthers and the temple), Castillo reverts to another Borgesian theme: the protagonist's chance to choose the form of his own death.[15] This text is thoroughly contextualized in its Buenos Aires setting and is laden with Borgesian echoes—in its language, in the digressive reflections of the characters, and in the philosophical generalizations they expound. Like "Réquiem para Marcial Palma," this is an antithetical version of "The South." The protagonist accidentally finds a train ticket at Constitution Station in Buenos Aires and decides to use it to begin a journey toward a destiny that was meant for "the other," a character he sees from the window of the departing train, searching his pockets for the lost ticket. Apart from these realistic details, the story subverts the idea of the choice of destiny. This human option becomes absurd when it is the result of a mere accident, a trivial impulse with irreversible results. Chance, here, is not the door to some epiphany or extraordinary revelation, as it often is in Borges.[16] On the contrary, it is the anteroom to damnation, as the chance event will become the cause of eternal solitude, a one-way ticket to a special kind of hell:

> Since that day I have walked thousands of times through this town, with its wretched square and empty streets, which were the death destined for another. . . .
>
> There is no leaf on any tree, no vein on any leaf, no stripe on any stone whose memory is not indelibly etched in my mind like the hand that now moves before my eyes. Nor is there any moss-covered brick in the furthermost corner of any house; nor any drop of water about to fall on the petal of a flower.[17]

15. Abelardo Castillo, *Las panteras y el templo* (Buenos Aires: Sudamericana, 1976).
16. I am referring to the concept of "signifying chance" as it applies to Borges.
17. Castillo, *Las panteras,* 89.

This is a peculiarly Borgesian kind of hell: intolerably lucid, infinite, frozen, without movement or future, dead. This is the opposite of the world of "The South," but it resembles that of "The End" in that it is a universe without markings, without traces of the passage of time, without differences: a hell to which the protagonist has condemned himself by chance.

Both of Castillo's texts introduce elements that were absent in Borges's stories: history, nonsignificant chance, circumstances that play a decisive role in the destiny of the protagonists. What was grotesque in the duel of the first text has become an ironic rendering of destiny in the second. In both stories the inexorable logic of the Borgesian text is called into question, but the characters no longer make conjectures; they remain the objects of historical forces that they cannot always understand and that they never try to systematize. Castillo brings the Borgesian proposal to a dead end and cancels the generalizing possibilities of the older versions. The new stories recount happenings in a world that is both familiar and alien, a world in which the imagination cannot always penetrate the opaque appearance of events experienced. Meaning is neither obvious nor even possible; and conjecture will not help mediate the empty textual spaces that perplex the speaking subject—who, in Castillo, is always present and audible as a witness who can account for but never explain what he or she perceives. Here Borges is subject to a peculiar kind of inquisition, resulting from this query about contextual meanings. The new stories are a sort of self-conscious simulacrum (*simulacro*) of the old master's stories. They imitate his discourse while they render intelligible and visible elements that were omitted in the original. This particular form of literary product vindicates Borges's own concept that one type of literature differs from another not so much in its text, but in the way it is read.[18]

Ricardo Piglia's novel *Respiración artificial* (Artificial respiration)[19] starts with a question: "Is there a history/story?" (*¿Hay una historia?*). The question points to the confluence of history as a consciousness of the past with history as a narrative function, and it insists upon a query that is only partially answered with a conditional statement: "If there is a history/story it begins three years ago. In April 1986, when my first book was published he sent me a letter." This beginning foregrounds the importance of both fiction and history in the novel, but it also

18. Cited in Jaime Alazraki, *Versiones. Inversiones. Reversiones. El espejo como modelo estructural en los cuentos de Borges* (Madrid: Gredos, 1977), 20.
19. Ricardo Piglia, *Respiración artificial* (Buenos Aires: Pomaire, 1980).

reflects a very prevalent concern in Argentina during the seventies: how to relate cultural production and sociohistoric events. This did not mean establishing causal relationships between literature and society; rather it meant considering how the sociohistoric informed the thematics and the form of discourse of the novel genre, and how this genre was placed in the literary tradition of Argentina. Piglia's novel resorts structurally and metaphorically to the figure of the archive. The text is made up of a corpus of preexistent data that must be interpreted by a chronicler-narrator. But unlike Borges's text, these data are not literary pieces. Quotes, files, testimonies, memories, letters, even the conversations of witnesses and listeners provide the novelistic material, foregrounding the importance of personal experience in what has become a collective project. Because the text does not provide a single new reading of these elements, each subjective interpretive effort responds to a series of collective confrontations between groups that are ideologically different, although not necessarily antagonistic. The novel takes note of these differences and distinguishes them as the essential elements that generate both opposition and dialogue, that include counterproposals that may recover what was lost, and that propose something new. Although the novel is set in 1979 and is narrated in the present, there are witnesses and fragments from a past that is thus rendered an open system, ready to be interpreted with a new optic. This operation allows the forging of a future where third positions can be enunciated and tried, where alterity can be given shape: a utopia, in sum, where truth can perhaps be lodged.[20]

Piglia, like Borges, problemizes the literary process itself, its modes of articulation and representation. But, unlike Borges, he places literary practice in the social realm, in the collective spaces of discourse and action, even at a time—the seventies—when historic events had pushed cultural practice to the most private places. Furthermore, in opposition to Borges, the modern fiction does not seek to be a reflection of the author's self; it does not rediscover the preselected. Instead, as in the case of Castillo, it allows the others to speak for themselves. Thus we listen to an old political figure analyze the failures of national history in his feverish memories. This particular character is a crippled man confined to a wheelchair who has stored the national past in his memory and experience. By dint of this knowledge and his capacity of analysis, he reminds us of many of Borges's decrepit sages who seem to hold an immense and occult power. But Piglia's sage is not a mystifying oracle or a statue like the old man in "The South." He is able to evoke the

    20. Fredric Jameson, "Marxism and Historicism," *New Literary History* 11:1 (1979): 41–71.

alliances and class conflicts of Argentina at the turn of the century, a time when he was himself a participant in the events he recalls. His knowledge is neither magical nor mysterious but the product of a long reflection on the possible options in our national past.

The narrator and the old man are relatives by marriage, a social contract. This type of relationship characterizes a new form of oblique genealogy that is freely chosen on the basis of common interests—the narrator and his distant relative are both interested in history and are both concerned with the life and biography of a common ancestor. But family history is not the paradigm of national history as in Borges; quite the contrary. While Borges's genealogy is one of frontier warriors and intellectuals, Piglia's fiction re-creates the personal history of the marginal, the exiled, the traitors to both the Federalist and the Unitarian causes— those who were seeking a third position not identified with either group.[21] The writer provides the voices of those not recorded in the official history except as a footnote or with a negative sign (as those who failed); those, in sum, who do not have discursive space in the authorized text. He makes audible the voices not only of crippled old politicians but also of failed professors; exiled noblemen with no profession; linguists with no language to make themselves heard in a new land—all representing a past and a history that have been totally obliterated by the empowered.

Furthermore, while Borges constructs his fiction out of quotes from books, Piglia fictionalizes quotes from subjects known to those who quote them. It is human experience that forms the basis for his novel, not textual readings. But there is some intellectual presence in *Respiración artificial:* a group of marginal thinkers who meet in the border town of Concordia, ready to cross the river into Uruguay if necessary. It is in this city (whose name evokes what was manifestly absent from the national discourse of the seventies) that they discuss national culture, intellectual figures of the past, national history, and poetic practice. These people give an account of culture as it is practiced in the periphery, far from the centers that generate and disseminate innovative ideas. It is interesting to observe how their very marginality offers them a fresh perspective. Their most revealing discussions are about the role of intellectuals in national history. They criticize the French writer Paul Groussac, who had immigrated to Buenos Aires, as the inauthentic European teacher of generations of Argentines. They also indict Pedro

21. Of the two main political parties in the second half of the nineteenth century, the Unitarians favored a centralized government dominated by Buenos Aires and an economy structured around trade with Europe, while the Federalists defended the interests of the interior provinces and their pastoral economy. The triumph of Justo José Urquiza over the forces led by Juan Manuel de Rosas at the Battle of Monte Caseros (1852) marked the defeat of Federalism.

de Angelis, the European-educated intellectual who put his skills at the service of the tyrant Juan Manuel de Rosas. In a way, Piglia is writing a novel in the style of Pierre Menard, since the modern text is a rewriting of older ones, given updated signification. In Piglia's novel the marginal thinkers consider this type of rewriting the most productive.[22] As their discussions progress, they call into question the assertion that Buenos Aires is the cultural aleph of the entire country; they also propose new readings of the national literature—arguing, for example, that Borges and Roberto Arlt, the styleless writer, have a lot in common in their debunking of useless erudition, a national vice. The marginal thinkers see Borges as the one who cancels the nineteenth-century tradition and Arlt as the one who initiates contemporary discourse. They not only criticize and evaluate past literary and intellectual figures but also re- cover certain peculiar forms of acculturation—the poor translations of foreign novelists that set the models for monolingual writers; mis- quotes; half-understood readings of foreign works—all of which con- tributed to shaping the national discourse in the most inclusive sense.

At this point, I need to clarify that, despite its manifestly inclusionary practice, *Respiración artificial* is a difficult novel to read. Its cultural ideology is at odds with its enunciation, which is highly allusive and thoroughly intellectual. An added difficulty lies in its veiled references to code words, a strategy that allowed for semantic extension at a time of heavy censorship. Furthermore, Piglia recognizes his debt to both Borges and Arlt when he defines parody as the most fitting literary form to represent modern life.[23] And parody is exactly how this author treats the quotes and readings of Borges. He deconstructs the Borges text, revealing the mechanisms that make it work, the conventions it up- holds. From this distance, he keeps the model always visible. In dialec- tic tension with the model, he proposes remaking it into a new cultural object with historical and cultural relevance for the seventies. It is not a matter of destroying the old text, but of updating it and, with some alterations, making it useful for younger generations. Even as parody questions the absolute truth of the original text, the new version has an obvious, close relationship with the original that prompted it. Piglia thus pays homage to his predecessor by identifying his work as relevant for younger generations, despite the necessary modifications.

Of the authors considered, Andrés Rivera is perhaps the most ideo- logically removed from Borges, yet he is the one who reveals the most obvious and frequent Borgesian markings.[24] He has written several

22. Piglia, *Respiración,* 157.
23. Ibid., 137.
24. María Teresa Gramuglio, "Escritura política y política de la escritura," *Punto de vista* 16 (1982): 28–29.

novels that re-create the life of the proletariat in Buenos Aires since the thirties. In his last three works, he has revealed a proclivity toward intertextuality with Borges's fiction, its themes, rhetoric, and literary topics. Like Piglia and Castillo, Rivera provides the historical context for Borges's texts and amends them accordingly, so as to better insert them in contemporary literary discourse. In *Una lectura de la historia* (A reading of history), a collection of stories from 1982, Rivera touches themes that are central to Borges's fiction and equally relevant to the moment of publication of the new book. Although the stories refer to various periods in recent national history, the dynamics of these pieces is the relationship between treason and power, crimes and politics, extortion and guilt. In short, the stories are characterized by violence, even in sexual relations. In the obsessively opaque text, Rivera reveals "a world in which gunmen can govern nations and practically govern cities" as he tries "to make . . . [his] feeble prose transport even the most cautious of readers to an alien, yet perhaps familiar setting."[25] The highly stylized prose establishes a tense dialectic with the epic of cruelty it articulates. There are abundant examples of the infamy and perversity that pollute social relations in situations of oppression. But, unlike Borges's text, Rivera's does not enunciate a universal history of infamy. His stories give instances of cruelty in specific circumstances, when evil is turned into a common occurrence, into a daily form of exchange. As he historicizes these events, evil is further trivialized as it becomes routine in the seemingly inevitable deterioration of human relations. In his later work *Nada que perder* (Nothing to lose), Rivera composes the biography of an immigrant union leader who has died.[26] He compiles it from the testimony of those who knew the deceased: his son, his wife, his union friends, those who shared his life at the factory and as a political activist. It is worth noting that Rivera, like Piglia, resorts to a fictitious biography in order to create a historical subject and that this biography is made possible by several other subjects who, from their memory of past experience, provide the materials that give meaning to the life of their dead friend. Thus the biography becomes a collective, collaborative project, the result of *heteroglossia* at many levels. Unlike the Borges text, this plurality of voices serves to provide a complex pattern of different voices accounting for coincidences in the subject as well as for contradictions and surprises. The new text reveals how the union leader, the biographic subject, evolved with the history of the labor movement in Argentina; how this struggle involved not

25. Andrés Rivera, *Una lectura de la historia* (Buenos Aires: Libros de Tierra Firme, 1982), 62.
26. Andrés Rivera, *Nada que perder* (Buenos Aires: Centro Editor de América Latina, 1982).

only members of the proletariat but also artists and writers, against a background of transplanted European traditions and antifascist movements transcending national boundaries. The different versions of the name of the subject, Reedson, act as markers of his various activities both as a private person and as a public actor, while the narrators' voices reveal the historical factors that converged in his life. These voices account for the displacements and necessary changes that befell the departed friend and those who knew him. For his life was consumed by a passion for liberty, and the techniques he adopted to reach this goal were varied. The narratives reveal not only the political strife he endured but also the forms of social interaction he practiced, including his enjoyment of art and the company of artists involved like himself in political struggle.

Rivera explores the proletarian population that thrived on the periphery of Buenos Aires, near the Maldonado Creek, where Borges had often placed his duelers. Rivera, like Castillo, gives an account of this neighborhood that differs from that of his predecessor, taking notice of the immigrant working class, the industrial waste, the poverty there.[27] As the protagonist's life seems finally to be authenticated by the word of people on the margins of society (immigrants and union leaders, committed artists, old friends), Rivera gives an ironic twist to the problem of authoritative discourse, since it is up to the nonauthoritative sources to give credence to Reedson's life. Originally, in the official rendering of his life, the fiction was induced from the seat of power; now it is up to marginal voices to reconstitute a valid historical subject: Reedson, the union leader.

The last work by Rivera that I want to analyze is his brief novel *En esta dulce tierra* (In this sweet land), set during the tyranny of Juan Manuel de Rosas, a historical period considered paradigmatic for the exploration of Argentine society since the appearance of Sarmiento's *Facundo*.[28] The narrative focuses on the persecution and the hiding of Doctor Cufré after the assassination of Manuel Maza, president of the House of Representatives (1839), and during the subsequent repressive measures of Rosas's police, the Mazorca. Rivera provides a conflict that

27. Rivera points out Borges's penchant for mystification and appropriates the rhetoric of his predecessor. He thus corrects him and recalls him in a double act of nomination: "a few yards from what had been the Maldonado Creek . . . where tough guys would talk through the point of a knife, according to Borges's doubtful prescriptions" (*Nada que perder,* 14).

28. Andrés Rivera, *En esta dulce tierra* (Buenos Aires: Folios, 1984). If the period of Rosas's dictatorship is the paradigm for dictatorial rule in Argentina's past, Sarmiento's *Facundo* (1845), as the biography of a representative *caudillo* (political boss) and as an analysis of the historical context in which such *caudillos* emerged, provides the model for the kind of historical critical assessment that some of the contemporary writers favor.

allows for a reexamination of role of the intellectuals in times of repression, as well as an obvious parallelism between the violence of that period and that of the recent military dictatorship (1976–1983). The text questions the value of the doctor's European education, of his civilized optics, in moments of uncontrollable violence. How can this man resist the affronts inflicted on him without going mad? Like Piglia's and Castillo's narratives, the novel gives the account of one more defeat, as Doctor Cufré suffers delirious madness while confined to the basement of his former lover's home. It would seem that defeat is the only discursive space available for historical narrative. Even the momentary victory of the Argentines against Brazilian forces at the Battle of Ituzaingó (1827) is seen as the beginning of a national decline, as an event that destroys both victors and vanquished, initiating the betrayal of the declaration of independence. All this is analyzed by Cufré, a man of reason, a doctor educated in France who returned to his own country despite his lack of faith in its historical destiny. His ambivalence is manifest as he answers his mentor in France: "Am I fighting against all hope? This is what it means to be an Argentine today."[29] The statement could well refer to many other periods in the not-too-distant past.

The narrative covers events that start when a small thin man, who later disappears, gives Cufré the news of the murder. Cufré is immediately found suspect. The narrative is made up of revelations, confessions, letters that must be burned, conversations that extend guilt and suspicion among those who hear them, false news spoken aloud and true news spoken in whispers—a bricolage of information in "this land that subjects its sons to horrifying rites and to the kind of suffering even the most wretched of the Czar's serfs would reject."[30] Cufré takes refuge in the house of Isabel Starkey, his former lover. Hidden in the basement, he must get in touch with his deteriorating body, with his former lover (who is not a very willing accomplice), with the outer world whose threatening echoes Isabel provides with glee. It is this part of the work that bears the most obvious Borgesian markings. Intertextuality pervades the entire narrative. Borges's diction—his idiosyncratic epithets and his entire set of rhetorical devices—is appropriated with the insistence of a parodic rendering, and the chapter on the events in the basement makes specific mention of "The Secret Miracle," Borges's tale of the preparation for death of the condemned Jewish writer Hladík. There are no secret miracles in Rivera's text, however, only a clandestine situation facilitated by a former lover. There are no covenants with God, no magic visions, no dreams that may bring epiph-

---

29. Rivera, *En esta dulce tierra*, 19.
30. Ibid., 17.

any. There are few metaphysical ponderings, and certainly no urge to justify life at the moment of possible death. There is, to be sure, the physical torture of confinement, of an enslaving body with its wastes and needs and unfulfilled desires. Cufré is not totally alone, as Isabel comes not only to clean him but also to read him news of the world beyond the basement. Isabel is "the other," the disembodied voice that reads a chronicle of the fraud and horror that go on outside, by the light of a candle. This candle is the only light in the musty cellar: the only light in Cufré's confinement appears in the text with obsessive repetition as "a dripping yellow eye." Cufré becomes delirious and imagines himself in an insane asylum, like the patients he visited daily with his mentor in France. The basement, the city, the country have become an immense lunatic asylum for him. There is no miracle here—no miracle is possible "in this sweet land." Yet confinement ends, as in Borges, with a solitary form of writing, as Cufré, the prisoner-patient, in his delirium thinks he is writing God's police file. Unlike in Borges, however, the deity has become the accused or the narrator's prisoner, not his deliverer. Such is the "miracle" of Rivera's text: the gratification of the sufferer who does not plead for divine guidance but condemns his Maker. This surprising end to the basement narrative cancels out any possibility of an idealist solution to the problem of destiny. It reinforces, on the other hand, the textual references to the materiality of physical suffering, to the deterioration of both mind and body, and it justifies the alienating and alienated escape at the end.

Yet this is not the conclusion of the novel. The last part consists of two possible, conjectural versions that could serve as epilogues. They are headed by the title *Pistas* (clues), and they offer possible solutions to what has become a mystery: what happened to the prisoner after his delirium? The two versions are two plausible answers. While different, they have an element in common in that they place the protagonist at the center of the Federalist struggle after the defeat of Rosas at the Battle of Caseros in 1852. In the first version, Cufré is seen allied to some of the fractured forces that held out in the interior and kept on fighting for Federalism, a system that was to be set aside forever. Cufré has allied himself once more with the vanquished, with the third position. It is important to note that Cufré will not end up joining the forces of his enemy's victors, the Unitarians who promoted the national political reorganization. Cufré will take up the role of the "other" to the very end, the third alternative, putting his medical skills at the service of the stricken General Varela as he withdraws to the mountains with his troops. The other version ends with Cufré's presence at the start of Sarmiento's presidency, in 1868, when Cufré presumably decides to descend once more to a cellar very similar to Isabel Starkey's. Thus

Cufré refuses to participate in Sarmiento's program, as he had refused to acquiesce to the Rosas regime. This ending centers the question of the function of the intellectual in history: neither with the Rosas, nor with his archenemy Sarmiento, but with the dreamers of the vanishing Federalist forces. Cufré "looked to the future, that abstraction which incites men like him to conspiracy and combat, and which survives defeat . . . with the unmistakable signs of utopia."

The book's epilogues are formed of fragments of others' discourse, of accounts by untrustworthy witnesses and unreliable chroniclers. There is in this part of the novel a plurality of conflicting signs that converge in the figure of Cufré, a strange, exceptional character, as he abandons the capital, the seat of political power, in order to join the resistance in the confines of the northwestern provinces. This could be an analogue of occurrences from the recent past, and it is undoubtedly an unofficial rendering of historical events that went unrecorded, of acts of faith, of commitment. Rivera produces a history of temporary failure and renewed faith in the struggle against abuses. Furthermore, this is a chronicle of continuous resistance against the excesses of power, in which the intellectual (the civilized person who returns from Europe) will take a central role, as Cufré did, not with Rosas's victorious enemies but alongside the persistent defenders of national federation. Thus Rivera's historical game is set—like Piglia's—on the historically marginal, not on the protagonists in the main struggles but on those who proposed alternatives to the two dominant sides. This particular perspective of Rivera's is the result not of some personal preference for the off-center or remote but of an attempt to reformulate options that were not taken or implemented in the national past. Cufré represents this perspective, and he embodies both a criticism and a review of the traditional conflicts in Argentine history, particularly of the role played by the intellectual.[31] Cufré's actions exemplify the intellectual's alliance with genuinely popular movements like those of Varela and El Chacho, the two military chieftains who continued the fight for federalism after the triumph of Urquiza at Caseros. His actions also allude indirectly to the lack of support for such movements among leftist intellectuals in more recent times.

With his conjectural double ending, Rivera resumes not only Borges's vocabulary but also one of his favorite narrative forms: the mystery or detective story. But what is most surprising is that these elements of style are used in a novel manifestly committed to a specific

31. Newman detects in Piglia's novel a revision and criticism of the position of the leftist intellectuals. Kathleen Newman, "Historical Knowledge in the Post-Boom Novel" (paper read at Tulane University in November 1985).

political and cultural ideology quite remote from Borges's own. While Borgesian markers are interspersed throughout the text, they do not act as forms of nonreality to place the conflict in the arena of the fantastic—quite the opposite. The highly allusive rhetoric serves to re-create loss: of anchor, of contextual consciousness, of a sense of real being. Hence the relevance of the lines at the end of the crucial chapter of confinement: "Leaning against the brick wall, what remained of Cufré took off its boots and socks. The smell from the feet of what remained of Cufré overpowered the cold pestilence which contained the voice of what was once Isabel."[32] The prisoner's diminished presence, his precarious condition, his likely disappearance, all converge in the neutral and disembodied "what remained of," a notation that alludes not only to the persecuted man but to his accomplice as well. History—both real and fictitious—becomes a paradoxical text in a series of enunciations with repetitive epithets and minimal variances, in narratives that convey opaque and often contradictory testimony. The literary resources are clearly Borgesian, but the aim is totally different. For Rivera is not trying to question the limits of reason or to produce an intellectual solution. Rather, he is trying to fathom the possible value of intellectual acts in specific historical circumstances. The protagonist proposes a new ethics for the members of his group, an ethics that "survives defeat . . . with the unmistakable signs of utopia." This is the new model, the opposite of Pedro de Angelis, who "sold his talent to the status quo, not to utopia."[33] Rivera intensifies the use of Borgesian rhetoric even as he makes it an ideology, producing for his own text an apocryphal lineage that has relevance for cultural resistance—as Borges had practiced within his circle—and for political and social activism as well.[34]

In conclusion, it is important to stress that the authors studied here recognize Borges as their literary predecessor, but that this recognition is predicated on difference. While they modify and reconstitute his discourse, they recognize in him certain features that need to be recovered. These would include Borges's lifelong interest in defining national culture; his use of irony (playfully intellectual in Borges, contesting and distancing in the younger writers); his criticism of misguided cultural projects and styles; and his vindication of certain fundamental texts in the national literary tradition (*Martín Fierro* for Borges; *Facundo,* Borges himself, and Arlt for the contemporary writers).

It seems odd that these literary descendants of Borges would identify him as the predecessor rather than Cortázar, who was so much closer

32. Rivera, *En esta dulce tierra,* 57.
33. Utopian project: analogous to an alternative, or third-position, national program.
34. The social markings of Rivera's text have been identified by Carlos Dámaso Martínez in "Historia entre la razón y el delirio," *Punto de vista* 24 (1985): 37–38.

to their own political ideologies. But if we consider that the writers of the younger generation are setting out to reconstruct culture, and with it a representative national literature, it becomes clear that Borges's work would be considered seminal to their own enterprise. Borges becomes a cultural object of extreme relevance as these writers assume the role of historical narrators. The relationship between the young and the old master is not dictated by subjective literary preferences. Rather, the link is based on the assumption that present and past represent two different types of cultural productivity, two forms of socialization for the intellectual, two possibilities of praxis that are confronted in the modern text in a quizzical mode. The past, with Borges as its representative in literary terms, will not be some inert body of concepts in need of interpretation. It has become an open, dynamic system that can be used to question and evaluate processes and cultural practices. This is made possible by the dialectical relationship between the modern text (which is set in a different historical and social context) and the Borgesian text (which is recalled). The dialectic relationship favors a new historical form of hermeneutics between past and present that can, as was the case with the fictional Cufré, spur the construction of a utopia, where the new generation of writers has chosen to place its works.

Robert Ross

"It Cannot *Not* Be There"

Borges and Australia's Peter Carey

*You're quite right when you suggest that it might be difficult to say
exactly how Borges may have influenced me, also right to suggest that
the influence is/was there. . . . It is there, it cannot* not *be there.*
—PETER CAREY, letter

On first reading Peter Carey's writing, I found it different from other
Australian literature, and I resolved this encounter with the unexpected
by making broad and perhaps obvious comparisons: Carey belongs
more to the world tradition than to the Australian; more specifically,
his work suggests South American writers, such as Borges and García
Márquez, or North Americans like Barth, Barthelme, Vonnegut, and
Kesey, or Europeans like Kafka and Camus—all facile enough parallels
to draw. In fact, Australian reviewers had already said much the same
about Carey's work, one observing, for example, that "his music is
more international . . . and echoes the upbeat rhythms of the three B's:
Borges, Barth and Barthelme."[1] The Australian critic Brian Kiernan
noted in a letter to me that reviewers in Australia often make such
sweeping statements about Carey, but critics there fail to develop these
generalizations because comparative literature is not generally pursued
in Australian universities either as a field of study or as an avenue of
criticism, except to a limited extent, comparing Australian writing with
American, British, and other English-language literatures. Thus there
exists no body of criticism on which to rely.[2]

Instead I turned to Peter Carey himself and in a letter asked the
questions one would often like to pose when setting out on a com-

1. Jim Legasse, review of *War Crimes* by Peter Carey, *Westerly* 2 (June 1980): 122.
2. Australian critics have reviewed Peter Carey's short stories but have not considered
them in critical essays. Two articles have appeared on the novels: Teresa Dovey, "An Infinite
Onion: Narrative Structure in Peter Carey's Fiction," *Australian Literary Studies* 11 (1983):
195–204; and Graeme Turner, "American Dreaming: The Fictions of Peter Carey," *Australian
Literary Studies* 14 (1986): 431–41. Both articles attempt to make connections between
Carey's work and what Turner calls "international forms." Neither dwells, though, on any one
"international" writer but more on the views of various postmodern critics.

parative study: had he in truth read Borges? If so, what part, if any, had Borges played in his own development as a writer? Carey replied, in the words of the headnote above, then elaborated:

> I remember the name of the friend who introduced me to Borges, remember the Melbourne bookshop where the first book (*Ficciones*) was purchased. . . . The bookshop was The Whole Earth Bookshop (God, could it *really* have been called that?) and its Hippy-poet proprietors ignored all the publishers' ideas on how the world of literature must be divided up and (illegally) imported paperbacks direct from the U.S. (Up until that time we could only read what London publishers decided.) . . . I shudder to imagine how the works of an erudite blind librarian might have been understood, misunderstood, as they were gulped down by a twenty eight year old Australian—recently embarked on the adventure of reading—who, I am sure, took them in long impatient draughts, better suited to simple spring water than such fragrant and delicate distillations.

Agreeable to further question-answering, Carey concluded: "I look forward to the inquisition."[3] Whether he used "inquisition" intentionally remains speculative, yet one cannot help but think of Borges's first book of essays, which he called *Inquisiciones* (1925), as well as of the later volume, *Otras Inquisiciones* (1952). Another of Carey's remarks, when read in a Borgesian light, suggests that image so much a part of Borges's world picture: the universe as a library, maybe even a bookshop. Did his first encounter with the great South American really occur in a store called "The Whole Earth Bookshop," Carey asks, seeming to hint at the irony involved in such a name.

A young writer, Carey has published two volumes of short stories, *The Fat Man in History* and *War Crimes,* and three novels, *Bliss, Illywhacker,* and *Oscar & Lucinda.*[4] With the publication of *The Fat*

3. Peter Carey, letter to author, October 22, 1986. I am in debt to Professor Brian Kiernan, University of Sydney, who introduced me to Peter Carey and offered encouragement. To Peter Carey, I am grateful for his clear replies to my sometimes muddled questions. I have quoted at length from Carey's response to "the inquisition." Perhaps foolishly I ignored his admission in one letter: "Is what I am saying the truth? Was this really the attraction [to Borges's writing] or am I simply trying to build an answer that will make us both happy?" But such are the hazards of the comparative enterprise, especially with the author looking over one's shoulder.

4. Peter Carey, *The Fat Man in History* (1974; St. Lucia, Australia: University of Queensland Press, 1979); *War Crimes* (1979; St. Lucia, Australia: University of Queensland Press, 1984); *Bliss* (1981; New York: Harper & Row, 1986); *Illywhacker* (New York: Harper & Row, 1985); and *Oscar & Lucinda* (New York: Harper & Row, 1988).

In a study of this length, it was not feasible to take up Carey's novels. First published in Australia, they have been issued in the United States by Harper & Row. *Bliss* is a richly comic novel about Harry Joy who survives a heart attack but discovers in the process that he has been living in hell. On one level more realistic than the short stories, *Bliss* continues to break down the barriers between fiction and life. In *Illywhacker* Carey reshapes Australian history, which

Man in History, he established himself, first at home and then abroad, as a highly original figure in Australian literature. In a review of that first book Frank Moorhouse, another innovator of Australian fiction, praised Carey's inventiveness and the freshness he had brought to Australian literature: "For some time now there has been a vacancy in the Sophisticated Fantasy Section of the Short Story Industry. It is my pleasure to announce that Peter Carey, 30, of Melbourne has been appointed to fill that position. He will also do allegories, fables, and astonishing tricks."[5]

Like Borges, Carey had inherited a national literature dominated by social realism. Before Carey's writing appeared another Australian, Patrick White, had altered irrevocably, through a series of impressive novels, the course of Australian fiction, which White himself early on described as "the dreary, dun-coloured offspring of journalistic realism."[6] Like White, who looked to the European tradition and wrote as though Australian fiction before him did not exist, Carey searched elsewhere for his models. That Carey's first book appeared in 1974 is significant, for a year earlier White had received the Nobel Prize for Literature, the first time an Australian had been so honored. Of course, White had been writing for nearly twenty-five years without much recognition from Australian critics who too often considered his metaphysical handling of Australian materials a violation of the social realism, bush humor, and other established conventions they admired. Once recognized by so prestigious a prize, White's work soon became acceptable to the most reluctant of his critics—at least publicly. So did other writing that broke away from the stock and often hackneyed accounts of such seasoned matter as life in the bush, family struggles on a sheep or cattle station, mateship, pioneering, and the labor movement. Gene Bell-Villada concludes that "Borges's best stories contribute a new praxis and sensibility" to Latin American fiction, and he praises this "fruitful artistic mode that breaks away from psychology and realism, which for some two hundred years have been the fundamental

---

Mark Twain called "the most beautiful lies." The narrator described himself as an *illywhacker,* an Australian slang term for a professional trickster or con artist. Certainly, Borges would have appreciated and approved of such a name for the storyteller. Not without its shadow of Borges, *Illywhacker* brings to mind more fully Gabriel García Márquez's *One Hundred Years of Solitude,* thus showing once again how Borges, on whom García Márquez in part relied, helped to establish modern Latin American literature and its international reputation. *Oscar & Lucinda,* which depicts a minister (Oscar) who is an inveterate gambler and thinks it is appropriate because believing in God is the biggest gamble of all, also has its Borgesian touches.

5. Quoted in Don Anderson, ed., *Transgressions, Australian Writing Now* (Ringwood, Australia: Penguin Books, 1986), 9.

6. Patrick White, "The Prodigal Son," *Australian Letters* 1 (April 1958): 37–40 (39).

materials of prose narrative."[7] In regard to Australian literature, much the same could be said of White, then of Peter Carey and the others who emulated White in his rejection of literary custom, and in their own ways let ripen in Australia a "fruitful artistic mode" resembling the one Bell-Villada saw take hold in Latin America.

Not many years ago, the question was frequently asked: Is there really an Australian literature? As a result of White's reception abroad, even before he received the Nobel Prize, and the international recognition accorded Australian writers in recent years, the faraway continent's distinctive literary voice now speaks with such clarity that the once scornful question has lost its edge. For instance, Tom Shapcott, director of the Literature Board of the Australia Council, has reported that during 1986 publications in the United States reviewed more books from Australia than from any other foreign country except Great Britain. Scores of Australian books, most often fictional works but occasionally a volume of poetry, now appear on major American publishers' lists each year, many of them faring well in the marketplace. According to editors and agents, the competition for Australian books has become keen among publishers in the United States.

This literary zest, stemming in part from government subsidy administered by the Literature Board of the Australia Council, has benefited Carey and his generation of writers, as have changes in worldwide publishing practices that make the books of international writers, especially those in translation, accessible to young Australians, who can now mature on a cosmopolitan literature. "I grew up in almost total ignorance of literature, the literature of my own country in particular," Carey recalls. When he began to read seriously he says that he did not turn to "the fiction written in, by, or about Australia" but became, as he described himself in a letter,

> a denizen of one of Borges' libraries—a great circular building crammed with unindexed books, its bulging shelves occasionally interrupted by tall thin windows through which one could see a brilliant ultramarine sky, dust from road works or quarries, a society founded by convicts where even those who now had big houses and expensive cars still carried, not the values of their apparent bourgeois status, but the values and prejudices of convicts. The society outside the library did not value writers, artists, singers, story tellers. It was a society that valued men who were good with their hands.[8]

Yet it is about this society that Carey most often writes, recording his

7. Gene H. Bell-Villada, *Borges and His Fiction* (Chapel Hill: University of North Carolina Press, 1981), 41.

8. Peter Carey, letter to author, April 6, 1987.

vision of it not in the "dun-coloured" tinge of the realist but in the broad
and vivid strokes of the mythmaker, the fabulist, the visionary, the
metaphysician.

In his twenties, during Australia's involvement in the Vietnam War,
Carey left Australia, which he then considered "a Client State . . . of the
American government." Abroad, he imagined himself "a citizen of the
world": "In Europe (Britain in particular) I had come 'home.' I had
returned to the culture from which I and two generations before me
had been exiled. I cannot tell you what a delight it was to see the
electric green grass between Dover and London or, for that matter, to
hold a copy of the Sunday *Times*—complete with colour supplement—
on my lap."[9] He came back to Australia, though, a country that he
admits he has always held a "great love" for but at the same time "feared
and loathed." After returning, he worked as an advertising copywriter,
lived part of the time in a commune, and started to write the fiction that
is neither Australian nor non-Australian, just as Borges's work is neither
Argentine nor non-Argentine. For both, although inhabitants of the
world library, are firmly grounded in their own particular countries
whose reality they enhance by traveling abroad in the country of the
mind, the country that Patrick White describes through Laura Tre-
velyan's confession in *Voss:* "Knowledge was never a matter of geography. Quite the reverse, it overflows all maps that exist. Perhaps true
knowledge only comes of death by torture in the country of the mind."[10]

This young Australian, growing up in "a society where," he says,
"artists were not only not valued but, often despised," found "a book
called *Ficciones*" and years later remembers that first reading when he
discovered "within its covers—stories of a potency . . . never dreamed
possible. The stories were magical, hermetic, creatures of the library.
They posited a world where books had power, where artists had power,
where story-telling mattered."[11] In retrospect, though, how do we determine the ways this journey into the country of the mind affected
Carey's writing? Like Borges, Carey demonstrates a strong sense of
nationality, for he makes full use of the peculiar materials his country
offers—its history, social oddities, geography; its people and their folklore—along with autobiographical and family matter. On the other
hand, like Borges, Carey can turn to any part of the world and call it his
own within that particular fiction. Yet for both writers the components
of a story—setting, plot, dialogue, character—derive their strength not
from faithful rendering of locale, not from the sources on which they

9. Ibid.
10. Patrick White, *Voss* (New York: Viking, 1957), 440.
11. Carey, letter, April 6, 1987.

draw, not from strong character delineation, not from the virtuosity of their prose, but from "truths painfully arrived at," as Carey defines the ancient art of story making.

Emir Rodríguez Monegal describes *Ficciones* as "perhaps the single most important book of prose fiction written in Spanish in this century."[12] To make such a claim for Carey's *The Fat Man in History* (1974) in relation to Australian fiction may be debatable, but certainly this book of twelve stories brought a singular newness to the Australian short prose narrative. Carey had presented himself as being "international," a label with which Australian critics often dub a writer who breaks the mold. Exactly what they mean by that appellation—at times complimentary, at times derisive—remains somewhat obscure, but I rather imagine they intend to suggest that the writer has looked to European and American literary figures, especially those considered postmodern, for his or her artistic mode, rather than to the Australian classic writers like Henry Lawson and Joseph Furphy, whose stature is comparable to that of Mark Twain and Bret Harte in the literature of the United States.

To return now to the original proposition—that Carey's work from the outset led me (and other readers) to think of Borges and those authors often associated with him; let us then ask, in what ways does Carey's fiction recall the Argentine master's? This is an obvious question in light of the knowledge that Carey has admitted to reading Borges and considering this literary experience an important element in his own formation as a writer. If it were possible, I would present here an impressive and all-encompassing list of characteristics to define the qualities that make Borges's fiction distinctive, then methodically apply them to Carey's writing. But no matter how thorough the search, first through the fiction itself, then through the abundant commentary on it, no such ordered list emerges. Donald A. Yates attempts just such a feat in his essay "The Four Cardinal Points of Borges." While admitting that "to ascribe to Borges's artistic world four key aspects, four cardinal points, is, to be sure, arbitrary," Yates hopes that with "any luck" his scheme will be "in some way telling."[13] And luck rides with him, as he compares the cardinal points to those of the compass and thereby provides an ordered way to look at Borges's work.

South on this compass stands for Borges's deep sense of Argentine nationality, not only in the way he makes use of indigenous materials

12. Emir Rodríguez Monegal, *Jorge Luis Borges: A Literary Biography* (New York: Dutton, 1978), 358.

13. Donald A. Yates, "The Four Cardinal Points of Borges," in *The Cardinal Points of Borges,* ed. Lowell Dunham and Ivar Ivask (Norman: University of Oklahoma Press, 1971), 25.

but also in his absorption and synthesis of borrowings from diverse sources—an easy assimilation Yates ascribes to the special type of Argentine *criollismo* that Borges represents.[14] Carey, a third-generation Australian, is also a *criollo,* born of European parents transplanted in the Southern Hemisphere. Bound to Australia, but ambivalent in his sentiments toward it, Carey, like all his countrymen of European descent, has always looked to the Northern Hemisphere and taken from it those elements required to complement his intellectual and artistic development. To call either Borges or Carey "Europeanized" or "international" may be a legitimate appraisal but not a disparaging one, as an examination of the next point on the compass will prove.

North, according to Yates, takes language and literature as its orientation. Borges has often said that the most significant feature of his childhood was his father's library of English books, which helped direct him toward a life of literature. Because Borges's writing makes use of other literatures, he admits to influences without hesitation, Yates notes, and then concludes, "Language . . . continues in [Borges's] later years to be a point to which he is oriented, a north by which he still guides himself."[15] Carey, too, recalls a library whose "bulging shelves" transported him to a world far beyond the one that "interrupted" through the "tall thin windows" of that "great circular building" in Australia (an apt description of the Victoria State Library in Melbourne). Like Borges, Carey does not hesitate to grant those books a place in his own writing, admitting easily that his eclectic reading led him into literary experiments of his own, some successful, others not. With many creative years ahead of him and with his literary success freeing him of other responsibilities, Carey now lives a life of language, derived in large part from "a north by which he still guides himself." In *Bliss,* Carey describes the talent of a great storyteller who gave to language a meaning that only his handling of it could impart: "The words of the story could be of no use to anyone else. The words, by themselves, were useless. The words were an instrument only he could play and they became, in the hands of others, dull and lifeless, like picked flowers or bright stones removed from underwater."[16] Thus the north of the compass alone would be useless, an observation that introduces the next point.

East on this literary compass is the cardinal point that represents what Yates calls the most "distinctive feature" of Borges's writing: "It could be described as a fascination with philosophical and metaphysical questions that manifests itself, in part, in the incorporation of

14. Ibid., 26.
15. Ibid., 27.
16. Carey, *Bliss,* 221.

these problems as elements of his prose fiction." Drawn more to the abstractions of infinity and identity than to the palpable substance of daily life with which he clothes these larger concerns, Borges has admitted that he is "quite simply a man who uses perplexities for literary purposes."[17] Carey recalls how, on discovering Borges's work, he had found storytelling that mattered, that gave artists power. No such phenomenon, Carey notes, had occurred in his country (where the tale and its teller mattered little) since the time, a century ago, when Australians took to their hearts Henry Lawson and his accounts of bush life. But Carey finds suspect even Lawson's fabled reception, and he wonders if the popular reports of "shearers and bushworkers reading Lawson by lanternlight may be the wishful thinking of city intellectuals."[18] Similarly, Borges found noteworthy that the literature celebrating the exploits of Argentine gauchos, the equivalent to Lawson's tales of bushmen, was in truth the creation of city writers—those urban intellectuals who claimed to speak in the style and voice of the gauchos. Lawson, like his Argentine counterparts, much preferred the comforts and relatively cosmopolitan atmosphere of Sydney to the bush he extolled. For both Borges and Carey, the storyteller and the story *matter*—their power is derived not from the faithful yet artificial recording of national myth but from the painful seeking of truth. This belief in the power of story is the province of the final point.

West on Borges's compass Yates considers to be "the strong, ever-present narrative ingredient of drama." This element he describes as assuming the form of vivid color, melodrama, mystery, tight plotting—those features that stand in for the psychological probing or exposition generally absent in Borges's work.[19] Likewise, Carey's stories are well constructed from a narrative standpoint, never employing the tricks of tedious psychological probing or dreary internal meandering. Instead, their dramatic events emerge swiftly in dazzling and mysterious ways. For one thing, both Borges and Carey show a penchant for depicting violence, a tendency Yates attributes in part to Borges's fondness for western films, gangster movies, and detective fiction. Carey, an Australian growing up in the fifties, most likely saw his share of American crime films and westerns. Both come from countries where violence has always played a significant role in everyday life. "I grew up in a country town," Carey explains, "where disagreements were always resolved physically,"[20] much in the same way, one might suppose, that Borges's *guapos* and *compadritos*—Argentina's native toughs—settled

17. Yates, "Cardinal Points," 27, 28.
18. Carey, letter, April 6, 1987.
19. Yates, "Cardinal Points," 28.
20. Carey, letter, April 6, 1987.

disputes and defended their honor. Another element of their narrative mode is comedy, a device that merges into the story as unobtrusively as it does in real life, sometimes intentionally, at other times accidentally. The first-person narrator, who so often appears in both writers' works, beholds the goings-on around him in a manner detached, ironic, and amused. He then reports his version of what he has seen, in tales that lack narrative pretensions and structural artifice but that display instead a self-disguised plotting and an enviable control of dramatic tension.

The four metaphorical points of the compass may now be transformed into the list of characteristics, albeit abbreviated, that I sought earlier. Both writers display a sense of nationality along with an awareness of the larger world. Their work reveals a broad reading, which they have incorporated. They take up the perplexities that trouble them and their fellows. And they both accomplish this through adherence to the rules that have always governed effective storytelling, so that their readers finish the fiction and are affected by it: remembering it, marveling at its power, and, because of its many-layered thematic texture, finding in it diverse, new, and private meanings.

With this compass in hand, let us venture into the literary territory of Borges and Carey, beginning with one of the stories from Carey's first volume, possibly the best known among them, "American Dreams." Set in a small Australian town during the fifties, the events unfold in a matter-of-fact way, recounted as a young male narrator's reminiscences. He tells how a respected townsman named Mr. Gleason one day orders his Chinese laborers to build ten-foot-high walls around nearby Bald Hill and then orders them to top the walls with broken glass and barbed wire and to build a mysterious construction inside. The years pass and the inhabitants of the town (which closely resembles those bush settlements depicted in countless stories from earlier Australian realistic literature) still do not find out what is hidden behind those walls; nor does the reader. Eventually Mr. Gleason dies and his widow orders the walls destroyed to reveal what the narrator calls "the most incredibly beautiful thing I had ever seen in my life." At first he only "breathed the surprising beauty of it," then he realizes that "it was our town," scaled down and "peopled," so that the townsfolk find themselves in familiar places performing daily tasks, their mundane, earthly lives caught in a miniature stroke of eternity.[21]

Although the town council soon asks Mrs. Gleason to destroy the model town "on the grounds that it contravened building regulations," their action comes too late, for the city newspapers discover the marvel, and the minister for tourism declares the site a tourist attraction,

21. Carey, *Fat Man,* 108–9.

promising that "the Americans would come, . . . take photographs and bring wallets bulging with dollars. American dollars." And they do arrive, the narrator reports, to examine and photograph the model town, then to compare it to the real one through telescopes, eventually leaving the miniature and descending into the life-size original to take additional photographs for which they pay a dollar each. But "having paid the money," the narrator concludes, "they are worried about being cheated. They spend their time being disappointed and I spend my time feeling guilty, that I have somehow let them down by growing older and sadder."[22] As the story opens, the narrator, who reveals what has happened after the fact, believes that the townspeople somehow offended Mr. Gleason, thus causing him to go to such lengths to settle his score with them. His revenge was to make them immortal; even worse, he forced them to look at their eternal selves while growing mortally "older and sadder."

"American Dreams" brings to mind any number of other literary works—Edward Albee's *Tiny Alice,* for one, in which a miniature of a house rests within that house, holding yet another replica, and so on. The wall that encloses Mr. Gleason's secret also has its parallels in the labyrinths that figure so often in Borges's fiction. The title, too, plays on and then perverts the tradition of the American dream. Once transferred to the bush town, the dreams turn materialistic and shoddy in their secondhand state, speaking only "of the big city, of wealth, of modern houses, of big motor cars,"[23] the wrong sort of dreams for people to use as vehicles for escape from their "poor kind of life" (as Borges describes the existence of people who are too sure about reality). In an interview, Borges observes, "If you're a materialist, if you believe in hard and fast things, then you're tied down by reality, or by what you call reality." Carey's townsfolk had tied themselves to such a reality even in their dreams, despite the fact that dissolving reality (which, Borges says, "is not always too pleasant") can mean that people "will be helped by . . . [the] dissolution."[24]

The picture of the tiny, disembodied townspeople caught in perpetuity, while time takes its toll on those whose lives served as models, brings to mind another of Borges's perplexities: what if man were immortal? Commenting on his story "The Immortals," Borges notes, "Such an idea as immortality would, of course, be unbearable. In 'The Immortals' we are face to face with people who are only immortal and nothing else, and the prospect, I trust, is appalling" (*AOS* 280). Like don

22. Ibid., 110, 113.
23. Ibid., 102.
24. Richard Burgin, *Conversations with Jorge Luis Borges* (New York: Holt, Rinehart and Winston, 1969), 142–44.

Guillermo's son or Dr. Narbondo's "immortals," the residents of the Australian bush town go on living in their own world, detached from the past, alienated from the present, impervious to the future. Carey has treated the same philosophical question that Borges often debated, and he has done so in a manner reminiscent of Borges by grounding his story in reality, then spreading over it a transparent covering woven from the strands of fantasy. In both cases, out of the remembrances of first-person narrators come stories that insist on their believability, for the narrators of "American Dreams" and "The Immortals" have, as Ana María Barrenechea says of Borges, erased "the boundaries between life and fiction," indeed the boundaries between story and metaphysical inquiry.[25] Extraordinary events have occurred, yet they seem altogether ordinary, set as they are in very commonplace contexts.

Each of the stories in Carey's first volume gains resonance when read in the light of this commonality of philosophical concerns and narrative structure, even when the relationship is limited to a single element of Borges's fiction: the labyrinth. In "Crabs" the labyrinth evolves into a drive-in movie theater where Crabs and his girl friend find themselves trapped—their captivity an outcome that is natural enough in the real yet fantastic world they inhabit. Another instance of a physical structure figuring prominently in relation to the story's metaphysical framework arises in "Life & Death in the South Side Pavilion." The narrator relates how he has been assigned to watch the horses living in the pavilion, both he and the horses being prisoners in this place of unexplained confinement. That the pavilion represents the narrator's mental labyrinth becomes evident once he tells of drowning the horses and describes them floating in the pool where they "bumped softly into one another like bad dreams in a basin."[26] The fat men in the title story of the collection find themselves shunned by a society that refuses to tolerate obesity. They are imprisoned not only in their fat but also in a bleak and colorless structure amid "high blocks of concrete flats and areas of flat waste land where dry thistles grow."[27] For Carey, the metaphor of the labyrinth emerges not only as a metaphysical structure that turns inward and devours itself but also as a physical entity, a concept realized in another of the stories, "Peeling." Here the narrator relates how he undresses a female companion and accidentally pulls a zipper that removes another layer to reveal a male body hiding beneath, and then another female body; finally "with each touch she is dismembered, slowly, limb by limb" until he loses hold and she falls to the

---

25. Anna María Barrenechea, *Borges: The Labyrinth Maker,* trans. Robert Lima (New York: New York University Press, 1965), 15.

26. Peter Carey, "Life & Death in the South Side Pavilion," in *Fat Man,* 40.

27. Carey, "The Fat Man in History," in *Fat Man,* 118.

floor, making a "sharp noise, rather like breaking glass." He discovers among the fragments "a small doll, hairless, eyeless, and white from head to toe."[28]

Carter Wheelock stresses that "Borges' much-noticed labyrinth, his symbol for the universe, is not the objective universe but the human mind." Both Borges and Carey suggest that once men discover they are lost in a mental labyrinth, entrapped and encircled by its mysteries, afloat in its chaos, helpless in its enclosure, they attempt to provide explanations. The traditional writer or the philosopher will form grave hypotheses to explain away the "Great Labyrinth," whereas Borges "stands above this attempt to account for the universe; his truth does not depend on the things that can be called true but on the assumption that nothing can be so called. For him the goal of thought is not knowledge, but distraction."[29] Extending this critical comment to Carey adds dimension to his stories, which repeatedly explain away mystery with distraction. Both writers derive one aspect of their comedy from this quality of distraction, by eschewing seriousness in the unraveling of the perplexities they behold.

Borges and Carey share another aspect of narrative structure, their handling of time. Most often Borges sets his tales in the past, but he narrates them from an immediate point of view as though recollecting the events as he records them. On the other hand, Carey's stories often occur in a hazy, remote future. Yet, like Borges, Carey relates the happenings from a past perspective, with an immediacy established to contrast with the vaguely defined past of the future about which he is talking. George R. McMurray, in his discussion of Borges's manipulation of time, concludes, "In the end, at the center of the labyrinth, inexorable lineal time prevails."[30] Both writers embrace this inexhaustible time, stretching backward and forward, and turn the past into immediacy, the future into long ago, the now into the infinite.

Much has been said about Borges's half-formed characters, a criticism that gains legitimacy only in light of the criteria for social realism. Borges, in an interview, talks about books that take characters as their focus (such as the work of Dickens), but he admits to admiring fiction in which "there are no characters," a judgment that he makes concerning the work of Franz Kafka and then applies to Henry James: "While if I think of James, I'm thinking about a situation and a plot. I'm not think-

28. Peter Carey, "Peeling," in *Fat Man,* 32.
29. Carter Wheelock, *The Mythmaker* (Austin: University of Texas Press, 1969), 67. For more on the importance of the labyrinth as a symbol for human thought, see André Maurois (*L* xiii); Wheelock, *Mythmaker,* 27.
30. George R. McMurray, *Jorge Luis Borges* (New York: Frederick Ungar Publishing Co., 1980), 106.

ing about people, I'm thinking about what happened to them."[31] Borges's stories do not conjure up the likes of Emma Bovary or David Copperfield, all flesh and blood; nor does any piece of Carey's short fiction. In spite of the adventurers, intellectuals, historical figures, murderers, wanderers, outsiders, and criminals of all sorts that inhabit Borges's and Carey's narratives, few, if any, stand out as characters. Instead, they stand as metaphors for ambiguous beings caught in a meaningless universe where they wander, trying to make some sense of its contradictory nature.

Let us look in particular at the wanderer, the picaresque figure found in earlier Spanish literature and, for that matter, in Australian literature. The role such a hero plays in Borges's and Carey's stories is exemplified by the narrator of "The Babylon Lottery." He opens his tale: "Like all men in Babylon I have been a proconsul; like all, a slave; I have also known omnipotence, opprobrium, jail." He goes on to recount other exploits, making known finally that he owes "this almost atrocious variety to an institution which other republics know nothing about, or which operates among them imperfectly and in secret: the lottery" (*F* 65). A capricious game dictates the destinies of the Babylonians, subjecting each to the disorder that chance sets in motion. The wanderer, leaving his life to such an unreliable determiner, evolves into everyman facing the vicissitudes of fortune through the ages.

Carey's "The Chance," which appears in *War Crimes,* provides a similar handling of the wanderer who also falls victim to the lottery's whimsical dictation of men's affairs. In a distant yet lineal time, as far in the future as Babylonia lies in the past, the narrator of "The Chance" opens his account of "the Genetic Lottery" three summers after the Fastalogians have arrived, succeeding the Americans, the previous occupants of this unnamed but perpetual "Client State." He explains that "for two thousand inter-galactic dollars (IG\$2,000) we could go in the Lottery and come out with a different age, a different body, a different voice and still carry our memories (allowing for a little leakage) more or less intact." A large part of the story develops the relationship between the narrator and a girl he meets. He fails to prevent her appointment with "the Genetic Lottery" and loses her, along with the illusion of permanency they have created amid the lunacy and fragmentation prevailing in those days. "So long ago. So much past," he concludes, describing himself as "a crazy old man, alone with his books and his beer and his dog. I have been a clerk and a pedlar and a seller of cars. I have been ignorant, and a scholar of note. Pock-marked and ugly I have wandered the streets and slept in the parks. I have been bankrupt and

31. Burgin, *Conversations,* 61.

handsome and a splendid conman."[32] "Because Babylon is nothing but an infinite game of chance," as Borges ends his story (*F* 72), the eternal wanderer remains helpless, whether he is the plaything of "the Company" or of "the Fastalogians."

Outlaws and desperadoes have long taken a dominant role in both Argentine and Australian literature, their exploits belonging, as Borges says in the opening of "The Challenge," "to legend or to history or (which may be just another way of saying it belongs to legend) to both things at once" (*AOS* 139). The gauchos from an Argentine past fascinate Borges, and he puts them to use not as traditional characters whose deeds he celebrates for their own sake but as representations of those whose "manly faith" and "chivalrous passion" was "in all likelihood . . . no mere form of vanity but rather an awareness that God may be found in any man." Their stories, he says, helped "men who led extremely elementary lives—herders, stockyard workers, drovers, outlaws, and pimps"—rediscover "in their own way the age-old cult of the gods of iron" (*AOS* 143).

Similar figures have found their way into the legends or history of Australia, namely the bushrangers, whose defiance of fate allowed them an escape from "elementary lives." To hardworking, often poor and dissatisfied, farmbound or citybound Australians, tales of the bushrangers' challenging of established order helped these ordinary folk discover for themselves "the age-old cult of the gods of iron." In "War Crimes," the title story of his second volume, Carey has found a new use for the paradigm of the bushranger, by transforming him into the ultimate capitalist, the one who sees that "business must go on." As the narrator of "War Crimes" gloats over his ruthlessness, he considers his code of honor not unlike the "manly faith" and "chivalrous passion" that set apart the gauchos and bushrangers. Once more, Carey has placed "War Crimes" in a far-off time when business must go on, even if its continuation depends on wandering capitalistic bushrangers who overcome all obstacles with violence. The narrator flaunts the peculiar religion created by the demands of capitalism, boasting to those whose "elementary lives" prevent them from similar action: "I am not mad, but rather I have opened the door you all keep locked with frightened bolts and little prayers." They lack courage, he tells them: "you sit in the front room in worn blue jeans, reading about atrocities in the Sunday papers."[33] Carey's modern-day bushranger, ironically cast in his futuristic role as the capitalist run amok, does, at the end of the story, hint that he, as Borges says of the gauchos, acted out of "no mere form of vanity" but

32. Peter Carey, "The Chance," in *War Crimes,* 76, 120, 121.
33. Peter Carey, "War Crimes," in *War Crimes,* 281, 280.

behaved more from "an awareness that God may be found in any man": "I wished I had been born a great painter. I would have worn fine clothes and celebrated the glories of man. I would have stood aloft, a judge, rather than wearily kept vigil on this hill, hunchbacked, crippled, one more guilty fool with blood on his hands."[34] But like the gauchos and bushrangers of Argentine and Australian history, he cast himself in the role of the outsider who cultivated violence and developed by necessity a code of courage that placed him above ordinary men: one part of him noble, standing aloof from his fellows; the other part, guilty and bloody, even a little bit foolish.

The stories contained in *The Fat Man in History* and *War Crimes* proved, as Frank Moorhouse said of the first collection, that Carey could do "astonishing tricks," learned in part, as we have seen, from Borges. Returning again to Yates's metaphor of the compass, we find that Carey followed the call of its four points. He proceeded in one direction to track his own ambivalent "Australianness"; then he traveled on another course through books that took him far beyond the provincial society where he only half belonged. Thus he prepared himself for further exploration: to investigate the perplexities he encountered and to chart unmapped territories in his native literary landscape.

The new generation of Australians, so much less restricted in national literary choices than their predecessors, greatly admires Carey's sophisticated fantasy. The widespread acceptance of this fantasy, in a literature once dominated by social realism, might make it possible someday to study Carey's effect on the Australian short story and demonstrate how he helped to alter its course. That traces of Borges's genius "cannot *not* be there," at least in the work of one writer, should assure that Australia's fiction will, as Moorhouse puts it, " 'go too far' and resist blandness."[35] The new work now appearing, much of it "international" in both mode and publication, suggests that Australian writers have taken up that challenge, just as Carey did a decade before.

34. Ibid., 282.
35. Frank Moorhouse, ed., *The State of the Act: The Mood of Contemporary Australia in Short Stories* (Ringwood, Australia: Penguin Books, 1983), 5.

Rafael Gutiérrez Girardot _____

Borges in Germany
A Difficult and Contradictory
Fascination

The reception of Borges's work in the Federal Republic of Germany has had to overcome many obstacles, the first and most persistent being a deep-seated prejudice against Latin American literature. In the unanimous opinion of those interested in it, Latin American literature had produced only three major works: *La vorágine* (The vortex; 1924) by José Eustacio Rivera; *Don Segundo Sombra* (1926) by Ricardo Güiraldes; and *Doña Barbara* (1929) by Rómulo Gallegos. These three works were not only considered to be the most outstanding; they were also seen as authentic expressions of Latin America's social milieu. Latin American literature had to be the expression of an untamed nature (Rivera), of the gaucho (Güiraldes), or of the barbarous plainswoman (Gallegos)—otherwise it was not Latin American literature. This prejudice had a precedent not merely in what Antonello Gerbi called the "dispute of the New World," but also in the Latin Americans' own evaluation of what constituted their *authentic* literature.[1]

At the end of World War II, this German appraisal of Latin American literature remained unchanged and, moreover, was relegated to a secondary place because the establishment of two Germanies in 1945 was characterized by a cultural paradox: a *Kahlschlag* or tabula rasa with regard to Germany's own past and, at the same time, a renewed awareness of European literature, which had been stifled by the Teutonic nationalism of the Nazis. (The work of writers like Gottfried Benn or Ernst Jünger, who had become contaminated by National Socialism or had been its involuntary forerunners—only to become its victims—was recovered as well.) In 1947, Hans Paeschke founded *Merkur,* the most influential journal in the Federal Republic until 1975; he gave the new publication this significant subtitle: "A German journal for European thought." In an atmosphere so focused on Europe, a Latin Ameri-

---

1. Antonello Gerbi, *La disputa del Nuevo Mundo* (Mexico: Fondo de Cultura Económica, 1960).

can literature rooted in Rivera, Güiraldes, and Gallegos could play no role: it seemed too exotically distant, too inferior. What could Rivera, Güiraldes, and Gallegos have to say to a German reader determined to reestablish lost links with Europe, to assimilate Proust, Gide, and Eliot, and to be informed about such contemporaries as de Rougemont and countless others?

In the same year *Merkur* was founded, Hans Werner Richter created what became known as the "Group 47." This informal association of writers gradually became the most important literary arbiter in Germany: the decisions taken at its meetings and the prizes it awarded all but replaced literary criticism. Its pronouncements attained canonical status in the eyes of the reading public. The group, and especially its creator and guide, Richter, attempted to overcome the tabula rasa with a new and demanding literature that would have nothing to do with the immediate past. The work of the most respected contemporary German writers—Günter Grass, Hans Magnus Enzensberger, Martin Walser, Ingeborg Bachmann, and others—resulted from this attempt. This is not the place to detail the problematics of a closed group, bound to a ritualized criticism that combined obscure aesthetic standards with an aversion toward dialogue (particularly dialogue with the new writers whose work was being judged). Nevertheless, with regard to the reception not only of Borges but also of other literatures, it is clear that Richter was hoping to renew German literature through the very evil he was trying to uproot: a peculiar nationalism hiding behind the mask of an after-the-fact antifascism.

The Tin Drum (1959), the novel that made Grass famous, is an example of this paradox. The book was awarded a prize by the "Group 47" at an October 1958 conference held in the town of Grossholzleute in Allgäu. What characterized not only the Grass novel but also most of the literature appearing under Richter's tutelage was an air (or as a German cosmopolite, following Jünger, would say, an "atmosphere") of small-town provincialism. The parodies Grass attempted in the book (parodies of the picaresque, of Goethe's bildungsroman *Wilhelm Meister,* of Heidegger's language), as well as its main character, all come across as deadly serious—they lack humor and fail as caricatures. There are many reasons this novel failed, but the most important is the atmosphere prevailing within Richter's group, an atmosphere of qualified renaissance and substantial provincialism that remained prevalent until well into the sixties. There was no room in it for Borges's work—not even for curiosity about his work. It would, nonetheless, be unfair to reproach Germany for blindness: in the same period, the Spanish reading public preferred the rustic nativism of Camilo José Cela's *The Family of Pascual Duarte* (1942)—which it considered literature—to *The*

Garden of Forking Paths (1942) and *Ficciones* (1944). It was thus a concept of literature and, even more, a concept of what constituted a fitting task for sense and reason that blocked the reception of Borges in postwar Germany.

Between 1948 and 1960, an "economic miracle" took place in Germany, bringing new values to society. These values were embodied in slogans such as "Prosperity for all," "Being there is everything" (referring to important happenings and entertainment events), and "No experiments" (what's sure is sure). These values implied a new, German self-understanding that energetically rejected the characterization that had made the country famous in the nineteenth century as "Germany, land of poets and thinkers." In the euphoria of full employment and prosperity for all, West Germany stifled anything that might raise doubts, or dredge up memories of the immediate past. "Germany is no longer a state," Hegel wrote in 1802.[2] The Germany of the "economic miracle" unconsciously added a second part to his statement: "It is an economy." In this atmosphere, the authors of most interest to the German public were not the ones rediscovered by such journals as *Merkur* or *Neue Deutsche Rundschau* but "edifying" writers like Romano Guardini, or easily understandable and semi-exotic ones like Ortega y Gasset. Guardini preached, Ortega prophesied, and criticism, irony, and humor fell by the wayside.

In 1958 this writer suggested to Ernesto Grassi, director of the famous *Encyclopaedia Rowohlt*, that he approach his publishers— among the most important in Germany at the time—with the idea of editing a selection of Borges's work in German.[3] The response to the proposal was surprising from a literary point of view, but it indicated that the publisher's reader knew his market. His verdict on *Otras Inquisiciones, Historia universal de la infamia, Ficciones,* and other works was, roughly, "This is neither understood nor of interest in Germany." A year later, possibly under the influence of a French collection, Karl August Horst published a translation of *Ficciones* and *El Aleph* under the title *Labyrinthe*.[4] The translation was all but ignored. In 1960, the cultural section of the Argentine embassy in Bonn published a series of mimeographed pamphlets on contemporary Argentine writ-

2. Georg Wilhelm Friedrich Hegel, *Schriften zur Politik und Rechtsphilosophie* (Leipzig: Meiner, 1913), 3.

3. Rowohlt was known for its innovative editorial policies. For example, it published two Expressionist anthologies: a prose collection, *Die Entfaltung,* ed. Max Krell (Berlin: Rowohlt, 1921) and the famous poetry anthology *Menschheitsdämmerung,* ed. Kurt Pinthus (Berlin: Rowohlt, 1920).

4. Jorge Luis Borges, *Labyrinthes,* trans. Roger Caillois (Paris: Gallimard, 1953); Jorge Luis Borges, *Labyrinthe,* trans. Karl August Horst (Munich: Hanser, 1959).

ers, which were sent to important German journals and newspapers. As a result, Hans Paeschke and Joachim Moras decided to devote an issue of their magazine to Borges (with the author of this article as guest editor) and to include in it a Borgesian text that would fit in with the "Europeanizing" philosophy of the journal. The text was "El escritor argentino y la tradición" (The Argentine writer and tradition).[5] It might seem, then, that Borges's reception, or recognition, in Germany began with *Labyrinthe*, which appeared in a second edition in 1962; the facts, however, were quite different.

The difficulties faced by Borges in Germany were not solely due to the exotic image of Latin American literature, or to the paradoxical provincialism of Germany's renascent postwar literature, or to the facile tastes of the reading public. There was yet another obstacle, considerably stranger than the others, and archetypally embodied by Horst himself. This obstacle had a scientific name: "neophilology" or, more specifically, "German Romance studies." In the years following World War II, this peculiar science was shaped and ruled by Ernst Robert Curtius, who in his famous book *Europäische Literatur und lateinisches Mittelalter* not only asserted the exclusive devotion of German Romance studies to Calderón but also praised Spain's cultural backwardness.[6] In his *Kritische Essays zur europäischen Literatur,* Curtius tried to bring himself up-to-date by including studies on Ortega y Gasset, Miguel de Unamuno, Ramón Pérez de Ayala, and Jorge Guillén.[7] But for the German reader interested in Spanish-language letters, the image imposed by Curtius continued to be narrow and extraordinarily partial: only those four contemporary writers could be added to the list of literary figures consecrated by earlier Romance scholars[8]—Calderón, Lope de Vega, Gracián, Cervantes, and the mystics, especially Teresa of Ávila. Aside from the work of those authors, there was nothing in Spanish-language literature that deserved attention; and if there was, it had to follow tradition or adapt to it.

This is precisely what happened to Borges's writing. The first German study to mention his name (and the French translation of his stories, *Labyrinthe*) was a work by Gustav René Hocke (a disciple of

5. Gutiérrez Girardot, "Jorge Luis Borges," *Merkur* 156 (1961): 171–78; Jorge Luis Borges, "Der argentinische Schriftsteller und die Tradition," *Merkur* 156 (1961): 118–26.

6. Ernst Robert Curtius, *Europäische Literatur und lateinisches Mittelalter* (Bern: Francke, 1948; 2d ed., 1954). The English translation is *European Literature and the Latin Middle Ages,* trans. William R. Trask (New York: Pantheon, 1953).

7. Ernst Robert Curtius, *Kritische Essays zur europäischen Literatur* (Bern: Francke, 1950). The English translation is *Essays on European Literature,* trans. Michael Kowal (Princeton: Princeton University Press, 1973).

8. Especially Karl Vossler in *Poesie der Einsamkeit in Spanien* (Munich: Beck, 1950).

Curtius) entitled *Die Welt als Labyrinth: Manier und Manie in der europäischen Kunst* (The world as labyrinth: Mannerism and manner in European art). In the first volume of his study—which owes much to Curtius's reevaluation of Mannerism in *Europäische Literatur*—Hocke says: "Jorge Luis Borges's *Labyrinths* [*sic*] has been published in a French translation. The narrations are composed in a very labyrinthine style, and say the following: [here Hocke gives two quotes, which are impossible to identify since they are translated into German from the French without any page references]. The 'hero' finds himself in a labyrinth [another quote follows describing the hero's growing terror and anguish]. This persistent fascination with the motif of the labyrinth in the homeland of Góngora is not surprising—Góngora died mentally deranged."[9] In the second volume of his study, called *Manierismus in der Literatur: Sprach-Alchimie und esoterische Kombinationskunst* (Mannerism in literature: The alchemy of language and the secret art of combination), Curtius's disciple adds: "The narrations of the Spaniard [*sic*] Jorge Luis Borges have the significant title of *The Aleph,* the Hebrew name for the letter 'A'. These stories are alexandrine in every sense of the word; they are also Gongorine, and consciously follow seventeenth-century models."[10] Borges is now Spanish and Gongorine, an imitator of literary models from seventeenth-century Spain. The description is not surprising: this was the mold into which Hocke had to squeeze Borges so that his prose would square with Curtius's nebulous notions of a European continuity based on topoi or on the "collective unconscious."

Hocke's evaluation of Borges's work influenced a peculiar kind of "literary criticism," the spur-of-the-moment criticism characteristic of many newspapers. These publications, faced with the need to comment on an ever-growing number of books, often resort to the repetition of two or three consecrated truths—usually whatever was first said about a particular author or work. In the case of Borges, the reference to the "alexandrine" quality of his prose was what fascinated the spur-of-the-moment commentators. (For reasons known only to God and Curtius, this quality was essential to the idea of European continuity.) Was Borges really "alexandrine," "Gongorine," "alexandrine-Gracian-esque"—a hallucinating Spaniard perpetuating the hallucinatory fascinations of seventeenth-century Spain? A number of answers come to

9. Gustav René Hocke, *Die Welt als Labyrinth. Manier und Manie in der europäischen Kunst. Beiträge zur Ikonographie und Formgeschichte der europäischen Kunst von 1520 bis 1650 und der Gegenwart* (Hamburg: Rowohlt, 1957), 103.

10. Gustav René Hocke, *Manierismus in der Literatur. Sprach-Alchimie und esoterische Kombinationskunst. Beiträge zur vergleichenden europäischen Literaturgeschichte* (Hamburg: Rowohlt, 1963), 22.

mind. The most evident and elementary is that Hocke was denied an impartial reading of Borges by the narrow horizons of German Romance scholarship, shaped as it was by Curtius's bias and by a pretense to omniscience and infallibility. There is, however, another answer, one that transcends the problem of the learned ignorance of German Romance scholarship. This answer is inevitably political.

The years between 1957 and 1962, the period of Borges's earliest reception in Germany, coincided with the conservative restoration and its peculiar correlative: the silencing, or perhaps more accurately, the reshaping of the immediate past. The process had unusual consequences. For example, the historiography of the resistance to Hitler took on a selective nature: the only ones who opposed him (so the argument went) were conservative Germans of various shades and types. Although the conservatives' anti-Hitler movement had been half-hearted or late in coming, it was now presented as the most efficient and promising. (Curtius was one of the outstanding conservatives of the restoration period, along with Rudolf Alexander Schröder, Reinhold Schneider, and the young writer Hans Egon Holthusen.) But German conservatism had been ambiguous, and it was in fact the so-called "conservative revolution" of the thirties (with Ernst and Friedrich Georg Jünger and the National Bolshevist Ernst Niekisch) that had involuntarily promoted ideas that later became part of the National-Socialist ideology. This conservatism had been unable to free itself either from the embrace of the Nazis or from tacit and at times open approval of the campaign against the democratic Weimar Republic. Thus, in the days of the restoration, conservatism provoked both pride and shame.

There was an attempt in those years to separate the "conservative revolution" from national socialism, since conservatism was trying to present itself as the link with Europe and the European future, forgetting or silencing the nationalist and antidemocratic elements that had previously characterized it.[11] As conservatism had given itself a future-oriented, Europeanizing face, its adherents—for example, Curtius's disciples, Hocke and Horst—were unable to understand any conservative thought not consonant with their own. Only in the seventies did conservatism finally examine its problems, dilemmas, and principles.[12] This explains why neither Hocke nor Horst (who had marked the beginning of Borges's reception in Germany) was able to perceive the affinities between the conservative bent of their master's thinking and

11. See Armin Mohler, *Die konservative Revolution in Deutschland* (Stuttgart: Vorwerk, 1950).

12. See M. Greiffenhagen, *Das Dilemma des Konservatismus in Deutschland* (Munich: Piepper, 1971).

the ideas of the "Spanish," "Gongorine," "alexandrine" Borges. The continuity of Europe (based on the persistence of certain topoi or on the "collective unconscious") had its equivalent in Borges's statement "Perhaps universal history is the history of a few metaphors" (*OI* 6), an idea repeated throughout his work. Also, a consideration of the similarities between Curtius's notion of European continuity and Borges's cyclical conception of world history would have inevitably brought to mind Spengler's *Der Untergang des Abendlandes,* a cyclically conceived work that had helped undermine the foundations of the Weimar Republic and was thus taboo in many circles.[13]

It is true that there are considerable differences between Curtius's and Borges's conservatism. Curtius, for instance, was not interested in philosophy. Since he ascribed to the idea of Spain's cultural "backwardness," he (like Dámaso Alonso) had an aversion to, indeed a fear of, philosophical speculation. Borges, on the other hand, was critical of this backwardness, justly blaming it for the absence of what he called "metaphysical terror" in Spanish-language letters (*ia* 182). Borges had to look elsewhere for his metaphysics—to Nietzsche, Schopenhauer, Berkeley, and the Greeks. Furthermore, unlike Curtius who wanted to enjoy the privileges and graces of the literary life but lacked the credentials, Borges had a cosmopolitan background that allowed him to become an unusually epicurean and hedonistic reader. Still, these differences should not prevent us from seeing how Curtius's German disciples might have initiated a fairer and more fruitful understanding of Borges had they followed the route of conservative thought. This omission, moreover, was important in determining Borges's reception in post-restoration Germany, the fervently neodemocratic Germany that grew out of the upheavals of the petite-bourgeoisie in 1968.

This Germany was preceded by another restoration: the heterodox, *großbürgerlich* Marxism of Theodor Adorno and Max Horkheimer of the legendary Frankfurt School. The rise to fame of this school began with Adorno's book *Prismen* (Prisms), published in 1955, the same year in which he also published—in strangely mutilated versions— several of Walter Benjamin's works.[14] Adorno popularized a deliberately complex, affected style, which gave an esoteric dogmatism to his writings. Perhaps because of this, he attracted Germany's intelligentsia

---

13. Oswald Spengler, *Der Untergang des Abendlandes* (Munich: Beck, 1920–1922). English edition, *The Decline of the West* (New York: Knopf, 1945).

14. *Großbürgerlich* is the German term used to describe a social class that in the Spanish-speaking world is called *la aristocracia del dinero,* the nouveaux riches, though in Germany this class has usually known how to harmonize commerce with culture. Theodor W. Adorno, *Prismen: Kulturkritik und Gesellschaft* (Frankfurt: Suhrkamp, 1955); Walter Benjamin, *Schriften* (Frankfurt: Suhrkamp, 1955).

and young people, who by 1961 were becoming disaffected with the restoration and thus increasingly politicized. The politicization—like Adorno himself—was not only confusedly leftist; it was also knee-jerkingly antifascist, displaying a selective sensitivity to the victims of right-wing regimes. This sensitivity, along with the growing cult of Che Guevara and Ho Chi Minh and the influence of Adorno's style and his discovery of Benjamin (a Jew persecuted by the Nazis), contributed to a stifling of interest in Borges. It was neither known nor made known that Borges had been pro-Jewish and anti-Nazi long before Germany's post-war antifascists, or that he had been persecuted by Perón, in large measure because of his views. These facts were also conveniently for-gotten later on, when Borges welcomed the takeover by the military in Argentina and accepted a decoration from Pinochet.

But the list of Borges's problems in Germany does not end here. After *Labyrinthe,* the Munich publishing house Hanser put out *Der schwarze Spiegel* (The black mirror) in 1961, while Frankfurt's Insel included a number of narrations from *Labyrinthe* in its prestigious Insel-Bücherei series, under the title *Der Zahir und andere Erzählungen* (The zahir and other stories) in 1964.[15] The translator of the title story, Eva Hesse, had a considerable reputation: she had translated Pound's *Cantos* into German and was respected as an expert in contemporary literature, particularly English literature.[16] But the link between Borges and Pound established through Hesse's translations could still not penetrate the strange barrier that was preventing Borges from succeeding in Germany. For Hesse herself, the work on his writings was not of central importance. Since she did not know what to do with him, since he did not fit into any of her literary categories, she quickly forgot him. (In fact, Borges might have been useful for Hesse's study on Pound: his appraisal of Nietzsche, like that of Pound's British "promoter," Thomas Ernest Hulme, is an essential chapter in the history of conservative thought and modern literature.)

For his part, Borges made sure to disorient his few German readers. During a German–Latin American literary colloquium in Berlin in 1963 organized by the Argentine embassy's cultural attaché, Ernesto Garzón Valdés, and by this author, Borges was asked what he thought about German translations of his works. He answered that they were better than the originals. Such a reply was confusing, to say the least, in the

15. Jorge Luis Borges, *Der schwarze Spiegel,* trans. Karl August Horst (Munich: Hanser, 1961), a translation of *Historia universal de la infamia;* Jorge Luis Borges, *Der Zahir und andere Erzählungen,* trans. Eva Hesse and Karl August Horst, afterword by Rafael Gutiérrez Girardot (Frankfurt: Insel, 1964).

16. Her monograph *Ezra Pound: Von Sinn und Wahnsinn* (Munich: Kindler, 1978) is a classic.

land of Eckermann's respectful conversations with Goethe. In the same year, the writer Horst Bienek, who had recently emigrated from East Germany and had attended the colloquium, made another attempt to decipher Borges. But during his interview, Bienek used the same mannerist, baroque, Spanish yardstick as Hocke and asked Borges about his relation to Gracián. "Yes, I like Gracián," was the answer.[17] (In his book *El otro, el mismo* [The other, the same], which appeared a year after the colloquium and his conversation with Bienek, Borges published an irreverent yet balanced poem on Gracián in which he demonstrated neither appreciation nor rejection, but rather astonished contempt.) The baroque Borges who was not baroque; the ironic Borges whose ironies were taken seriously; the Spanish Borges who was Argentine; the author of pieces like "El hombre de la esquina rosada" (Streetcorner man), which was included in *Der schwarze Spiegel* and should have been the delight of all the European consumers of gauchesque exoticism—who was this Borges? Was he a (Borgesian) fiction?

The first doctoral dissertation on Borges to be written in West Germany was devoted to answering these questions.[18] The author, Ernst E. Behle, attempted to clarify the problems posed by Borges's early ultraist, or avant-garde, period as well as to elucidate his concept of man, time, and space. To do so, he had to confront the reigning view of Borges as a mannerist-baroque writer, the view put forward by Hocke and by Borges's translator, Horst (see the epilogue to *Labyrinthe* [1959]). The reading of Borges presented by these two critics derived from Curtius's notion of "latent mannerism" as a permanent (ahistorical) characteristic of the literature of the Romance-speaking peoples—a notion that was itself part of the larger concept of *Völkerpsychologie* (a psychology typical to every people), whose chief exponent was the German Wilhelm Wundt. The pressure of this and other received teachings (such as the previously mentioned preference for seventeenth-century Spain) explains why Behle, using Bienek's conversation with Borges as evidence, asserts that the early Borges was a mannerist. Still, after examining the "baroque" characteristics that Horst underlines in Borges's work, Behle ultimately concludes—following Ana María Barrenechea, José Luis Ríos Patrón, and this writer—that Borges is not a mannerist.[19] His need to "confirm" the dominant reading of Borges, through a discussion of Hocke's and Horst's impressionistic thesis, exemplified the type of resistance that new Latin American authors had

---

17. Horst Bienek, "Coloquio con Jorge Luis Borges," *Humboldt* (Munich) 24 (1965): 45–50 (50).

18. Ernst E. Behle, *Jorge Luis Borges: Eine Einführung in sein Leben und Werk* (Bern: Lang, 1972).

19. Ibid., 90–91.

to overcome in Germany, particularly authors like Borges, who did not fit into the mold propagated by German Romance studies. Though this first doctoral dissertation on Borges deserves credit for conceding to the Latin Americans the right to speak for themselves and to evaluate their own literature (a right all too often denied them by German critics), it reveals the shortcomings that resulted from the bias toward nineteenth- and twentieth-century Latin American literature and from the ignorance of the achievements and innovations of this literature since independence.

"I disbelieve in literary schools," Borges wrote in the introduction to *El oro de los tigres* (The gold of the tigers; 1972), "which I consider to be didactic simulacra intended to simplify what they teach; but if I were forced to say from where my poems derive, I would say from *modernismo* [the fin-de-siècle renewal of poetry and prose initiated by the Nicaraguan poet Rubén Darío]. That great freedom . . . renewed the many literatures whose common instrument was Spanish and, . . . of course, reached Spain itself."[20] German Romance scholarship was unaware—and is still unaware—of the importance of *modernismo* in the history of Spanish-language letters. It had no need to be aware of *modernismo,* since Vossler had already decreed that Gracián marked the beginnings of modernity in Spain, because Gracián had failed to quote a single poem in his *Criticón.* He had thus anticipated Hegel's thesis about the "death of art," that is, about the inception of modernity.[21] If modernity had in fact been announced by Gracián, what room could there be for Darío's *modernismo* or for Borges's writing? If the German image of Spanish-language literature did not include any Latin American literature prior to the so-called classic novels by Rivera, Gallegos, and Güiraldes, how could Darío and Borges be called leading artisans of Hispanic letters?

These problems of Romance studies in Germany were, as already noted, not confined to Borges. After having suffered the isolation imposed by the Nazis, Romance scholarship faced the formidable task of incorporating and understanding unfamiliar literatures and literary periods. But it had at its disposal only outmoded tools—the time-honored models of the Spanish Golden Age, the Italian Renaissance, or the French Classical era. These were totally inadequate for studying eighteenth-century Spanish literature, nineteenth-century Spanish and Latin American writing, or most of all Latin American literature of the contemporary period. Before any successful critical work could be

---

20. Jorge Luis Borges, *Obra poética: 1923–1977,* 3d ed. (Madrid: Alianza Tres; Emecé, 1983), 365.

21. Vossler, *Poesie der Einsamkeit,* 310.

undertaken, room had to be made for new ideas and new modes of analysis. That was precisely the thrust of Hans Robert Jauss's path-breaking study, "Literary History as a Challenge to Literary Theory."[22] This is not the place to undertake an evaluation of Jauss's *Rezeptions-ästhetik* (aesthetics of reception); what is clear, however, is that *Rezeptionsästhetik* did not confront some of the central problems of German Romance scholarship: its narrow scope and more importantly its resistance to change and innovation. For example, German Hispanists were interested in the so-called Boom in Latin American literature. But instead of looking at it historically, they considered it to be a spontaneous aberration of the sixties—an aberration that reinforced the exotic image of Latin America and the well-worn German nostalgia for the far-off: *Fernweh.*[23] "Magical realism," "primitive mythology," "civilization or barbarism": these were the catchwords and the criteria used to define the Boom. Borges, of course, did not fit this image; he also did not fit the label automatically placed on all members of the Boom Club, a leftist label that often hid a suspicious irrationalism of a fascist cut.[24]

The fact that Borges was not a man of the left to a great extent shaped his image in the eyes of the German public. In September 1976, on the occasion of Borges's visit to Madrid, Walter Haubrich, the correspondent for the widely read conservative daily *Frankfurter Allgemeine Zeitung,* published an article based on the visit with the title "Dichter sollte man erschiessen: Die seltsamen Ansichten des Jorge Luis Borges" (Poets should be shot: Jorge Luis Borges's strange views).[25] The title supposedly referred to comments made by Borges about Federico García Lorca. But what it revealed in fact was a painful lack of critical penetration, an intellectual dishonesty, a total unawareness of Borges's characteristic irreverence, and a complete ignorance of the simplest facts of literary sociology. According to Haubrich—who had been invited to teach courses on the contemporary Latin American novel at the Universidad Internacional Menéndez Pelayo in Santander—Borges had said, "The circumstances of Lorca's death were very advantageous for him. It is very good [*es muy favorable*] for poets to die this way. Besides, Lorca's death allowed Antonio Machado—who was a better

22. Hans Robert Jauss, *Literaturgeschichte als Provokation* (Frankfurt: Suhrkamp, 1970). The English translation is "Literary History as a Challenge to Literary Theory," in *Toward an Aesthetic of Reception,* trans. Timothy Bahti, intro. Paul de Man (Brighton, Sussex: Harvester Press, 1982), 3–45.

23. Wolfgang Reiff, *Zivilisationsflucht und literarische Wunschträume* (Stuttgart: Metzlersche, 1975).

24. Rafael Gutiérrez Girardot, "Der dritte Versuch: Kritisches zur Rezeption lateinamerikanischer Literatur," *Merkur* 31 (1977): 172–78.

25. Walter Haubrich, "Dichter sollte man erschiessen: Die seltsamen Ansichten des Jorge Luis Borges," *Frankfurter Allgemeine Zeitung,* July 10, 1976, p. 23.

poet—to write an excellent poem on the death of Garcia Lorca."
Haubrich's brilliant conclusion from these statements is: "Kill the poets,
so that good poems may be written!" And this conclusion is glossed
with an air of didacticism typical of many German correspondents in
Latin America: "Immorality and cynicism disguised as aesthetic commentary could not have been expressed more crassly."[26]

There is no doubt that Lorca's execution by Franco's forces, and his
conversion into a martyr, privileged his writings and his poetry. In his
comments, Borges alludes to this indisputable fact, albeit with his usual
irony. But Haubrich, with characteristic Teuto-democratic, postrepub-
lican seriousness, goes on to derive a commandment from these comments—poets should be shot—and completely distorts Borges's intent.

Haubrich's attack on Borges is buttressed by another, related issue
that has impeded Borges's reception not only in Germany: the matter of
his support for rightist regimes. The journalist takes Borges to task for
having said during the same visit to Madrid: "Democracy is only a
superstition. Franco benefited his people. . . . I completely agree with
Chile's military junta." Haubrich correctly assumes that such views
prevented Borges from winning the Nobel Prize for Literature, adding
that awarding the prize to the author of *The Aleph* would have been
seen by Latin Americans as a "premeditated provocation." This does
not prevent Haubrich from recognizing that "Jorge de Borges [*sic*] is
one of the few living authors to whom contemporary literature owes a
debt of gratitude for his enduring innovations in literary style and narrative technique. Many writers in Latin America and Europe have benefited immeasurably from Borges's influence."[27]

What are the reasons for this German hypersensitivity to Borges's
declarations of support for Franco, Pinochet, and Argentina's former
military regime? Why do those critics, incensed by Borges's statements,
refuse to address Neruda's Stalinism, or the tacit and sometimes overt
support of the United States, the Catholic Church, local elites, and even
elements of the middle class, for these same totalitarian regimes? Postwar German society has not forgotten but has repressed its shock at the
support given to the Nazis by such prominent members of the intelligentsia as Martin Heidegger and Carl Schmitt, to name only two
among many. The rise of national socialism was "blamed" on these
intellectuals instead of on much of the middle class, on skilled labor,
Catholic political groups, and the industrial barons. Under normal circumstances, few people would have known who Heidegger was; but
when the time came to lay the blame for the rise of Hitler, it was "clear"

26. Ibid.
27. Ibid.

that he had been the one largely responsible. Little attention was paid to the philosopher's retraction, to his admission one year after his affiliation with Nazism that he was wrong. Here was a scapegoat; little else mattered. As for Borges, his was understood as a replay of Heidegger's case: the intellectual betraying his society, *la trahison des clercs*.

The matter of Borges's social commitment greatly influenced the review of the German translation of *El libro de arena*, "Literatur über die Literatur über die Literatur" (Literature on literature on literature), written by one of West Germany's most serious, socially aware, and independent critics, Walter Boehlich. Boehlich, a former disciple of Curtius, had turned against the master's teachings, espousing instead a peculiar form of Marxist criticism suitable only for Latin America. In his review, which appeared in the moderately liberal *Süddeutsche Zeitung,* the country's second most important daily, Boehlich voiced opinions about Latin America that were not very different from those of Haubrich and much of the German left. He confessed, for example, that he read Borges with a "mixture of repugnance and fascination." While based on dreams (guided dreams that have nothing to do with *social* reality), Borges's literature is fascinating because it still reflects certain aspects of reality that should not be eliminated. In addition, albeit to a lesser extent, Borges's dreams bespeak a certain cultural context, and this context cannot be done away with in the real world. Nonetheless, Borges is repugnant because he is "deeply reactionary"—not conservative, as he has long claimed. Those who ignore this fact, or who are not bothered by it, necessarily read his works in a "highly inaccurate way."[28]

At this point Boehlich makes one of those mental leaps so frequent in Curtius. Instead of referring to Borges's writings, where this "reactionary conscience" is supposedly to be found, he quotes the statements made by the author in Madrid, those statements that a year earlier had occasioned Haubrich's distortions. Nevertheless, Boehlich recognizes that Borges's importance comes from his contributions to "Argentine Spanish, which cannot be appreciated by German readers; first, because translations of Borges into German are no more than approximations, and second, because literary German long ago reached the level to which Borges has raised Argentina's literary idiom."

These comments demonstrate that it was not the "politically indifferent" readers of Borges who understood his works in a "highly inaccurate way," but rather Boehlich himself. Had he bothered to read

---

28. Walter Boehlich, "Literatur über die Literatur über die Literatur," *Süddeutsche Zeitung* (Munich), October 12, 1977, p. 18. All citations in the next three paragraphs are from this article.

Borges's precursors Sarmiento and Darío as well as Borges (essays such as "Las alarmas del doctor Américo Castro"), he might have refrained from underlining the author's merits as a "renewer" of Argentine Spanish. Yet the circumscribing of Borges to the Argentine milieu did not prevent Boehlich from pointing out that he is "the most European of Latin American writers," since he is removed from his country and the social reality of his continent by his education and upbringing. The question the critic did not consider was: how could Borges renew something from which he was completely estranged?

Boehlich goes on to make a related accusation: "Borges has consistently reproduced European themes and cultural patterns. These have more to do with the abstractions of universal literature . . . than with his Latin American circumstance. He has lived in books; has written on and according to books; has imitated and rewritten books; and has incorporated into his work what others have written before him." The implication of all this, of course, is that there is no room for universal literature on the South American continent. And since Latin America has no room for universal culture, this culture, which includes "the mystical and the fantastic, Old English and Old Germanic literature, the Arabian Nights, and the world of ancient myth," can only be considered "adventurism" in an Argentine context. Consequently, Borges must be taken to task for doing what European writers (including German writers like Jean Paul and Arno Schmidt) have done: for writing on and according to books; for imitating, incorporating, and reworking the writings of others.

Although Boelich, speaking from a leftist perspective, advocates a literature committed to politics and change for Latin America, his views on the relevance of European culture in a Latin American setting reveal the same type of incredulity found in an essay on Darío written by the conservative scholar Sir Cecil Bowra.[29] But despite their doubts—doubts not untinged by a residual racism—both Bowra and Boehlich have to recognize Darío's and Borges's literary merits. What is clear is that neither critic has a solid knowledge of the historical-literary realities of the Hispanic world, and that some of their judgments are patently absurd. Boehlich, for example, thinks that Borges really considered Hitler to have been a philanthropist.

Boehlich said that his reaction to Borges was a mixture of fascination and repugnance. But the reaction was, in fact, more a mixture of prejudice and blindness to reality—the reality that Latin America can, and does, have a literature with European characteristics, but with a unique and universal voice. Such prejudice is not new. Gerbi has traced its

29. Cecil Bowra, *Inspiration and Poetry* (London: Macmillan, 1955).

persistence from Buffon to Schlegel to Schopenhauer, while Edmundo O'Gorman has studied its presence in the thinking of Ortega y Gasset, who claimed, "America has no history; it is Nature."[30] This notion, which O'Gorman termed "the calumny of America," in many ways underlies the reception in both Germanies of Borges and of Latin American literature as a whole.

The most recent phase of this reception began in 1976. That year, the Association of German Publishers and Booksellers decided to feature Latin American literature at the Frankfurt Book Fair. One of the highlights of this effort was a book entitled *Materialien zur lateinamerikanischen Literatur* (Materials on Latin American literature), published by Suhrkamp, a house that had gradually become aware of the impact of the Boom and had begun to republish earlier translations of Latin American writers. The volume was edited by Mechtild Strausfeld-Salcedo, who held a doctorate from the University of Bonn, and it opened with an essay on Borges.[31] The book was a huge success largely because it was presented at the fair, in a paperback edition. (It is still the principal introductory text on contemporary Latin American literature used at many German universities.)

But the author of the opening essay on Borges was neither German nor Latin American. He was George Steiner, whose essay collection *Extraterritorial* had been published by Suhrkamp in 1974. The collection, characterized by the same erudite superficiality later perfected by Steiner in his *Antigones* (1984), included a piece on Borges with the Borgesian title "Tigers in the Mirror."[32] The piece seemed to have been authored by Carlos Argentino Danieri; it presented Borges as an aleph who, although discovered late, "belonged" to Steiner with the intimacy of a childhood friend. The essay also had factual errors—the date of Borges's translation of Virginia Woolf's *Orlando,* for example. But the preciseness of Steiner's information was largely beside the point; and so was Borges. What was really involved was business, pure and simple, a commercial transaction using Borges's name. Steiner had created an aura of expertise around himself, and his publishers were taking advantage of it to promote the sales of their new (and better-forgotten) book.

"Retirado en la paz de los desiertos / con pocos, pero doctos libros juntos, / vivo en conversación con los difuntos / y escucho con mis ojos

30. Gerbi, *Disputa del Nuevo Mundo;* Edmundo O'Gorman, *Fundamentos de la historia de América* (Mexico: Imprenta Universitaria, 1942), 85.

31. Mechtild Strausfeld-Salcedo, *Materialien zur lateinamerikanischen Literatur* (Frankfurt: Suhrkamp, 1976).

32. George Steiner, *Extraterritorial* (New York: Atheneum, 1976) and *Antigones* (Oxford: Clarendon, 1984).

a los muertos" (Away, amid the peace of deserts / With few, but learned books, / I live conversing with the shadows / and with my eyes hark to the dead). These words, written by Quevedo in exile, are highlighted by Borges in his introduction to an anthology of poetry by this exceptional Spanish writer.[33] Boehlich took Borges to task for having lived in and written on books, for having devoted his life to "harking to" the dead—which Boehlich erroneously interprets as *returning* to the dead. Steiner, on the other hand, deprived his contemporaries, and future generations, of seeing Borges as one of those dead—as an author of books. This was because the sales strategy adopted by Suhrkamp— which could be called "intertextual advertising"—turned Borges into a commodity, with little concern for what he had to say. Borges had generally resisted the prevailing tendency toward the commercialization of literature. In addition, the controversy generated by his political opinions helped keep discussions of his work on a level where (paradoxically) the emphasis was on quality and literary content rather than on popularity or sales potential. Now, through the aura of discovery that Steiner gave to Borges (with the encouragement of Suhrkamp's owner), the controversial and admired Argentine became a luxury item, a sort of gaucho tiger, the property of certain, select beings.

The commercial transformation of Borges led to two unhappy circumstances: the publication of a poor German edition of his complete works and the appearance of the first generation of young "experts" on Borges. These developments were closely linked. For example, Claudio Magris, who had written an epilogue to one of the volumes of Borges's complete works, published a curious homage to his "victim" (and steady source of income) on the occasion of Borges's eightieth birthday (1979). The article appeared in West Germany's largest weekly, Hamburg's *Die Zeit,* under the title "Triumph und Tragödie eines reaktionären Schriftstellers: Monotones Preislied" (Triumph and tragedy of a reactionary writer: Monotonous hymn). In the article, Magris asserts that Borges is "always an author of anthologies. His most significant books are finely-compressed concentrations of essential moments and absolute revelations, a series of highpoints of a purity so perfect that it lacks the necessary values of everyday reality." In other words, Borges is not a realist writer. Magris seems to have no knowledge of the history of Spanish literature—or of German literature. He also appears to be influenced by the intimidating terminological narcissism that Adorno made current. Thus he notes that Borges "is an obstinate agro-

33. Jorge Luis Borges and Adolfo Bioy Casares, eds., *Francisco de Quevedo: Antología poética* (Buenos Aires: Emecé, 1948); rpt. in Jorge Luis Borges, *Prólogos, con un prólogo de prólogos* (Buenos Aires: Torres Agüero, 1975), 125.

conservative who can perceive the bare facts only from a distance, only when they are described by someone who can see them in their illuminating appearance, which Borges's blind eyes can no longer discern." His indignation at the reactionary Borges further induces him to create the following non sequitur: "The will to freeze provisional reality and to propound it as the static religion of a never-changing life is there because of the sterility of that which forces us to compassion in the face of man's suffering." Magris concludes, however, "Borges is a great literary creator when, moved by our transitory and irreplaceable individuality, he forgets the indifferent identity of things. This nostalgia for life makes it possible for Borges to overcome the small-minded obduracy of a reactionary, and to understand the dignity of every human being—of the dark Indian, prouder than a Caesar, and of the barbarian, who can teach pride and loyalty to the missionary."[34] In the end, then, Borges is a reactionary who is not a reactionary.

These obfuscations were due not only to Magris's limited knowledge of Hispanic literary history, to his aping of Adorno's style, and to his lack of familiarity with Borges in the original. They were also due to his purpose in writing on Borges, which was to sell a product. That is why he makes use of the fascination/repugnance motif already associated with the author and already proved successful in marketing merchandise. Indeed, Magris closes his pitch with an American figure sure to attract his consumers: the "dark Indian" who has consistently fascinated the civilized German.

In 1980, Munich's Hanser Publishers began to publish Borges's complete works using previous translations by Horst, Curt Meyer-Clason, and others.[35] The editor in charge of the project was Gisbert Haefs, who had presented a short, barely passing master's essay on Borges while studying at the University of Bonn. As part of his studies, Haefs participated in a seminar on German translations of Borges. One of the translations the seminar examined was Horst's version of "Hombre de la esquina rosada" (Streetcorner man), included in *Der schwarze Spiegel.* Horst had rendered the Spanish *en un oscuro* (on a dark horse) as "darkness," and *prendas de plata* (silver ornaments) as "stolen silver." (The references are to the story's protagonist.) Haefs's "corrected" rendering for the complete works added the word *tipptopp* to these phrases, distorting the original even more. The dictionary definition of *tipptopp* is "dressed up, very elegant"; but at a certain moment in the

34. Claudio Magris, "Triumph und Tragödie eines reaktionären Schriftstellers. Monotones Preislied. Zum 80 Geburtstag des argentinischen Schriftstellers Jorge Luis Borges," *Die Zeit* (Hamburg), August 24, 1979, p. 35.

35. Jorge Luis Borges, *Gesammelte Werke,* ed. Gisbert Haefs, 11 vols (Munich: Hanser, 1980–1983; rpt. 1987).

sociopolitical development of the Federal Republic, the stage when it was known as the "Mommy State" (1959–1966), *tipptopp* acquired other connotations. Primarily through the influence of advertising, *tipptopp* became associated with a cozy, maternal domesticity and with the appliances and furnishings that helped create these blissful surroundings. This newer meaning of the term was diametrically opposed to the context of Borges's story, where the protagonist's manly presence was being described. Such mistakes and stylistic aberrations filled Haefs's edition, prompting Günter W. Lorenz to comment in a review: "The translator would have been more successful had he used Buenos Aires as his encyclopedia rather than the dictionary of the Royal [Spanish] Academy of the Language. By so doing he might have avoided a good many misinterpretations; he might have also been able to reproduce the duplicitous buffoonery of the two jokers from the River Plate region far more faithfully."[36]

Lorenz's observations are correct and insightful. Still, Haefs's basic problem was not ignorance of Borges's Latin American context. His fundamental error had a long history in Germany; it was summed up by Hegel in a draft of a letter to Johannes Heinrich Voss, the translator of Homer: "Luther made the Bible speak German, as you did Homer. This is the greatest gift that can be given to a people; for a people is uncultured, and it cannot perceive the excellence of what it recognizes as truly its own until it comes to know it in its own tongue."[37] Hegel's prescription for *Verdeutschung* (Germanization) was successful in such cases as Wieland's and Schlegel's translations of Shakespeare, Reinhardt's translation of Sophocles, Voss's rendering of Homer, and Gries's version of Calderón because the translators were thoroughly familiar with the authors and respected their work. (In the case of Calderón, what was underlined was his strangeness and the oriental flavor of his writing [this was pointed out by Goethe]; the fact that the endings of some of his works were undeniably vulgar and that he was a reactionary was never aired.) Further, the translators had recourse to a body of criticism that facilitated their task. All this was not so when it came to Latin American literature in general and to Borges in particular. As a result, the Germanization of these texts did not make them speak German but rather falsified them in an attempt to make their social content conform to the exigencies of German society.

An instance of this problematics of falsification—which is also a problematics of discrimination—is the treatment of the words *Señor*

36. Gunter W. Lorenz, "Ein einmaliges Zeugnis dichterischer Zusammenarbeit: Borges, Bioy Casares und ihr Doktor Domecq," *Die Welt* (Hamburg), May 31, 1985, p. 16.
37. Georg Wilhelm Friedrich Hegel, *Briefe von und an Hegel,* ed. J. Hoffmeister (Hamburg: Meiner, 1952), 1:99.

(Mr./Sir) and *indio* (Indian). These words are generally left untranslated in German versions of Spanish texts, even though they have German equivalents. The effect is a total distortion of meaning, with *Señor,* which is a common form of address or a term of courtesy, taking on an exotic flavor that adds "local color" to the text. The same happens with *indio.* The fact that in works translated from English, the German equivalent, *Indianer,* is used suggests that in the German mind there is a difference between the North American and South American Indian: the *indio* is a strange being, a quasi-beast for which there is no zoological designation, yet another exotic touch of local color. There are multiple examples of similar Germanizing maneuvers that deform Hispanic reality in the interest of subjugating it to a variety of ingrained prejudices and social conventions, foremost among them *Besserwisserei* (knowing-it-all-better), both a cause and effect of that provincialism known as "Eurocentrism." This resistance to accepting and respecting Latin American and particularly Borgesian literature, to Germanizing it (in the Hegelian sense), is, however, capped by another, even greater obstacle: Borges challenges every received paradigm; he upsets every commonplace and banishes all *modorro* (drowsiness), to put it in Quevedo's words.

Germany, the country that suffered most in World War II and that was shaped by the rivalries of the Cold War; the country whose postwar reconstruction was directed by Walter Ulbricht and Konrad Adenauer, both characterized by rigid, schematic ways of thinking; the country most sensitive to its immediate past, a past that, together with the structures of the present, formed a Gordian knot—this Germany was hardly ready to accept the cynical rupture of preconceived notions that is Borges's literature. Borges challenged the sacred cows of the left by praising Franco, Pinochet, and Videla, and the left (together with the neodemocrats) reacted with irritation and reproach. Borges, whose early inclinations were toward anarchism, challenged the hallowed teachings of the right in a more subtle fashion by turning his writings into a continual questioning of the theological basis of Hispanic society. Significantly, Borges's ironic observations about the parasitic anachronism of Argentina's military leaders were never publicized in West Germany. These observations, applicable to Latin America as a whole, were marked by a conciseness and a penetration unmatched by many sociologists studying the "cancer" of military dictatorship. Had his comments been known, what would have remained of the "reactionary" Borges, of that facile and obstinate image that allowed its proponents to proclaim an antifascism after the fact, or to rend their neodemocratic garments? The complex political history of the Federal Republic and the deep-seated prejudices against the New World were the primary obstacles to a balanced reception and to an enriching Germanization of Borges's work. This occurred in a fundamentally conservative nation that was not yet a State but an Economy, that had renounced its past as a land of "poets and thinkers" but was still searching for an identity amid the shadows of old structures and the labyrinths of political mistrust.

In October 1982, the German press had an opportunity to take another look at Borges when he visited Heine's homeland at the invitation of the West German government. Borges gave a number of interviews, yet only one literary critic, the independent, open-minded Marcel Reich-Ranicki, knew how to ask him the right questions and to do him justice. Reich-Ranicki noted that Borges had not received the Nobel Prize but added: "Second-class writers have always enjoyed the favor of the selection committee in Stockholm. The prize was not awarded to the Swede August Strindberg but to the Swede Selma Langerlöf; not to the Norwegian Henrik Ibsen but to the Norwegian Björnstjerne Björnso; not to the Frenchman Marcel Proust but to the Frenchman Anatole France; not to the Russian Isaak Babel but to the Russian Ivan Bunin; not to the Germans Franz Kafka or Bertolt Brecht but to the German Herman Hesse." Borges, however, had no need for such consolation, since he was "an artist who had been extremely self-aware for over half a century, and who had not let anything lead him off the right track."[38]

Reich-Ranicki's summary of his conversation with Borges emphasized the author's interest in Heinrich Heine and Ernst Jünger, two writers who appear to be total opposites when examined with the criteria usually applied to Borges. (Their biographies seem to confirm this.) But were they really antipodal? The revolutionary Heine made this caustic, little-known statement about the course of a revolution: "The heads that philosophy used to reflect on [to prepare] the revolution could later be chopped off for any reason. But philosophy would have never been able to use the heads chopped off by the revolution had the latter preceded the former."[39] Jünger's work, as politically complex as Quevedo's, has been labeled "profascist" or "pre-Nazi." Yet if we examine this work objectively, it becomes evident that it has nothing to do with such irrationality. It is, rather, the work of a "conservative anarchist," for whom dream and adventure constitute the most appropriate way to uncover what underlies surface reality and to avoid all forms of boredom and rigidity.[40] "Let us be alert in the face of the great

38. Marcel Reich-Ranicki, "Borges, der blinde Seher," *Frankfurter Allgemeine Zeitung*, October 10, 1982, p. 23.

39. Quoted in Karl Löwith, ed., *Die Hegelsche Linke* (Stuttgart: Frommans, 1962), 39.

40. H. P. Schwarz, *Der konservative Anarchist* (Freiburg: Rombach, 1962).

danger that life may become something habitual," Jünger wrote in his antitheological work, *Das abenteuerliche Herz* (The adventurous heart), succinctly expressing his point of view.[41]

To the pseudo-ideologues, Borges's interest in these two German writers was further illustration of the "tragedy of a reactionary." But, in reality, it was an indication of an extremely independent intellectual stance, a fact that Reich-Ranicki pointed out in his piece, significantly entitled "Der blinde Seher" (The blind seer). For Borges, both Heine and Jünger represented that independence of spirit which he consistently cultivated in his works. In addition, each author stood for one important aspect of such iconoclasm: Heine for irony, and Jünger for adventurous fantasy.

Reich-Ranicki's comments in his article were brief. But his interview presented, for the first time in West Germany, an image of Borges that the German public could understand and accept, an image that, without distorting Borges's distinctive personality, suggested significant connections between Borges and German literature. Interestingly, Reich-Ranicki's Polish-Jewish background probably gave him a broader perspective on Borges. It was this perspective that indicated a path for a fruitful Germanization of his literature. The desired change in Borges's reception did not come about, however. Although Reich-Ranicki emphasized the primacy of lyricism in Borges's writings and reiterated the autonomy of literature in the face of any and all political ideologies, the obituaries published on the occasion of Borges's death gave no indication that anyone was interested in developing Reich-Ranicki's suggestions, particularly the idea of using Borges's German affinities as access to the work of an author so blindly admired and so conscientiously rejected. Perhaps the German reception of Borges is no exception.

Translated from the Spanish by Pilar Martín

41. Quoted in Armin Mohler, ed. *Die Schleife. Documente zum Weg von Ernst Jünger* (Zurich: Die Arche, 1955).

Françoise Collin _____

The Third Tiger; or,
From Blanchot to Borges

Can one read Borges in French? This would be a legitimate question with respect to any translated writer, but referring to Borges it takes on a particular pertinence. His language is not just a language approximately transcribable into French; it is a language within which different languages debate among themselves: Spanish with Argentine, or the Argentine inflection of Spanish; the vernacular with the classic; the modern with the archaic; European with American—even though all these languages merge in the sovereign mastery of his writing. French can reflect this debate among languages only with difficulty because French is a metropolitan, even academic language in which tensions are perceived as infractions. French considers itself a Latin language, but it is the Latin of the Roman Empire, not the Latin of South America.

The best French translations of Borges by necessity operate a reduction of the text; they must pare it down. Or else they impose a transference such as the one undertaken by Ibarra, who explains his procedure: it consists in turning the decasyllabic original of the poems into alexandrines, with all the latter's inherent references to classicism.[1] But in its passage through the linguistic medium, it is still Borges's transcultural nature that resists a purely French reading—as it seems, by the way, to disturb a purely Argentine one.

Regardless of difficulties in translation, Borges's work has been and is for France a wellspring of reference, limited though it is to a certain milieu. I would first like to elucidate the reasons for this phenomenon. Subsequently, I shall try to go beyond those reasons by choosing as the revealing criterion the reaction of one of Borges's most attentive commentators, Maurice Blanchot.

Following Roger Caillois, to whom we owe the first translation, Maurice Blanchot drew attention to Borges with a brief text devoted to him in 1955 under the title "L'Aleph" in *La Nouvelle Revue Française,* a text later included in *Le Livre à venir*.[2] It doubtless helped acclimatize

1. Néstor Ibarra, preface to Jorge Luis Borges, *Oeuvre poétique 1925–1965* (Paris: Gallimard, 1970), 9–23 (11).
2. Maurice Blanchot, *Le Livre à venir* (1959; Paris: Gallimard, 1971).

Borges to the French mode of reading by providing the reader with some keys that, while still familiar, opened access to the literary *étranger/étrange* (foreign/strange) Borgesian universe.

NIHILISM

Borges's belated reception in France in the fifties and sixties[3] lies at the heart of a general reflection on *modernity,* a term that in this context designates a break with the reassuring traditions of post-Renaissance literature, and in particular with those of the novel as it was constituted and fixed during the nineteenth century. This genre included necessarily and simultaneously a story, developed in a register of linear, if more or less complex, concatenations; characters of explainable, coherent psychology; and a socially determined milieu. The totality formed a coherent whole with precise contours, an object with a claim to restitute "reality," drawing its value from its own fidelity to that claim. This definition must seem a caricature, but it is necessary to caricature, or at least to schematize, in order to bring out a difference.

Modernity marks a break with this conception of the work. It was not a brutal break, rather a break that originated in French literature itself with Mallarmé and the question of the Book, or with Proust, who unsettles narrative structure and imposes the question of temporality. Foreign writers such as Kafka and Joyce also accelerated this break.

The French writers of the fifties and sixties, vaguely grouped under the category of the *nouveau roman,* have little in common (how can we group together Robbe-Grillet and Beckett, Nathalie Sarraute and Claude Simon, Robert Pinget and Marguerite Duras?) apart from their common challenge to forms and genres and, in particular, narrative structure—all of which goes hand in hand with the suspicion harbored against the very concept of literature. This suspicion works in favor of the concept of *écriture,* an essential writing that transcends genres.

Such a radical challenge of formal concepts logically cannot stop at that of the "author." As Gérard Genette writes in homage to Borges:

> Depuis un siècle et demi, notre pensée—et notre usage—de la littérature sont affectés par un préjugé dont l'application toujours plus subtile et plus audacieuse n'a cessé d'enrichir mais aussi de pervertir et finalement d'appauvrir notre commerce des Lettres: le postulat selon lequel une oeuvre est essentiellement déterminée par son auteur, et par conséquent *l'exprime.*

> (For a century and a half our thought—and practice—of literature have been affected by a prejudice whose ever more subtle and daring application has

---

3. Jorge Luis Borges, *Fictions,* trans. Paul Verdevoye and Néstor Ibarra, pref. Néstor Ibarra (Paris: Gallimard, 1951; rev. 1967, 1968, 1971, 1974); Jorge Luis Borges, *Labyrinthes,* trans. Roger Caillois (Paris: Gallimard, 1953).

never ceased to enrich, but also pervert, and finally impoverish our dealing with Letters: the postulate that a work of literary art is essentially determined by its author, and consequently *expresses him*.)[4]

The crisis of expression in literature is nothing but the crisis of its claim to "figure" reality (to re-present it). Literature does not refer to a reality that supposedly gives an account—as if language were nothing but a more or less refined tool in the service of what *is*. Language is, rather, self-constitutive: it states what it does and it does what it states. The resemblance it produces is always that of a semblance.

This implicit or explicit reflection developing around literature is accompanied, though perhaps not in an immediately perceivable way, by a movement of thought that, following Heidegger, denounces the Western metaphysical tradition, a tradition that conceives Being (and any being) as an object of mastery and seizure within the framework of a dialectical, finalized history.[5] In a short article, it is impossible to give an account of this critique of metaphysics and the diverse forms it takes in contemporary French philosophy, from Foucault to Deleuze and from Derrida to Lyotard; and it is impossible to detail the links between that critique and the psychoanalysis of Lacan or the structuralism of Lévi-Strauss. Yet there is no doubt that it contributed in its own way to the development of the revolutions in art and literature and, more generally, in language since the beginning of our century.

The locus of the encounter between literary and philosophical currents that proved decisive for the problematics of modernity was the

4. Gérard Genette, "La Littérature selon Borges," *Cahiers de l'Herne* 4 (1981): 323–27 (325).

5. Translator's note. In spite of the author's subsequent statement that philosophical explanations would lead too far, it may be appropriate to elucidate as quickly as possible what appears to be a crucial hinge, not only concerning the link between Heidegger and Blanchot, but as a major epistemological turning point reflected also by Borges.

Heidegger's distinction between *das Sein* and *das Seiende* is hard to render in English where such a substantivization of present participles and of verbs in the infinitive can only be expressed by the same gerund. English lacks the possibility of saying, for instance: "the to be." *Das Sein* (being) refers to the immutable essence of what "goes through" (*durchgehen*), that in which participate all phenomenological beings in their *Seiendheit* (quality of being phenomenologically).

While both writers think in a Heideggerian mood, Borges poeticizes that mood, while Blanchot's way is to keep halfway between philosophical and poetic language. For Heidegger, furthermore, thought conceived as constitutive of a subject is logically and ethically problematic: when I as a thinking subject think (of) something, I constitute it as an object in my field; I appropriate it, make it my own. Heidegger, following in the footsteps of Nietzsche, "revaluated" all "property values" of the subject by thus deconstructing it, an intuition that finds its extreme manifestation in Derrida. The questioning of the status of the (transcendental) subject ipso facto calls into question the finality of history, since there will be no willing, "whole" subject to will history's direction.

work of certain writers who had read Mallarmé, Joyce, and Heidegger with care. Blanchot is the most eminent among them. It is in the crucible of his reading/writing, which refrains from any explicit problematics, that their osmosis takes place. But this encounter acquires its full meaning only because it seems to respond to a mysterious call: to reflect a corpus of fiction that developed since the publication of *Thomas l'obscur* (1941), in narratives that owe nothing to the novelistic genre and that are not without affinities with Borges, narratives with a labyrinthine or plural structure, offering substance for thought rather than for vision or feeling, erasing a world rather than constituting one.[6]

While the importance of Maurice Blanchot is acknowledged in the French literary milieu, it remains ignored, or at least underestimated, abroad. The reason is that Blanchot—in marked distinction from so many contemporary writers and philosophers—occupies no glamorous sociocultural position. He exists by virtue of his work alone. In a media-obsessed era, he neither bolsters his work by an exterior gesture nor attempts to safeguard it—directly or indirectly—except in the most minimal sense, by publishing it.

Nevertheless, *écriture,* or quintessential writing—the concept that has met with such tremendous success in the United States and has become an intellectual fashion to the point of acquiring the status of a restrictive critical technique, deconstruction—owes its initial impulse to Blanchot. Difference—what became Derrida's "différance"—is determined by the concept of the *ne-uter* (neuter, literally neither the one nor the other).[7] "De cette différence qui fait que, parlant, nous différons de parler, les Grecs les plus anciens ont eu le pressentiment qu'elle était la dure, l'admirable nécessité en vertu de laquelle tout s'ordonnait" (This difference which accounts for the fact that, while speaking, we differ from speech was already vaguely felt by the most ancient Greeks as the hard, admirable necessity by virtue of which everything in the world is regulated).[8]

Language, and more precisely writing, attests to the impossibility of unity and totality. Its itinerary is without beginning and without destination, always moving toward the unknown—a movement of wandering (*errance*) and error devoid of foundations. To write is to enter into nonpower, to be related to what is never-present or what is present

6. Maurice Blanchot, *Thomas l'obscur* (Paris: Gallimard, 1941).

7. Françoise Collin, *Maurice Blanchot et la question de l'écriture* (Paris: Gallimard, 1971), 190–221.

8. Blanchot, *Le Livre à venir,* 119. Translator's note. Again the Hegelian/Heideggerian linguistic rendering of ontology. Here *sprechend* (speaking) is a phenomenological state, while *das Sprechen* or *le parler,* which I translate as "speech," should rather be "the to speak." *Das Sprechen* is eidetic, while "speech" would still be phenomenological.

only in the mode of absence. To write means to be denied all claims to knowledge and power; it is to abandon oneself to renouncement and to the never-ending. It is the acceptation of always being "differred."[9]

Language as writing is hence not a particular incident of human adventure proper to certain individuals. It attests the structure of all being, abandoned as it is less to death as a single happening than to a ceaseless dying. Its essence is the inessential. The final word, the last word, the key word does not exist. This is why we never finish speaking or writing, since we speak and speak again, ceaselessly.

Borges, to be sure, does not follow the same paths, does not resort to the same concepts. But like Blanchot and within the space of that same rupture of modernity, through his narration and meditation, he challenges metaphysics or the question of totality, of "absolute knowledge," and the notion of the (authorial) subject.[10] And the inflation of the book, symbolized by the library and everything it claims to be, is actualized only by its own derision. The whole matter is an infinite system of relations and references that reflect each other as in a play of mirrors. No reading can ever embrace and absorb it; no eye can ever focus steadily on its center. "La vérité de la littérature serait dans l'erreur de l'infini," comments Blanchot, "le monde perverti dans la somme infinie de ses possibles" (The truth of literature would be in the error of the infinite, the world perverted in the infinite sum of its possibles).[11] This is symbolized by the aleph, contemplated in the depth of a cellar. The essence of the world is "a small iridescent sphere of almost unbearable brilliance . . . little more than an inch," reflecting a multitude of images. "I saw the teaming sea; I saw daybreak and nightfall; I saw the multitudes of America; I saw a silvery cobweb . . . I saw, close up, unending eyes . . . I saw a woman in Inverness whom I shall never forget . . . I saw the cancer in her breast . . . I saw a summer house in Adrogué and a copy of the first English translation of Pliny" ("The Aleph," *BAR* 161).

For Blanchot as for Borges, "The book is in principle the world . . . and the world is a book."[12] The priority of the book over life is due to the overflowing by the infinite of the possibility of the finite. The Borgesian library, in its paradoxical dimension, does not imply for human-

9. Translator's note. Here the author uses Derrida's (Heidegger-style) play on the double meaning of *différer:* (1) to be different, a qualitative notion, and (2) to put off or delay, a temporal notion. Writing as "différance" does both.

10. Translator's note. The Hegelian concept of "absolute knowledge," or rather the condition of its possibility, is "shattered at its foundations"—Derrida's *sollicité*—by thinkers of the Nietzschean-Heideggerian-Derridian lineage.

11. Maurice Blanchot, *L'Espace littéraire,* 4th ed. (Paris: Gallimard, 1955), 125.

12. See "On the Cult of Books," *OI* 120.

kind the impossibility of knowing all and seeing all within the limits of particularity; it pushes humankind toward the orgy of knowing and seeing as an explosion of limits. When one deals with the book or with books, one enters a relationship with the impossible and with nothingness. The book has neither beginning nor end, neither center nor margins; far from constituting an "Orient," be it an unreachable one, it disorients.[13] By making a sign, by causing signs to proliferate, the book undermines meaning.[14]

To say that writing as the unfolding of the imaginary comes first is to state the priority of the interminable and ceaseless. It is on this "ceaselessness" that the certitudes of reality and human behavior inscribe their cutting marks; they do so in order to reduce the infinite to finite slices and the impossible to a sum of possibles within the finalized objectives of life in society.

> La différence entre le réel et l'irréel, l'inestimable privilège du réel c'est qu'il y a moins de réalité dans la réalité, n'étant que l'irréalité niée, écartée par l'énergique travail de la négation et par cette négation qu'est aussi le travail. . . . C'est ce moins, sorte d'amaigrissement, d'amincissement de l'espace, qui nous permet d'aller d'un point à l'autre, selon l'heureuse façon de la ligne droite.

> (The difference between the real and the unreal, the inestimable privilege of the real is that there is less reality in reality—which is nothing but negated irreality—set aside by the energetic labor of negation, and by that negation inherent in the very labor. . . . It is this "less," a kind of growing lean or shrinking of space, which allows us to go happily from one point to another along a straight line.)[15]

Such a conception of the book is, for Blanchot at least, the empire of writing over the book, its questioning from within. The book is a semblance of an object that resists all objectification. The multiplication of books, their accumulation, their endless referring to each other make their nonmeaning burst (*éclater*).[16] When one enters the book, begins communication with the book, when one has access to the library, one is sent back to one's folly, one's unreason—an unreason that

---

13. Translator's note. Instead of "Orient" or East one might speak of "North," since the compass is one of the essential Borgesian symbols ("Death and the Compass" for instance), which Borges's irony empties of their essence as symbols.

14. Translator's note. Another reference to Hegel, *Die Zeichen machende Phantasie* (Sign-making fantasy), *Enzyklopädie der geistigen Wissenschaften*, #457. In French, *faire signe* can have frivolous, erotic connotations.

15. Blanchot, *Le Livre à venir*, 119.

16. Translator's note. *Eclater* is another example of the intentional use of a double meaning, which allows both acceptations to apply: *l'éclat* is both explosion and brilliance, simultaneously destroying and making visible.

is not the other or the contrary of reason but the only possible reason. The potential totalizing closure promised by the universal library is substituted by an infinity without margins—the "bad" infinite in the Hegelian sense.

The meticulous classification, the catalog, then the catalog of the catalogs, all bring out the folly of any pretense to order, much more than they reveal or establish an order. Space cannot articulate time. The essence of writing is that there is neither center nor periphery, neither right nor left.[17] There is no before or after, no past or future. All orientations are reversible. What has been is to come.[18] Nothing is definitely achieved. Nevertheless everything has already been said, gone through. This is why there is no history of literature, no more than there is virgin territory in literature. The staking out of the territory is not so much circular as it is labyrinthine, for the circle could still be taken as a figure of totalizing final achievement. Whoever starts writing/reading feels conscious of a beginning, but that beginning is a rebeginning.

Thus one easily perceives not only that writing cannot refer to reality as a stable foundation but also that it is, on the contrary, the exercise of the nonfounded, of the absence of any foundation, be it subjective or objective. Being without origin, writing has no initial point to attach itself to. It reads and rereads—as witnessed by Borges, in his enormous, never-appeased cultural appetite and also in his own text—thus turning every writer into a writer of writers, a reader through whom the works of the writers reflect themselves as in an infinite gallery of mirrors.[19] This is a practice that in other works of visual and literary art takes the form of collage, a technique of modernity that itself points to what is *à venir,* what is to come, to supersede it; the postmodern.

Alien to truth as it is alien to reality, literature is thus an immense mirage, a hallucination, an art not of resemblance or mimesis but of semblance. Even when it makes an effort to say what is, it subverts what is, it *appears.* One must understand in the proper sense that it is fiction. But fiction is not a doing in the sense of fabrication, not even in

17. Translator's note. See de Lailhacar, "The Mirror and the Encyclopedia," in this volume. Both Blanchot and Borges sacralize writing. It is no coincidence that Roland Barthes, for instance, stresses "negative theology" when characterizing that very "break of modernity" which is Collin's concern. The modernist iconoclasts appear as essentially religious atheists.

18. Translator's note. This *à venir* means "to come," and, of course, what is to come is a book, Blanchot's *Le Livre à venir.* Here, too, there are both Heideggerian and Christian connotations: for example, "advent" is the period preceding the Coming of Christ.

19. Translator's note. Once more the Heideggerian connection: Hölderlin as "the poet of poets." The inscribing of texts into or onto a text corresponds to the notion of intertextuality coined by Julia Kristeva or, in a slightly different acceptation, to Gérard Genette's palimpsest.

the sense of creation.[20] It makes nothing come about (*advenir*), nothing but itself. The words do not say the thing; they do not constitute the thing either. They are this "in-between" of a navigation without a compass, the space between sky and earth, sky and sea, by which humanity learns to maintain itself in the unreal as in its only place. This accounts for the fantastic register of some layers of Borgesian narrative fiction whose function is to witness to the nonmeaning of any resemblance between words and reality. Borgesian fantastic does not attempt to give a glimpse of some surreal more real than the real.

Priority of the book or of language over the real, not as a foundation but as the absence of any foundation; totality disintegrating into the infinite; beginning that absorbs itself in the rebeginning; collapse of the subject into the neuter or the "one" (not the first number but the impersonal pronoun): these are a few of the themes through which Blanchot and Borges confront the metaphysical security transmitted by Western knowledge. The possibility of the object, and at the same time of the subject, becomes questionable in this confrontation because there is no constituting subject, no author, either human or divine, no center or origin with which the world can define itself. Where one speaks (where it is spoken), nobody speaks. To write/read is to be exposed to the dispossession of the real and also of oneself as subject. The one who writes/reads ceases to be somebody, a subject securely grounded in the identifying marks of personal existence, to become an impersonal pronoun, one. The writer/reader is abandoned to anonymity—or to the plurality of names, becoming somebody/nobody by becoming everybody.[21] The author is dispossessed of authority and is transformed into a name that is just a word among the words inscribed on the page—nothing but a word in a book.

> According to Hume, we ought not to say "I think," because "I" is a subject; we ought to say "it is thought," as one says "it is raining." In the two verbs we have an action without subject. Instead of saying "I think, therefore I am," Descartes should have said "something thinks" or "it is thought," because the "I" supposes an entity, and we have no right to suppose the existence of such an entity. One should say: "It is thought, therefore something exists."[22]

20. Translator's note. Collin refers here to the literal meaning of the word *fiction:* from Latin *facere* (to make), corresponding to Greek *poiein* (*poiesis;* to make, to do); a "making" or "make-believe."

21. Translator's note. Another "significant" etymological duplicity: in French, *la personne* is "the person," while *ne . . . personne* is "nobody." Collin, following Heidegger's "crosswise erasure," wants the two terms to cancel each other out, yet to stay there simultaneously.

22. Jorge Luis Borges, "La inmortalidad," *Borges, oral* (Buenos Aires: Emecé/Belgrano, 1979), 31–32.

It is this impersonality that makes a quotation out of every written text. One author is always inhabited by another. It is not I who writes but the other, in a perpetual movement of substitution.

Linear and progressive temporality as inscribed in the notion of history is a construct of Western thought: "We know that chronology and history exist, but they are primarily Western discoveries. There are no Persian histories of literature or Indian histories of philosophy, nor are there Chinese histories of Chinese literature, because they are not interested in the succession of facts" ("The Thousand and One Nights," *SN* 50). Just as space has no center, time is not oriented but is the dispersion of *The Thousand and One Nights;* that is, the dispersion of that which cannot be numbered, that which is always in excess over what can be divided into numbers—one plus thousands.

What we experience, then, with Borges as with Blanchot—and what interests Blanchot in Borges—is a rejection of the "one" (here not the impersonal pronoun but the first number as a single, closed, totalizing entity). "C'est le plus indéfini, essence de l'imaginaire, qui empêche K. (dans Kafka) d'atteindre jamais le château, comme il empêche pour l'éternité Achille de rejoindre la tortue, et peut-être l'homme vivant de se rejoindre lui-même" (It is the indefinite more—the essence of the imaginary—which prevents K. [in Kafka] from ever reaching the castle, as it eternally prevents Achilles from rejoining the tortoise, and perhaps man while alive from rejoining himself).[23]

Blanchot, elucidating Borges not only by his commentary but also by the proximity of his own work to that of Borges, discovers and perhaps stresses in the work of the latter what one could call his nihilism in the Nietzschean sense. It is a specific nihilism, for in Borges *mise en abyme,* the emptying or hollowing out of fullness, of totality, of the library, is always accompanied by the nearly physical pleasure taken in the presence of the book, of all its presence—a pleasure that redeems absence.[24]

A KIND OF JOY

What is striking from the first moment one approaches these oeuvres is that, despite the proximity of their narrative structures and themes, they reflect a profound difference in mood and color. To analyze this difference, however, would be the task of psychoanalysis. The general connotation of Blanchot's work is one of gravity and mourning. In

23. Blanchot, *Le Livre à venir,* 119.

24. Translator's note. *Mise en abyme (abîme)* is originally—and significantly—a printer's term, designating the hollowing or engraving of the mold for a letter: the essence is in the negative. The term, first used as a semimetaphor of writing by André Gide, became a household word in poststructuralism with Barthes, Derrida, and so forth.

contrast, Borges's work radiates a kind of jubilation, which is diffused in disparate lines of irony and lyricism, which explodes in fireworks of images, a passion for detail. "I believe literature to be . . . a kind of joy," he writes[25]—an affirmation one could hardly impute to Blanchot. The centerless space opened up by literature is perceived by Blanchot in the mode of loss, by Borges in that of play—space of shadow or space starred with luminous points. The Blanchotian imaginary is a closed-in universe that takes refuge in rooms or corridors; the Borgesian imaginary, in spite of its subterranean, labyrinthine side, opens itself to a city or a landscape. One is sedentary, the other is cosmic and cosmopolitan.

These differences can already be noticed in the relations entertained with literature and philosophy by the two great readers, the two men of culture. While Blanchot proceeds work by work, his entire intelligence geared to the heart of each of them individually, Borges short-circuits epochs, authors, and quotations, mixing them in one and the same text in a nearly provocative freewheeling that might be qualified as "postmodern." He does not hesitate to rewrite the whole history of philosophy on half a page. Thus, in his lecture on immortality he states (in a characteristic manner): "Today these concepts of soul and body are for us subject to caution. *Let us summarize the history of philosophy* . . . Locke said . . . Then Berkeley said . . . Then comes Hume . . . Descartes should have . . . Fechner says that . . . the eminent master Saint Thomas Aquinas. . . . "[26] He continues his obstacle course, jumping from Goethe to Tacitus, to Pythagoras, to Plato, to Pascal, to Shakespeare—to name but a few.

Borrowing citations, even entire works, swapping literary paternity, playfully assembling and disassembling texts from the past, arranging them in new perspectives: all this has innovative value for Borges. *Imitatio Christi,* if attributed to Joyce or Céline, produces immediate meaning, a reading. To create is perhaps, as it is for Duchamp, to displace objects, not to constitute them. To think is to combine preexisting objects and put them into a new context. As Rodríguez Monegal notes:

Peut-être les spéculations métaphysiques ou théologiques de Borgès manquent-elles de toute valeur philosophique. Il est probable que Borgès n'ait pas ajouté une seule idée nouvelle, une seule intuition durable au vaste corpus compilé par les occidentaux et les orientaux depuis les méditations des présocratiques ou les passives hallucinations de Boudha. Mais elles sont fondamentales pour comprendre le sens final de son oeuvre créatrice.

(It is possible that Borges's metaphysical and theological speculations are

25. Borges, "La inmortalidad," 21.
26. Ibid., 31–33 (my emphasis).

devoid of any philosophical value. In all likelihood he has not added a single
new idea, not one lasting intuition to the vast corpus compiled by East and
West, from the meditations of the pre-Socratics or the passive hallucinations
of Buddha. But they are fundamental for the understanding of the final
meaning of his creative work.)[27]

Is it candor or impertinence (doubling the pertinence), this random,
all-encompassing convocation of the general panorama of thought, a
convocation put to the service of Borges's intuition of and obsession
with time? Erudition by its sheer weight becomes the balancing rod for
this tightrope walker. It is a "gay science," understandably dazzling the
gazer/reader.[28] His strings of affirmations do not belong to the order of
truth but to that of evidence—evidence to which one may remain
insensitive, but which one can neither discuss nor link to any proper
origin. This evidence forms part of the sleight of hand in Borges's text,
where it finds its legitimacy. Locke or Berkeley is from then on Borges.
His prodigious memory, the memory of the blind, is not a necropolis; it
bathes the past in the present. Even at a distance of centuries, Borges
deals only with the living. He passes Plato and Shakespeare in the
street. He chats with them in the café around the corner. For him, to
write is to give rise to a new original. This is his passion for the radical
deconstruction of historicity, his way of abolishing past and future in a
present that itself has no existence other than that of an infinitely
reflecting mirror.

Borges thus at once invites us to follow him and not to take him too
seriously. In his view, the sacred character of the book is always put into
question by the rabbi's cat:

> There was something too untoward in the Golem
> for at his approach the rabbi's cat
> would hide. (This cat does not appear in Scholem
> but I intuit it across all these years.)
>   ("The Golem," *BAR* 275)

The rabbi's cat—the harmlessness of the familiar—strolls into the grave
seriousness of the library. Its presence evokes the irony of detail, perhaps also animality's irreducible resistance to culture, like that of Baudelaire's cats.

By the French reader, at least, Borges's literary work has been identified mainly with his stories, and, as we have seen, the stories were
situated at the crossroads of the ideological debate on modernity. This

27. Emir Rodríguez Monegal, "Borgès essayiste," *Cahiers de l'Herne* 4 (1981): 343–51
(345).

28. Translator's note. The reference is to Nietzsche's *Die fröhliche Wissenschaft* (1882).
The English translation is *The Gay Science,* trans. Walter Kaufmann (New York: Vintage,
1974).

drew attention away from the importance of his poetic creation, as well as from the vibrancy of his images in the case of the stories, and from all that did not lend itself to being melted down into a philosophical tale. But Borges's irony, which undermines any attempt at unification, has not only a negative power liberating writing from the unicity of the idea; paradoxically it also produces a lush efflorescence of images and sensations that are deployed in a minor key within the stories but with full freedom in the poems.

This luxuriance constitutes a kind of inversion of nihilism, or is its positive version. The celebration of the finite is the luminous side of the coin whose other side is the perception of the infinite. The proof of dispersion comes about in Borges (not in Blanchot) through an intensification of the presently lived moment, giving it a certain quality of eternity. The concentration of the unlimited in one instant transforms distress into jubilation. This movement could be interpreted as mystic in the framework of Western thought. But it does not contain the element of transcendence implied by that thought. One must rather locate it in its Oriental version, an Orient to which the writer makes explicit reference.

To Blanchot the only alternative to the limitlessness of language and to wandering is the limit imposed by world-historical projects. For Borges there is a version of the unlimited that maintains him within the finite: the infinite experience of the finite, condensed into a single moment or captured in a detail. Consequently, to trust and abandon himself to the finite does not mean to hide the unlimited but to apprehend it in a mode different from that of the labyrinthine itinerary or the accumulation of the library. Perception is a form of refutation of knowledge (*savoir*), as powerful as the cacophony of "knowledges" (*savoirs*).

In speaking of this intellectual infatuated with words, how else can one explain the reflux of things tangible, the irruption of concrete and banal everyday elements, into the labyrinth that is the book? How else is one to account for his abandoning himself to the pursuit of all that is iridescent and rainbow-like? How to account for his way of saying "I," an "I" emptied of all pretension to substance? How to account for the poetry? This is the way life penetrates his text: Buenos Aires, the sea, birds, faces, swords, stars, the "diversity of beings"—and "Another Poem of Gifts." Equally consistent with this is the calm inscription of oneself within a lineage, the presence of ancestors, warriors, thinkers. "For Reason will never give up its dream," he says.[29]

The rehabilitation of the finite obliges us to consider in a new light the relationship between book and life, as established by Borges's work.

---

29. Jorge Luis Borges, *Selected Poems 1923–1967*, ed. Norman Thomas di Giovanni (New York: Delacorte/Seymour Lawrence, 1972), 199.

While that work decidedly advocates the priority of book over life, the impossibility of ever reaching things—or of reaching them only in the guise of words—is experienced as a never-vanquished nostalgia. While writing/reading deprives one of life, the fascination with life remains.

The book is marvel and the book is horror. The library as universe is both open space and prison. Everything is in the book and everything is missing. Writing is royalty and it is infirmity. Words exile the body. In the library, the body is no longer present except as an excluded element, a remainder: "To the left and right of the hallway there are two very small closets. In the first, one may sleep standing up; in the other satisfy one's fecal necessities" ("The Library of Babel," *L* 51). Thus, Borges's relationship with literature remains that of a nonsurmounted, nonsurmountable tension, words simultaneously offering the thing and taking it away. Borges experiences the presence of the book in the double register of inebriation and pain, which makes him write:

> The rose is in the letters of "rose"
> and the length of the Nile in "Nile"
> (*BAR* 274)

but also, at the same time:

> I, who have been so many men, have never been
> The one in whose embrace Mathilde Urbach swooned.
> ("The Regret of Heraclitus," *Dt* 92)

Borges reflects this insurmountable tension, this duplication of schemes, lucidly—and, as always, ironically—in a poem devoted to the tiger. Everywhere in his work the tiger occupies the place of a sacred animal, a focal point of all tensions. He belongs to the archaic phantasmagoria of a Borges who, as a child, was fascinated by a tiger kept captive behind the bars of a zoo. The tiger is the animal that pierces Borges's work from all sides, setting his dreams free.

The living tiger, however, the jungle tiger with his striped coat, is in words never more than a domesticated tiger:

> Against the symbolic tiger, I have put
> the real one, whose blood runs hot,
> and today, 1959, the third of August,
> a slow shadow spreads across the prairie,
> but still, the act of naming it, of guessing
> what is its nature and its circumstances
> creates a fiction, not a living creature,
> not one of those who wander on the earth.
> Let us look for a third tiger . . .
> ("The Other Tiger," *BAR* 282)

The debate between literature and life, word and thing, is experienced and expressed by Borges under the aspect not only of the object but also of the subject, or at least of the author: Borges against Borges. The experience of writing is always what gives him life and what deprives him of it, in a doubling of himself that he relentlessly witnesses:

> It's to the other man, to Borges that things happen. I walk along the streets of Buenos Aires, stopping now and then—perhaps out of habit—to look at the arch of an old entranceway or a grillwork gate . . . I live, I let myself live, so that Borges can weave his tales and poems, and those tales and poems are my justification. ("Borges and I," *BAR* 278–79)

The conclusion is a pirouette that expresses both the writer's victory and his defeat, his essential perplexity: "Which of us is writing this page I don't know" (*BAR* 279).

When, in *Nueve ensayos dantescos* (Nine essays on Dante) he evokes Beatrice's definitive retreat into beatitude, Borges indicates what, however, separates the real Dante from the narrator Dante: "The scene was imagined by Dante. For us it is very real; for him it was less so (reality for him was that first life, then death snatched Beatrice from him)."[30] The narration aesthetically transposes the violence of the experience to a sublime level. Dante the narrator sings; Dante the man suffers.

Borges's work thus fully affirms the primacy of literature and language and, at the same time, ceaselessly rejects it in the nostalgic longing for a life devoid of words. The body inscribes itself in the symbolic as in its own absence—a fact to which writing masterfully attests.[31] "I shall remain in Borges, not in myself (if it is so that I am someone)" (*BAR* 279). The subject of writing defeats the subject of experience.

The fascination of Borges's work lies in this, which is its heart: language is reference to language, and literature inscribes itself into the space of literature, of literatures, as the perpetual new beginning. But language is also reference to the "other" of itself, to the "real." We must therefore read the work in that double register. If the first has been the most striking and remains so for the reader, it cannot erase the always present second register. It is Borges the writer who triumphs, but the other Borges does not stop shouting out through him.

Could it be poetry, through its lyricism, that does justice to the one as well as to the other? May one imagine that in poetry the conflicting

30. Jorge Luis Borges, *Nueve ensayos dantescos,* intro. Marcos Ricardo Barnatán, pref. Joaquín Arce (Madrid: Espasa Calpe, 1982), 161.

31. Translator's note. To Borges and Blanchot, viewing everything not only metaphorically but also quasi-literally as writing, the expression "the body inscribing itself" may seem natural. Not until Derrida, however, was this seemingly idiosyncratic perception given ontological explanation: everything is marked, everything is a trace, so even speech and other impressions and imprints are *archi-écriture,* that is, they correspond structurally to the essence of writing.

imperatives of feeling and thinking, living and telling, are harmonized?
Is it the poetic space where word and perception merge, or almost do?

The inability to seize things, the inability to live an experience
(which is also the inability to make things emerge from words) is without doubt inherent in the human condition; it belongs to the ontological structure of the human and is a mark of mortality, of dying. But in
Borges's work this inability is also lived as a singular destiny, or through
that destiny. A psychoanalytical reading of his entire work would surely
benefit from the study of Borges's relationship with his mother, whom
he never really left. (His is the common fate of many writers, as if,
contrary to current theory, our symbolizing capability were linked to
the mother, and not to the separation from her, as the first imposition of
Law in our lives.) In Borges's work, the absence of life is linked to the
absence of the body, of the sexed body, relegated to a beautiful, wild
animality—as though the body could gain existence in its own right
only in violence. (The line between love and war in the virile tradition,
and more precisely still in the Latin tradition, is certainly not alien to
that perception.) We thus find in Borges the traditional bipolarization
of woman as virgin–distant lady (Beatrice), and as whore. The impossibility of the "third woman" is correlative to the impossibility of the
"third tiger," which doubtlessly explains the rather general absence of
amorous sentiment from Borges's work. But this attitude is not specifically Borgesian. It pervades all (masculine) Western literature, a param-
eter of the dichotomy between soul and body as established by Greek
and reinforced by Christian thought. Borges's work is in its special way
heir to this tradition: the feminine is marked as absence, a presence
structured as a hiatus. May one advance the hypothesis that the besti-
ary, so important in his work, represents displacement and drifting?[32]

It is true that, through one aspect of his work (the most visible and
most commented on in France), Borges is instrumental in the break
caused by modernity in the history of European literature, a break that
amplifies into the questioning of Western metaphysics. But it is also
true that an entire aspect of his work escaped general notice—that
which one could call Oriental in its thought and sensibility. But the
Orient here can be identified with no empirical Orient; it is the metaphor through which shines everything that focuses on the dazzling

32. Translator's note. "Displacement" is a psychoanalytical term, as in Freud's dream
work. Here is a crucial link between psychoanalysis and Saussurean linguistics that, as the
author states, lies at the heart of the debate on modernity. *Dérive* (drifting) and *dérapage*
(sliding), as of a boat adrift or an anchor not holding, refer also to the slipping of the signified
from under the signifier in the Saussurean sign: the essential semantic instability.

power of the finite, sole carrier of the infinite.[33] There is simultaneously Buddhism, Judaism, and even perhaps the exuberance of the Latin American Baroque. It is this side of the work that infuses the rest with its color, the side where mirror reflections no longer vanish into the darkness of the labyrinth. Here nihilism becomes poetic intensity. To be sure, there is nothing, but everything is in that nothing, and in that little. By relinquishing the pretension to sense or meaning, the senses become lighted, aroused, and illuminated: everywhere the gods are present. The condensed time of the instant, an instant linked to a specific here and now, takes precedence over the dispersed time of the interminable, the maze of the temporal labyrinth; the infinity of the immobile takes the place of infinite wandering; the emptiness of a thought, a perception, substitutes for the proliferous convocation of knowledge. "Not a single day goes by in which we are not for an instant in paradise," he says.[34] Héctor Bianciotti attributed this "instant of paradise" to Borges's encounter with María Kodama, an encounter that, though late in his life, never ceased to reverberate in his writings.

Borges's work comprehends more than one register. One may explain this fact by the transcultural, even cosmopolitan character of the author. Yet one should not understand it as a sort of uprootedness or aesthetic syncretism, but rather as a crossbreeding where several traditions and many roots intertwine. This explanation, however, cannot dissimulate the existence of that more secret and radical tension affecting Borges's very relationship with writing and, more generally, with culture. This tension, constitutive of his being as a writer, leaves intact within the skeptical intellectual that grand and simple lover who never forgot "the old, elementary joy of the rain."

Translated by Christine de Lailhacar

33. Translator's note. The use of Heidegger's term *durchscheinen* (to shine through) seems appropriate here.

34. Cited by Héctor Bianciotti, in his preface to Jorge Luis Borges, *Neuf essais sur Dante*, trans. Françoise Rosset (Paris: Gallimard, 1987), 9–19.

II
A New
Critical Idiom

Jaime Alazraki

Borges's Modernism and the New Critical Idiom

In his essay on Modern Man, Jung has observed that although "many people call themselves modern—especially the pseudo-moderns—the really modern man is often to be found among those who call themselves *old-fashioned*."[1] I doubt very much if Jung's category of modern man befits Borges. Writers like Musil, Beckett, or Cortázar come much closer to this definition—up to the point of providing an illustration for Jung's profile. But I cannot think of anybody who has more strongly claimed to be old-fashioned, and who has more consistently defended his right to be so than Borges. When asked about contemporary authors or more fashionable trends of thought, he has invariably replied that he is not to blame if he was born in this century, adding: why should one pick his literary preferences among twentieth-century writers when one has thirty centuries of literature from which to choose? Supporting this seeming eccentricity, André Maurois has pointed out, rather hyperbolically, that "Borges has read everything, and especially what nobody reads any more" (*L* ix). Similarly, in an interview with William Buckley, Borges has been held responsible for reintroducing Americans to American writers—but to nineteenth-century American writers. "Borges reminds me," says Alfred Kazin, "not of contemporaries, not of any novelists, but of Poe and Melville, of Emerson and Thoreau, even to their 'immaturity.'"[2]

Being old-fashioned in an age that worships contemporaneity is an expression of modernity because, according to Jung, "to be 'unhistorical' is the Promethean sin, and in this sense modern man is sinful."[3] As for Borges, only when he stopped aping seventeenth-century Spanish writers, from Saavedra Fajardo to Quevedo and Gracián, did he begin to write the prose for which he is now known. He refers to those early

From Jaime Alazraki, *Borges and the Kabbalah* (Cambridge: Cambridge University Press, 1988), © 1988 by Cambridge University Press, reprinted with permission

1. Carl G. Jung, "The Spiritual Problem of Modern Man," in *The Portable Jung,* ed. and intro. Joseph Campbell, trans. R. F. C. Hull (New York: Viking, 1971), 456–79 (459).
2. Alfred Kazin, "Meeting Borges," *New York Times Book Review,* May 2, 1971, pp. 4–5, 22 (5).
3. Jung, "Modern Man," 458.

years as his baroque period: "I used to write in a very baroque and ostentatious style. Out of timidity, I believed that if I wrote in a simple way, people would think that I did not know how to write. I then felt the need to prove that I knew many rare words and that I was able to combine them in a very startling fashion."[4] Borges was then playing the role of being a modern writer, and by doing so he was at most a pseudo-modern. He was honoring a Spanish tradition against which he would eventually wage a fierce war, but even this was a form of attitudinizing. If "an honest admission of modernity means voluntarily declaring oneself bankrupt, taking the vows of poverty and chastity in a new sense, and—what is more painful—renouncing the halo of sanctity which history bestows," as Jung has asserted,[5] then Borges's modernity as a writer begins with his own admission of the bankruptcy of the Spanish language in his 1927 essay "El idioma de los argentinos" (The language of the Argentines), with his acceptance of the poverty of literature as a whole and with his acknowledgment that "perhaps universal history is the history of the diverse intonation of a few metaphors" (*OI* 9). The consequence of the first verification is the notion of style as "total efficacy and total invisibility" ("Eduardo Wilde," *ia* 158); and the conclusion of the second, the idea that the writer's task is less to invent new metaphors than to rewrite the old ones.

Borges was able to derive these two fundamental tenets only after he moved from a limited and provincial outlook on literature to a more cosmopolitan one. He remained old-fashioned in the sense that while reading Joyce he thought of Góngora—as he wrote in an essay of 1925—and while reading Kafka he was able to trace his precursors back to Zeno, Kierkegaard, Lord Dunsany, and Robert Browning.[6] Borges resisted the dazzling and bewildering impressions that modern writers leave on us. Instead, he read them as updated versions of those few metaphors Homer coined once and for all. Raymond Queneau has said that "all literary work is either an *Iliad* or an *Odyssey*."[7] Much earlier, Borges advanced a similar thesis: "The *Iliad*," he wrote in *Historia de la eternidad* (A history of eternity), "was composed some three thousand years ago; during this vast lapse of time every familiar and necessary affinity has been noted and recorded.

---

4. James E. Irby, "Encuentro con Borges," *Vida universitaria* (Monterrey, Mexico), April 12, 1964, pp. 7–16 (14). Unless otherwise noted, all translations from the Spanish are my own.

5. Jung, "Modern Man," 458.

6. Jorge Luis Borges, "El *Ulises* de Joyce," in *Inquisiciones* (Buenos Aires: Proa, 1925), 25, and "Kafka and His Precursors" (*OI*).

7. Quoted in Gérard Genette, *Figuras: retórica y estructuralismo* (Cordoba, Argentina: Nagelkop, 1970), 187.

This does not mean, of course, that the number of metaphors has been exhausted; the ways of stating or hinting at these hidden sympathies are, in fact, limitless" (*He* 74). Later, he would arrive at a conclusion that is a direct effect of this early finding: "Perhaps it is a mistake to suppose that metaphors can be invented: the real ones, those that formulate intimate connections between one image and another, have always existed; those we can still invent are the false ones, which are not worth inventing" (*OI* 47).

Borges reads literature not as an archipelago of isolated texts but as a written continent that comprises one single text. This holistic approach leads him to the views of literature that form the backbone of his essay "The Flower of Coleridge," where he quotes Valéry as saying, "The history of literature should not be the history of the authors and their work, but rather the history of the Spirit"; and where he refers to Shelley, who said, "All the poems of the past, present, and future are fragments of a single infinite poem" (*OI* 10). The ultimate inference of this reasoning is the statement that "one literature differs from another not so much because of the text as for the manner in which it is read" (*OI* 164). The writer's task is therefore to read those few metaphors anew; to rewrite the *Quixote,* as did Pierre Menard; or, as John Barth put it, referring to that story, "to write an original work of literature, the implicit theme of which is the difficulty, perhaps the unnecessity, of writing original works of literature."[8] Literature as a formal game? Literature as a verbal algebra? Literature as a mere syntactics? Yes. Such is the sweeping conclusion that closes Borges's short piece "Elementos de preceptiva" (Elements of rhetoric): "Literature is fundamentally a syntactical event" ("Ep" 161).

The article was published in *Sur* in April 1933, the same year in which most of the stories later to be collected in *A Universal History of Infamy* (1935) appeared in *Crítica.* The two conclusions presented in the short note defined two basic elements of Borges's more mature concept of literature: first, the place and function of each word or group of words as the unit that conditions the effective or ineffective performance of a text, and therefore "the validity of rhetoric as a discipline of literary analysis" ("Ep" 161); and second, the formulation, in a nutshell, of a theory of literature that views writing as rewriting. I believe that Borges's modernity stems from these two main assumptions: one deals with language and the other with syntax or structure as the text's basic raison d'être.

As early as 1927, Borges defined "total efficiency and total invisibility as the twin perfections of any style" (*ia* 158). At the time he

8. John Barth, "The Literature of Exhaustion," *Atlantic* (August 1967): 29–34 (31).

pronounced this dictum, it was only a desideratum since he was still writing in the same mannerist style he was castigating and rejecting. Only with the narratives of *A Universal History of Infamy* did he put this theoretical machinery to work. There are, of course, some differences between the prose style of *Inquisiciones* (1925) and the prose of *El idioma de los argentinos* published three years later: less pompous words, less showy neologisms, less tortuous constructions, but still a rather heavy and obtrusive prose. The last essay in the second collection, the one that gives the book its title, comes close to the prose of the first essays of *Discusión* (1932), written in the late twenties. It is not yet the compressed and free-flowing style of his more mature prose; there are still residues of the old style, but one can easily notice a gradual cleansing of the baroque arabesques of his early writing.[9] By 1933, year of the publication of the first stories of infamy, and in spite of what he later said in the preface to the collection ("The very title of these pages flaunts their baroque character" [*UHI* 11]), he was able to write a more restrained, smooth, and balanced prose.[10]

The metaphysical perplexities of his later fiction are still missing in this collection, but one recognizes the basic traits of his masterful prose—a transparency one is tempted to call invisible and, at the same time, the subtle use of a clockwork of stylistic devices. Five years after he defined what style ought to be, he produced a prose that was the skillful praxis of that earlier program.

The stories of infamy are also important on a different account. They represent the first instance in which Borges applied the literary strategy initially disclosed in the short note of 1933, namely that "literature is fundamentally a syntactical event" ("Ep" 161). In the preface to the

9. See the following paragraphs extracted from his essay "La penúltima versión de la realidad" (The penultimate version of reality) of 1928 and included in *Discusión:* "Gaspar Marín, who practices metaphysics in Buenos Aires"; "I believe the opposition between the two insuperable concepts of space and time to be fallacious. I am certain that the genealogy of this error is illustrious"; "I wish to complement these two illustrious imaginings with my own, which is (both) a derivation and a facilitation" (Jorge Luis Borges, *Discusión* [Buenos Aires: Emecé, 1957], 42–44).

10. If those pages could be called baroque, they are so only in the sense defined by John Barth: "While his own work *is not* Baroque, except intellectually (the Baroque was never so terse, laconic, economical), it suggests the view that intellectual and literary history has been Baroque, and has pretty well exhausted the possibilities of novelty" (Barth, "Literature of Exhaustion," 34).

As an example of this new, more tempered prose, read this passage from "The Dread Redeemer Lazarus Morell": "At the beginning of the nineteenth century (the date that concerns us), the vast cotton plantations along the river were worked from sunup to sundown, by blacks. These blacks slept on dirt floors in wooden cabins. Apart from mother-child relations, kinships were casual and unclear. They had first names, but they made do without family names. Nor could they read" (*UHI* 21).

1954 edition of *A Universal History of Infamy,* he wrote: "These pages . . . are the irresponsible game of a shy young man who dared not write stories and so amused himself by falsifying and distorting the tales of others" (*UHI* 11–12). Yet the method for writing adopted in this first collection would become a permanent feature of his poetics of fiction. When he wrote the preface of 1954, he already knew (if one is to take his explanation at face value) that he was going to remain shy for the rest of his literary career—but he turned this shyness into his most daring weapon.

What Borges said about his tales of infamy applies to his entire narrative work. After *Ficciones* and *The Aleph,* he repeated, in the same apologetic tone of the 1954 preface, that he was rewriting what others had already written: "Everything I have written could be found in Poe, Stevenson, Wells, Chesterton, and some others."[11] One is tempted to dismiss this and similar declarations as sheer modesty, or perhaps false modesty. The truth is that the statement is neither literally accurate nor completely false; it is, rather, a casual formulation, with modesty as its dress, of what can be regarded as the cornerstone of his poetics. He is saying informally what he very carefully formulated in the essays quoted earlier, namely, writing as rewriting.

Throughout prologues and comments, Borges tirelessly restates this central notion. About the novel *The Approach to al-Mu'tasim,* which his story reviews, he said that it shows "the double tutelage" of Wilkie Collins and Farid ud-din Attar. About the "Library of Babel," he wrote: "I am not the author of this narrative; those curious to know its history and its prehistory may interrogate a certain page of Number 59 of the journal *Sur,* which records the heterogeneous names of Leucippus and Lasswitz, of Lewis Carroll and Aristotle" (*F* 15). Of "The Circular Ruins," which is a recasting of the legend of the Golem, he said: "Lewis Carroll gave me my epigraph, which may have been the story's seed" (*AOS* 193). Of "Streetcorner Man": "This story was written under the triple influence of Stevenson, G. K. Chesterton, and Josef von Sternberg's unforgettable gangster films" (*AOS* 190). Of "Death and the Compass": "Should I add that the Hasidim included saints and that the sacrifice of four lives in order to obtain the four letters imposed by the Name is a fantasy which dictated the form of my story?" (*F* 105). Of "The Life of Tadeo Isidoro Cruz (1829–1874)": "This tale is a gloss of the gaucho poem *Martín Fierro,* written by José Hernández in 1872" (*AOS* 195). Of "The End": "Apart from one character . . . —Recabarren—nothing or almost nothing is . . . an invention of mine; everything in it is implicit in

11. James E. Irby, Napoleon Murat, and Carlos Peralta, *Encuentro con Borges* (Buenos Aires: Galerna, 1968), 37–38.

a famous book, and I have merely been the first to reveal, or at least, to declare it" (*F* 105). Of "Three Versions of Judas": "In the Christological fantasy . . . I believe I perceive the remote influence of Leon Bloy" (*F* 106). The postscript to "The Immortal" registers interpolations, intrusions, or thefts from Pliny, De Quincey, Descartes, and George Bernard Shaw. Of the story "The Immortals," Borges said: "Blake wrote that if our senses did not work—if we were blind, deaf, etc.—we would see things as they are: infinite. 'The Immortals' sprang from that strange idea and also from the verse by Rupert Brooke: 'And see, no longer blinded by our eyes' " (*AOS* 203). Of "The Dead Man": "Azevedo Bandeira, in that story, is a coarse divinity, a wild and mulatto version of Chesterton's incomparable Sunday (chapter 29 of *Decline and Fall of the Roman Empire* tells a destiny similar to Otálora's but by far greater and more incredible)" (*AOS* 171). Of "The Other Death": "The eleventh-century churchman Pier Damiani grants God the unimaginable power of undoing the past. This idea gave me the start for my story" (*AOS* 197).

One can find similar acknowledgments for most of his stories. It would be wrong to take them as demonstrations of sheer intellectual probity or mere modesty. They are of a piece with his proposition of literature as "the diverse intonation of a few metaphors," stated in a sketchy yet unequivocal way in the short note of 1933. In the afterword to the English translation of *Doctor Brodie's Report* he reiterates: "William Morris thought that the essential stories of man's imagination had long since been told and that by now the storyteller's craft lay in rethinking and retelling them. . . . I do not go as far as Morris went, but to me the writing of a story has more of a discovery about it than of deliberate invention" (*DBR* 123). Unknowingly, Borges was placing himself at the very center of one of the most modern approaches to literary theory.

The Russian Formalists strove to define literature in terms similar to the ones enunciated by Borges. They believed that texts are not born in a vacuum but evolve from other texts. What changes is less the ideas elicited by them than the new syntax that governs the rewriting of the old text. Eichenbaum, for instance, found that Tolstoy had created the new Russian novel following the direct legacy of the eighteenth-century novel; Osip Brik ascertained that the vaudeville writer Belopiatkin was reborn in Nekrasov. They also concluded that Blok canonized the themes and rhythms of the "Gypsy Song"; that Chekhov bestowed literary status to the *Budilnik,* a comic newspaper in nineteenth-century Russia; and that Dostoevski brought the devices of the dime novel to a level of literary norm. Their overall conclusion was that "new forms come about not in order to express new contents but in order to replace old forms."[12] More tightly even, Viktor Shklovsky in his essay "Art as Artifice" gives further and rather surprising support to Borges's own outlook on literature as "the diverse intonation of a few metaphors." Shklovsky's comment sounds like a paraphrase of Borges's notion:

> Images originate nowhere, they belong to God. The more one gets to know a period, the more one is persuaded that those images that were considered as a creation of this or that poet were taken by him from another poet almost without any modification. The task of poetic schools is none other than the accumulation and revelation of new devices for disposing and elaborating the verbal material, and it consists in the disposition of the images rather than in their creation. Images are there once and for all, and in poetry they are remembered rather than utilized for thinking.[13]

Although Shklovsky's article was published as early as 1917, it is most unlikely that Borges knew it. The doctrine of the Formalists was not known in western Europe until the forties, when Jakobson moved to the United States and one of his students, Victor Erlich, published (in 1955) the first book-length survey of the movement. One is forced to conclude that Borges was working on his own and that he arrived independently at conclusions similar to those reached by the Formalists. Besides, critical theory was for him a subsidiary undertaking intended to sharpen his own awareness as a writer. He did what the Formalists did not do: he incorporated some of his ideas about literature into his creative writing, thus amalgamating theory and craft.

 If one thinks of French structuralism as a consequence and derivation of Russian Formalism—and Lévi-Strauss was the first to acknowledge the debt of his anthropology to Vladimir Propp and the members of the *Opoiiaz*—it is understandable that Borges's notion of literature as syntax overlapped with the structuralist concept of literature as a system (Barthes). It is also understandable that a structuralist critic such as Gérard Genette should read Borges with so much fascination and conviction. Genette echoed Borges's enthusiasm for the idea of all literature constituting a single text, and relying on this assumption he proposed the following definition: "Literature is a coherent whole, a congruous space in whose interior the works touch and penetrate each other."[14] He further supported his definition with the notion of writing as rewriting developed by Borges in the essay "For Bernard Shaw": "If I

12. *Readings in Russian Poetics: Formalist and Structuralist Views,* ed. Ladislav Matejka and Krystyna Pomoroska (Cambridge: MIT Press, 1971), 32, 29.
    13. Quoted in *Teoría de los formalistas rusos,* ed. Tzvetan Todorov (Buenos Aires: Signos, 1970), 56.
    14. Genette, *Figuras,* 186.

were to read any contemporary page as it would be read in the year 2000, I would know what the literature would be like in the year 2000" (*OI* 164). Genette quotes this sentence as the foundation for a structuralist theory of literature.

In the first part of "Elementos de preceptiva," Borges undertakes the stylistic examination of a *milonga* (a precursor of the tango), discovered "in a rural grocery store near Arapey, at the beginning of 1931." He leaves to Spitzer, he says, "the original aesthetic experiences which determined it" ("Ep" 158); he simply seeks to explore its verbal effectiveness. What this example shows, Borges concludes, together with the analysis of two lines from the tango "Villa Crespo," is that "a subtle interplay of changes, clever frustrations and supports defines the aesthetic fact; those who neglect or ignore it, ignore literature's raison d'être" ("Ep" 159). In 1933, Borges was showing that poetic functions are not exclusive attributes of literary texts; they can appear in either a *milonga* or a tango—or even in an anonymous inscription written on a street wall.

Roman Jakobson was to say and do something similar in 1960. To prove that "the linguistic study of the poetic function must overstep the limit of poetry," he examined the various phonetic and morphological functions operating in the structural system of the election catch phrase "I like Ike."[15] For Jakobson, poetics, as the discipline that deals with problems of verbal structure, sees literature the way Borges did in 1933—as a syntactical makeup. In the same essay, Jakobson warned that "the terminological confusion of 'literary studies' with 'criticism' tempts the student of literature to replace the description of intrinsic values of literary works by a subjective, censorious verdict."[16] At the conclusion of his 1933 note, Borges voiced a similar warning: "If there is no single word written in vain, if even a popular *milonga* is a world of attractions and rejections, how to elucidate . . . the 1056 quarto pages attributed to a Shakespeare? How to take seriously those who judge themselves as a whole, without any method other than a loud emission of terrifying praises, and without examining a single line?" ("Ep" 161).

I would like to add that when Borges postulated in 1927 "total invisibility and total effectiveness as the twin perfections of any style" (*ia* 158), he was anticipating Camus by twenty-four years. It was not until 1951 that the author of *The Rebel* wrote, "Great style is invisible stylization, or rather stylization incarnate."[17] Two years later, Roland

15. Roman Jakobson, "Linguistics and Poetics," in *Style in Language,* ed. Thomas A. Sebeok (Cambridge: MIT Press, 1960), 350–77 (357).

16. Ibid., 351–52.

17. Albert Camus, *The Rebel: An Essay on Man in Revolt,* trans. Anthony Bower, foreword by Herbert Read (New York: Knopf, 1967), 271–72.

Barthes studied this trend against artistry in contemporary French fiction and coined the formula "writing degree zero." What he said was a restatement and a development of Camus's basic point: "This neutral writing achieves a style of absence which is almost an ideal absence of style . . . ; it deliberately foregoes any elegance or ornament; it is the mode of a new situation of the writer, the way a certain silence has of existing."[18] More straightforward, more matter-of-fact, Borges has been saying the same since the twenties and has been putting this principle to work in his own writing since the thirties. But Borges lived in Buenos Aires, not in Paris, and he was an Argentine who did not have the prestige and the weight of a literature that, like the French, had been dominating the European scene since the eighteenth century. Recognition came late, but the seed of Borges's modernity was already implanted in his early writing.

When Borges's work was translated into most of the European languages and became better known in Europe and the United States, his fiction and essays turned into a driving force in modern letters. Some critics have seen Borges's place in contemporary literature as a new example, which has "served to release the influence of his own master, Kafka, and even such different writers as Beckett and Robbe-Grillet."[19] More important to our topic is the fact that one of the most recent approaches to have made its way into the critical arena after structuralism found its spokesman in Borges. I am referring to intertextuality. (Borges wrote the story that became the metaphor and the credo of the new method, "Pierre Menard, Author of the *Quixote*." Recall also what he had said in the preface to *A Universal History of Infamy* to the effect that he was not the author of the stories, but merely their counterfeiter.) Intertextuality is—in oversimplified terms—the study of the relationship between two or more texts, one that functions as a model or "hypotext," and a second or "hypertext" whose production is based on the first. The most important book on the method to have appeared so far is Genette's, *Palimpsestes: La Littérature au second degré* (Palimpsests: Literature in the second degree), published in 1982. Genette borrowed his title from a passage in "Pierre Menard, Author of the *Quixote*," and on page 452 there is an indirect acknowledgment of that fact.[20] The debt to Borges is further recognized throughout Genette's

---

18. Roland Barthes, *Le Degré zéro de l'écriture* (Paris: Seuil, 1953). The English translation is *Writing Degree Zero,* trans. Annette Lavers and Colin Smith (London: Jonathan Cape, 1967), 83–84.

19. Morris Dickstein, review of *City Life* by Donald Bartheleme, *New York Times Book Review,* April 26, 1970, pp. 1, 38–43 (1)

20. Gérard Genette, *Palimpsestes: La Littérature au second degré* (Paris: Seuil, 1982). In that passage, Borges notes: "I have reflected that it is permissible to see in this 'final' *Quixote*

book. On page 296, he defines the method he owes to Borges:

> Attribuant à d'autres l'invention de ses contes, Borges présente au contraire son écriture comme une lecture, déguise en lecture son écriture. Ces deux conduites, faut-il le dire, sont complémentaires, elles s'unissent en une métaphore des relations, complexes et ambigües, de l'écriture et de la lecture: relations qui sont bien évidemment—j'y reviendrai s'il le faut—l'âme même de l'activité hypertextuelle.

> (By attributing the invention of his stories to others, Borges, on the contrary, presents his writing as a reading; he disguises his writing as reading. The two procedures are, of course, complementary; they merge into a single metaphor of the complex and ambiguous relations between writing and reading. These relations—I will return to this if necessary—are most evidently the heart and soul of hypertextual activity.)

Borges always had a keen interest in and a strong attraction to the classics.[21] After his brief participation in the Spanish brand of the avant-garde, *ultraísmo,* and later in his more mature period, he gave blunt signs of impatience toward modern writers. If as early as 1925 he translated into Spanish "the last page" of Joyce's *Ulysses,* since the fifties, as his blindness became more advanced, he turned more and more into the past: he began the study of Old English and Old Norse; returned to his favorite Victorian writers; kept rereading the classics; and became disdainful and even vitriolic about the moderns. He did his best to be seen and known as old-fashioned. Ironically, he became not only a "classic of modern fiction," as John Barth defined him, but also the guru of modern literary perception.

---

a kind of palimpsest, through which the traces—tenuous but not indecipherable—of our friend's 'previous' writing should be translucently visible" (*L* 44).

21. See Jorge Luis Borges, "Sobre los clásicos," *Sur* 85 (1941): 7–12.

Gerry O'Sullivan _____

The Library Is on Fire
Intertextuality in Borges and Foucault

Jorge Luis Borges and Michel Foucault—the blind librarian and the archivist—seem, at least at first, to resist one another's company. Borges, after all, was no genealogist seeking to disentangle the subtle and rhizomatic movements of *pouvoir* (power)—indeed, many of Borges's Argentine detractors have dismissed the writer as inconsequential because of his inattention to questions of politics and power—and Foucault had little if any interest in the writing of so-called fiction. To speak of "influence" in either direction would render a disservice to the respective projects of these two elusive nonauthors. Borges spurned the mantle of authorship on more than one occasion, choosing instead to refer to himself as an encyclopedist or "simply a man of letters." Foucault, on the other hand, preferred to call himself a cartographer, a "dealer in instruments, an inventor of recipes."[1]

But the proper name *Borges* does appear—and somewhat conspicuously—upon one of the latter's many recipe cards. Two years after the appearance of a special issue of *L'Herne* (1964) dedicated to Borges,[2] Foucault opened the preface to his monumental study *Les Mots et les choses* (The order of things) with the following observation: "This book first arose out of a passage in Borges, out of the laughter that shattered, as I read the passage, all the familiar landmarks of my thought—*our* thought, the thought that bears the stamp of our age and our geography—breaking up all the ordered surfaces and all the planes with which we are accustomed to tame the wild profusion of existing things." The passage, which threatened to "collapse our age-old distinction between the same and the Other,"[3] was drawn from Borges's

Material included in this article appeared previously in *CEA Critic* 46 (1984): 3–4 and is reprinted with permission.

1. *Simply a Man of Letters: Panel Discussions and Papers from the Proceedings of a Symposium on Jorge Luis Borges Held at the University of Maine at Orono,* ed. Carlos Cortínez (Maine: University of Maine at Orono Press, 1982), 1–26; Alan Sheridan, *Michel Foucault: The Will to Truth* (London and New York: Tavistock, 1980), 224.

2. *Jorge Luis Borges: L'Herne* (Paris, 1964).

3. Michel Foucault, *The Order of Things: An Archeology of the Human Sciences* (New

"The Analytical Language of John Wilkins," a tale involving a rather bizarre taxonomy of animals attributed by one Dr. Franz Kuhn to a Chinese encyclopedia entitled *Celestial Emporium of Benevolent Knowledge*. The animals are classified in a seemingly random fashion and according to seemingly random characteristics—frenzied, tame, belonging to the emperor, drawn with a very fine camel-hair brush, and so on. The system, which appears ostensibly to be no system at all, is unnerving in its ability to suggest, if not the plausibility, then at least the startling possibility of other discursive formations and classificatory arrangements. Borges's parable throws us into the realm of what Foucault has called the "heterotopia" that, unlike the consolation of order promised by utopias, desiccates speech and undermines syntax, stopping "words in their tracks" and contesting "the very possibility of grammar at its source."[4]

One such heterotopic trope found in both the Borgesian canon and the Foucauldian project (particularly with regard to the so-called archaeological period) is that of the library or archive. In both cases, the archival metaphor suggests the undermining of unities once held to be inviolable in both historical and literary studies—seamless canons; isolate and individual works of genius; linear chronologies; myths of ends and origins; and the enduring presence of privileged, and ultimately authoritative, authorial voices. Such centers or centrisms have long maintained their explanatory, and transcendentally validated, hegemony in history and the human sciences, and these disciplines are in turn undermined by the intertextual dispersion at work in, and suggested by, the figure of the library. As Eugenio Donato has noted, the labyrinthine libraries constructed by Borges are indicative of a particular topography of memory operative in the poems, essays, and *ficciones*. Here, the library "systematically emblematizes its own representational memory as diffuse, non-ordered, without origin and without end," suggesting a nonprivileged type of memory or, to use Foucault's language, "counter-memory."[5]

Intertextuality, the product of the *glissement* (shift) traced by Barthes in "From Work to Text," not only subverts the "internal" constitution of meaning secretly situated within a text and awaiting liberation by hermeneutical strategies but also undercuts the external or referential dimension of discourse.[6] In the Foucauldian archive, such categories as

York: Vintage, 1970), xv.

4. Ibid., xviii.

5. Eugenio Donato, "Topographies of Memory," in *Man of Letters,* 99–114 (104–5).

6. Roland Barthes, "From Work to Text," in *Textual Strategies: Perspectives in Post-Structuralist Criticism,* ed. Josué Harari (Ithaca: Cornell University Press, 1979), 73–81 (73, 77).

meaning and reference (as in reference to a world, a subject, or a sovereign consciousness) are displaced by the proliferation of discursive irregularities. Foucault turns away from transcendental and anthropological guarantees for the continuity and certainty of meaning, memory, history, and language and deals instead with the functional materiality of the *énoncé,* the statement. "Language," as he observes in *The Archeology of Knowledge,* "in its appearance and mode of being, is the statement. . . . The enunciative analysis does not lay down for linguistic or logical analysis the limit beyond which they must renounce their power and recognize their powerlessness; it does not mark the line that encloses their domain; it is deployed in another direction, which intersects them."[7]

The enunciative domain is neither delimited nor controlled by metaphysical regularities occurring within or without a given constellation of texts. Instead, we are faced with the exteriority or materiality of discourse wherein "there is no subtext. And therefore no plethora. The enunciative domain is identical with its own surface." This principle of exteriority renders problematic both traditional historical and structural analyses, insofar as it denies the possibility to free-floating or readily available "facts" on the one hand, and the unity of sign and signifier on the other. Archaeological analysis invites us to question language, "not in the direction to which it refers, but in the dimension that gives it; ignore its power to designate, to name, to show, to reveal, to be the place of meaning or truth, and, instead, turn one's attention to the moment—which is at once solidified, caught up in the play of the 'signifier' and the 'signified'—that determines its unique and limited existence."[8] It could be said that Foucault here reworks the temporal dimension of Heideggerian *Ereignis,* the radical eventfulness of the *es Gibt* (the "giving-ness" or "there is" of being) so that the focus is no longer the historicity of understanding, but rather the site or domain of discourse itself—the materiality of statement, the density of discourse, the "space" of the archive.

For all intents and purposes, the student of hermeneutics becomes an archivist, and the double movement of understanding and misunderstanding that characterizes hermeneutic phenomenology is displaced by the fragility of statements as they are traced and charted in their emergence and disappearance. Hence Foucault, like Borges, seems to revel in the logic of the found document.[9] In an interview with Charles

7. Michel Foucault, *The Archeology of Knowledge,* trans. A. M. Sheridan Smith (New York: Pantheon, 1972), 113.

8. Ibid., 119, 111.

9. See especially Michel de Certeau's tribute to Foucault: "[Foucault] visited books just as he went around Paris on bicycle, around San Francisco or Tokyo, with exact and vigilant

Ruas regarding his essay on Raymond Roussel, for example, Foucault points out that the study emerged "completely by chance" and as the result of a visit to the Librairie José Corti to purchase an unrelated, and long-since-forgotten, volume in the summer of 1957. While waiting for Corti to end a prolonged conversation with a friend, Foucault happened upon a series of yellowed volumes issued by the Librairie Lemerre, among which he discovered a copy of Roussel's *La Vue*.[10] Prior to cataloging the documents and fragments collected and published as *I, Pierre Rivière* . . . , Foucault notes that the materials, discovered in the Archives du Calvados, were "come across" in the course of research on the "practical aspects of the relations between psychiatry and criminal justice."[11] Likewise, the introduction to the stories of Herculin Barbin, a nineteenth-century hermaphrodite later celebrated in a piece of medicopornography written by Oscar Panizza, traces the intersections between a memoir—that of Barbin herself—and a fictionalized account written after Panizza's possible discovery of the original document in a German library in 1882.[12]

The Foucauldian principle of exteriority demands that we concede the contingency of knowledge as well as the reality (or materiality) of discourse with recourse to a founding subject or other such transcendental constructions. Similarly, in the work of Borges, we find what John Updike has characterized as a confession of artifice, an understanding or meaning as constituted by the dispersion and chance inter-

---

attention, poised to catch, at the turn of a page or street, the spark of some strangeness lurking there unnoticed. All these marks of otherness, whether 'minuscule lapses' or enormous confessions, were for him citations of an unthought. . . . When he discovered them he would roll with laughter. . . . His other works seem to have the same origin: bouts of surprise (in the same way there are bouts of fever), the sudden jubilatory, semi-ecstatic forms of 'astonishment' or 'wonder' which have been, from Aristotle to Wittgenstein, the inaugurators of philosophical activity. . . . Hence his complicity with the great detectors of the surprises of language and the chance events of thought, from the Sophists down to Roussel or Magritte" (Michel de Certeau, "The Laugh of Michel Foucault," in *Heterologies: Discourse on the Other,* trans. Brian Massumi [Minneapolis: University of Minnesota Press, 1986], 194–95).

10. Shortly thereafter, Foucault, noting a remarkable resemblance between the prose styles of Roussel and Robbe-Grillet, recalls meeting the latter in Hamburg in 1960. The two proceeded to the Hamburg Fair, where they wandered through the "fun-house maze of mirrors." This event, Foucault suggests to Ruas, was the material for the beginning of Robbe-Grillet's *Dans le labyrinthe* (Michel Foucault, *Death and the Labyrinth: The World of Raymond Roussel,* trans. Charles Ruas [New York: Doubleday, 1986], 171–73).

11. Michel Foucault, *I, Pierre Rivière, having slaughtered my mother, my sister, and my brother . . . : A Case of Parricide in the 19th Century,* ed. Frank Jellinek (New York: Pantheon, 1975), vii.

12. Michel Foucault, *Herculin Barbin: Being the Recently Discovered Memoirs of a Nineteenth-Century Hermaphrodite,* trans. Richard McDougall (New York: Pantheon, 1980).

section of surfaces rather than as something preexistent or somehow hidden beneath the skin of the text.[13] As Borges has written in "The Wall and the Books": "Music, states of happiness, mythology, faces scored by time, certain twilights, certain places, all want to tell us something, or told us something we should not have missed, or are about to tell us something. This imminence of a revelation that does not take place is, perhaps, the aesthetic fact" (*PA* 92). The metaphysical assurance that our interpretive gestures will, somehow, cause the curtain or veil of language to part, revealing a shining and prediscursive adytum, is undercut by Borges's reliance upon possibility—the always imminent revelation, the "elegant hope" proffered by the narrator of "The Library of Babel": "I venture to suggest this solution to the ancient problem: *The Library is unlimited and cyclical.* If an eternal traveler were to cross it in any direction, after centuries he would see that the same volumes were repeated in the same disorder (which, thus repeated, would be an order: the Order). My solitude is gladdened by this elegant hope" (*L* 58). Borges here, in effect, restates Foucault's case regarding enunciative analysis—the line traced by the hypothetical "eternal traveler" does not engender a sovereign theoretical position that encloses the discursive domain. Rather, the line doubles back, intersecting the library and creating a contingent, but seemingly eternal, "Order."

While the notion of the archive suggests for Foucault the density of discursive practices (as opposed to the great mythical book of history in which the visible characters are merely translations of lines of thought formed in another time and place),[14] Borges's metaphors similarly suggest the exteriority of texts—libraries, books, encyclopedias, manuscripts, dictionaries, *grimoires.* The heterotopic force of the metaphor of the library cannot be underestimated in the writings of Borges, and these normally austere and reassuring places become, in his hands, fantastic and terrifying labyrinths of paper. Having himself worked in the Biblioteca Nacional, the Argentine National Library, Borges is well aware of the almost gothic sense of horror that faintly illuminated and seemingly endless rows of shelves are capable of evoking. Borges's most thorough biographer to date, Emir Rodríguez Monegal, was once taken on a jaunt through the dark corridors of the National Library by the blind librarian who rushed from stack to stack, around corners and through passageways, leaving Rodríguez Monegal confused and exhausted. "Finally," remembers Rodríguez Monegal, "I come to understand that the space in which we are momentarily in-

---

13. John Updike, "Author as Librarian," *New Yorker,* October 30, 1965, pp. 223–46.
14. Foucault, *Archeology of Knowledge,* 128.

serted is not real: it is a space made of words, signs, symbols. It is another labyrinth." He continues:

> Borges drags me, makes me quickly descend the long, winding staircase, fall exhausted into the center of darkness. Suddenly, there is light at the end of another corridor. Prosaic reality awaits me there. Next to Borges, who smiles like a child who has played a joke on a friend, I recover my eyesight, the real world of light and shadow, the conventions I am trained to recognize. But I come out of the experience like one who emerges from deep water or from a dream, shattered by the (other) reality of that labyrinth of paper.[15]

It could be said that Rodríguez Monegal's description of his dash through the National Library constitutes something of a countertrope for Plato's myth of the cave. Rather than encountering the blinding light of truth, Rodríguez Monegal still seems to be immersed in the dream, or nightmare, of the library. The real world of light and shadow becomes a simulacrum, and the order of referentiality is temporarily suspended. In spite of the vertigo effected by these haunting labyrinths, Borges remains oddly attracted by the lure of the library, "the enveloping serenity of order, time magically desiccated and preserved" (*Dt* 21). Being a site of dispersion, the library overturns hierarchies and traditional oppositions, leaving only ambiguity and undecidability. The library simultaneously repels and attracts, discloses and obscures, promises knowledge and yet often yields only confusion, as Rodríguez Monegal discovered. For Borges, paradise is not a garden but a library—a library attained, as he observes in "Poem of the Gifts," when he was blind. And this, as Borges once explained to Alastair Reid and John Coleman, is not the irony of "Poema de los dones," but rather God's irony (*BEC* 118).

In the figure of the library, intertextuality usurps extraverbality, the archive replaces rhetoric, and we are left to deal with a world of seemingly infinite self-referentiality, of perfect repetition and actuality.[16] Such is certainly the case with Foucault's essay "Fantasia of the Library," which deals with Flaubert's *Temptation of Saint Anthony*. Foucault observes that this book, unlike any book before it, finds its locus within the realm of knowledge itself, existing "by virtue of its essential relationship to books."[17] For the first time, the world of the fantastic finds its domain not in nature or the heart, but rather in the bound

15. Emir Rodríguez Monegal, *Jorge Luis Borges: A Literary Biography* (New York: Dutton, 1978), 431.

16. Edward Said, *Beginnings: Intention and Method* (New York: Basic, 1975), 92.

17. Michel Foucault, *Language, Counter-Memory, Practice: Selected Essays and Interviews*, ed. Donald F. Bouchard, trans. Donald F. Bouchard and Sherry Simon (Ithaca: Cornell University Press, 1977), 91.

volume, in the library where books dream other books. And such an intertextual aesthetic of accumulation has its precursor in *Don Quixote,* the first reversal of the Renaissance's logic of resemblance.

In *The Order of Things,* Foucault locates Cervantes's knight-errant at an epistemic juncture, a shift in the texture of knowledge occurring with the onset of the so-called Classical Age. Don Quixote's quest is a search for similitude, but his benchmark is not the "prose of the world" itself, but rather the book. Don Quixote, then, "reads the world in order to prove his books" rather than vice versa, wandering in the newly opened space that now exists between words and things. Hence, *Don Quixote* is according to Foucault the first modern work of literature because "in it we see the cruel reason of identities and differences make endless sport of signs and similitudes."[18] Words, having broken their old alliance with things, now occupy a new and sovereign state— that of literature—and resemblance is driven into the concomitant regions of madness and the imagination. The postmodern turn, initiated by Flaubert's *Temptation,* takes this one step further, allowing for the likes of Kafka, Pound, and Borges. Just as Manet's *Déjeuner sur l'herbe* and *Olympia* were the first "museum" paintings, composed not as a response to Raphael and Velázquez but rather as acknowledgments of "the new and substantial relationship of painting to itself, as a manifestation of the existence of museums and the particular reality and interdependence that paintings acquire in museums,"[19] so too did Flaubert compose the *Temptation* as a bow (or at least a nod) to the library.

Both Manet and Flaubert self-consciously erect their art within the archive, and painting is consigned to its own "squared and massive surface" while all literary works are confined to "the indefinite murmur of writing."[20] Hence, what Manet is to the site or space of the museum, Flaubert is to the library. *The Temptation of Saint Anthony* is linked to a vast world of print rather than to a region of stable referents external to discourse and extends the space "that existing books can occupy" by recovering, hiding, displaying, combining, and fragmenting them. It initiates the vast conflagration of intertextuality that will enable Mallarmé to write *Le Livre.* Indeed, as Foucault contends, the library is now on fire.

For Borges, the single volume gives way in much the same manner to a textual network or, as he describes it in "A Note on (toward) Bernard Shaw," an infinite dialogue. "A book," says Borges, "is not an isolated

18. Foucault, *The Order of Things,* 47–48, 49.
19. Foucault, *Language, Counter-Memory, Practice,* 92.
20. Ibid.

being: it is a relationship, an axis of innumerable relationships" (*L* 214). Such is the case with one of Borges's later works of short fiction entitled "The Book of Sand." Here, an unassuming Bible salesman appears at the door of a rather myopic narrator who is, for all intents and purposes, Borges himself. The salesman, dressed in gray and of nondescript bearing and features, possesses a book with an infinite number of pages. Leafing through the cloth-bound volume, the narrator discovers that the pages are numbered in a seemingly random fashion (he discovers page 40514 opposite page 999) and that illustrations appear and disappear with each and every turn of a page. The stranger asks the befuddled narrator to find the first and last pages, but each time he attempts to put his thumb on the flyleaf, pages are mysteriously generated between the cover and his hand. In response to the potential buyer's incredulity and shock, the Bible seller explains, "It can't be, but it *is*. The number of pages in this book is no more or less than infinite. None is the first page, none the last. I don't know why they're numbered in this arbitrary way. Perhaps to suggest that the terms of an infinite series admit any numbers." Then, thinking aloud, the stranger adds, "If space is infinite, we may be at any point in space. If time is infinite, we may be at any point in time."[21]

It is not surprising that Borges, with delicious irony, would make the bearer of such a book a Bible salesman. The Bible, after all, remains the West's exemplar of and for textual unity, and "The Book of Sand" assumes the character of the Bible's sinister Other—a book that, almost demonically, resists closure. The book of sand is rightly described as a "nightmarish object, an obscene thing that affronted and tainted reality itself."[22] Driven by fear of chaos and an overwhelming terror of the irrational, Borges's narrator decides to lose the volume, appropriately enough, in the Argentine National Library.

Suggested by the Borgesian library and the Foucauldian archive is what Foucault has described as a discursive "disease of proliferation"— the seeming inability of language to avoid repetition, reduplication, and multiplication. Death acts as both limit and center in discourse, and we write, as Blanchot has observed, "so as not to die."[23] Language mirrors itself against the dark backdrop of death, doubling and redoubling itself ostensibly to infinity. Repetition, pure serialism, and multiplication continually threaten to displace the metaphysics of identity and representation, making a mockery of them. As Borges wrote in

21. Jorge Luis Borges, "The Book of Sand," in *The Book of Sand,* trans. Norman Thomas di Giovanni (New York: Dutton, 1977), 117–22 (117–19).

22. Ibid., 122.

23. Cited in Foucault, *Language, Counter-Memory, Practice,* 53.

"The Draped Mirrors": "As a child I felt before large mirrors that same horror of spectral duplication or multiplication of reality. Their infallible and continuous functioning, their pursuit of my actions, their cosmic pantomime, were uncanny then, whenever it began to grow dark" (*Dt* 27).

Throughout the tales, Borges inserts mirrors among books in order to hint at a seemingly impossible infinity of words and pages. The shelves in "The Library of Babel" are arranged "in an indefinite, perhaps infinite, number of hexagonal galleries" (*L* 51) and these are reflected in a mirror by the entranceway, which in turn only increases the sense of vertigo by insinuating that the library might indeed be both limitless and periodic. Books and mirrors are conjoined elsewhere in the *ficciones,* most notably in "Tlön, Uqbar, Orbis Tertius," wherein the elusive volume of the *Anglo-American Cyclopaedia,* containing an extended treatment of the history and literature of the mythical nation of Uqbar, is first discovered upon the conjunction of a mirror and an encyclopedia. Borges insinuates himself into this particular story as author, recalling an alleged conversation with his collaborator, Adolfo Bioy Casares, concerning an observation once made by one of the heresiarchs of Uqbar that both mirrors and copulation were monstrous because they only served to increase the number of men. Looking up from their table, Borges spies a set of the *Anglo-American Cyclopaedia* reflected in a mirror that has "troubled the depths of the corridor." The volume fails to provide any information regarding Uqbar and, contrary to Bioy Casares's claim, does not contain the quotation cited by Borges's guest. Undaunted, Bioy Casares later calls Borges from Buenos Aires to announce that he has in fact discovered the volume—and article—in question and proceeds to produce the text for examination. The rather lengthy essay, replete with suggestions for further reading and research, painstakingly describes a region that seems to refuse verification and corroboration in spite of an evening spent in the National Library searching for supporting materials.

Rather than rehearse the entire tale, suffice it to say that the alleged conversation between "Borges" and "Bioy Casares" sets a series of bibliographical searches in motion, searches that themselves engender commentary and speculation on topics ranging from dialectics to idealism. Such intertextual meanderings are not limited, however, to the intertextual apparatus of "Tlön, Uqbar, Orbis Tertius" but extend rhizomatically to a "world" of other texts. As Rodríguez Monegal has pointed out, the citation that sets both search and story in motion is not to be found in an encyclopedia but is rather a distorted quotation lifted from another of Borges's own stories, namely "The Masked Dyer,

Hakim of Merv," which first appeared in *A Universal History of Infamy* (1935).[24] The search for supporting facts leads us, inevitably, to other fictions, and every attempt to isolate evidence outside language carries us back into a library strewn with mirrors. Such a configuration renders suspect our most cherished metaphysical oppositions—inside/outside, text/commentary. Indeed, the encyclopedia in question is presented in the story as a "literal but delinquent" reprint of the 1902 edition of the *Encyclopaedia Britannica,* and, ironically, Borges's interlocutor, Bioy Casares, once collaborated with Borges on a collection of literary essays attributed to a fictional critic of the Charles Kinbote variety and entitled *Chronicles of Bustos Domecq*.

When texts mirror other texts rather than a stable and external reality, the effect is heterotopic, to use Foucault's language, and the mimetic relationship between text and world is radically altered. Like Borges, Foucault is well aware of the destabilizing, decentering power of mirrors:

> The mirror is, after all, a utopia, since it is a placeless place. In the mirror, I see myself there where I am not, in an unreal, virtual space that opens up behind the surface; I am over there, there where I am not. . . . But it is also a heterotopia in so far as the mirror does exist in reality, where it exerts a sort of counter-action on the position that I occupy. From the standpoint of the mirror I discover my absence from the place where I am since I see myself over there. Starting from this gaze that is, as it were, directed toward me, from the ground of this virtual space that is on the other side of the glass, I come back toward myself; I begin again to direct my eyes toward myself and to reconstitute myself there where I am. The mirror functions as a heterotopia in this respect: it makes this place that I occupy at once absolutely real . . . and absolutely unreal.[25]

The mirror, and very often facing mirrors, betokens infinity while undermining representation. Mirrors are, and remain, real objects that merely suggest representation, and this leads Foucault to draw a parallel between the incessant doubling offered by polished surfaces and the self-representation of language in writing, which drives us into the virtual "space" of reduplication and repetition: "Since writing refers not to a thing but to speech, a work of language only advances more deeply into the intangible density of the mirror, calls forth the double of this already doubled writing, discovers in this way a possible and impossible infinity, ceaselessly strives after speech, maintains it beyond the death which condemns it, and frees a murmuring stream." In order to illustrate this point, Foucault chooses as his exemplary text Borges's "The Secret Miracle," in which Jaromir Hladík, a Czech writer con-

24. In Cortínez, *Man of Letters,* 188.
25. Michel Foucault, "Of Other Spaces," trans. Jay Miskoweic, in *Diacritics* 16:1 (1986): 22–27.

demned to die before a Nazi firing squad, is granted another year to live in order to complete his masterwork. Just as the guns converge on Hladík, the entire universe is brought to a halt in answer to a prayer. Suspended between life and a certain and always impending death, Hladík's work "is a drama where everything is necessarily repeated: the end (as yet unfinished) taking up word for word the (already written) beginning, but in such a way as to show the main character, whom we know and who has spoken since the first scenes, to be not himself but an imposter [sic]." As Hladík writes, he produces a "great, invisible labyrinth of repetition, of language that divides itself and becomes its own mirror. When the last epithet is found (also the first since the drama began again), the volley of rifle fire, released less than a second before, strikes his silence at the heart."[26]

Against the metaphysics of representation, Foucault posits discourse and duplication, the library and the mirror. In the heterotopic domain of the archive, all of our idealisms are undermined as knowledge confronts its Other in the sheer materiality—and artifice—of discourse, of a writing that is always and already inhabited by death. Writing has become a game forever ahead of itself in which the writing subject continually disappears and is dispersed in the midst of the interplay. This is the fate of the author, the traditionally "author-itative" guarantor of place, meaning, and unity. The author has become what Foucault calls an "author-function," merely a configuration or construct, and the tendency in some forms of criticism to reconstruct or recover an author's intentions remains ensconced in the tradition of Christian exegesis which attempts to ascertain the value or authenticity of a given text by gauging the holiness of its author.[27] Borges's "Pierre Menard, Author of the *Quixote*" foregrounds the problem of authorship by attempting to re-create a fictitious author by reference to an equally fictitious compendium of nonexistent books, sonnets, essays, and treatises. Borges then proceeds to critique Menard's strange attempt at composing not merely another *Quixote,* but rather the *Quixote*—line for line, word for word, page for page. The method was simple: Menard vowed to "know Spanish well, to reembrace the Catholic faith, to fight against Moors and Turks, to forget European history between 1602 and 1918, and to *be* Miguel de Cervantes" (*BAR* 99). Borges skillfully parodies the dream of Romantic hermeneutics embodied in Kant's (and later Schleiermacher's) credo: "To know an author better than he knew himself."

The hermeneutic thrust is, more often than not, confounded by the

---

26. Foucault, *Language, Counter-Memory, Practice,* 56.
27. Ibid., 127.

proliferative character of language and subverted by intertextuality. Foucault has noted that, prior to Sade's consecration as an author, his many papers were little more than repositories for the myriad fantasies he spun during his confinement in prison. The logic of the proper name can only contain and control so much before it finds itself overtaken by excess. "If we wish to publish the complete works of Nietzsche," Foucault asks, " where do we draw the line? Certainly, everything must be published, but can we agree on what 'everything' means?"[28] Given the traditional coordinates, "author" and "work," shall we then proceed to include appointment reminders, addresses, and laundry bills in the name of completeness and totality—or, to use Derrida's favorite example, a fragment found among Nietzsche's unpublished papers that reads, "J'ai oublié mon parapluie"?[29]

At this juncture, the author vanishes like the disintegrating dreamer dispersed into the increasing materiality of his own phantasm in Borges's "The Circular Ruins." The excesses of intertextuality and the proliferation of discourse seem to overtake such organizing and totalizing centers as the work and the author; as Roland Barthes has noted, this is most certainly the case when one concedes that every text is, always and already, the intertext of another text.[30] The work as classically understood—as defined object, as creation of genius—is now to be understood under the category of "Text," a category that traverses and transgresses traditional divisions and boundaries. The work sits upon a library shelf, occupying a specific book-space, while the Text is plural, resisting the various myths of filiation—source, origin, genius, and influence. The notion of a unified and singular oeuvre remains a creation of monism and stands opposed to plurality and difference. Indeed the Text might, as Barthes winkingly suggests, take its motto from Mark 5:9: "My name is legion, for we are many."[31]

Language, at least as it is treated by both Borges and Foucault, will not and cannot be forced into continua of unity, continuity, and identity. We are left instead with the unsettling trope of the library with all of its attendant characteristics—plenitude, serialization, the exteriority of language, the infinity of words. Borges's libraries are mazelike suggestions of infinity, housing finite beings forever reading by an incessant and insufficient light. They are worlds atomized and vacant; as John Updike has written, "Perhaps not since Lucretius has a poet so

28. Ibid., 118.
29. Jacques Derrida, *Spurs: Nietzsche's Styles/Eperons:Les Styles de Nietzsche,* intro. Stefano Agosti, trans. Barbara Harlow (Chicago: University of Chicago Press, 1979), 122–43.
30. Barthes, "From Work to Text," 77.
31. Ibid., 80.

definitely felt men to be incidents in space."[32] Likewise, Foucault, in the conclusion to *The Order of Things,* foresees the end of "Man"—that empirico-transcendental doublet, dubbed the Subject, erased like a face "drawn in sand at the edge of the sea."[33] Against the threat of difference, we have erected laws of sameness. While clinging desperately to the need for constancy and unity, Borges presents us with the horrible fancy of the library, the "vast contradictory library, whose vertical deserts of books run the incessant risk of metamorphosis, which affirm everything, deny everything, and confuse everything—like a raving god" (*BAR* 96).

32. Updike, "Author as Librarian," 223–46.
33. Foucault, *The Order of Things,* 387.

Suzanne Jill Levine

Borges and Emir
The Writer and His Reader

In the next essay, "Borges and Derrida: Apothecaries," Emir Rodrí-guez Monegal refers to the essay "Borges: The Reader as Writer" as a blueprint, a rehearsal—an *essai* in the etymological sense—for the literary biography, commissioned in English by E. P. Dutton, which he had begun to write. In "The Reader as Writer," Emir developed the "theory that Borges preferred reading over writing as a way of denying authorship, that is, a way of not admitting the paternity of his work"—a theory based on a lifetime of practice, of reading (with) Borges. In Emir's words: "All that Borges writes becomes reading, that is, liter-ature, fiction."[1] Emir quotes Borges's preface to his earliest volume of verse, *Fervor de Buenos Aires* (1923), as characteristic of the maestro's ironic stance on authorship: "If the pages of this book offer some felici-tous line or other, may the reader pardon me the discourtesy of having claimed it first. Our inconsequential selves [*nuestras nadas*] differ but little: the circumstances that you are the reader and I the writer of these exercises is accidental and irrelevant."[2] The undermining of authorship, of individual personality (*nuestras nadas*), the equation of reader and writer—Borges's ironic, modest, self-effacing mask—served as the (ab-sent) center around which Emir was to weave his biography.

To write the biography of "such a one" was already a Pierre Menar-dian task because Borges's life was books. As he said in his "Auto-biographical Essay"—which was written originally in English and served as the palimpsest upon which Emir elaborated his biography—"If I were asked to name the chief event in my life, I should say my father's library. In fact, sometimes I think I have never strayed outside that library" (*AOS* 209). How was he to write the biography of such a seemingly passive Bartleby, for whom bachelorhood was synonymous with celibacy?

---

1. Emir Rodríguez Monegal, "Borges y Derrida: boticarios," *Maldoror* (Montevideo) 21 (September 1985): 123–32 (125).
2. Quoted in Emir Rodríguez Monegal, "Borges: The Reader as Writer," *TriQuarterly* 25 (Fall 1972): 102–43 (106). This was a special issue titled *Prose for Borges*.

But every history is a story, every life conceals a drama to unfold, and Emir found this drama/trauma in Borges's rhetoric of reading. Why was Borges so intent upon denying his creative paternity? Emir tells us that Borges had practiced writing (until nearly age forty) as a son: "Father had led him to fulfill a literary destiny" that Borges senior did not have the ambition or the resources to accomplish himself. Borges did not choose to become a writer but rather was created a writer by his father; to call himself a creator, to supplant father, was a violent act tantamount to parricide.

Violence did occur, however. Borges survived an accident "on Christmas Eve of 1938—the same year my father died" (*AOS* 242), causing a head-wound (I was present in 1970 when Emir asked Borges to show him the scar), after which the direction of his writing would radically change. After this "symbolic suicide" or "masked parricide," Emir shows and tells us, Borges the author of *Ficciones* was born. This turning point provides the dramatic seed that Emir the biographer cultivates, a story of passage from son to father, not biological father (a destiny Borges foregoes) but literary father, who not only overshadows his biological father (a failed novelist) but who also subverts his father's voice by writing a different type of fiction, nonpsychological, "critical and even fantastic."[3] As this literary father, Borges (posing as a mere reader) created not only a body of writing but a literary space: readers and writers like Emir Rodríguez Monegal and Adolfo Bioy Casares and, as Emir has shown us, at least three generations of writers—Julio Cortázar, Carlos Fuentes, Guillermo Cabrera Infante, Reinaldo Arenas. In brief, Borges became the father of the new Latin American novel.

Borges's relation to himself as father/son, to the Other, even to the supreme Being as Author (we are all a dream dreamed up by some perverse god who is also a dream) remains an enigma, however, one that Emir—a persistent, perspicacious Theseus in Asterion's labyrinth, armed with a formidable critical mind and an encyclopedic knowledge of literature, his Ariadne's thread—perhaps went furthest in deciphering. Emir knew he was dealing with a perverse and slippery father figure, and it was precisely this challenge which drove him on.

Borges worked through the relationship with his father-creator in complex ways, by making him into one of his "sons"; by reinventing him in such story/essays as "The Enigma of Edward Fitzgerald" and "An Examination of the Work of Herbert Quain"; and, more directly, by immortalizing his father Jorge Borges through his own fame and name. This complex relationship extended itself to *the* father, Literature: Bor-

---

3. Emir Rodríguez Monegal, *Jorge Luis Borges: A Literary Biography* (New York: Dutton, 1978), 326.

ges, as Emir made us see, neutralized the "anxiety of influence" by inventing his own as well as "Kafka's precursors." Borges, in his selective praise for forgotten, marginal, or minor writers, virtually rewrote the canon, but the possibility lurks that his praise (or his negligence) could be taken as some sovereign irony.

He also related in complex and perverse ways to his sons—like Emir and Bioy Casares, his readers and interlocutors—who rewrote him or "fathered" him. When Borges calls Bioy Casares one of the greatest writers of the twentieth century—with which I and many readers may agree, particularly if greatness is not equated with radical experimentalism on the model of Joyce or Pound—is he damning him or praising him? No matter how much Borges insisted in interviews that Bioy was the "secret master," that it is the fathers who learn from the children, the fact remains that Bioy is known as the disciple, Borges the mentor. Indeed many readers still consider Bioy a character invented by Borges in "Tlön, Uqbar, Orbis Tertius."

Though he would protest that he never read the books written about him (including Emir's), Emir's psychoanalytic reading of him in the biography did not escape Borges, whose aversion for Freud's "sordid" reduction of human complexity to a sexual complex is well publicized. Borges's final homage to Emir, "Borges y Emir," written a month before Emir's death, can—like all his texts—be read in more than one light. Allow me to translate:

> In the United States, I'm not sure if at Yale or Columbia, Emir Rodríguez Monegal told me that he intended to write my imaginary biography, to write not about what had happened but about what could have happened.
>
> I told him he could do a better job than I since he had spent a good part of his life studying me, goodness knows why. To me it seems perverse, an enormous waste of time. But, in any case, he was the one who knew "my works"—not works as far as I'm concerned, only a series of rough drafts which have been published. He has spent his life studying, reading, rereading, analyzing these pages, inventing their undeserved merits. He also knows all the dates of my personal history, while the only date I know is 1899. I don't remember it of course since no one can remember the moment of his birth—although, according to psychiatrists, memory includes one's life before birth, which seems to me a bit excessive. So I told Emir that he could do an admirable job, and people tell me that he did. I haven't read this book because it is as embarrassing to read about oneself as it is to hear people talking about one. There is not a single book by or about me in this house, except one that is written in Chinese ideograms. So that I am not acquainted with Emir's book but those who are say it is excellent, which must be so since it doesn't refer to my relatively poor real life but to an imaginary life which has to be much richer; so that I am grateful to Emir Rodríguez Monegal for this book and, moreover, I can speak of him not only

as a scholar and a writer but as something much more important, as a friend. I believe that friendship is really one of the supreme passions of our countries. Perhaps the most significant. . . . For example, in *Martín Fierro,* what is so interesting about the lives of two deserters—one from the army, the other from the police who takes sides with the outlaw he is supposed to arrest? Precisely what one feels here is that a friendship exists between these two criminals. Well, I'd simply like to add that I would like very much to see Emir again, to thank him for his book that I am not worthy of reading. I would like to be in Montevideo, soon, to see him again.
Buenos Aires, October 22, 1985[4]

Love and gratitude are expressed here (even in the humorous analogy of the friendship between "two criminals" who are also two gauchesque literary heroes), but there is also a playful tinge of mockery—the allusion to psychiatrists, a typically oblique Borgesian dig that buries not only Emir but all Borges analysts in one fell swoop—a supreme indifference in the guise of an extreme modesty.

All of which only proves Emir's theory that Borges had become a perverse ironist to exorcise his father's power over him. But where does Emir reflect himself in this shifting mirror where castrating fathers are self-effacing sons and vice versa?

At the tender age of fifteen, like Bioy at seventeen, Emir found in Borges a literary master for his intellectual apprenticeship. Emir reminisced about this encounter in an interview shortly before his death:

I discovered Borges in a woman's magazine *El Hogar* (Home) in which Buenos Aires society ladies appeared copiously photographed in their furs, flanked by their dogs, husbands and chauffeurs. In the midst of . . . advertisements for hand creams . . . there appeared these book reviews signed by someone named Borges. The section was called *A Reader's Guide* and here Borges would treat his readers—a public which did not yet exist—as if they were Borges, commenting on Kafka's *Metamorphosis,* or publishing a biographical sketch of Spengler, or a review of *Finnegans Wake.* . . .

Suddenly, I discovered a wonderful gentleman who had read all the books in the world and who, above all, liked the books I liked and thousands of others I didn't know, but I already liked them because he did. . . .

This encounter transformed my life. Borges led me to read critically, at a sophisticated level previously unknown to me.

I had already read a lot of literary criticism, Henríquez Ureña, Alfonso Reyes, Dámaso Alonso, Menéndez Pelayo, Menéndez Pidal, Bello, Rodó, the great critics of the Spanish language; but they were old if not old-fashioned. And here, on the other hand, was this wild man who'd say, for example, "I never managed to finish *Madame Bovary*" or "I don't consider collecting books one of my superstitions." He would not hesitate to claim that the most famous author in the world bored him to tears or to exalt Paul Groussac

4. Jorge Luis Borges, "Borges y Emir," *Jaque* (Montevideo), November 7, 1985.

because he was amusing. Borges—more than any other writer—made me feel free, made me see that literature was a very personal passion, a game, a joyous epiphany.[5]

But at the same time that Emir—a humble disciple—discovers a literary mentor, he also creates him: Emir was probably the first reader of *El Hogar* (outside of Borges's small circle of *Sur* friends) to seek out the largely invisible "visible" work of this eccentric book reviewer, to make sure that Borges—despite the Author's ultimate nonexistence—did exist. Indeed to say that he found Borges in *El Hogar* was a little like the claim made by the character Bioy Casares that he had discovered a new planet in the pirate edition of an encyclopedia, in "Tlön, Uqbar, Orbis Tertius," Borges's intricate parable about a reader's discovery (or invention) of not only a book but a world.

Thus, at the same time Emir (whose father was really a stepfather) found a superliterary father who would cast a decisive shadow on the rest of his life, as a literary critic he helped create a writer. He continued to do so all his life, most notoriously during his *Mundo Nuevo* years, "midwifing" the birth of writers such as Gabriel García Márquez, Guillermo Cabrera Infante, and Manuel Puig—just like his father/son, Borges, who (by digging them out of obscurity) made primary figures out of secondary figures like Marcel Schwob, Paul Groussac, and Macedonio Fernández. In order to create oneself, one has to create one's father; Borges seemed to be doing so by praising the insignificant and damning the greats—both delighting and irritating many readers in the process. The Peruvian critic José Miguel Oviedo recently expressed a slight irritation at Emir—in an otherwise enthusiastic review of *Ficcionario*—observing that Emir's "unnecessary familiarity" in calling Borges "Georgie" (his English nickname since childhood) was a form of trivializing Borges.[6] José Miguel did not take into account (at least in print) that there is a double edge to this affectionate name-calling, that somewhere in his own necessarily parricidal nature Emir—like Borges in his arbitrary yet methodical debunking of the patriarchs—was reducing the old man to size, son-size. Emir too was a parricidal parodist, mocking and paying homage in the same breath, a perverse practitioner of that lethal and precious mode, irony.

In Emir's essay on his two "pharmacists" he again rereads Borges—this time as Derrida's precursor—and examines, through this perspective, Derrida's revision of Plato's "Pharmacy," which pivots on the pun

5. Martín Caparrós, "La última entrevista con Emir Rodríguez Monegal," *Culturas,* November 17, 1985, pp. 1–2 (my translation).
6. José Miguel Oviedo, review of *Ficcionario, Vuelta* 118 (September 1986): 36–38 (37). *Ficcionario* is Emir's anthology of Borges's works based on the English edition, in collaboration with Alastair Reid, titled paronomastically *Borges: A Reader.*

pharmakon (meaning both drug and poison) and its similarity with *pharmakos* (scapegoat). Derrida recounts Plato's recounting of a tale told by Socrates about an ancient Egyptian myth that reveals writing to be secondary and subversive. In this myth a king rejects writing, recommended to him by his son as a remedy for oblivion and necessary to record the deeds of history; the king says "no" because, on the contrary, it will make humanity forgetful: the people will depend on writing rather than memory. The king's voice, his oral word, is all that is needed. In this myth it turns out that the Egyptian god of writing, Thot, is also the god of death, and that the king's son's writing signifies the subversion of his father's power, the absence (or killing) of the father. But Derrida concludes—in his reading of Plato's commentary—that all these opposing forces are one, that Thot (or Theuth) is the Other of the father, is the father and the subversive replacement. The god of writing is at once father, son, and himself.

When Plato "repeats" Socrates, writing the father's words (as I am now writing Emir's), there is an inevitably different intonation, a subversion that Plato recognizes in saying, finally, that one must not write because one's writing will fall into the hands of the public (of a reader who rewrites). His prophecy comes true: Derrida, Borges, Emir all rewrite, kill, immortalize the father who in turn has "seduced" his son with words.

It is poignant that Emir's last essay portrays his favorite writer as he who gave him both remedy and poison, life and death. This healing and destroying power of language, of the father's word is the common plot of all writers and readers. Emir, the "Borges Reader," both gave himself life (as a literary critic) and submitted himself to the god of death—like all men and women, the silent as well as the vocal.

Borges ironically outlived his younger critic—the frail old man ultimately the stronger—but not by long; curiously enough, their final mortal destinies, their warriors' ways of confronting death with life, were not dissimilar. As if the two had been one, each traveled to a beloved city of his past, Emir to Montevideo to make his final peace with his country, Borges to neutral Geneva, the city of his adolescence—where he experienced, according to Emir's biography and to one of his last poems, his greatest joys and conflicts; where he, as an Argentine, as a citizen of the world, perhaps felt most at home. Both married at the last moment, to have a happy ending, turning life's drama into a fable whose meaning we have yet to decipher.

Borges and Derrida

Apothecaries

I.

I've always found it difficult to read Derrida. Not so much for the density of his thought and the heavy, redundant, and repetitive style in which it is developed, but for an entirely circumstantial reason. Educated in Borges's thought from the age of fifteen, I must admit that many of Derrida's novelties struck me as being rather tautological. I could not understand why he took so long in arriving at the same luminous perspectives which Borges had opened up years earlier. His famed "deconstruction" impressed me for its technical precision and the infinite seduction of its textual sleights-of-hand, but it was all too familiar to me: I had experienced it in Borges *avant la lettre*. That is why, when "La Pharmacie de Platon" appeared in numbers 32 and 33 of *Quel Tel* (1968), I glanced at it reverentially, confirmed the two epigraphs from Borges which reinforced section 3 ("L'inscription des fils"), and went on to something else. Some time later, while I was visiting Severo Sarduy in Senlis, I saw him going over the essay with a fine-tooth comb; I also recall exchanging some words with him about its importance. Still, I did not (then) feel compelled to decode Derrida in order to reach Borges. The publication of "La Pharmacie" in book form (*La Dissémination,* Paris: Seuil, 1972) reintroduced the text to me in a more detailed version, but one which I could again only read in fits and starts. I was more interested in the volume's prologue ("Hors livre, préfaces"), where I recognized some of Borges's ideas on the subject. I made so many detailed notes on it that—as I recall—I was left without any energy to read the rest of the book. At the time I was already involved in writing, or inventing, a literary biography of Borges for a New York publishing house.

In 1971, as a rehearsal for that biography, I wrote an extremely lengthy piece, "Borges: The Reader as Writer," which was published in

Originally published as "Borges y Derrida: boticarios," in *Maldoror* (Montevideo) 21 (1985): 123–32. © 1985 by *Maldoror*. Translated and published with permission. English translation published in this volume for the first time.

a special issue on the Argentine author ("Prose for Borges," *TriQuarterly* 25, Northwestern University, Evanston, Illinois, Autumn 1972). There I developed the theory that Borges had preferred reading to writing as a way of denying *authorship*, that is, of admitting to the paternity of his works. Educated by his father in the writer's calling, he had practiced it as a son; in so doing he avoided parricide. But on the death of his father in 1938, and after an accident on Christmas Eve of the same year, Borges committed symbolic suicide in order to conceal the parricide and to be free to begin writing his most important fictions: "Pierre Menard" (1939), "Tlön, Uqbar, Orbis Tertius" (1940), and others. These, however, continued to be masked as exercises in reading. The essay contained the germ of what I would later develop systematically in *Jorge Luis Borges: A Literary Biography* (New York: Dutton, 1978); only in this work, the psychoanalytical investigation, supported by ideas of Freud, Melanie Klein, and Lacan, would be much more exhaustive.

If I had then read "La Pharmacie de Platon" with some care, I would have discovered that by a different though parallel route Derrida had succeeded in producing the same "model": writing as symbolic parricide. Perhaps it was better that I hadn't read it. I probably would have been seduced to the point of being prevented from achieving a different development, but one more adequate to the specific problem of Borges's literary biography. Another thing which kept me from a more detailed reading of Derrida was the publication of several articles in which attempts were made to establish links between the French philosopher and the Argentine writer. I am referring specifically to the studies by Mario Rodríguez and Roberto González Echevarría. While Rodríguez gives a general panorama of the affinities between the two and applies Derridean principles to the reading of some Borgesian texts, González Echevarría concentrates specifically on "La Pharmacie." In the case of the first critic, however, the reading is not sufficiently painstaking to justify invoking a method known above all for its textual fanaticism and microscopic criticism. In the case of the second, the passages from Borges that Derrida uses in the third chapter of the essay are adequately identified (though Barbara Johnson had previously made the identification in her English translation of *La Dissémination* [1981]),[1] and some interesting questions are raised about the deeper links which might be established between the two authors. But González Echevarría completely misses the analogy between the parricide of

1. Translators' note. In preparing the translation of Rodríguez Monegal's essay, we have found it useful to consult the English version of "La Pharmacie de Platon," entitled "Plato's Pharmacy," in *Dissemination*, trans. Barbara Johnson (Chicago: University of Chicago Press, 1981).

writing that Derrida, departing from Plato, proposes and Borges's symbolic parricide. He also fails to see the distinction (made very clear by Derrida) between *pharmakon* (drug/poison) and *pharmakos* (scapegoat). On page 208 of his article he uses them as synonyms. Mario Rodríguez's textual reading is also superficial. For example, commenting on a passage from "The South" in which the protagonist, Juan Dahlman, takes a train (or dreams that he is taking a train) to go to the South, Rodríguez talks about the fact that "the grandeur of the landscape distracts him from his reading." A critical examination of the story reveals that the landscape is anything but magnificent and that Borges—here as realistic as Balzac—limits himself to a description of the ugliness and desolation of the pampas.

These and other less than Derridean exercises in reading (there is one by Monique Lemaître which is frankly incoherent) fortified me in my resolve to steer clear of this path. I had to allow the Derridean itch to subside before undertaking a double reading based on other premises. The decision was a wise one, I think. Some years ago I read Derrida again; I once more examined his "kinship" with Borges; and I was able to discuss the subject with him personally. The fortuitous circumstance that we shared the same university (Yale, in New Haven) for a few weeks every year made this possible. On one occasion I participated in the discussion on "Pierre Menard," one of the primary readings for his seminar. More recently I took advantage of his stay in Yale to give a course on Paul de Man in order to conduct a formal interview. (It took place in Ezra Stills College on May 2, 1984.) That interview has served as an incentive for this article, a double reading of Borges and Derrida whose interlinear design makes use of the operative principle of deconstruction. The intent here is not to produce another exercise of the "Borges, precursor of Derrida" variety. My study proposes another path.

II.

One of the main themes in "La Pharmacie de Platon" (though not the only one) is the identity between reading and writing, a theme which Borges had developed paradoxically in his "Pierre Menard, Author of the *Quixote.*" Another, more related to Derrida's earlier speculations in *De la grammatologie* and *L'Ecriture et la différence,* is the contrast between writing (dead knowledge) and the voice (living knowledge). A third is the opposition between writing/myth and logos/dialectic. All of these had already been dealt with in the previous work of the French philosopher. This is not the place to examine their ramifications in the aforementioned essay. I would prefer to concentrate on parts 2 and 3 of "La Pharmacie," which are devoted to a very detailed analysis of a fragment from Plato's *Phaedrus* where the myth of Theuth (Thot or Zot), the god of writing, is introduced; this myth, as Derrida points out, is one of the two strictly original ones in Plato, in spite of its very obvious Egyptian background.

In Plato's text, which Derrida reads in León Robin's translation (Collection Guillaume Budé), injecting interpolations and variants of his own, Socrates relates that he has heard that in a certain region of Egypt there was an ancient divinity, Theuth, who was the first to discover the science of numbers—calculation, geometry, and astronomy—as well as the art of backgammon and dice and, above all, writing (*grammata*). It is precisely this invention that will be the focus of the ensuing analysis. Socrates also notes that at that time King Thamous, whose god was Ammon, reigned in Egyptian Thebes. When Theuth appeared to demonstrate his arts to the king, a dialogue ensued in which the ruler seemed little disposed to accept the validity of such inventions. Theuth's argument that writing would make Egyptians more capable of remembering and that both memory and instruction would find their remedy (*pharmakon*) in this new art was disputed by the king, who believed that it would make them even more forgetful, since they would no longer depend on memory but on writing for the recording of the past.

At this point Derrida freezes the scene from Plato and reflects: the king occupies the position of the god Ammon, and from this position he refuses to recognize the *value* of writing—that is, he does not validate it with his spoken word. The king does not know how to write, but this ignorance does not demean him in any way because he does not need to write: he speaks, he says, he dictates, and his word suffices. Therefore the god-king-who-speaks acts as a father. He rejects the *pharmakon* (writing) to better watch over it. This father converts his child into writing. The specificity of writing, says Derrida, would thus refer to the absence (negation) of the father. This absence can be manifested in diverse modalities: to have lost one's father, through natural or violent death, through parricide; then to solicit the assistance, possible or impossible, of the paternal presence, to solicit it directly or to claim to get along without it, and so on. The conclusion is obvious: the desire of writing is indicated, designated, and denounced as the desire for orphanhood and parricidal subversion. The *pharmakon* is a poisoned present. (The other meaning of the word in Greek is poison.) While the spoken word is alive and has a father, writing is not an orphan but a slayer of the father. This parricide, let me make clear, may be repressed or declared.

The two epigraphs from Borges appear in part 3 of the essay, framing the one from Joyce ("like a sandwich," as Derrida wryly remarked during our interview). In the first, which is from "Pascal's Sphere"

(*Otras inquisiciones,* 1952), Borges specifically refers to "Thoth, who is also Hermes"; in the second, from "Tlön, Uqbar, Orbis Tertius," he notes that one school declares that writing is produced by "a subordinate god in order to communicate with a demon." As for Joyce, in *A Portrait of the Artist as a Young Man* he makes his protagonist, Stephen Dedalus, feel a mysterious affinity with the man-falcon whose name he bears, and with Thoth, the god of writers. At this purely thematic level, the relationship among the three epigraphs seems obvious. That it is not quite so is evidenced by González Echevarría's failure to perceive a more complex relationship, one hidden by the overt links.

For his part, Derrida dedicates this third section (which is entitled, let us remember, "L'inscription des fils: Theuth, Hermes, Thot, Nabû, Nebo") to underlining several important facts. For example: the permanent identity of the god of writing and his function was precisely that of working at the subversive dislocation of identity in general. This is an eminently Borgesian theme, whose early traces can be found in an essay included in *Inquisiciones* ("La nadería de la personalidad" [The nothingness of personality], from about 1925); and whose most famous developments appear in his mature work ("Borges y yo" [Borges and I]; the piece on Shakespeare, "Everything and Nothing"). Another suggestive aspect of Theuth which Derrida glosses is his being the eldest son of the sun-god Ra, who engenders through the mediation of the word (not of writing), and whose name, Ammon, means the Hidden. Derrida also points to the homology between Theuth and Hermes (noted in the epigraph from Borges). Plato never mentions this homology in his dialogue, but in Derrida's text Thoth-Hermes retains his traditional role of messenger-god, of clever intermediary, extremely cunning, ingenious, and subtle enough to always steal away. The signifier-god, as Derrida calls him.

Once again, Derrida emphasizes the fact that writing only reproduces a divine thought: it is a second and secondary word. Thoth can become the god of the creative word only by metonymic substitution, by historical displacement, and in some cases by violent subversion. Writing thus appears as a supplement of the word, and, at times, as its substitute, a substitute capable of "doubling" for the king, the father, the sun, and the word, distinguished from these only by dint of being a representation, a mask, a repetition. Hence King Thamous was right: the *pharmakon* of writing was good only for *hypomnesis* (re-memoration, recollection, consignation) and not for *mneme* (living, knowing memory).

The god of writing is the god of death. In all the cycles of Egyptian mythology Thoth presides over the organization of death. It is he who measures the life span of men and gods.

Here the opposition between the spoken word (living) and the written word (dead) is found once again. Derrida thus concludes that Thoth (or Theuth) is the father's *other*—the father, and the subversive movement of replacement. He does not allow himself to be assigned a fixed role in the play of differences. Sly, slippery, and masked, a schemer and a fraud, like Hermes he is neither king nor servant, but rather a sort of *joker,* a floating signifier, a wild card that puts play into play; the *trickster* of whom Northrop Frye also speaks.

This summary of some of the themes discussed in chapters 2 and 3 of "La Pharmacie" is deliberately arbitrary. I have stressed what pertains most to Borges, leaving aside (among many other things) the tantalizing reference, in note 17, to the effect that the entire essay is "but a reading of *Finnegans Wake,*" a work that is, of course, not mentioned in the text, and which could only be remotely alluded to in the epigraph from Joyce's *Portrait of the Artist.* But since we are dealing with the inclusion in "La Pharmacie" of the epigraphs, and other texts by Borges cited more obliquely, we shall for the moment abandon the temptation to follow Derrida into the Joycean labyrinth. The Argentine writer provides enough grist for our mill.

III.

It is quite possible that Derrida was then only familiar with some of Borges's essays in *Otras inquisiciones,* and with the anthology which Roger Caillois published under the title *Labyrinthes,* which included some of Borges's most famous stories and several important essays. At least, that is what he now remembers. He recalls reading Borges in French around 1961–1962. The first time he quotes him in one of his essays is in a piece on the philosophy of Emmanuel Levinas entitled "Violence et métaphysique" (1964). On page 137 of *L'Ecriture et la différence* (which contains the essay) the same sentence from "Pascal's Sphere" is cited twice (this time, however, indicating the bibliographic source). The first version reads: "Perhaps universal history is the history of a few metaphors"; and the second, more complete version: "Perhaps universal history is the history of the diverse *intonation* of a few metaphors" (Derrida's emphasis). This subtle variation in the quotations, which in Borges's text are separated by an entire essay but in Derrida's only by several lines, reveals a device characteristic of Derridean writing: nuanced repetition which is really reiteration, in the manner of Gertrude Stein's "A rose is a rose is a rose is a rose." When asked why she wrote "A rose . . . ," Stein replied that the first rose was not the same as the second, while the second differed from the third and fourth. By the mere fact of being reiterations, with an *intonation* which is inevitably different, Stein's roses and Borges's quotations say something more: there is a supplement.

Recalling his readings of Borges during the 1984 interview, Derrida stated categorically: "Il m'a séduit" (he seduced me). He also pointed out that after 1968 he had rarely read Borges again, or at least he had read only what was already familiar to him. This should not deter us from examining some selected commonalities between the texts of these two writers. Before moving into a more detailed analysis, however, I would like to mention another anecdote which Derrida told me in confidence. He said that a short time earlier, while he was at the airport in Ithaca, on his way back from a lecture at Cornell, he saw Borges, who had also been speaking there. He wondered whether or not he should go over and greet him, since he knew who Borges was, but assumed Borges had never heard of him (which was, sadly, the case). In the end, the desire to meet Borges overcame the feelings of inhibition typical to this kind of situation. Derrida went over to Borges, introduced himself as a reader and admirer, and the two spent the rest of the trip to New York chatting like old friends. I was already familiar with the story (it had made the rounds at Cornell), and I was also familiar with Borges's old habit of declaring his lack of acquaintance with the work of writers whom he met. When Sartre came over to tell him that he was his reader, and that he had published his stories in *Les Temps Modernes,* Borges replied that he was very sorry, but he had never read any of Sartre's works.

But more than the reading or the direct quoting of Borges, it seems important to underline the similarities in outlook between the Argentine writer and the French philosopher. For anyone who knows his Borges, the summary of "La Pharmacie" offered above is filled with tantalizing allusions. On a purely biographical level, Borges himself has recounted in his "Autobiographical Essay" (written in English with the help of Norman Thomas di Giovanni and included in the American edition of *El Aleph,* 1971) how from childhood he had been destined by his father to be a writer, a vocation which the elder Borges had been unable to fulfill due to the early onset of blindness. The voice of the father, then, orders the child Georgie to practice writing. This writing avoids parricide precisely because it finds sanction in the father's presence, to which it submits. But scarcely had his father died in 1938 when Borges underwent a ritual of symbolic suicide. He hit his head against an open window frame in a dark stairway—the incident is fictionalized in "The South"—and began to write his boldest fictions. These fictions were destined to destroy or deconstruct forever that very same literature which his father had so admired but had failed to bring into fruition. The parricide implicit in writing is thus carried out precisely at that moment when, in the absence of the father (of the father's voice), Borges became an orphan.

Through a different path, after a detailed analysis of "Pierre Menard," I had reached a similar conclusion. My point of departure was Borges's refusal to consider himself to be the author (father) of his work, and to reveal himself only under the mask of reader (son). With evidence from other texts ("The Masked Dyer, Hakim of Merv" [*A Universal History of Infamy,* 1925]; "Tlön, Uqbar, Orbis Tertius" [*Ficciones,* 1944]), I demonstrated Borges's insistence on characterizing mirrors and fatherhood as abominable, since they multiplied the number of men. Again, he was assuming the mask of the son. I had finally reached the conclusion that Borges could write (be an author) only if he persuaded himself—falsely, after all—that he was not the author but the reader of his own texts.

The affinity of this reading to the one applied by Derrida to the *Phaedrus* is obvious, as are the differences in the philosophical density of both interpretations. When I mentioned this affinity to Derrida during our interview, he assured me that he had no knowledge at all of the circumstances of Borges's life, even though he was very familiar with "Pierre Menard." (We had even discussed it in one of his classes several years earlier.) During the same interview I also mentioned to Derrida how in my literary biography of Borges I had used a complementary, though different approach to explain this paradox. There, I had parted from the basic childhood situation: the acquisition of language. Using the work of Melanie Klein as well as Didier Anzieu's reading of Lacan in an essay on Borges, I had succeeded in clarifying the problem of Georgie's bilingualism. Georgie had acquired Spanish from his mother and English from his maternal grandmother, Fanny Haslam de Borges, and his father, [Jorge] Guillermo. This bilingualism produced a split which would give rise to the theme of the double in Borges's work; it was the origin of a double voice which ordered his entry into writing. While Borges was Georgie, he was convinced that Spanish was an inferior language, his mother's language and the language of the servants, almost always Galician immigrants. English, on the other hand, was a superior language, his father's and grandmother's language, the language of the "library of unlimited English books" in which he claims to have grown up. But what is most significant is that when he began to write—after some attempts in Spanish, English, and even French—he finally opted for Spanish. If Georgie was Anglo-Saxon, Borges would be Hispanic, and his entry into the world of literature would be carried out under the banner of the Sevillian avant-garde.

There is an element here that, up to a certain point, was barely present in "La Pharmacie": the maternal element. As Melanie Klein points out, it is the mother's mouth that gives the breath of life and the word. This word is spoken and directed at the child when he is still an infant (that is, when he still doesn't talk); it thus differs radically from the word of the father, who later orders writing. Nevertheless, it is not disconnected from her. In chapter 9 of "La Pharmacie," Derrida had already referred to the "receptacle," the "matrix," the "mother," the "nurse" as the place in which writing is inscribed. There he notes: "It would be proper to compare the receptacle to a mother, the model to a father, and the intermediate nature between both to a child." And a bit further on: "Inscription is thus the production of the son." Only to conclude: "Platonism is both the general rehearsal (literally in French, "la répétition générale") of this family scene and the most powerful effort to master it, to silence its noise, to conceal it by drawing the curtains over the dawning of the West." This passage serves as the link between *pharmacy* and *home,* suggesting that while Plato privileges the first, he inscribes the second in the text of his *Phaedrus* only by indirection. That explains why the long essay concludes with a "myth," only now not a Platonic but a Derridean one: Plato leaves his pharmacy for the countryside and soliloquizes about the connections between writing, the calendar, dice (*le coup de dés* with its Mallarmean associations), theatrical effects, the *glyph* (the name of a journal published by Johns Hopkins for which Derrida writes), and so on. His meditation concludes with a quotation from the Second Letter in which Plato states that it is necessary to learn things by heart, and not to write, since writing ends up falling into the public domain. He also states that he has not written a thing, that there is no work by Plato (here he coincides with Borges, who refuses to admit to having "authorized" any work). "What now carries his name (says Plato), was written by Socrates in the prime of his youth." The last part of the letter is even more Borgesian: "Farewell and obey me," he tells his correspondent. "As soon as you have read and reread this letter, burn it." This the correspondent did not do, thus thwarting the reticent author's designs for fame-through-destruction (*pretensiones erostráticas*).

Such coincidences are inevitable, since we read Derrida and Plato through Borges. As he himself had indicated in "Kafka and His Precursors," it is impossible to avoid reading anachronistically. Imbued as we are with Borges, we recognize him in every previous or parallel text. In the 1984 interview Derrida observed with gentle irony that when one is very close to a text one sees only the coincidences. What is curious is that during the interview Derrida appeared somewhat removed from his own *pharmacie.* He now seems uncomfortable with the very homogeneous (*grécisé*) quality of the text and observes with self-deprecation: "Ça fait un peu le Parnasse." His comment is correct with reference to *Glas,* which is composed much more freely, in the style of a collage; but it is slightly exaggerated in the case of "La Pharmacie," given the essay's rich texture and the density of its allusions. The myth of the pharmacy, in which Plato himself is seen as the pharmacist, opens up the autobiographical perspective on to infinity; in the inscription of the pharmacist Plato, the pharmacist Derrida is also inscribed, and, as I hope to have shown, the pharmacist Borges. Or the apothecary (*boticario*), to naturalize it more into our language.

BIBLIOGRAPHIC NOTE

Part I. A Spanish version of the article, "Borges: The Reader as Writer," appears in my book *Borges: Hacia una lectura poética* (Borges: Toward a poetic reading; Madrid: Guadarrama, 1976). The title of the book is the result of a careless error on the part of the publisher: the original title read: *Borges: Hacia una poética de la lectura* (Borges: Toward a poetics of reading). The article by Mario Rodríguez, "Borges and Derrida," was published in the *Revista Chilena de Literatura* (Santiago), April 13, 1979; González Echevarría's piece, "BdeORridaGES (Borges y Derrida)" is included in his book *Isla a su vuelo fugitiva* (Island fugitive from its course) (Madrid: José Porrúa Turanzas, 1983).[2] Monique Lemaître's "Borges . . . Derrida . . . Sollers . . . Borges" appears in *40 inquisiciones sobre Borges* (40 inquisitions on Borges), a special issue of *Revista iberoamericana* (Pittsburgh), July–December 1977, pp. 679–82. The course on Paul de Man, subtitled "*Logos* in Translation," focused on an analysis of the sections on Nietzsche and Rousseau in the distinguished critic's *Allegories of Reading;* on his study, "Autobiography as De-facement," the text on Hölderlin that appears at the end of *Blindness and Insight;* and on another of his essays, "Sign and Symbol in Hegel's *Aesthetics*." The rest of the seminar was devoted to an analysis of texts by Heidegger, Kant, and Schelling.

When we were once discussing his colleague and friend's untimely death, Derrida told me: "Pour moi, Yale c'était Paul de Man" (For me, Yale was Paul de Man). Indeed, the famous school of literary criticism about which so much is said now was nothing more than a somewhat heterogeneous collection of personalities (Harold Bloom, Geoffrey Hartman, J. Hillis Miller, in addition to Derrida and de Man), who seemed to be united for reasons more negative than positive, as Derrida himself noted in the interview. "We had common enemies; we were a group rejected by others, formed by the antagonism of others."

2. Translators' note. An English version, "Borges and Derrida," has since been published in Harold Bloom's collection *Jorge Luis Borges* (New York: Chelsea House, 1986).

In spite of some shared ideas, the differences among them were more evident than the similarities, the contradictions more obvious than the areas of agreement. "What interested me," Derrida said during our conversation, "was the existence of a kind of common frame of reading which took a number of conventional truths as its starting point; these were deconstructed in different ways." Today the group has disbanded. De Man's death has left Derrida without a truly worthy partner with whom to dialogue. For his part, Bloom has become independent, even hostile. Only Hartman and Hillis Miller continue to dialogue fruitfully.

But even with regard to them, Derrida injected a note of dissidence. "Shelley, c'était de la famille pour eux" (Shelley was like family for them), he said, in a clear reference to readings which don't carry the same weight outside the English-speaking world. This dissension is also evident in the volume enthusiastically compiled by Geoffrey Hartman under the title *Deconstruction and Criticism* (New York: Seabury, 1979). In it, only the Americans can comfortably quote the poets of their language; although de Man and Derrida explicitly refer to Shelley, it is obvious that they are not members of the family. On the other hand, one can see the distance separating the foreigners from the Americans within their common deconstructive endeavor in Paul de Man's ironic review of Harold Bloom's allegories in *The Anxiety of Influence* (another topic that Borges had previously demythified in "Kafka and His Precursors").

Part II. The edition of Plato which Derrida uses is the complete works in León Robin's translation (Paris: Les Belles Lettres, 1944). This is a bilingual edition, best known for its publication under the auspices of the Association Guillaume Budé. I have preferred to quote from it, translating into Spanish; I have also preferred to translate directly from Derrida's text in order to stay closer to the literal sense (*la literalidad*) of his words, rather than to use the Spanish version by José Martín Arencibia (Madrid: Fundamentos, 1975). For Borges's texts, I have used the *Obras completas* (Complete works; Buenos Aires: Emecé, 1974). This edition is full of errors, but it is the most readily available.

Part III. In the first part of my literary biography of Borges I analyze in detail the problem of bilingualism and its psychological significance; the third part of the book thoroughly investigates the 1938 Christmas Eve accident and its literary and biographic consequences. A Spanish version of this work (originally published in English) is soon to be published by the Fondo de Cultura Ecónomica (Mexico).[3]

Translated by Paul Budofsky and Edna Aizenberg

3. Translators' note. It has since appeared under the title *Borges: una biografía literaria* (Mexico: Fondo de Cultura Económica, 1987).

Herman Rapaport _____

Borges, De Man, and the
Deconstruction of Reading

In "The Resistance to Theory," Paul de Man asked, "What is meant when we assert that the study of literary texts is necessarily dependent on an act of reading, or when we claim that this act is being systematically avoided?"[1] Unlike many critics who presuppose a notion of consistency-building wherein the act of reading is unified in an aesthetics of reception or in what Wolfgang Iser has termed *Rezeptionstheorie,* de Man believes that the act of reading is always divided between interpretive constructions that, because of their undecidability, in Jacques Derrida's sense, often resist unification.[2] By "resistance to theory," therefore, de Man means the resistances inherent in the act of reading (itself a conflict of interpretations), which frustrate the ability to make the hermeneutical decisions that clarify the determination of meaning in a literary work. It is this critical conflict that compels one to resist a self-consistent theoretical model of a given text even as one is driven to elucidate a text's meaning or mode of signification. As is well known, "The Resistance to Theory" specifically makes this argument in terms of considering "the uncertain relationship between grammar and rhetoric," themselves complex hermeneutical formations that cannot be reconciled into any unified account able to describe a literary work. De Man says, "The argument can be made . . . that no grammatical decoding, however refined, could claim to reach the determining figural [or rhetorical] dimensions of a text." In other words, there are rhetorical elements whose function cannot be grammatically defined. Conversely, de Man argues that there are grammatical features that also elude rhetorical understanding. Rhetorical readings "do not lead to the knowledge of an entity (such as language) but are an unreliable process of knowledge production that prevents all entities, including linguistic entities, from coming into discourse as such."[3]

Given the incommensurability between such complex interpretive formations, one cannot achieve generalizations or master critical nar-

1. Paul de Man, "The Resistance to Theory," *Yale French Studies* 63 (1982): 3–20 (15).
2. Wolfgang Iser, *The Act of Reading* (Baltimore: Johns Hopkins University Press, 1978).
3. De Man, "The Resistance to Theory," 16, 20.

ratives that would systematically determine the truth of a literary text. De Man's approach is ironic, of course, in that it is fully aware of the phenomenological implications: those who champion the possibility of a well-formed theory of reading that might be able to resolve the conflict of interpretations arising in the act of literary comprehension are exactly those who appear to adopt what Edmund Husserl called the "natural attitude" of perception, which as theory can only be "a piece of description *prior to any theory*."[4] Thus any serious theory, in de Man's sense, would have to be aware of those interpretive resistances emerging as complex hermeneutical constructions that, although experientially identified in the "natural attitude," would, at a much more analytical and self-conscious level, discourage a unified field of cognitive synthesis and thereby frustrate theory.[5] In *Ideas Pertaining to a Pure Phenomenology,* Husserl himself specifically declines to entertain "theories." "We keep theories . . . strictly at a distance," he says, underscoring by the word *theory* a notion of "supposed unities of validity."[6]

From de Man's perspective this allergy to theory paradoxically characterizes the theoretical itself. De Man expresses reluctance, as Minae Mizumura notes, "to reduce the text into something that is identical to the experience of reading."[7] For de Man, identification is an expression of the "natural attitude" and underwrites what is known today as the humanist tradition. De Man's resistance to theory rejects a tradition that takes for granted values based upon the readerly principles of identification such as those expressed by Sainte-Beuve when he argued that a classic work of art is characterized by "order, wisdom, moderation, and reasonableness," or what he called "simplicity and majesty." Invoking Buffon's *Discourse on Style,* Sainte-Beuve laid the groundwork for much twentieth-century critical reception when he argued that a literary work must have clarity and unity of design, despite whatever digressions might be introduced, and that it is the purpose of such works to enrich the mind by encouraging it to take "one more step forward . . . in that heart where all seemed known and explored."[8] For Sainte-Beuve, as for many twentieth-century readers, the act of reading implies a certainty of interpretive comprehension and a common under-

4. Edmund Husserl, *Ideas Pertaining to a Pure Phenomenology and to a Phenomenological Philosophy* (The Hague: Martinus Nijhoff, 1982).

5. It is of interest that Jorge Luis Borges himself resisted systems and theories: "I reject all systematic thought because it always tends to deceive (*tiende a trampear*). A system necessarily leads to deceit." *Entrevistas con Jorge Luis Borges* (Caracas: Monte Avila, 1970), 116.

6. Husserl, *Ideas Pertaining to a Pure Phenomenology,* 56.

7. Minae Mizumura, "Renunciation," *Yale French Studies* 69 (1985): 81–97 (95).

8. C.-A. Sainte-Beuve, "What Is a Classic?" in *Critical Theory since Plato,* ed. H. Adams (New York: Harcourt Brace Jovanovich, 1971), 556–62 (558, 557).

standing based on systematic principles of establishing identification, of which the canon, the masterpiece, clarity, or a teleology expanding the already known are but a few examples. For de Man, however, these practices will always be but "a piece of description *prior to any theory*" even if, as in Mizumura's summary of de Man's position, "no reading can come to being without an attempt to identify one's experience of reading with the text, that is, without assuming the readability of the text."[9] For de Man, then, a theory of reading is a hermeneutics eluding the preconception that no aporia or impasse exists between the act of reading and the readability of a text.

No literary writer, perhaps, has self-consciously explored this problematics in more detail than Jorge Luis Borges. Yet, whereas de Man subverts Sainte-Beuve's humanist preconditions for reading or interpretation by carefully deconstructing metaphysics, Borges does much the same by intensifying and exhausting metaphysical strategies. Certainly, from a deconstructive perspective it may seem peculiar that Borges's obsession with mirrors, mystical tracts, divine manifestations, magical beasts, and the like would facilitate a writing that reflects a resistance to reading so closely approximated by de Man's critical positions, even if, of course, Borges's resistance to reading is developed somewhat more thematically than de Man's. Still it would be difficult to find a literary author whose texts are as directly engaged in what appears to be a de Manian project as are those of Borges. No doubt, this is hardly an accident of culture, given that much twentieth-century literature has been exploring modes of readerly reception that are alternatives to the humanist model, especially in Latin America, as evidenced not only by Borges but also by Manuel Puig, Gabriel García Márquez, Julio Cortázar, and many others. However, Borges's fiction is unique in the rigorous systematicness of a narrative that, while acceding to theory, tells the story of its own deconstructive unreadability. Borges, like de Man, searches for such a story in the texts of antecedent authors and uses texts like *objets trouvés* that can be situated in a very systematic discourse in order to demonstrate various aporias of interpretation and expose the act of reading as resisting theoretical closure and readerly identification. Most striking is how close Borges's logical strategies are to those used by de Man in *Allegories of Reading*[10] and the extent to which they render indeterminate the separation between literature and criticism, an indeterminacy that affects those practices of identification enabling us to read without resistance, what we might call our reading/theory.

9. Mizumura, "Renunciation," 95.
10. Paul de Man, *Allegories of Reading* (New Haven: Yale University Press, 1978).

It is interesting that, during the early sixties, de Man himself wrote a short review on Borges's stories entitled "A Modern Master." Although this review by no means develops in any detail the sort of problematics that concerns us here, it does show de Man's clear fascination with Borges's writings in terms of what he calls layered reflections in which "the complication is pushed so far that it is virtually impossible to describe." De Man clearly recognized that "style in Borges becomes the ordering but dissolving act that transforms the unity of experience into the enumeration of its discontinuous parts."[11] Perhaps it is the word *act* which is most significant, since it is nothing less than the interpretive effect or readerly consequence of style, which results in resistance to comprehensibility. Indeed, part of what I will develop here are two demonstrations to show how Borges's resistance to reading can be interpreted from the perspective of the later de Man, first in terms of what de Man called "figure" and second in terms of what he called "allegory." Particularly important will be how Borges and de Man resist reading and theory for the sake of a writerly limit where, as we will see in Borges's texts, a death of literature is established as the necessary condition for the perpetuation of literature. This limit dissolves the difference between literature and criticism (that is, what belongs to literature and what exists beyond it) and the metaphysical as opposed to the antimetaphysical, even while insisting upon their differences; and this fact marks an aspect of contemporary theory that resists interpretive closure, or (to put it in a more properly ambiguous way) reading theory.

I.

In Borges's "The God's Script," we are introduced to a narrator who is the last of the Aztec priests. Having been confined in a prison, he says, "Impelled by the fatality of having something to do, of populating time in some way, I tried, in my darkness, to recall all I knew" (*L* 170). The place of the priest's confinement is a dark circular space with a dividing wall and a barred window in between. The priest is on one side of the wall; a jaguar is on the other. "Endless nights I devoted to recalling the order and the number of stone-carved serpents or the precise form of a medicinal tree" (*L* 170). Far from leaving the parameters of a metaphysical tradition saturated with magical talismans, secret scripts, powerful formulas, and fetishized objects, the priest enacts them in the most metaphysical of ways—by pure thinking. His recollections and reconstructions are so intense that only hours after thinking them can he begin to interpret what they might mean.

11. Paul de Man, "A Modern Master," *New York Review of Books,* November 19, 1964, pp. 8–10 (10, 9).

Hours later I began to perceive the outline of the recollection. It was a tradition of the god. The god, foreseeing that at the end of time there would be devastation and ruin, wrote on the first day of Creation a magical sentence with the power to ward off those evils. He wrote it in such a way that it would reach the most distant generations and not be subject to chance. No one knows where it was written nor with what characters, but it is certain that it exists, secretly, and that a chosen one shall read it. (*L* 170)

As the last remaining priest of a ruined civilization, the narrator believes it has been left to him to decipher and interpret the script, if only he can reconstruct the text of his ruined culture. He gradually comes to believe that the text has been placed in the cell next to him: the pattern of the jaguar. But in spending endless years in deciphering this text, the priest, Tzinacán, reaches an odd enlightenment, an ecstatic revelation—indeed, one suspects it is madness—in which the god has been disclosed and the script revealed. To utter the script would make the priest all powerful and would release him from prison. "But I know," he says, "I shall never say those words, because I no longer remember Tzinacán" (*L* 173). In recollecting the script, Tzinacán has been himself effaced; therefore, there is no subject left who can "performatively" read the script in such a way that its god will avenge the Aztecs.

In Borges's text, the metaphysical apparatuses of thinking have been overloaded, and typically characteristic oppositions (like subject and script, culture and nature, recollection and forgetting, enlightenment and madness) have become destabilized. To decipher the god's script, the priest must first sacrifice himself as an interiorized consciousness wherein identifications are made. He must undergo the deprivation of self so that he may accede to a consciousness outside itself, a consciousness that is nothing less than script itself. In *The Space of Literature,* Maurice Blanchot describes this condition of the written: "The writer belongs to a language which no one speaks, which is addressed to no one, which has no center, and which reveals nothing. He may believe that he affirms himself in this language, but what he affirms is altogether deprived of self." In Borges, too, the performer of the script affirms his own being as that of a belonger-to-the-script and in the process forgets and therefore destroys his former self. This is, of course, a violation. Again, notice Blanchot's remarks: "In the work, the artist protects himself not only against the world, but also against the requirement that draws him *out* of the world. The work momentarily domesticates this 'outside' by restoring an intimacy to it."[12] In Borges's story this is exactly what does not happen to the priest, who composes

12. Maurice Blanchot, *The Space of Literature,* trans. Ann Smock (Lincoln: University of Nebraska Press, 1982), 26, 53.

or recollects the script of god, an exteriority parallel to what Blanchot discusses. For what happens in this story is that the priest—metaphorically the writer or scribe—deprives himself of intimacy and interiority. His whole project is to get outside the prison, and in a sense he succeeds.

Another way to consider this "outside" or exteriority is suggested by two statements of Michel Foucault in *Madness and Civilization:* first, "for the nineteenth century, the initial model of madness would be to believe oneself to be god, while for the preceding centuries it had been to deny god"; and second, "madness is the absolute break with the work of art; it forms the constitutive moment of abolition, which dissolves in time the truth of the work of art; it draws the exterior edge, the line of dissolution, the contour against the void."[13] In the Borges story, the priest is the figure for the threshold between art and madness, between the legible and the illegible, the illuminated and the insane, man and beast. In fact, he is the chiastic figure that maintains an indeterminate relationship between these terms. As such, the priest maintains the threshold between rational account and insane experience. Indeed, in this story, and as the Foucault passages suggest, the rational may very well only work in the service of madness—the belief that one has become god, the drawing toward the exterior edge, the moment of dissolution. The figure rides the margin between readability and illegibility, subject-centered interiority and writerly exteriority, intense interpretive understanding and lethargic, forgetful concealment approaching the nonconsciousness of the jaguar. For Borges, this is the aporia of man's relation not only to god but also to other men who are hostile. It is odd that in the act of being avenged, the avenger and the act are deconstructed, as the metaphysics of interpretation becomes the narrative of its own illegibility and impossibility. This has the ironic effect of turning back on the priest the same apparatuses of destruction that he wishes to direct toward his enemies. For by achieving the condition of the jaguar (the exterior), the priest is in a condition of being that expresses only lassitude and fatigue in the face of its own destruction. "That man [the priest] *has been he* and now matters no more to him, if he, now, is no one. This is why I do not pronounce the formula, why, lying here in the darkness, I let the days obliterate me" (*L* 173). The "I" at this point is, quite evidently, but a placeholder for he-who-is-one-and-no-one, an I-and-not-I. It is the pronoun through which the metaphysics of scripture, the interpretation of the holy, or the enactment of the magical is canceled in the very gesture of its coming about. It is as if,

13. Michel Foucault, *Madness and Civilization,* trans. Richard Howard (New York: Random House, 1965), 264, 287.

by passing through the most metaphysical of religious conceptions, the priest comes back to himself as a not-himself and, as such, resists transcendence, knowledge, and power. Rather, "he" accedes to the thingness of script, the condition of the jaguar, the solitary existence of a man rotting in a cell. Has this "he" achieved enlightenment or mere delusion? This is the question the narrative leaves wholly undetermined.

Given this approach to the story, the priest may be viewed as the figure for a resistance to interpretation or reading, a resistance which ensures that the Borges story is itself the narrative of its own unreadability. The story, then, is an enactment of the destruction of those grounds upon which readers make identifications from within a determinate perspective. This locus is no less than an interiorized subjectivity on which a Cartesian hermeneutics is established. Borges's text, however, in initially sighting this locus in the priest, works to undermine its certainty by making the priest into a figure of what de Man calls "hypallage," a trope that links two incompatible interpretive structures. The priest as figure decenters our reading by invalidating his own authority as a centralizing Cartesian consciousness or stable perspective to which all the information in the story must be reduced.

Indeed, even the function of priest as figure is peculiarly decentered because the possibility of this function is threatened by the moves of the narrative, insofar as the telling of the story negates the possibility of the story's (that is, the figure's) existence. This feature of the tale is brought out especially in the remarks concerning the loss of the narrator in a labyrinth of dreams figured forth as the multiplication of grains of sand, for it is in this *mise en abyme* that the story itself fails recoverability or even narrativity. In passing through what one might call the death of narrative, the narration of the figure (the priest) accedes to the god's script and, in so doing, is divested of all Cartesian characteristics. As *mise en abyme,* the text we are reading is the script of an unrecoverable agency, figure, or god. And the narrative, therefore, emanates from what Blanchot views as the exteriority or "beyond" of the "subject" as figure. What makes the Borges story deconstructive is that the relationship between interiority (or selfhood) and exteriority (or otherness) is left so undecidable that the figure of the priest functions as a threshold or limit where the narrative becomes the story of its impossibility to occur. As threshold between two states that can assert neither their difference nor their identity (which is reflected in the inability of the figure of the priest to separate sleep from wakefulness), the narrating figure of the priest succumbs to a de-figuration and obliteration wherein the narration itself is dashed. It is here that the rhetorical function of the priest as figure is undermined by the grammatical or structural function of the tale, as a story enacting de-figuration. The figure of the priest, then, marks a resistance to reading from the side of grammar or structure and ensures that our understanding of the text cannot reconcile the conflict of interpretations concerning modalities of interiority and exteriority, figuration and de-figuration. At the same time, however, by having to acknowledge the priest as a figure of hypallage that is deconstructive and undecidable, we might be able to bring into better relationship those aspects of Borges's story (its grammatical or narrative structure) that might otherwise elude comprehensibility. That is, if the rhetorical function of the priest is undermined by the grammar or structure of narrative, it is also true that the rhetorical figure of the priest as hypallage labors to help us read and understand this deconstructive operation. As that which resists reading, the figure also rhetorically facilitates it.

II.

There are, of course, other narratives by Borges in which the resistance to reading is structured similarly to "The God's Script"—for example, "Borges and I," "Paradiso, XXXI, 108," and "Parable of the Palace" from the collection *Dreamtigers,* and "The Maker" and "The Enigma of Edward Fitzgerald" from *Ficciones.* Yet one can find another sort of narrative in Borges's work that approaches somewhat more strongly a resistance to reading, along the lines of what de Man called "allegories of reading." One of the best examples is Borges's "Forms of a Legend" from *Other Inquisitions.*

By "allegories of reading," de Man had in mind the literary counterpointing of narratives in texts by authors like Rousseau or Proust, which had the effect of debilitating interpretation. In the essays on Nietzsche in *Allegories of Reading,* de Man isolates the figures of Dionysus and Apollo as characteristic of two major arguments that, when counterpointed, result in correspondences that resist the construction of a theory of narrative interpretation, even as just such a theory is being established in the counterpointing of the arguments themselves. In discussing this critical approach by de Man, Geoffrey Hartman has written that it "goes right through the problem of ideology to that of theology," because de Man reaches "the point where [theory] must break with representational values." Such statements by Hartman alert us to the probability that, although de Man's critical practice is overtly antimetaphysical (the texts he chooses for analysis are written by authors who are themselves inherently skeptical of this tradition), its consequences are, nevertheless, theological or metaphysical in nature. Furthermore, Hartman notes that both "Derrida and de Man reduce this continuous figuration [the allegory of reading] to the concept of *writing:* and they fashion a mode of criticism helplessly ironic in its emphasis on displacement, on words rather than the Word."[14] That is, de Man's allegorical method of critical speculation moves very much in the same direction as does Borges's narrative: toward what is exterior, or, as Michel Foucault puts it in "La Pensée du dehors" (Thinking from without), toward an opening to a language from which the subject is excluded.[15] It is here, Foucault has said, that the being of language appears only in the disappearance of the subject and that language as theology can be thought. In fact, Foucault has argued that such a thought has surfaced in the mystic texts of Christianity; that it is by passing through a certain metaphysics that the "outside" of thought becomes accessible as simulacra, in whose recursiveness the subject has "lost its place" and hence is not capable any longer of reading mimetically. De Man, who is largely concerned with recursiveness, approaches an extreme exteriority when he notes, toward the end of *Allegories of Reading:* "Fiction has nothing to do with representation but is the absence of any link between utterance and a referent, regardless of whether this link be causal, encoded or governed by any other conceivable relationship that could lend itself to systematization."[16] Fiction is precisely that which is outside or exterior to a representational notion including the Cartesian subject; fiction is the resistance to reading and theory announced by an absence or elision that substitutes for the subject, which has lost its place. It is in this effacement of the subject that the allegory of reading is situated as a thinking-from-without.

In Borges's "Forms of a Legend," the narrative mimics a scholarly essay that outlines, in the most schematic of terms, various ways in which the legend of Siddhartha's finding the way has been culturally transmitted. It does not take long to realize that the way of the Buddha here is nothing less than the differences between the various stories of his coming to enlightenment. Each variant functions as an allegory of reading, wherein interpretation is both facilitated and obstructed by the interactions between the narratives. Although the narrator appears to be looking for the true legend, it becomes evident that the effect of all the variants is to erode the authenticity and authority that any such perception of origins might at first have held for the researcher. It is as if the absence of the story were the story. In "The God's Script," the impulse of the priest to enact the power of text turns back on itself so that the priest, in becoming one with the script, occupies an illustrative

14. Geoffrey Hartman, *Criticism in the Wilderness* (New Haven: Yale University Press, 1980), 111, 111–112.

15. Michel Foucault, "La Pensée du dehors," *Critique* 229 (1966): 523–46.

16. De Man, *Allegories of Reading,* 292.

or exemplary position which is "nonperformative," whereas in "Forms of a Legend" exemplary modes of understanding narrative are turned back on themselves so that they appear to have the capacity to enact. The thing enacted is the figure of the Buddha that, like the priest in "The God's Script," could be viewed as a deconstructive figure of hypallage. Yet, the priest in "The God's Script" was the narrating subject of the story, whereas the Buddha is obviously the narrated object in "Forms of a Legend." Again, the priest was given from the side of interiorized conscious reflection—indeed, the prison cell emphasized this perspective—whereas the Buddha is given from the exteriorized position of a more allegorical discourse, in the variants of a legend he has not himself articulated and from which the subject has been excluded.

Because of the writerly exteriorization of thought in "Forms of a Legend," it goes almost without saying that the narrator's attempt to reconcile all the variants by locating a common denominator will end in failure. Rather, what this narrator notices is a network of parallel accounts that, although addressing a similar story (of a young prince's going out into the world and encountering various types of sufferers), only manage to corrupt their purpose by making deviations or by incorporating interpolations from sources clearly other than what the narrator thinks the original story must have been. Whereas a preliminary examination of only a few accounts serves to declare the nature of the Buddha fairly clearly, a much more rigorous examination undermines almost completely an illustrative or exemplary understanding. The Buddha as figure is a horizon of interpretive performances that comprise not only each account but also, more importantly, the relating of these accounts by way of allegorical superimposition. For example, the narrator cites a text called *Barlaam and Josaphat* (Josaphat = Bodhisat, Bodhisattva), which, according to the narrator, is a Christian corruption and allegorical transposition of the Siddhartha story. And this corruption imports into the Buddhist context the problem of what Christ knew as man. Indeed, the narrator admits, nothing could be more corrupt or alien from the standpoint of the Asian materials, yet the narrator will show that this misreading is transferred back to the Asian context in yet another corruption entitled the *Lalitavistra,* which takes up precisely this problematics of what Siddhartha "knew" even when kept "ignorant" in the palace from which he sets out on his journeys. Is it that a Western digression or misreading contaminates Asian tradition, or that, by some peculiar mode of indirection, a Western text has allegorically brought out one of the deeper spiritual problems implicit in the Buddhist literature? Evidently, the ability to "read" is undecidably facilitated and obstructed. Yet, in *The Lalitavistra,* the narrator reads that "the Buddha . . . directs each stage of his destiny" (*PA* 125).

The religious problem of incarnation and knowledge is posed as a most serious question at that very moment when the status of scriptural understanding has been put into question by the narrator's cross-referencing of accounts. As if to solve this contradiction, the narrator says, "To my mind, the enigma deserves another solution" (*PA* 126). In fact, he will offer us various answers: for example, the Buddha is both eternal and temporal, so he can very well create the four sufferers who will provide him with answers in his incarnation as Siddhartha; or, "we need merely remember that all religions in Hindustan, and Buddhism most particularly, teach that the world is illusory" (*PA* 126). The life of the Buddha is a dream, the earth another dream, and so on.

> Siddhartha chooses his country and his parents. He fashions four forms which will fill him with astonishment. He disposes that another form declare the meaning of the first four. All this is reasonable, if we assume that it is a dream of Siddhartha's; even better if we think of it as a dream in which Siddhartha plays a part (as the leper and the monk play a part), but a dream no one actually dreams, because, in the eyes of Northern Buddhism, the world and the proselytes and Nirvana and the wheel of transmigrations and the Buddha are all equally unreal. No one is extinguished in Nirvana, as we read in a famous treatise, for the extinction of innumerable beings in Nirvana is like the disappearance of a phantasmagoria which a magician at a crossroads creates by occult art; in another place it is written that everything is mere emptiness, mere name, including the book which says so and the man who reads it. (*PA* 126–27)

Most peculiar about this account is its paratactical layering of explanations. How do we get, for example, from the narrator's idea that the Buddha is a dream, the earth another dream, to the statement about Siddhartha choosing his country and parents? Why is it reasonable that Siddhartha's choices depend upon himself being the dreamer, since dreamers are not so much inventors of what is said in a dream as passive recollectors of previous events? And what would make the account even more reasonable if the dream were dreamt by no one? Here the reason given, "because, in the eyes of Northern Buddhism, the world and the proselytes and Nirvana and the wheel of transmigrations and the Buddha are all equally unreal" (*PA* 126–27), is not so much an explanation as an assertion pulled out of scripture, a paratactical overlay. What occurs in this explanation, then, is a piling up of disjunct and fragmentary statements that contribute to placing the Buddha "under erasure," as Jacques Derrida might say,[17] by suggesting not only that the

---

17. Jacques Derrida, *Of Grammatology,* trans. G. Spivak (Baltimore: Johns Hopkins University Press, 1977).

legend of Siddhartha is constituted within a *mise en abyme* of dreams within dreams but also that the agency of dreaming is not someone but, rather, the textual phenomenon or scriptural evidence, which suggests that "the vast forms and the vast ciphers . . . are only vast and monstrous bubbles, emphasizing Nothingness" (*PA* 127). Here, once more, we achieve an exteriority of consciousness or subjectivity marked by the name: Buddha. It is an exteriority or (to put it even more radically) a nothingness achieved by the way that "the unreal progressively riddles the story," the way in which various scriptural fragments paratactically form a layering of texts or allegories of reading wherein the figure of the Buddha, in its "erasure" or canceling out as a "constative" textual element, takes charge as a performative entity—to the extent that it is as nothingness that the Buddha directs his destiny as the narrative of his own unreadability and unrecoverability. That this narrative is, in itself, not nothing but something reflects how undetermined or undecidable the ontological grounds of reading have become, in what is again a very religious and mystical context where one might expect metaphysical or ontological certainties to prevail, despite the paradoxes usually associated with Eastern thought.

Like "The God's Script," this account problemizes the figures of narrative assertion. But, whereas in "The God's Script" it was the grammatical or structural ordering of the narrative itself that deconstructed the rhetorical figure of the text (the priest), in "Forms of a Legend" the weight of deconstructive pressure rests largely on the rhetorical figures whose effect is to play havoc with the grammatical or structuring features of the legends. In recalling the speech-act vocabulary of de Man's *Allegories of Reading,* we find that in Borges a constative (or exemplary) mode of utterance expressed by the figure of the scholar-narrator has been undermined by the performative (or enacting) mode of utterance that belongs to the figure of the Buddha.[18] Conversely, it is also

---

18. De Man's use of the terms *constative* and *performative* loosely follows J. L. Austin's definitions in *How to Do Things With Words* (Cambridge: Harvard University Press, 1962). However, it is quite helpful to consult Kent Bach and Robert M. Harnish's discussion of the terms in *Linguistic Communication and Speech Acts* (Cambridge: MIT Press, 1979). Constative speech acts are "illocutionary"; they have the intent of establishing belief in the addressee. This is different from "locutionary" speech acts that function at the level of information and are not directed in such a way as to convince an addressee. Illocutions, then, have a rhetorical force that locutions do not. Performative speech acts differ from constative ones in that they enact something. Although the addressee does not have to believe the intent or force of a performative speech act, Bach and Harnish still view performatives as illocutionary and categorize them as either "effectives," which make changes in institutional states of affairs (the granting of a university degree, the vetoing of a congressional bill), or "verdicatives" (judgments that have binding import, as in a court of law). These are illocutionary insofar as such performatives presuppose general social consent and belief. In "Forms of a

true that the performative is in turn undermined by the constative. Since both the performative and the constative are largely illocutionary modes of utterance that elicit belief on the part of an addressee, they are inherently rhetorical. Particularly interesting is that, not unlike de Man in *Allegories of Reading,* Borges develops a rhetoric of the figure in which illocution is itself undecidably divided into figures of the performative and the constative, which in achieving a certain illocutionary force also manage to undermine the determinableness of narration, meaning, authority, and belief. However, at the same time, this conflict of performative and constative utterances suggests that something profound has been said.

Because the narrator's constative authority is most in doubt at those moments when the legends are being most scrupulously explicated and because the Buddha's performative strength is fulfilled at the moment we perceive him acceding to nothingness, we discover that the figure of the narrator is most illusory when it becomes most present as voice and erudition and that the figure of the Buddha, which operates under the aegis of erasure or figment, is established as most real and present when it performs the differences of the legends and becomes the vanishing point where these legends appear to converge as one. The question is, finally, whether the narrator is not the Buddha, or whether the Buddha is not just the erudition of the narrator. Such paradoxical crossings are especially important not only because they function as figures whose effect is to de-figure the figure by means of undecidability but also because the grammar, structure, or forms of the accounts cannot sustain such a rhetorical impasse, even as such forms make it possible for us to read the constative and performative figures as the impossibility of achieving a readability of scripture.

Indeed, "Forms of a Legend," with its rhetorical undermining of grammar, could be viewed as an inverse counterpoint to "The God's Script," with its grammatical undermining of rhetoric, suggesting that together these stories are allegories of reading that are embedded one within the other. Given such an allegorical performance, and given our orientation to it as a fugal counterpoint to de Man's own critical practices, we are ourselves necessarily committed to a performance (or

---

Legend," the Buddha has performative force insofar as Hindu and Buddhist religions are institutions that reflect the Buddha's power of performing "effectives" (granting enlightenment) or "verdicatives" (establishing ethical and spiritual judgments). Borges is well aware that this sort of performative action is highly problemized in Eastern thought. Although, from a de Manian perspective, terms like *constative* and *performative* are used in a general sense, one could draw from the much more defined and structured account of Bach and Harnish to establish a more elaborate account of Borges's story, something there is neither the space nor for my rhetorical aims the necessity to do here.

rather re-performance) of certain literary and critical strategies, in whose interplay the resistance to theory is itself enacted. The consequence of being drawn to work in terms of performance, for the sake of enacting and defining the resistance to theory, is that the difference between criticism and literature is itself called into question. In commenting on Borges and de Man, therefore, it appears that we are fated by respect for the subversion of the difference between literature and criticism to reenact a resistance to a critical reading, which would purport to separate itself or take distance from its subject matter in the name of a unified account wherein the impasses to comprehension are explained away. But what is the fate of reading, in the context of this performative conjunction of literature and criticism in which a certain resistance inheres? What is the fate of that necessary performance-as-theory in which the difference between literature and criticism is called into question?

III.

Fiction as we find it in the writings of Borges has, according to de Man, nothing to do with representation. Rather it is the absence of any link between utterance and referent. Yet it is an absence that has been achieved through reference and language. It is, to use Gerald Graff's phrase, a literature against itself. No doubt such a literature turns away from the humanist notion of writing that Sainte-Beuve had in mind when he turned his attention to valorizing the classics and the problemized assumptions about reading that the canon of such classics presupposed.[19] Through Borges, it becomes especially clear that de Man's concern with a resistance to reading or even theory is closely connected to a literary movement of which Borges is a major part—a movement wherein the literary work, by exacerbating various humanist interpretive assumptions, broaches what Blanchot viewed already in the early fifties as a writing-beyond-writing. From Blanchot's perspective—and this is a perspective de Man and Borges implicitly share, I think—it is not so much that literature turns against itself in some sort of reified destructive moment but that literature is inherently resistant to what Husserl called "supposed unities of validity." This is not because literature is somehow perverse but because, as Blanchot says, "whoever devotes himself to the work is drawn by it toward the point where it undergoes impossibility."[20] This impossibility is achieved at that limit where the writer undergoes self-effacement in the service of a

---

19. Gerald Graff, *Literature Against Itself* (Chicago: University of Chicago Press, 1978); Sainte-Beuve, "What Is a Classic?"

20. Blanchot, *The Space of Literature,* 163.

writing in whose exteriority the subject-as-author is excluded. At that limit the writer must submit to a certain death of the author in order to be heard. Blanchot asks, therefore, what it means to speak from beyond oneself, to speak from beyond the grave and yet not be dead, to write during a darkness whose night is a terrifying exteriority wherein the writer is extinguished even as he is heard.

> Whoever believes he is attracted [by the night in which literature is written] finds himself profoundly neglected. Whoever claims to be in the thrall of an irresistible vocation, is only dominated by his own weakness. He calls irresistible the fact that there is nothing to resist; he calls vocation that which does not call him, and he has to shoulder his nothingness for a yoke. Why is this? Why do some embark upon works in order to escape this risk—to elude rather than respond to 'inspiration,' constructing their work as a burrow where they want to think they are sheltered from the void and which they only build, precisely, by hollowing and deepening the void, creating a void all around them?[21]

In other words, the writer should not avoid that moment when the impossible limit of being/nonbeing is apprehended in the exteriority of a language beyond the author's finitude or being. Writers should not turn away from a dark or blind moment when reading and writing turns on itself in such a manner that the sanity of the writer is at risk in the service of a writing-beyond-writing. Borges, de Man, and Blanchot articulate a resistance to reading, which is that resistance of the limit invoked by Blanchot in *The Space of Literature*. This resistance is nothing other than the space that is literature and, as such, determines the act of reading or comprehending as one that is not easily recoverable, as a construction whose ontology guarantees epistemological or hermeneutic smooth sailing. Rather, it signals interpretive difficulties whose problematics, as Blanchot demonstrates, is not at all as divorced from the existential condition of the writer as one might at first assume. This is not to say that the condition of the writer is the unifying ground upon which a reading of literature must ultimately rest, but rather that this condition is itself resistant to theory, and problematic as reading. Indeed, for these writers it is precisely the condition of identification (as that readerly horizon through which the writer is made to appear as unifying ground) that is capsized in the articulation of literature as a critical deconstruction, even as such a deconstruction itself is always already literature. Just as Borges and Blanchot presage the death of literature, by way of a critical intervention that undermines the assumptions inherent in normative practices of identification, so de Man presages the preservation of that very literature, by way of writing a text

21. Ibid., 170.

(such as *Allegories of Reading*) whose strategic and overdetermined counterpointings accede to a verbal architecture for the sake of a certain literary monumentality. What we might call the Sartrean "situation" of the writer is a function of this literary/critical chiasmus—a chiasmus in which inheres a marked resistance to reading and to the literature/theory difference, as if that theory itself (in traditionally being resisted by a literary temperament)[22] is that which resists separation from the literary act of writing and from the condition of being a writer, and a reader. What is meant by the death of literature may very well be but the resistance to the assumption that criticism and literature, theory and art, can be separated. If this is so, then the act of reading (in which the traditional assumptions of identification are given up) broaches yet another moment of identification, that of theory and art, criticism and literature. Yet this moment is not one that is recoverable as an "act of reading" or as an essentialist truth buried in the intersection of critique and text. Instead it is a moment reflected as a limit, whose significance puts an end to identification as synthesis, stasis, determinability, or *clôture*. Hence, this limit discloses a "figuration" that problemizes the identities of and differences between literature and theory and threatens the act of reading itself in its very coming to pass. To read Borges and de Man together is, indeed, to enact this limit as a resistance to theory and as the death of literature, a double negativity under whose sign both literature and criticism are bound.

22. One thinks of Roger Shattuck, *The Innocent Eye* (New York: Washington Square, 1986).

Christine de Lailhacar

The Mirror and the Encyclopedia

Borgesian Codes in Umberto Eco's *The Name of the Rose*

I. *SPECULUM SPECULORUM*

"I began writing *The Name of the Rose* in March 1978, prodded by a seminal idea: I felt like poisoning a monk." Quite a seminal idea, indeed, announced in the *Postscript to* The Name of the Rose.[1] One may recall Derrida's antilogical—or poetically logical—mock-etymological play with the Latin word *semen* (seed, sperm) and the Greek *semeion* (sign) as based on their common function of *dissemination,* a potential spreading of intertextual/genetic reproduction.[2]

The empirical reality grown from this significant seed is a book of fiction presented *in exergum* as "a manuscript—naturally." Eco needed the mask of an innocent medieval chronicler to protect himself from the monster of the encyclopedia: his own encyclopedic knowledge and the intertextual mirroring between books in a real or imaginary library, that is, himself as reader. The same authentically medieval manuscript read by, say, Vincent de Beauvais and Umberto Eco would be as different a text as Cervantes's *Don Quixote* is different from Pierre Menard's *Don Quixote,* because the later reader reads the same text through the prism of all those texts that came to superpose themselves on that "hypo-text" like new inscriptions on a palimpsest.[3] Every writer creates his precursors, as Borges remarked in connection with Kafka. But this mask of innocence is the mask of an earlier mask, a *speculum speculi* (mirror of another mirror). In *Don Quixote,* the empirical author resorts to the alibi of a manuscript found by chance, that manuscript being the trans-

1. Umberto Eco, *Postscript to* The Name of the Rose (New York: Harcourt, 1984); Umberto Eco, *The Name of the Rose* (1980; New York: Warner, 1984). All further citations to *The Name of the Rose* are to this edition and will be given parenthetically in the text.

2. The following works have also been consulted in the elaboration of this essay: Jacques Derrida, *L'Ecriture et la différence* (Paris: Seuil, 1967); Jacques Derrida, *Marges de la philosophie* (Paris: Minuit, 1972); Emir Rodríguez Monegal, *Borges: Hacia una interpretación* (Madrid: Guadarrama, 1976); V.-L. Saulnier, *La Littérature du Moyen Age* (Paris: PUF, 1948).

3. Gérard Genette, *Palimpsestes: La Littérature au second degré* (Paris: Seuil, 1982).

lation of a manuscript written centuries earlier in forbidden, forbiddingly mysterious characters that elicit all the less faith in their truth as they are traced by some infidel. The missing parts of that manuscript—absence of meaning—are as significant as the existing ones, if not more so, because here the logical category of necessity—the necessary limitation to what is still present—gives way to that of possibility, or *speculation* (from the Latin *speculum,* mirror, or imagination, fiction). So the first manuscript is more than doubtful as a chronicle, and many symptoms lead to thinking that it was initially fiction, mirror image, *speculum mentis* (mirror of a mind). In the case of *The Name,* the initial discovery is that of a "faithful" translation by a monk of a fourteenth-century manuscript. Eco's tongue-in-cheek pretension to historical reconstitution of the universe and events reported in the manuscript of Dom Adso de Melk resembles the reconstitution of the universe of "Tlön, Uqbar, Orbis Tertius," whose discovery Borges attributes to "the conjunction of a mirror and an encyclopedia," and which is a "*labyrinth* destined to be *deciphered* by men . . . built with the rigor of chessplayers" (*F.S* 13, 35, my emphasis). So *The Name* is fiction on absent fiction, since the translation disappears and no trace of the original can be found. Eco reports having discovered, however, a quotation from the original in a Spanish translation of a Georgian manuscript (all the connotations associated by Russians with *gruzin* [Georgian] by themselves form a code). He discovered this manuscript by chance in a noncoded library, the random collection of books of a street bookstall in the Borgesian city of Buenos Aires, and it was entitled "On the Use of Mirrors in the Game of Chess"—chess, that game of games with its infinite forking possibilities, like the threads of a nonwritten novel.

That this fiction on absent fiction, *The Name,* became an unprecedented best-seller and, when turned into a film, was projected on the screen in innumerable copies, appears a prime example of Borgesian ontological sleight of hand. When speaking about "himself," Borges consistently turns the fantastic into reality and turns everything concerning his "real" or biographical being into the unreal in an iridescent sort of aleph. The sign, in particular the written letter or combination of written letters such as the name *Borges,* stands in ordinary perception for an already existing object. In Borges's universe—a universe made of books—the sign not only precedes but creates the eventually existing object. The thing is mirrored before it exists. In Eco's case, at the time of my writing, the object exists in reality—a fake monastery, a (re)construction in cardboard for the purpose of shooting the film in northern Italy. The "antecedent"—what we first perceive—is a cardboard copy; the original. . . . Semiotics is indeed "diabolical" (from the Greek *diaballein,* to throw across, put upside down, invert) in its practice of inversions: what I perceive as a sign is an antecedent; the original cause I infer from that antecedent is the "consequent." In *The Name,* there are as many ontological, chronological, logical, and moral inversions of conventional order as there are in Borges's fictions.

What could be more tempting for the middle-aged medievalist Eco than the mask of the naïveté of a fourteenth-century Benedictine novice's belief in a *Liber Mundi,* the creed that everything can be read as a divine book, a godly sign? Such an ideal state of the world is an ideal basis from which to create Borgesian referential havoc.

A verse by Alanus ab Insulis (Alain de Lille) is quoted early in the novel by the narrator Adso's master, the Franciscan William of Baskerville (18), and this sets the foil: a simple correlational code for the interpretation of the world.

> Omnis mundi creatura
> Quasi liber et pictura
> Nobis est et speculum.

(Every creature of this world is to us a book, picture, and mirror.)[4]

This *speculum* reflects theology's most famous "mirror"—Saint Augustine mirroring Saint Paul (1 Cor. 13:12) with "Nunc videmus in speculum in aenigmate, tunc facie ad faciem" (Now, in this world, we see truth in a mirror as enigma; then, in the other world, we shall see it face to face). Eco does not quote it but shrewdly disperses intertextual shards of that mirror throughout his text.

The novel's dynamics are determined by the way of seeing (*videmus*), of reading signs as "enigmas" in the mirror of the here and now, that is the pragmatics of inference and interpretation and the use of codes.[5] The propelling force is a counterpoint: on the one side is Jorge de Burgos, a diabolically inverted image of the blind seer, the Tiresias figure who, in conventional literature, is always wise and good. He stands for fanatic defense of dogma and consequent hatred of philosophy and the inquisitive mind; on the other hand stands William of Baskerville, pre-Renaissance emancipated "scientist," disciple of Roger Bacon, and certainly the disciple of semiotician Umberto Eco, as we may infer from his numerous paraphrases of passages from Eco's works.[6] Baskerville starts his investigation into truth (the truth of a crime) by

4. All translations from Latin and Spanish are mine.

5. Regarding *enigma,* the American edition's translation as "riddle" does not render the different Greek acceptations of the word (Aristotle's in particular), which are important in the context of *The Name.*

6. Works such as: Umberto Eco, *A Theory of Semiotics* (Bloomington: Indiana University Press, 1979); *The Role of the Reader* (Bloomington: Indiana University Press, 1984); and *Semiotics and the Philosophy of Language* (Bloomington: Indiana University Press, 1984).

inventing a plausible hypothesis, chosen from one of the "possible worlds." This is what we call "speculation": an activity not too far removed from fiction.

Thus it is the supposed rigor of science (based on syllogisms) which leads to the reading of books, any books, in the spirit of *opera aperta,* an attitude justified in typically Eco-esque intertextuality by Saint Paul himself, quoted by Saint Augustine, quoted by Vincent de Beauvais: "Quod genus litterarum non cum credendi necessitate, sed cum iudicandi libertate legendum est" (We should read certain books not with the unconditional acceptation [the necessity] of faith, but with the freedom of judgment).[7]

a. Speculum historiale

The Middle Ages are retrospectively a golden age for semioticians. They represent the apogee of monoreferential meaning, and of signification and its crisis. Virtue was to act like a copying monk, respectful only of what had already been written, to the exclusion of creative, or even critical, thought (the sin of intellectual pride). The late period of the Middle Ages chosen by Eco was torn by the conflict between Augustinianism (what today one would call "conservative") and Thomism (what today one would call "polluted" by "integrationist" tendencies), which reconciled Christian theology with the teachings of pagans like Aristotle and was transmitted, to make it worse, by the infidels. This led to the crisis where the solid, closed unity of signified and signifier became fissured (*entamé* would be Derrida's word), implying a partial loss of secure meaning, which cannot be recuperated. Signification opens up. On the other hand, copying and quoting rely on *auctoritas*—a single, authoritative source—and in conflictual dialogue quotes were the major, if not the only, weapon. Thus the Middle Ages were *the* era of intertextuality.

The Middle Ages, furthermore, were the era of the *summae* (the complete enumeration, the comprehensive world view), fascinating to both Borges and Eco, while ours today could be called a *speculum fractum* (fragmented mirror). This is why I structured this essay vaguely on the model of Vincent de Beauvais's *Speculum quadruplex* or *speculum maius* (fourfold or greater mirror). To judge from its title page, there could be no more major exponent of the medieval craving for wholeness:

Speculum quadruplex: naturale, doctrinale, morale, historiale.

In quo totius naturae Historia, omnium scientiarum Encyclopaedia, moralis

7. Vincent de Beauvais, *De eruditione filiorum nobilium,* ed. Arpad Steiner (Cambridge, Mass.: The Medieval Academy of America, 1938), xv.

philosophiae thesaurus et actionum humanarum Theatrum amplissimum exhibetur; ita ex optimorum auctorum elegantissimis sententiis *inter se concatenatis contextum opus* [my emphasis].

The fourfold mirror: natural, doctrinal, moral, historical.

In which the history of all nature, the encyclopedia of all sciences, the treasure of the philosophy of morals, and the immensely vast theater of human actions will be exhibited; thus the work is *woven together* (*texted together*) from the best authors' most elegant sentences, *concatenated* among themselves.[8]

There could be no more modern definition of intertextuality either.

De Beauvais, most typical authority for the background image of contextual frame, is my *auctoritas,* then. In fact he, like the host of other *auctoritates,* is a code in the works of Borges and Eco. Human actions and events, such as a crime, may be explained by inference from what these authors stand for. As such, from dogmatic authority as authors, these authors became quasi-characters in the fiction: actors (*auctor-actor*). Given both Borges's and Eco's mathematical inclinations, Alanus ab Insulis corresponded better as the favorite scholastic encyclopedist because of his mathematical and axiomatic method. Overt and covert references to him and citations from him abound in the works of both. How could Borges not have loved Alanus whom he connects with the most desirable thing in the world for a writer, the aleph? Alanus studied the pseudohermetic *Book of the Seven Wise Masters* (hardly a holy *auctoritas*), from which he took the theological rule "deus est sphaera intelligibilis cuius centrum ubique, circumferentia nusquam" (God is an intelligible sphere whose center is everywhere and whose circumference is nowhere), perhaps the sentence most frequently quoted or alluded to by both Borges and Eco in connection with semiotics.[9] Besides, Alanus was concerned with one Arabic word: *chifre* (zero), which has entered our languages as *cipher,* replacing one element of a plaintext by an element taken from another signifying system in the "correlative code."[10] Alanus thus leads directly to what one could call Borges's "negative semiotics."

Lastly it is no coincidence that Eco chose to reconstruct that very late period of the Middle Ages when the dispute over *universalia* (nominalism) had reached its peak and no coincidence that William of Basker-

---

8. Vincent de Beauvais, *Speculum quadruplex sive speculum maius. Opera Theologorum Benedictorum. Bibliotheca Mundi,* integral copy of the original edition of a 1624 manuscript (Graz: Akademische Verlagsanstalt, 1964/1965), title page.

9. Ernst Robert Curtius, *Europäische Literatur und lateinisches Mittelalter* (Berlin: Franke, 1948), 125.

10. Eco, *Semiotics and Philosophy,* 165.

ville, disciple of the *doctor admirabilis* Roger Bacon is a contemporary of William of Occam, *doctor invincibilis,* the main representative of nominalism. Occam's answer to the conflict over *universalia* was that general notions are only words or names (*nomina*) by which similarities are brought together—ultrasemiotic. *The Name of the Rose,* significantly, ends with the words "Stat rosa pristina nomine, nomina nuda tenemus" (The rose stays fresh in the name, we have only the name). As to the name *Baskerville,* it is a sign that stands for a sign, namely a letter type named after the eighteenth-century British typographer John Baskerville. The "Model Reader" may, however, prefer a more recent and popular intertextuality: the detective (or sign interpreter) Sherlock Holmes solving the enigma of "The Hound of the Baskervilles," with the help of his faithful companion, Watson (Adso).

Umberto Eco has never hidden his fascination with Borges. The list of parallels in the ways of thinking of the two authors is inexhaustible. I am speaking of parallels or affinities, because it would be neither Borgesian nor Eco-esque (significantly, Eco lacks the semantic capacity of adjectivization) to speak of "influence," to present the older author as a father figure. This would presuppose a conventional notion of anterior/posterior time and the corresponding causality—particularly when finding ourselves in the scholastic universe with its *post hoc, ergo propter hoc,* an a priori that both Borges and Eco tend to dissolve. There is no anxiety of influence, but there are affinities or common obsessions that could be subsumed by one—unholy—name, considering all its connotations: Babylon.

Babylonia: that is the birth of the written sign, those pictographic clay tablets of fifth millenary B.C. Ur. It is the mysterious correspondence of numbers, origin of the Cabala where the aleph becomes the microcosm of the alchemists, miniaturized multiplicity, the *multum in parvo.* It is synonymous with the world's most ancient profession, the *mulier amicta* (fallen women), and with the corresponding male fantasy, and so it is a model of the Apocalypse of Saint John. It is, above all, those wondrous labyrinths where one code or assumed reference leads to another ad infinitum, as in an encyclopedia: libraries that are "mirrors of a universe" to be penetrated only through secret corridors by means of codes; ciphers; cloaks that are full of treacherous clues where a crime can be committed and its traces lost.[11] Significantly, the imaginary continent of Uqbar is speculated to be a "region of Iraq or Asia Minor" (*F.S* 14), formerly Babylonia or Assyria. Most of all, Babylon is language in general, its betrayal of meaning, its confusion, explosion, and final "dis-semination." "Penitenziagite!" obsessively mumbles the

11. Ibid., 172.

repulsive false monk Salvatore, the diabolically inverted image of the Savior, the escapee from the heretic hordes of the *fraticelli* (those disciples of the far from *dolce,* [far from sweet] Fra Dolcino), the plebeian Antichrist whose final trial was to be a "mirror of atonement for the edification of others" (135). "Penitenziagite" is neither Latin nor Provençal but the "Babelish language of the first day after the divine chastisement, the language of primeval confusion" (48).

Above the entrance of the library, that *speculum maius* or mirror of the universe, are inscribed the ominous signs: MENE, MENE, TEKEL— God has numbered the days of your kingdom, that is, the rule of mono-referential meaning (188). You are weighed and found wanting: there is always an absence of meaning; meaning is never full or closed. A dictionary always refers to another of its own entries in an endless cyclic tautology.

MENE, MENE: latter-day Daniels, Borges and Eco are interpreters of signs, or preferably interpreters of that sign-making fantasy that Hegel in the *Encyclopedia of Sciences* calls *Mittelpunkt* (center). They interpret with a religious, if sometimes invertedly religious (blasphematory), zeal close to a killer instinct. This is the second reason I hesitate to speak of Borges as a father figure to Eco, lest I accuse Eco of parricide: the killer monk in *The Name* is Jorge de Burgos.

b. Speculum aporiae

In order to bring a murderously fascinating subject down to a manageable size, I have considered several possible orders—monkish ones preferably—but each degenerated into an impossible world. Ideally, this essay should take the shape of a *speculum quadruplex,* juxtaposing four parallel columns of texts—like Derrida's *Glas*—where *The Name* would be the first column, since it is "visible" (like that part of the work of Pierre Menard which was "visible," hence "natural" evidence). Borges's collection of *Ficciones,* divided into two parts, "El jardín de senderos que se bifurcan" (The garden of forking paths) and "Artificios" (Artifices), together with *El Aleph,* would be some *speculum mentis:* the second column. Patristic and scholastic writings mirrored in the "nature" of *The Name* would be a *speculum doctrinale:* the third column. The fourth column would consist of Eco's theoretical writings and might be a *speculum meditationis* on man as a semiotic animal.

These four columns of texts should then be mounted like stiff posters on pivots and, as *perpetua mobilia,* should turn incessantly but at variable speed, like four Calder mobiles, so that in accordance with the law of probability, every aspect of each of them faces at some point in time every aspect of all the others. Or it could be something in the spirit of Raymond Lulle, who "prepared himself to solve all the world's arcanes by means of a machinery of concentric, unequal and girating discs" (*BAR* 65). That is decidedly too much to ask of a printer. And since with that I already find myself in a three-dimensional universe, my principle of order may just as well be "a sphere whose center is everywhere and whose circumference is nowhere." I got that idea as an antecedent—my first perception of it, which for me as reader or detective perverts conventional chronology and dissolves the logic of cause and effect—in Borges's *Aleph*. It appeared later (in the sequence of my readings) in the work of Alanus ab Insulis (*auctor-actor* in *The Name,* where I met him again) and also in *Le Roman de la rose,* whose title is an anagram of *The Name of the Rose:* Jean de Meun quoting Alanus's "theological rule" (of doubtful origin, as we saw): "God is a sphere whose center. . . ."[12] It's that simple.

c. Speculum humilitatis

Seized by metaphysical vertigo at the prospect of such an undertaking, I chose linearity over sphericity—praised be the Lord that written texts are by nature—*naturaliter*—linear. I can only summon the reader to follow the monastic order of *The Name* and to detect in it the forking paths, all the not-actualized possibilities or possible developments that were sacrificed at every turn in the labyrinth, when one direction was chosen over some other possible one in accordance with some code, the result being as aleatory as a lottery—that of Babylon, for instance. So the reader has to speculate on all the possibilities of a not-(yet)-written novel.

d. Speculum Iacobi Bondis

On the gaudy cover of the American paperback edition, *The Name* is hailed as the greatest mystery novel ever.[13] The illustration is taken from the illuminated manuscript of a Spanish Apocalypse, as the copyright page informs us, and shows an angel throwing hail on a courtly scene of musicians and dancing couples—in the courtyard of a Benedictine abbey. This entertainment-style Apocalypse forms the background for the portrait of a very American macho-looking monk hold-

12. The rule can be found in Abbé Jacques Paul Migne, *Patrologiae cursus completus,* series latina, 221 vols. (Paris, 1844–1855), PL CCX 627 A, cited in Curtius, *Europäische Literatur,* 357.

13. Some people expressed astonishment at Eco's fascination with the popular character James Bond, insinuating that for a detective-semiotician there exist more appropriate, more sophisticated detective stories. Actually, Eco is interested in the narrative structures in Fleming and in characters like James Bond and Superman as socio-psychological phenomena to be investigated semiotically (Umberto Eco, *Travels in Hyperreality* [New York: Harcourt, 1986], 144–72).

ing an expensive baccarat rose in his hand. It is a mystery novel, true, but the word *mystery* is "undecidable." The mystery of Christ's incarnation cannot be interpreted. *Corpus Christi* is an object *credendi necessitatis;* its only evidence is in the Scriptures. The mystery of a crime can be solved by a detective/decipherer interpreting signs as indices, *corpora delicti.* His mode of action will be inference and speculation *iudicandi libertate* about possible worlds, "assumed states of affairs or possible course of events depending on propositional attitudes."[14] But what if the crime is committed in the name of Christ? Then there is a "nice, complicated knot" whose "unraveling" (476) needs first a look to the Scriptures, not only the holy ones, but any *auctoritas,* even if it is infidel.

The difference between a detective and a cleric interpreting scriptures lies in the degree of respect for the *auctoritas* of signs in general. While the former will consider any material to be indices, the latter (unless he is exclusively devoted to *traditio,* like Jorge de Burgos) will look for the signifying intention (*Bedeutungsintention* in Husserl's sense)—even that implied in the material trace, but, more obviously so, in the written mark. As William of Baskerville says: "Books are not made to be believed, but to be subjected to inquiry. When we consider a book, we musn't ask ourselves what it says, but what it means" (380). What it "means" is what it "wants to say," its *vouloir-dire.*[15]

William of Baskerville, just like his homologue Lönnrot in Borges's "La muerte y la brújula" (Death and the compass), is at first misled by the tendency to presuppose too much signifying intention (or intention to conceal, which comes to the same thing). They are too narrow in their speculation on possible entailments of these presupposed intentions. Obnubilated by meaning, by what they perceive as codes taken from books, Baskerville and Lönnrot tend to discard one possible world: the one of mere contingency.

Possible attitudes toward signs cover the whole spectrum: from humble, self-forgetting copying of signs of revealed truth, the attitude of the copying monk (repetition only, not transposition according to any code, much less interpretation), to hermeneutics (highly coded, hence restricted interpretation) and heuristics (the art of finding new elements by methodical hypotheses, the freedom of projecting and rejecting possible worlds and the corresponding codes). Heuristics implies the legitimacy of an *als ob* (as if) philosophy,[16] which comes close to fic-

14. Eco, *The Role of the Reader,* 219. The American translation of *The Name* leaves out a semiotically crucial passage concerning "possible worlds" on p. 110. Other such significant lacunae of the manuscript occur on pp. 120 and 279.

15. Jacques Derrida, *Positions* (Paris: Minuit, 1972), 23.

16. Hans Vaihinger, *Die Philosophie des Als Ob* (Berlin: Reuther and Reichard, 1911).

tion, Borgesian fiction in particular, that is, glosses on imaginary plots or enigmas. With this technique, one may reconstitute an unknown horse, for instance, or rewrite a nonread and possibly nonexisting book. This type of heuristics may be, and usually is, combined with empirical inferences.

Thus, those who find in *The Name* what allured them on the paperback cover, namely, the most fantastic mystery story ever, are right. So are those who find in it the most fantastic theological and ontological dialectic or *The Battle of the Books*. The link is semiotics; witness Adso's ambiguous promise to "leave to those who will come after . . . signs of signs, so that the *prayer of deciphering* may be exercised upon them" (4, my emphasis).

"What a magnificent librarian you would have been, William," Jorge de Burgos grudgingly admits (567) to the heuristic, Anglo-Saxon, empiricist investigator Baskerville—William of Baskerville, or James Bond, alias Sean Connery, in the "intermediality" (if you allow that neologism for something like inter-media-textuality) of the screen-mirrored novel. Nothing could be more Eco-esque than that ironically compressed compilation of incongruous identities, probably sufficient reason for Eco to sacrifice Baskerville's initial physical image, which is strongly suggestive of Don Quixote: tall, skinny, "having perhaps seen fifty springs" (9), and certainly ingenious. Isn't Baskerville, after all, a Knight of the Woeful Countenance, relentlessly fighting some Knight of the Mirrors in the pursuit of the utopia of reality?

I doubt whether my postulate that crime investigation and theology are functionally homologous unqualifiedly applies. I do not know about their reversibility—whether James Bond would have been "a magnificent theologist." But there is more involved than a mere analogy of method. It is a certain mode of being determined by a common finality: the quest for truth, or Truth. The capital question is whether to capitalize (or not) one letter of the alphabet—out of which arises an unfathomable world of difference, as in the change from minuscule *n* to minuscule *t* in the *nunc* and *tunc* of Paul mirrored by Augustine.

II. *IN AENIGMATE*

a. Speculum naturale

We tend to identify nature and reality as what *is there*: the *materia prima* or *hyle* offered to empirical observation in contradistinction to the products of the mind. The latter come to inscribe themselves on that material basis. In a Borgesian—or Benedictine—universe, the *hyle* consists of books. In *Historia universal de la infamia* (A universal history of infamy), Borges gives the "biographies" of gangsters, slave traders, and murderers. Each story is presented as real, that is, based on books. It is in that sense that I understand *speculum naturale* here, even at the risk of Nature's complaint (*Planctus Naturae* by . . . Alanus).

This *speculum* seemingly differs from that of Adso, who finds "the praise of the Creator sung by the dog and the ox, the sheep and the lamb and the lynx" (339). But actually it is the same: Adso is seeing nature in terms of a book, precisely the *Speculum naturale* by Vincent de Beauvais, who is the *auctoritas* of my speculative order but referred to only once in *The Name,* in connection with the ox. The same holds for Adso's own *speculum amoris:* what is nature? The wretched girl's hair "is a flock of goats that lie along the side of Mount Gilead" (291). Her "neck is the tower of David," and more such biblical delights arouse Adso. A girl of flesh and blood is more exotic a world than what Adso has interiorized of Solomon's world—just as Eco, according to his own confession, is "at home in the 'real' world of the Middle Ages while knowing the contemporary world only through the intermediary of television." The monks recognize the abbot's concrete, living horse they see every day only when the ideal, literary image of horse is invoked, when William of Baskerville has "reconstituted his inexisting memory of it on the basis of books." "Big eyes, flaring nostrils"—that is the code of the finest Arabian horse, as established by Isidore of Seville of the school of Chartres (19). It is absolutely natural that the horse bears the name of an ass taken from Nigellus Wireker's *Speculum stultorum* (fool's mirror) and is meant to kick the Parisian theologians, who are the bêtes noires of Roger Bacon and Oxford.

Eco denies the capacity of the ordinary mirror to produce signs, because the semiotically necessary relation between an antecedent pointing to a consequent is not given, and because "the mirror image is present in the presence of a referent which cannot be absent."[17] The mirror is a mere prosthesis—like William's "forked pin holding two almonds of glass," which is Adso's perception of his master's eyeglasses (82). Therefore it cannot be used to lie, whereas signs can. It is this impossibility of corruption that explains the fascination with mirrors of the greatest thinkers, from Plato to Notker Balbulus, all of whose incorruptible mirrors are offered to us for our edification and moral improvement.

Such priestly zeal can hardly be imputed to Borges or Eco, who are more interested in mirrors that can lie. In "La muerte y la brújula" detective Lönnrot's speculation, which adopts a talmudic text as a code for the interpretation of the criminal's scheme, leads him correctly and fatally to the house of the criminal, which, like our Benedictine abbey,

17. Eco, *Semiotics and Philosophy,* 214, 216.

"had an abundance of useless symmetries and maniacal repetitions . . . Lönnrot multiplied himself infinitely in mirrors facing each other" (*F.S* 157–58). These are mirrors that are used in order to lie. Instead of leading to close observation, to truth, they create confusion, just as the library of the abbey is used to hide knowledge rather than to radiate it, which infuriates William of Baskerville, the lover of enlightenment. Here the diabolic mind of Jorge de Burgos uses a combination of distorting mirrors and hallucinatory drugs to protect the forbidden part of the library, coded as *finis Africae*. That code refers to a place where the most dangerous pagan and infidel authors are hidden, in order to keep them "nullius animi curiositate violata."[18] No one should come close to those pillars of Hercules that are possibly decodable as the legendary threat to the simple sailor—in other words, Gibraltar, where *finis Africae* meets Europe in Spain, whence the infidels subdued Christianity, corrupting it with mathematics, optics, cryptography, and the thought of the Jew Maimonides, of Averroës, Avicenna, and through them Aristotle. Jorge's very Catholic city of Burgos was to become instrumental in the Reconquest, the Inquisition, and the resulting delay of free, humanistic thinking. For the defense of the forbidden, *finis Africae,* Jorge de Burgos, matching his adversary's training in Eco's semiotics, seems to have taken the recipe directly from *Semiotics and the Philosophy of Language*:

> Freaks, distorting mirrors.
> Mirror images are not signs and signs are not mirror images. And yet there are cases when mirrors are used to produce processes which can be defined as semiotic.
> The first peculiar case is that of distorting mirrors whose amazing effects were already observed by Arab [!] physicists and in *Le Roman de la rose.* [!][19]

Hallucinatory substances, such as certain herbs, possess the undecidable quality of healing and poisoning, designated by one Greek word, *pharmakon* . . . in that they are like books, like writing in general, as we discovered in "Plato's Pharmacy," a Derridian/Platonic intertextual play later grafted onto *The Name.*[20] The combined effects of treacherous glasses and treacherous grasses at the approach of *finis Africae* are further enhanced by the mirror of art, the marginalia of various Moorish/Christian Apocalypses depicting the *mulier amicta* and—knockout for Adso—the *Speculum amoris.*

Finally our detective team "owes to the conjunction of a mirror and

18. Beauvais, *De eruditione,* 55.
19. Eco, *Semiotics and Philosophy,* 217.
20. Jacques Derrida, *La Dissémination* (Paris: Seuil, 1972), 70–197 (78–79).

an encyclopedia the discovery" not of the imaginary continent of Uqbar but of *finis Africae* and the ever-elusive forbidden book, that "purloined letter," lost, found, and lost again (*F.S* 13). Among all the possible interpretations of the code "Supra idolum viginti quatuor" (Above the mirror four are watching), the interpretation taking "idolum" for eidolon was the right one. It resulted from the speculation that Venantius was thinking in Greek. This is an operation of "overcoding" (taking into account Venantius's psychological particularity and his state of mind at the moment of encoding). Indeed, eidolon is not only "image" and "mirror," but also something like "ghost." So *finis Africae* was beyond the distorting mirror where, with the additional conditioning by the herbs, Baskerville and Adso perceived themselves as "ghosts." Unlike others who before them had been scared away by that experience, they found the *finis* toward which tended the whole eschatological structure of *The Name:* the revelation of the criminal plot (enigma), the apocalypse of the "mirror of the universe," the destruction by fire (*ekpyrosis*) of the library.

It is in the nature of an encyclopedia to be unlimited; in that of a mirror to be limited, to have a frame. The frame of *The Name* (which as an encyclopedia is nothing less than a history of eternity, "a delicate and secret mirror of what happened in their souls" [*He* 35]) is the beginning of the absolute Beginning, the first words of the genesis according to Saint John and the end, the speculated, absolute, extreme end (*eschaton*), the Apocalypse of Saint John. In order to mirror the *multum in parvo,* or rather *infinitum in parvo,* Eco chose a more humanly accessible possible world with a parody of the use of time in the so-called realist novel. Here, the human frame within the cosmic frame is the clichéd beginning of the first chapter: "It was a beautiful morning at the end of November." But that reasonable *modus ponens* (way of positing a proposition) is immediately blown up by the division into seven days, the time of the Creation. Those seven days, piously subdivided into "primes," "terces," are a possible *speculum naturale,* because it is conceivable they were lived by conceivable individuals in the historical anno Domini 1327.

The cosmogonic frame finds its symmetry in the *speculum doctrinale* of the first and last confrontation between the two great antagonists William of Baskerville and Jorge de Burgos. The first dialogue sets the doctrinal problematics; the last resolves it in the *Revelation* (Apocalypsis). The "use of mirrors in the game of chess" determines the moves where Jorge de Burgos has a decisive advantage: he knows exactly the rules of the game and the identity of the antagonist. William of Baskerville does not know either—he can only make inferences from fragmentary and unreliable evidence; he can speculate, trying and rejecting various possible codes, deciphering various cryptographs; and he can invent:

> "We would have to test them all, and others besides. But the first rule in deciphering a message is to guess what it means . . . A rule of correspondence has to be found."
> "Found where?"
> "In our heads. Invent it." (191–92)

To invent is to "assume a fictional world (state of affairs, course of events) as the real one. . . . Both worlds, though modally different, depend on inferential walks."[21]

But such fiction risks an excess of attributed meaning, an overinterpretation of contingent data. An encyclopedist mind, in particular, is susceptible to falling prey to the demon of analogy, to causality, to seeing connections where there are none. Lönnrot's and Baskerville's single flaw is their tendency to project into a situation a coherence corresponding to a code. Thus they become, unwittingly, the ones who set the rules of the game to which diabolically complacent counterplayers conform. Within this framework, the fanatic, blind Jorge de Burgos sees clearly—as if *facie ad faciem*—while the enlightened scientist, even when helped by an optical prosthesis, is groping his way from enigma to enigma. In fact, Adso does not quite know what exactly his master is searching for, and occasionally suspects him not to know himself, especially when Baskerville declares himself to be "close to the solution but not to know which one" (367).

The Borgesian/Babylonian notion of the library as labyrinth is concretely actualized in the Benedictine library, in conformity with Eco's blueprint of the encyclopedia as labyrinth. It corresponds to the third type of labyrinth (as opposed to Theseus's linear Greek labyrinth and the Germanic *Irrgarten* or maze). It is a "net . . . or *meander* . . . whose main feature is that every point can be connected with every other point, and when the connections are not yet designed, they are, however, conceivable [possible worlds]. A net is an unlimited territory . . . *it has neither center nor outside*."[22] This is strangely reminiscent of "a sphere whose center is . . ."

"*Blindness is the only way of seeing* [locally] and *thinking means to grope one's way*." This is Eco's description of the only way of coping with the "myopic algorithm" represented by this type of labyrinth. It is obviously the blind Jorge de Burgos who impersonates this art. He is thus the master of this "universe of semiosis" that is "the universe of

21. Eco, *The Role of the Reader*, 217–19.
22. Eco, *Semiotics and Philosophy*, 81 (my emphasis).

culture which must be conceived as structured like a labyrinth . . . according to a network of interpretants [and that] is virtually infinite."[23]

This universe of semiosis is, then, an endless network of forking paths where the interpreter must choose his future direction at every node. This is why the ideally open book would be a novel containing all possibilities of development. To write such a novel is synonymous with building a labyrinth—which is precisely the endeavor of Ts'ui Pên, governor of Yunan in "El jardín de senderos que se bifurcan" (*F.S* 106).

b. *Speculum doctrinale*

As Borges is "The God of the Labyrinth," according to Jean Ricardou,[24] the passages about labyrinths are key points linking Eco's semiotic theories to his novel. The novel was an accident, the fruit of his abandoning himself for once to "sheer narrative pleasure" (xviii)—that *goût fabulateur* (taste for telling stories) or Bergson's *fonction fabulatrice* (fiction-making function), which seems an escape from the rigor of codes. "Hier bin ich Mensch, hier darf ich's sein" (Here I am a human being, here I can be) as Goethe's Faust exclaims with relief after leaving his study for a pleasant walk outside the medieval city walls on Easter Sunday. But beware: *fabula* is one of the translations of Aristotle's *enigma*. Baskerville repeatedly insists that precisely the *als ob* (as if) faculty of fiction is necessary to the detective interpreting signs; that imagination, grafted onto skeptically ventured hypotheses, guarantees him against the danger of ideological bias. Baskerville refuses to take for the absolute truth the "local" view that is available at a single node of the net. "Local" (Husserl would say "regional") truths are always parochial, discriminating, oppressive, and xenophobic: the contrary of genuine *cat'holicism* (oriented toward the whole world, *orbis et urbis*) and of ecumenical *aggiornamento* (the openness of the mind and adaptation to history). Baskerville reads signs and their combinations as *opera aperta*. He rejects dogma—the closed, circumscribed, intellectual, or religious region that established *auctoritate* as universally and absolutely binding; the totalitarianism of a "great inquisitor" or a Jorge de Burgos.

To Baskerville's skeptical mind, the direct equivalence assumed by the *Liber Mundi* is acceptable at best at a very indirect metaphorical level, as a metaphor of a metaphor of a metaphor joined by metonymic contiguities. To him truth lies not in signs alone but in the relation between them (599). When he has finally found the code of Venantius's

---

23. Ibid., 82, 82, 83 (my emphasis).
24. *L'Herne: Jorge Luis Borges* (Paris, 1964): 25–26.

cryptogram (the notes on the forbidden book), he still possesses only signs of signs. The following Greek text consists of mysterious references. Yet "this page is the only possible starting point in re-creating the nature of the mysterious book, and it's only from the nature of that book that we will be able to infer the nature of the murderer" (341). Fragments of references to a nonread book, like those to the unknown and possibly nonexisting continent of Uqbar, evoke in Baskerville's mind a *déjà lu* (already-read), however faint. "Books speak of books; it is as if they spoke among themselves" (342) is his definition of intertextuality. But, even if he remembers, he will not be able, without an idea of the contextual frame, to re-create that unknown book using only other ones he did read. And since that context is the very reason for hiding the book, the contextual selection is most important. It is most likely to be of a doctrinal nature, since in the abbey life (nature) and the teachings of the books coincide. Starting the argument the other way round, this assumption may in turn yield an insight into the nature of the book. The conjecture—books as origin of the crime—is more to Baskerville's taste than a banal explanation based on empirical facts. This, as Borges's detective Lönnrot tells the police commissioner, expressing the stubborn quixotism of all intellectuals in the world, would be:

> possible, but not interesting. You will object that reality does not have the slightest obligation to be interesting. I will say that reality is not obliged to be interesting, but hypotheses are. In the one you improvised, mere coincidence accounts for almost everything. Here we are faced with a dead rabbi; I would prefer a purely rabbinical explanation, not the imaginary mischiefs of a banal imaginary criminal. (*FS* 149)

The newly deciphered zodiacal cryptogram and the fragments of Greek having as yet not yielded an interesting hypothesis and being heterogeneous in relation to his tentatively adopted, (interesting) code (the Apocalypse), Baskerville goes on expecting things to happen in accordance with the sequence of Saint John's book ("The first angel sounded the first trumpet"), just as Lönnrot goes on conforming to references to the *Tetragrammaton* ("The first letter of the Name has been articulated" [*FS* 150]). Unfortunately for them, so do their respective counterplayers, who have understood the schemes imputed to them, the imaginary code. They post factum cloak their actions—which were prompted by sheer contingencies of reality—into the bookish logic imagined *ante factum* by the interpreters. "There was no plot" (enigma), Baskerville realizes at the end, "and I discovered it by mistake" (599). This is strictly speaking an agrammatical statement, a semantic paradox, yet it is the truth. This is characteristic of Borges's and Eco's flawless juggling of ontology. "I understood," says Scharlach the crimi-nal to Lönnrot, "that you conjectured that the Hasidim had sacrificed the rabbi. I devoted myself to the justification of your conjecture" (*F. S* 161).

Actually, Scharlach and Jorge de Burgos are super–model readers of *opera aperta,* which Eco defines as "a syntactico-semantic-pragmatic device whose foreseen interpretation is a part of its generative pro-cess."[25] But both in "La muerte" and in *The Name* there is a Borgesian inversion (*Aufhebung*) of authorship. One may just as well consider Lönnrot and Baskerville as model readers—but of a nonwritten text. More exactly, they are writing glosses on imaginary texts. Their adver-saries subsequently re-create the text from these fragments. Thus Lönn-rot and Baskerville, believing that they deal interpretatively with the text, actually deal with it generatively.

It is the professional criminal investigator Lönnrot who becomes the fatal victim of his own theologico-heuristic bias, by which he sticks to the letter of talmudic scriptures with the zeal of the neophyte, simply because a spiritual explanation mirrors a more interesting possible world than accidental events. Baskerville, in contrast, is saved by his discovery in extremis that he must switch codes. From now on he has to re-create the text by overcoding it; by taking Jorge de Burgos's psy-chological and, above all, doctrinal attitudes into account as well as his hatred of philosophy and his fear of laughter. These are "uncoded determinants of interpretation."[26]

What distinguishes Borges's and Eco's detective fiction from ordi-nary mystery stories is the intertwining of the three types of codes explained by Eco—paleographic, correlational, and institutional.[27] The correlational code (such as the Morse code or a cryptogram) is, in its simplest form, a system of equivalences. There is an encoded mes-sage, and the decoder's competence consists in the knowledge of the transcriptional rule. "Transcriptions can be realized by either transposi-tion or substitution."[28] An example of transposition would be the ana-gram. For instance, *Le Nom de la rose* is a partial anagram of *Le Roman de la rose,* the quintessential French novel. Thus the correlational code by far exceeds the possibilities of simple equivalence, considering all the intertextual mechanisms, all the connotations, interpretative pos-sibilities, and psychological effects unleashed by association—both in the encoder (his *Bedeutungsintention*) and in the reader (his reception) since both are determined by all possible conditioning and contexts.

25. Eco, *The Role of the Reader,* 3.
26. Ibid., 22; Eco, *A Theory of Semiotics,* 129.
27. Eco, *Semiotics and Philosophy,* 165.
28. Ibid., 172.

Here, we are already in the domain of overcoding. Psychological and ideological determinants of interpretation (which by their very nature are uncoded) call for overcoding, which is usually a supplementary practice to the three basic codes, just as "undercoding" is the rough application of an insufficiently understood code.[29] In the ordinary mystery story correlational codes prevail in the interpretation of signs and indices. Yet the most simple mystery, pushed a bit in Borgesian fashion, may lead to a vertigo of codes and diabolic inversion. *Don Quixote* by Cervantes is clearly a consequent of *Don Quixote* by Pierre Menard.

It is the degree of complexity in interaction (or mirroring) between the three types of codes, their subcodes, and their kaleidoscopic combinations that distinguishes Borges's and Eco's stories as ontological, quasi-metaphysical sleights of hand, relegating the criminal mystery to the rank of a pre-text (in both the chronological acceptation and the moral one of *mauvaise foi* [bad faith]). The mystery is a pretext, just as the Middle Ages can be. There are "ten little Middle Ages" perceived by Eco, one of them "the Middles Ages as pretext." Each of these ten little Middle Ages can be unearthed in *The Name,* to mention only the characteristic "expectation of the millennium."[30]

All such semiotic considerations lead Baskerville to finally seek the possible motivations of the crimes in the clashing doctrines concerning the Book of Books. The very first words pronounced by Jorge de Burgos at the first encounter with Baskerville and Adso form the doctrinal key sentence, "Verba vana aut risui apta non loqui" (87). These are the words of austere Saint Benedict of Nursia, founder of the Benedictine order.[31] His rule (an institutional code) was for the monk "not to pronounce words that are vain or susceptible to produce laughter." In the "game of chess" against Baskerville, Jorge de Burgos's quote of Benedict's rule is the opening move. He plays white, the purely dogmatic. Baskerville's ecumenism in contrast is contaminated, if not quite by black magic, at least by Moorish science and a corrosive tendency toward humor. Indeed, it does not escape the blind seer that Baskerville comes "from another order," and he seems to refer to more than just the classification of the various official Christian orders. For Jorge de Burgos, the world has but one order, so coming from another order is belonging to the Antichrist.

As a rule, totalitarian fanatics destroy even the faint sympathy or admiration one might possibly feel for their sacred fire by the inevitable

29. Eco, *A Theory of Semiotics,* 129.
30. Eco, *Travels in Hyperreality,* 68, 72.
31. Curtius, *Europäische Literatur,* 385.

use of blackmail. Jorge de Burgos reminds Adso of a namesake, Adso of Montier-en-Der, author of the *Libellus de Antichristo,* a warning that, according to Jorge, had not been sufficiently heeded, and he menaces: "He [the Antichrist] is coming! Do not waste your last days laughing" (93).

William and Adso have heard this prophesy not only from the diabolically inverted blind seer but also from others. One of them was Salvatore, the inverted image of the Savior, with his Babelish "Penitenziagite," his "Watch out for the *draco* [dragon] who cometh in futurum" (47), and, in the same breath, "Jesus venturus est [will come] et les hommes must do penitenzia" (49). They perceive the same prophesy later in the distorted mirror of senile Alinardo's mutterings. With all these fragments supporting Jorge de Burgos's prophesy, the psychological atmosphere—an unstructured code—becomes compelling.

Whereas among the other Benedictine monks and their Franciscan and Dominican visitors the doctrinal conflict arises mainly around the question of whether Jesus could have owned property (the Lord's poverty reported by the apostles singularly contrasts with the opulence of His servants in the abbey), Jorge de Burgos's violent concern is with laughter as an emanation of the Antichrist. Baskerville, his tolerance taking into account all possible worlds, points to Christ as the Son of Man and draws the Aristotelian inference of the possibility of His laughter, since "laughter is the proper of man" (108). But blind Jorge de Burgos's ultralucidity always makes him identify his enemy; he knows he has one infinitely more dangerous than Baskerville. Like any master player, he has studied the other's techniques and learned the history of all his moves by heart. So he is prepared to ward off the blow: "Quomodo ergo eo uti non potuit? Forte potuit, sed non legitur eo usus fuisse" (Why is it impossible that He could have laughed? He perfectly could have. But it is not written that He ever made use of that possibility).[32] Characteristically valuing the letter over the possibility of interpretation, he replies, "The Son of Man could laugh, very possibly so, but it is not *written* that he did" (108). The twelfth-century compiler (*compilator*) Petrus Cantor, whom he quotes, could not have listed in his *Verbum abbreviatum* (the abridged Word) a sentence more ideally exploitable by semioticians of possible worlds than precisely that "forte potuit sed non legitur eo usus fuisse."

Jorge de Burgos's linking of laughter with the imminence of the Apocalypse and the already-felt presence of the Antichrist within the community constitutes one panel of the *speculum doctrinale.* The other panel is Baskerville's prehumanistic trust in the freedom and

---

32. Ibid., 424.

responsibility of man through the acquisition of knowledge, not exclusively in the service of theology as demanded by Augustine, Hieronymus, and others, but for its own sake, *animi curiositate*.[33]

In Jorge de Burgos's universe, in contrast, doubts do not exist. His harangue to the respectfully assembled hosts and visitors, the papal delegation, is the apotheosis of dogma:

> In this community the serpent of pride has coiled. . . . Our work is the preservation of knowledge. Preservation, I say, not search for, because the property of knowledge as a divine thing is that it is complete and has been defined since the beginning. . . . There is no progress . . . but a most continuous and sublime recapitulation. . . . There is only to gloss, preserve. (482)

So where would there be a place for laughter? Who feels like laughing when "the cycle of the universe is about to be fulfilled?" (485). But what is the beast Jorge de Burgos is after? Is it intellectual pride, emancipation from mere recapitulation, independent thinking, *animi curiositas*? Or is it laughter? In fact, it comes to the same thing. Not for the simple, whose laughter is the result of a full stomach and a lot of wine. But intellectual pride and laughter are linked, and that combination will be allowed only over Jorge de Burgos's dead body—literally. Laughter is either vulgar or perverted, a nervous spasm of the diaphragm. It cannot be good, that is, put to the service of God. And if it is possible that some *auctoritas* presented laughter as something positive, something helping us understand truth, it is not written that any real *auctoritas* has ever done so. Some fools or infidels may have done so. If there were written proof of a work on laughter by a serious *auctoritas,* it would have to be hidden, if necessary destroyed, including all clues leading to it. Someone like Jorge de Burgos is bound to perceive laughter as an emanation of the Antichrist: it is uncanny not only because it cannot be coded into any equivalence but also because it dissolves all codes, codexes, laws.

Here is the link between laughter and intellectual pride: the self-confidence of the searcher. He may suddenly find himself confronted with something incongruous—two semiotic systems, incommensurable but partly superposed (what Julia Kristeva calls *position en catastrophe*), the overlapping part being unaccounted for in either system. This produces the comic, such as the comic of certain incongruous enumerations relished by Borges and Eco, or the effect of Adelmo's illuminations of marginalia representing human beings with animal heads and vice versa (partly superposing two systems like two grids). Did Adso not feel that these marginalia "*naturally* inspire merriment, though they were commenting on holy pages" (86, my emphasis)? But since

33. Beauvais, *De eruditione,* xv.

there can be only one system—the one given by the prophets and commented on by the Church fathers—there can be no *position en catastrophe. Verbum unum et sanctum.*

Baskerville, however, perceives that "it is through the excess of virtue itself that the forces of hell prevail" (584):

> I have seen [the Antichrist's] face tonight: Jorge's face. In that face deformed by the hatred of philosophy I saw for the first time the portrait of the Antichrist . . . who does not come from the tribe of Judas or a far-away country. The Antichrist can be born from piety itself, from the excessive love of God or of the truth, as the heretic is born from the saint. . . . Fear prophets, Adso, and those prepared to die for the truth, for as a rule they make others die with them, before them, at times instead of them. (598)

One cannot help thinking of all those terrorist suicide squads that have been sent out to the world by the great warlords of Holy Wars, who themselves usually manage to survive the Holy War, to become as old as Khomeini did in any old or new Middle Ages.

Is the answer, then, the systematic doubt inherent in unlimited semiosis? This may lead away from bloody sanctity and toward a bloodless, spineless secular relativism—"Possible, but not interesting." But that is a moral question, and writers and philosophers throughout the ages have accommodated themselves rather well to the absence of morals. What they are unable to bear is the absence of form—form that can be apperceived, reduced to a scheme, mirrored by some *speculum,* translated into signs; recuperated in order to satisfy the instinct of the semiotic animal. "If this abbey were a *speculum mundi,* you would already have the answer," says Baskerville. "But is it?" asks Adso. "In order for there to be a mirror of the world, it is necessary that the world have a form," concludes William (136). That is the melancholy resignation of somebody who, nevertheless, goes on in his quixotic pursuit of signs of truth, the Knight of the Woeful Countenance, the figure who is loved by more people than any other because he makes people laugh more than any other. "Perhaps the mission of those who love mankind is to make people laugh . . . *to make truth laugh,* because the only truth lies in learning to free ourselves from the insane passion for the truth" (598, my emphasis).[34]

Earlier I showed the functional homologies between detective and semiotic practices and suggested a link between their common characteristics and theology. That link is the presupposition of an order, of

34. Michel Foucault indicates a text by Borges as the birth place of his seminal book *Les Mots et les choses,* "dans le rire qui secoue à sa lecture toutes les familiarités de la pensée" (in the laughter that shatters, while reading it, all the habits of thought). Michel Foucault, *Les Mots et les choses* (Paris: Gallimard, 1966), preface.

one single "absolute signified" (a Husserlian term) from which to derive signifiers and to devise codes for the relations between them.[35] Semioticians and detectives, even if accepting unlimited semiosis, must first act *as if* such an order existed, so as to be able to give an orientation to their pursuit and to decide about even its most elementary steps. But, in addition to the *as if* element, which is an element of *fiction,* what the semiotic instinct leads to is the eternal, basic dilemma of faith: "It is hard to accept the idea that there cannot be an order in the universe, because it would offend the free will of God and His omnipotence. So the freedom of God is our condemnation, or at best, the condemnation of our pride. But how," asks Adso, "can a necessary being exist that is totally a texture of possibles?[36] What difference is there, then, between God's absolute omnipotence and primal chaos? . . . Is it not demonstrating that God does not exist?" (600). Baskerville reacts to this with an expressionless (blind) look—across his optical prosthesis (same category as the mirror, according to Eco) and answers with an aporia. He knows only so much: we must go on acting *as if, in aenigmate.*

III. *FACIE AD FACIEM*

"I want to see the second book of the Poetics of Aristotle" (567). In the final showdown between the two grand antagonists the forbidden name has at last been pronounced. Jorge de Burgos has been waiting for William of Baskerville in the labyrinth's most forbidden place, *finis Africae,* beyond the mirror, just as the criminal Scharlach was waiting for the final face-to-face encounter with Lönnrot in the labyrinth of the house of the mirroring symmetries, both criminals having acted *as if* they were following the plan imagined by their counterplayers.

Never before has Jorge de Burgos condescended to the revelation of his secret: not to those he manipulated with contempt like pawns on a chessboard. Having at last found in Baskerville an adversary worthy of himself—William has re-created the unknown book on comedy by the same technique he used before to re-create the unknown horse—Jorge de Burgos makes his confession: not one of humility, but one of pride. Such is, indeed, the power of the Antichrist that human vanity almost makes the two men forget the tragic series of deaths and the divine Word itself, object of their gigantic fight, over their mutual quest for admiration of their strategies, their semiotic competence. The most startling diabolic inversion in this deadly face-to-face encounter be-

35. Edmund Husserl, *Husserliana, Gesammelte Werke* (The Hague: Martinus Nijhoff, 1950-).

36. I am deviating here from the English translation, "polluted with the possible," preferring the French one of "tissu de possibles," a texture of possibles, something "woven" together, as Beauvais's *contextum, concatenatum.*

tween two sworn enemies is that there arises something like affection, a mutual identification born from the interpenetration of their beings in their finally true confessions—something almost suggesting love. This is not the banal love of the victim for the torturer, since the positional values in that game are undecidable. It is not the identification of analyst and analysand, since subject and object of this "text" are intertwined. It may be, as it clearly is in the confrontation between Scharlach and Lönnrot, the complicity or "cooperative activity performed by the reader in actualizing a text."[37] This is a *reflexive* (mirror) phenomenon, since *auctor, actor,* and *lector* regularly exchange positions as in a courtly minuet. It certainly is, and on both sides, pride. Pride brings us close to those we deem of equal rank.

Intertextual competence and the interpretation of signs that is based on it, *semiotics,* reveal themselves at the end of the novel as the criterion of their self-assessment and token of their pride. As its name (*onoma,* word, sign) indicates, *The Name* is a book on *semiotics* (science of signs). Signs, in relation to truth and as indices of various futures, are the theme of Borges, of all of his *ficciones.* Then, why is the word *semiotics* never pronounced or written? Because:

> In a riddle whose theme is chess, what is the only forbidden word?
> The word "chess." (*F.S* 114)

Why had Jorge de Burgos shielded, at the price of mass murder, that very book, one of several ones dealing with laughter, the one dealing with the soul-purifying, healing qualities of laughter? Because it was by the *Philosopher,* by the one who has diabolically inverted the true "image of the world" transmitted by the Church fathers (576). The manuscript of the second book of Aristotle's *Poetics* (of which the only copy in the world is in the abbey's library) had been discovered in Spain long ago and hidden in *finis Africae* by Jorge de Burgos. From William of Baskerville, who "writes" that second book in a manner comparable to the technique of Pierre Menard, we learn that it is a complement to Aristotle's known book on tragedy, that is, dealing with comedy and satire. As tragedy was said to purify our feelings in a catharsis produced by fear and pity, comedy is supposed to have a correlative effect, because "by inspiring the pleasure of the ridiculous it arrives at the purification of that passion." In other words, laughter has an edifying function beneficial even to the most pious Christian, and that is the heresy to be combated by fire and sword.

The manuscript, which had reached the Christian world through the intermediary of infidels, is, significantly, bound together with and hid-

37. Eco, *The Role of the Reader,* 39.

den under an Arabic and a Syriac text. Being by the Philosopher, if accessible, it would have a formidable power: "What in the villain is an operation of the belly would be transformed into an operation of the brain" (577). Like any reactionary, Jorge de Burgos is elitist: "The simple must not speak. This book would have justified the idea that the tongue of the simple is a vehicle of wisdom. This had to be prevented. Which I have done" (582). To Jorge de Burgos, this book has the spiritual "poison of a thousand scorpions." So he imbued its pages with a physically lethal poison as strong as that of a thousand scorpions, stolen from the herborist's collection of *pharmaka* and coming from the infidels.

"You are the Devil," William of Baskerville says in an ultimate inversion, launching against Jorge de Burgos his own accusation of pride. "The Devil is the arrogance of the spirit, faith without smile, truth that is never seized by doubt" (581).

In that final encounter of the diabolically perverted collaboration where the identities of hunter and victim, author and reader, become undecidable, or where as coauthors they comply with each other's plans, Scharlach is more obliging than Jorge de Burgos. He directly executes Lönnrot by way of the strict execution of the plan for an alternative possible world involving another labyrinth imagined by the latter. Lönnrot's cooperative suggestion that Scharlach, when he kills him next time, use not a quadrangular lozenge as a scheme but the linear labyrinth of the Greek (the Theseus labyrinth as described by Eco)[38] is loyally executed by application of the optimal linear possibility: a gunshot.

Jorge de Burgos, too, is thoroughgoing in his faithful execution of both his own plan and the one imputed to him by William of Baskerville. By swallowing the pages imbued with the poison of a thousand scorpions, he hides the forbidden book forever. By throwing Adso's oil lamp on a disorderly pile of books, he sets off the *Apocalypse*.

IV. *EUCALYPTOS*

Eu-kalyptos means that which is well hidden, protected from revelation (*apokalypsis*), and from *animi curiositatis*. What code should one apply in the interpretation of Borges's obsession with that plant, the most innocent *pharmakon* against sore throats? Should one start by trying a sentimental or aesthetic overcoding—the eucalyptus tree being the most genuinely Argentine plant, its gracefully moving silhouette a distinguishing accent of subtropical landscapes, "The South" in particular, a childhood attachment, one of Borges's habits of memory, "the

38. Eco, *Semiotics and Philosophy*, 80.

balsamic eucalyptus" around the large, rose-colored house? (*F.S* 196). Or are these leaves, turning leathery once they have fallen from the tree (*codex* originally means "stem"), reminiscent of parchment, suggesting fragments of manuscripts that rustle when you walk through them? On his way to the fatal encounter, Lönnrot "walked forward between the eucalyptus, stepping on confounded generations of broken, rigid leaves" (*F.S* 157). Confounded generations of leaves (pages), that is, intertextuality.

On the "last leaf" of the *(Name of) The Rose*, we see Adso, now a grown man, his feet shuffling through the parched parchments in the circular ruins of what was once the library of the abbey, the citadel of wisdom, the pride of Christianity. He is in search of signs of signs: "At the end of my patient reconstruction I had before me a lesser kind of library made up of fragments, quotations, unfinished sentences, amputated stumps of books" (609).

The signs of signs are well hidden (eu-kalyptos) as if by Jorge Luis Borges, so that they may become open to interpretation, speculation, fiction. We definitely have to eliminate the institutional code that leads to the single truth as a possibility for Borges's associations with eucalyptus or any other matter. To Jorge de Burgos's fanatic defense of the taboo of the sacred (institution, *traditio, auctoritas*) where there is "no progress . . . but only preservation," William of Baskerville might have answered in Borges's words: "The theologians affirm that the conservation of this world is a perpetual creation, and that the verbs 'to conserve' and 'to create,' so inimical here, are synonymous in Heaven" (*He* 35). A man who could unite those two verbs in practice was not yet born and is probably *innascibilis* (unable to be born), to use one last time a word, a marvelously agrammatical adjective, of Alanus ab Insulis. It could be Borges who might have invented a character "unable to be born." A possible world where such a character could conceivably live would be inaccessible to our world view of reference, our encyclopedia. But then, *innascibilis* is an attribute of God.

With Borges, however, one is led to believe in the "nascibility" of a possible world created only in order to produce a book.

III
In Dialogue
with Other Writers

Jerry Varsava

The Last Fictions
Calvino's Borgesian Odysseys

Attitudes toward the three components of literary exchange—the author, the text, the reader—have undergone fundamental alteration during the last two hundred years. In this century, critics and writers alike have come to question traditional views of literary production and innovation. Historically, many authors—notably certain of the Romantics—have emphasized the individual as the wellspring of literature. Though rarely stating as much, Romantic poetics implies for the author a social and cultural disembodiment. Here, literary endeavor succeeds where it escapes the mundane, where it embraces one or more absolute psychic conditions—the "aesthetic purity" of Schiller, or Shelley's "freedom of spirit," or the Emersonian "sublime vision."[1] Two important propositions are at the base of these various notions of authorial transcendence, namely the author's belief in his own divinity and the consequent view that the individual author originates textuality. Though usually fashioning a less ethereal rhetoric, nineteenth-century novelists also emphasize the personality of the author. Hawthorne, for example, in the estimation of Henry James, is a "beautiful, natural, original genius" whose life was free of "worldly preoccupations and vulgar efforts," whose work was "as pure, as simple, as unsophisticated" as his life.[2] One suspects James would have found these epithets accurate descriptions of his own life and work. Even Zola, in his manifesto on naturalism, admits a role, if muted, for "genius" and "personality."[3]

Early in this century, important essays—"Romanticism and Classicism" by T. E. Hulme and "Tradition and the Individual Talent" by T. S. Eliot—criticize Romantic and neo-Romantic poetics for their celebra-

1. Friedrich Schiller, *The Aesthetic Education of Man, in a Series of Letters,* trans. Elizabeth M. Wilkinson and L. A. Willoughby, in Hazard Adams, ed., *Critical Theory since Plato* (New York: Harcourt, 1971), 418–31 (428); Percy Bysshe Shelley, "A Defense of Poetry," in Adams, *Critical Theory,* 499–513 (503); Ralph Waldo Emerson, "The Poet," in Adams, *Critical Theory,* 545–54 (551–52).

2. Henry James, *Hawthorne* (New York: Collier-Macmillan, 1966), 155.

3. Emile Zola, "The Experimental Novel," trans. Belle M. Sherman, in Adams, *Critical Theory,* 647–59 (sec. iv).

tion of intuitionism and novelty. The assault continues today, but with different emphases. Structuralism, with its emphasis on the text, and poststructuralism, with its emphasis on the reader, also neglect the author and subvert claims of authorial originality and authorial divinity. Thinkers as diverse as Barthes, Foucault, Ricoeur, and Gadamer have all made significant revisionist statements on authorship, emphasizing the text-reader axis over the author-text and author-reader relationships. Though some readers of contemporary fiction, in focusing narrowly on discontinuity and radical innovation, still underestimate the historicity of reading and writing, interest in textuality and concern for the reader are indeed dominant trends today.

The two writers that concern me here are postmodern in their repudiation of the author, in their emphasis on literary tradition and the reader. Indeed, their narrative theories scoff at the very notion of authorial genius. Before looking at specific fictions and the narrative theories that support them, I offer a point of clarification. My title identifies Calvino's last fictions—*If on a winter's night a traveler* and *Mr. Palomar*—as "Borgesian odysseys," that is, emulations of a "trip" already taken by a specific author. My metaphor may seem to imply a narrow notion of influence wherein certain psychological compatibilities between Calvino and Borges have led the former to mimic the latter. Theirs is not, however, a son-father relationship. Such an interpretation of Calvino's work would not square well with the authors' own views on writing and philosophizing as expressed within and without their fiction. Tradition, literary and philosophical, is the seminal force in the work of each one.

Both Calvino and Borges are classicists, writers who find continuity a more potent force than its opposite, writers who see writing as an act of conservation. As Borges notes in "The Flower of Coleridge," "For the classical mind, the literature is the essential thing, not the individuals" (*BAR* 165). For Calvino and Borges, the author is less demiurge than craftsman, his work a product less of intuition than of erudition and toil. Calvino addresses the "personality" issue in his major theoretical statement, "Notes towards a definition of narrative form as a combinative process," whose essential tenets (and less than terse title) recall Barthes's "Introduction to the Structural Analysis of Narratives": "In the process of writing, the author's 'I' gets dissolved. The so-called 'personality' of the writer is bound up with the act of writing: it is a product and a manner of writing. . . . What the terminology of the Romantics classed as genius, talent, inspiration, or intuition is simply a writer who finds his way empirically, by taking short cuts."[4] Or, to allegorize one of

---

4. Italo Calvino, "Notes towards a definition of narrative form as a combinative process,"

Borges's short stories, the author, like the people of Tlön, acts not with the discipline of an angel but with that of a chess player (*F* 34). And as Calvino and Borges themselves note, as their fictions exemplify, ludic metaphors best describe their narrative practices.

I.

Literature, for both Calvino and Borges, is a complex intertextual field. In this field conventions cluster to define genre and subgenre. A literary work takes on generic and subgeneric shape according to its position within this field of clusters and interstices. The bias here is clearly, though not exclusively, structural. As master parodists Calvino and Borges are singularly adept at mapping routes across this intertextual field. As master parodists with variegated interests, each very capably obscures generic borders. In their parodies, authorial personality recedes into the background, supplanted by the personality of literature itself as well as by that of the reader. Indeed, the protagonists of *If on a winter's night* and many Borgesian short stories—notably those of *Ficciones*—are precisely literature and the reader.

If on a winter's night problemizes the act of reading. The novel is a random collection of incipits overlaid with a continuous unifying plot. The ten incipits draw from narrative tradition and serve as a celebration of plagiarism. A catalog of the subgenres represented indicates the novel's stylistic breadth: the spy thriller, failed realism, the Austro-German diary tale, revolutionary melodrama, *film noir* narrative, the novel of introspection, the Poe-esque story of mystery and suspense, the erotic oriental novel, the Borgesian fantasy, and Gogolian surrealism. These ten incipient novels provide the fictional plane of reference for *If on a winter's night*. Calvino achieves structural unity by overlaying the ten incipits with a metafictional plot told in the second person to a male character identified simply as "you, Reader."

The metafictional plot advances through the numbered chapters that, variously, precede, introduce, and comment retrospectively on the ten incipient novels. The metafictional plot involves the search for the original, "authentic" text that the protagonist has encountered at the outset of *If on a winter's night*. With a distinctly Borgesian reflexivity this "original" text is entitled *If on a winter's night a traveler* and is authored of course by one Italo Calvino. An error at the bindery has violated the integrity of the protagonist's copy of *If on a winter's night a traveler*. In lieu of the complete text the protagonist confronts an

---

20th Century Studies 3 (1970): 93–101 (95). For a more detailed discussion of Calvino's narrative theory than I offer here, see my "Calvino's Combinative Aesthetics: Theory and Practice," *The Review of Contemporary Fiction* 6:2 (1986): 11–18.

assembly of first chapters. He stomps off to his bookseller to exchange this defective text for an integral one and so begins his quest for the "real" text. In his quest, the protagonist engages a kaleidoscopic world, which offers up finally no indisputably authentic text but does provide him both with the impetus to question his reading practices and with a wife, Ludmilla (known throughout the novel as the "Other Reader").

In using these well-worn conventions of romantic melodrama and detective fiction to structure the metafictional plot, we see the instability of Calvino's irony. He refuses to offer a definitive last word on fiction-writing or fiction-reading. His self-parody is intentional. He acknowledges writing to be parasitic—not just the writing of others, but his own as well. Through unstable irony and self-parody, he aligns himself with Borges and other postmodernists. *If on a winter's night* endorses the view of the narrator of Borges's "The Library of Babel," who remarks that "to speak is to fall into tautologies" (*F* 86). Clearly, the free-floating irony of Calvino and Borges feeds on their deeply ingrained stylistic self-consciousness as well as on their capacious knowledge of literary history. Given these factors, self-parody becomes inevitable. In discussing Thomas Pynchon and Norman Mailer, Harold Bloom expresses a preference for Pynchon because "a voluntary parody is more impressive than an involuntary one."[5] Though I, like Bloom, would not wish to make exclusionary choices, Calvino and Borges remain nonetheless exemplary in their conscious self-effacement, in their respect for the sophistication of their readers.

As my necessarily reductive gloss of Calvino's novel points out, *If on a winter's night* has a degree of structural involution not found in any single Borgesian fiction, though it might be argued that, taken whole, Borges's fiction has comparable complexity. Also, metafictional commentary in Calvino's novel is overt and hyperbolic, unlike in Borgesian fictions. These are clearly differences more of degree than of kind, however. Calvino and Borges are kindred spirits with similar views on authorship, textuality, and the reader.

I have noted above that literature and the reader are the real protagonists of the fiction under consideration here. To clarify this point and to establish the nature of the text-reader relationship, I *borrow*—a sanctioned mode of scholarly plagiarism—a concept developed by Michael Riffaterre and other semioticians. Riffaterre defines *intertextuality* as "an operation of the reader's mind": "Intertextuality necessarily complements our experience of textuality. It is the perception that our reading of the text cannot be complete or satisfactory without going through the intertext, that the text does not signify unless as

5. Harold Bloom, *A Map of Misreading* (New York: Oxford University Press, 1975), 38.

a function of a complementary or contradictory intertextual homologue."[6] An intertext, Riffaterre suggests, is a body of texts and textual fragments that shares a lexicon and syntax with the text we are reading. A reader can use a single intertext—itself a motley of borrowed conventions—to render *If on a winter's night* and many Borgesian stories explicable. The readerly elaboration of an intertext recalls Borges's project in "Kafka and His Precursors": "Once I planned to make a survey of Kafka's precursors. At first I thought he was as singular as the fabulous phoenix; when I knew him better I thought I recognized his voice, or his habits, in the texts of various literatures and various ages" (*BAR* 242). Readers understand given works of literature by contextualizing them within the intertextual field(s) with which they are familiar. In his brief study of Kafka's precursors, Borges founds a reading of Kafka on the basis of an intertext that Borges, not Kafka, has inscribed. Here, as in Riffaterre's theoretical statement, intertextuality is a readerly observation related to texts, not to authors per se. Borges concludes his short piece on Kafka by noting that, in the correlation established between a given work and the tradition that precedes it, "the identity or plurality of men matters not at all" (*BAR* 243).

A number of conventions characterize the intertext that provides the reader joint entry into the fiction of Calvino and Borges. Like "Tlön, Uqbar, Orbis Tertius" and "The Garden of Forking Paths," for example, *If on a winter's night* considers an enigmatic text. In "Tlön, Uqbar, Orbis Tertius," the narrator attempts to solve the riddle posed by the discovery of the eleventh volume of the *First Encyclopaedia of Tlön*. His investigation succeeds finally in conflating the actual world and the "fantastic" realm of Tlön. The narrator's limited resolution of the Tlönian mystery engenders epistemological ambiguity rather than certitude. Textuality also remains puzzling in "The Garden of Forking Paths," whose very title seems a fitting metaphor to describe the reader's pursuit of an intertext. In this story the like-named novel of Ts'ui Pên, the narrator's ancestor, presents a number of mutually exclusive scenarios, a model adopted in *If on a winter's night* (not to mention Thomas Pynchon's *The Crying of Lot 49* and Robert Coover's "The Babysitter" and *Spanking the Maid*). On an explicit fictional plane, "Tlön, Uqbar, Orbis Tertius" and "The Garden of Forking Paths" pre-

6. Michael Riffaterre, "Intertextual Representation: On Mimesis as Interpretive Discourse," *Critical Inquiry* 11 (1984): 141–62 (142–43). In this essay Riffaterre applies his notions of intertext and intertextuality to short poems (William Carlos Williams's "The Red Wheelbarrow" and Wordsworth's "Composed Upon Westminster Bridge, September 3, 1802") and textual fragments from novels by Dickens. Riffaterre's concern is with both tropic play and register shift. In contrast, my application of his concepts is more "macrostructural," focusing on the interaction of generic conventions.

sent worlds resistant to causal analysis and linearization, while on an implicit metafictional plane both works induce the reader to question his or her reading practices. Similarly, *If on a winter's night* involves an act of textual detection, a search for an indisputable, authentic text with an indisputable, authentic significance.

Reader-as-detective is an appropriate analogy when discussing the Calvino-Borges intertext. Both Calvino and Borges pay tribute to such popular genres as the parable, science fantasy, and the fictions of mystery, detection, and adventure. Borges documents his respect for G. K. Chesterton, H. G. Wells, Nathaniel Hawthorne, and Robert Louis Stevenson in reviews and lectures as well as mimetically in his fictions. Furthermore, in *Six Problems for Don Isidro Parodi,* which was co-authored with Bioy Casares, Borges pays homage to Poe's Monsieur Dupin. For his part, Calvino, in one of his last interviews, admits to sharing the predilections of Borges for popular narrative forms.[7] In *If on a winter's night,* he explores the technical formulas of various popular forms, but it is the narrative of detection that provides the generic umbrella for the novel in toto. Like the detective, the protagonist in *If on a winter's night* seeks clues that will allow him to naturalize the incongruities he encounters while investigating the textual mystery of *If on a winter's night a traveler.* Like traditional detectives (and the Royal Canadian Mounted Police), the traditional readers want to "get their man," to delineate a pattern that decodes references and establishes connections. The narrator in *If on a winter's night* mocks this desire: "The thing that most exasperates you is to find yourself at the mercy of the fortuitous, the aleatory, the random, in things and in human actions. . . . In such instances your dominant passion is the impatience to erase the disturbing effects of that arbitrariness or distraction, to re-establish the normal course of events."[8] Just like the mutually exclusive conjectures in "Tlön, Uqbar, Orbis Tertius" and the random voice of chance in "The Babylon Lottery," the multiple plots in *If on a winter's night* defy all efforts to straighten things out.

Another feature of the Calvino-Borges intertext is what we might call "generic counterfeiting," that is, a parodic re-presentation of set genres. With generic counterfeiting comes a confusion of readerly expectations. Here, the unstable irony of the postmodernist takes the literary work beyond the limits of the pastiche that merely aims at "improving" the reader's tastes, at replacing certain standards with others. In "Pierre

7. Ian Thomson, "In the Heat of the Moment: A Conversation in Rome with Italo Calvino," *London Magazine* 24:9–10 (1984–1985): 54–68 (66).

8. Italo Calvino, *If on a winter's night a traveler,* trans. William Weaver (New York: Harcourt, 1981), 27.

Menard, Author of the *Quixote*," Borges fictionalizes a traditionally nonfictional form, the scholarly article/review—a practice that, incidentally, we also find in Vladimir Nabokov's *Pale Fire*, John Updike's *Bech: A Book* ("Appendix B"), Stanislaw Lem's *A Perfect Vacuum: Perfect Reviews of Nonexistent Books*, and Gilbert Sorrentino's *Mulligan Stew*, for example, as well as in *If on a winter's night*.

In the latter, we encounter an absurd bibliophilic world where linguists wrangle over the authenticity of an unfinished novel written in a modern dead language, where publishers mismatch book signatures, where hacks pirate the fiction-writing formulas of other hacks. In short, this is a world where, as the fictive novelist Silas Flannery notes, "there is no certitude outside of falsification."[9] Again, the attacks on such traditional notions as textual authenticity and generic purity unsettle the reader, who is led to question the issues of authorship and genre. Generic counterfeiting is a central interest for Calvino and Borges, one that they explore systematically in their fictions.

Allied to their fascination with generic counterfeiting is their mutual interest in the notion of literature as a closed system and, consequently, in the possibilities for innovation that such a system allows. In "The Library of Babel," the narrator comments on "the formless and chaotic nature of almost all books" (*F* 81). There is a curious paradox here. The Library of Babel offers an exhaustive catalog of texts. The library codifies the conventions of textuality. Yet, notwithstanding the implications of *limit* inherent in any list, the narrator goes on to call the library infinite. How does one reconcile limit with infinitude? The narrator offers a solution to this apparent paradox: "*The Library is limitless and periodic*. If an eternal voyager were to traverse it in any direction, he would find, after many centuries, that the same volumes are repeated in the same disorder (which, if repeated, would constitute an order: Order itself)" (*F* 81–82). Here, of course, another paradox smiles quizzically at the reader: order in disorder, disorder in order.

In his theoretical essay "Notes," Calvino also investigates the issues of textual limit and infinitude. On the one hand, he acknowledges that literature is nothing more than a "set of variations on a finite stock of functions and functors." On the other hand, however, innovation and freedom occur where literature becomes "a form of combinative play." He elaborates on this curious paradox of constraint-in-freedom, of limited infinitude: "Since our mind is a chessboard on which thousands and billions of pieces are continuously in play, we would never be able

9. Ibid., 193. The name "Silas Flannery" conjures up, of course, another master parodist, Flann O'Brien.

to play out all the possible games with them in our life-time, even if it lasted as long as the created universe. But we also know that every one of those games is implicit in the code of all cerebral games in general."[10] Notwithstanding his informed remarks here on the subject, Calvino's fiction expresses his narrative aesthetics yet more eloquently. Much of Calvino's fiction, particularly his later work, exhibits what he calls the *ars combinatoria.* In these works he uses commonplace phenomena as generators of textuality. In *The Castle of Crossed Destinies* (1969; 1973), for example, he uses two decks of tarot cards; in *Invisible Cities* (1972), he manipulates numerical patterns; and in *If on a winter's night,* as has been noted, he mixes sets of narrative conventions drawn for the most part from popular fiction.[11] In each instance the textual generator is tired, prosaic, and "familiar," yet in each instance it yields a fiction that is vibrant, imaginative, and novel.

II.

If on a winter's night describes the pursuit of textual truth. Calvino's last novel, *Mr. Palomar,* is also about the pursuit of truth, but this is a more general truth, the truth of worldly appearances and the surreptitious meanings such appearances do and do not harbor. In each novel, knowledge—its essence, its acquisition—presents itself as problem. Calvino provides a catalog of various responses to the task at hand, a hermeneutic one in *If on a winter's night,* an epistemological one in the case of *Mr. Palomar.* At the conclusion of *If on a winter's night,* Reader listens as a number of theories of reading are outlined: affectivism, formalism, allegorization, intertextualism, myth criticism, psychoanalytical interpretation, the exegesis of "concealed" meanings. In *Mr. Palomar,* the reader accompanies the protagonist on an intellectual journey as he works his way through the empiricist-idealist dialectic, a journey that ends with Palomar embracing neither, but rather a descriptive phenomenology bereft of confidence and any real emotional succor. There are, of course, noteworthy differences between the two works. Where *If on a winter's night* is overtly metafictional, *Mr. Palomar* is more traditional, depicting the ruminations of its eponymous protagonist through third-person narration in the present tense. In considering the problem of knowledge, while eschewing direct authorial commentary, *Mr. Palomar* resembles important Borgesian fictions. Both Calvino and Borges construe knowledge as a matter of human desire and local perspective and dramatize the protagonist's epistemo-

10. Calvino, "Notes," 97, 101, 94–95.
11. Italo Calvino, *The Castle of Crossed Destinies,* trans. William Weaver (New York: Harcourt, 1979), and *Invisible Cities,* trans. William Weaver (New York: Harcourt, 1974).

logical quest. Although Calvino in *Mr. Palomar* and Borges in most of his short stories seem to promote alternative epistemologies—materialism for Calvino, idealism for Borges—they are linked by a common realization that all attempts *to know* are quixotic gestures illustrating at once human limits and the inscrutability of the world.

Although published in 1979 and 1983, respectively, *If on a winter's night a traveler* and *Mr. Palomar* were written at the same time. In March 1984, eighteen months before his death, Calvino pointed out in an interview a key difference between the two. While *If on a winter's night* considers textual interpretation, *Mr. Palomar* responds to "the problematic of nonlinguistic phenomena," to how one reads that which is not written but which merely occurs in nature, in society, in oneself.[12] In the metafictional novel epistemological issues are subtly presented through the problemizing of the reading act, whereas we confront these issues directly in *Mr. Palomar,* through the protagonist's introspections on the nature of the world. As Calvino's brief, postscriptive guide indicates, *Mr. Palomar* has three thematic areas, each with its own rhetorical nuance. Chapter 1, "Mr. Palomar's Vacation," is descriptive and details Mr. Palomar's visual experiences of natural phenomena; chapter 2, "Mr. Palomar in the City," presents short narrative vignettes of the protagonist's attempt to interpret cultural-anthropological phenomena; and the final chapter considers the protagonist's metaphysical meditations and ends with his death. Characteristic of the structural geometry of Calvino's later work, each of the three chapters has three sections and each section has three subsections.

Throughout the novel Mr. Palomar tests the efficacy of empiricism, its capacity to weave the disparate into a seamless narrative that explains all. In the three sections of chapter 1, Palomar considers phenomena within three given fields—the beach, his home garden, and interplanetary space. At the beach, he analyzes not " 'the waves' . . . but just one single wave: in his desire to avoid vague sensations, he establishes for his every action a limited and precise object."[13] So far, so good. But Mr. Palomar immediately encounters difficulties isolating a single wave within a ceaseless flux of water. A given wave does not exist in vacuo; it has a relationship to a myriad of other phenomena. Further, in attempting to define "wave-ness," Mr. Palomar realizes that, although there is identity among waves, there are also elements of singularity. Impatience and anxiety overcome him. Perhaps a shift of focus will help. He observes not the waves themselves but the reflux of waves that

12. Gregory Lucente, "An Interview with Italo Calvino," *Contemporary Literature* 26 (1985): 248–53 (248).

13. Italo Calvino, *Mr. Palomar,* trans. William Weaver (Toronto: Lester and Orpen Dennys, 1985), 3.

have already crashed upon the shore. This inversion of perspective leaves him wondering if, in fact, movement is not generated from the beach outward.[14] In substituting the subsequent for the antecedent, will Palomar be able to undo the already done, "to make the waves run in the opposite direction, to overturn time, to perceive the true substance of the world beyond sensory and mental habits"?[15] No, Palomar yields to common sense and wonders about phase two of the operation, the linking of the part to the whole, the extending of his knowledge about waves to the entire universe.

Palomar's concern for an exhaustive explanation of the universe threatens to compromise his philosophical materialism, to make of it a metaphysics.[16] Empiricists have traditionally set themselves modest goals, the understanding of a wave, say, rather than of the force that moves all, the primum mobile, for example.[17] In an indirect interior monologue, Palomar expresses his nostalgia for a first principle: "What a relief it would be if he could manage to cancel his partial and doubting ego in the certitude of a principle from which everything is derived! A single, absolute principle from which actions and forms are derived? Or else a certain number of distinct principles, lines of force that intersect, giving a form to the world as it appears, unique, instant by instant?"[18] In the beach section, a first principle of sorts suggests itself to Palomar. While swimming one evening, he marvels at the reflection the sun casts over the sea at dusk. What, he asks, is the ontological status of this reflection, this "sword of the sun"? He quickly dismisses his first thought

14. Throughout *Mr. Palomar,* the foregrounding of background is used recurrently to present the familiar in an unfamiliar light. Thus, for example, the spots on a giraffe are construed, not as spots, but as a black coat marred by bleeding veins (80), and the communicative dimension of silence is emphasized over that of sound (103–4). Borges, of course, is a master manipulator of focal inversions, which he uses to violate expectations and to provoke speculation and fantasizing in the reader.

15. Calvino, *Mr. Palomar,* 7.

16. Mary Tiles, in *Bachelard: Science and Objectivity* (Cambridge: Cambridge University Press, 1984), identifies another way in which scientific method can easily metamorphose into its seeming antithesis: "If it is empirically interpreted scientific theory which sets limits on the possibility of experimental knowledge, this means that scientific theory itself sets the limits of possible experience and in so doing can force changes in conceptions of reality and in standards of objectivity. This is crucial because it makes metaphysical (world-view) revision part of the cognitive process of science" (212–13).

17. Comte, in his introduction to positive philosophy, criticizes the pursuit of first causes, finding it characteristic of the theological tenor of "primitive philosophy": "The inner nature of being, the origin and end of all phenomena, are precisely those [questions] that our intelligence undertakes in that primitive state, while all the truly soluble problems are looked upon as almost unworthy of serious consideration" (Auguste Comte, *The Essential Comte,* trans. Margaret Clarke, ed. Stanislav Andreski [London: Croon Helm, 1974], 22).

18. Calvino, *Mr. Palomar,* 16.

that the reflection is the sun paying personal homage to him. He considers at length two other alternatives.

His first hypothesis suggests the Berkeleian idealism that Borges so often discusses. Palomar notes, "Everyone with eyes sees the reflection that follows him; illusion of the senses and of the mind holds us all prisoners always."[19] The resistance of the table to his knock establishes its facticity for Berkeley; in obliging the beholder to shade his eyes, the reflection confirms, for Palomar, that it *is*. Borges glosses Berkeley's philosophy in "New Refutation of Time": "Berkeley denied matter. That does not mean, it should be understood, that he denied colors, odors, flavors, sounds, and contacts. What he denied was that, outside of those perceptions or components of the external world, there was an invisible, intangible thing called matter. He denied that there were pains that no one feels, colors that no one sees, forms that no one touches" (*BAR* 186). For the idealist, or the *immaterialist* as Berkeley called himself, *being* is conferred through *perception*. After stripping Berkeleian idealism of Berkeley's god, we find a philosophy maintaining that human perception "moves" all. Since everything has its origin in perception, perception itself becomes a de facto first principle (though an idealist would not use such language). Palomar plays out the idealist position: "'All this is happening not on the sea, not in the sun,' the swimmer Palomar thinks, 'but inside my head, in the circuits between eyes and brain. I am swimming in my mind; this sword of light exists only there; and this is precisely what attracts me. This is my element, the only one I can know in some way.'"[20] At the conclusion of this meditation he will revert to his earlier materialism, but the epistemological quandaries that preoccupy him at the beach will remain with him until his death at the end of the novel.

Borges is also interested in modes of conceptual patterning. Like Calvino, he is concerned both with the process through which particular modes of thinking are given voice and with their fallibility. In many of his fictions, protagonists express great faith in both the existence and the accessibility of a single ordering principle. In "The God's Script," for example, Tzinacán, the magician of the pyramid of Qaholom, in an epiphanic moment experiences the ineffable for which, he tells us, such "poor and ambitious words" as "*all, world, universe*" serve as mere "shadows or simulacra" (*L* 171). For the mystic, epiphany serves as a kind of epistemological deus ex machina, a deliverance from the problem of knowledge. A similar epiphanic moment occurs in "The Aleph," when the narrator comes face to face with the origin of all, the

19. Ibid., 14.
20. Ibid., 15.

aleph, the first letter of the Hebrew alphabet and the godhead in the Cabala. In the aleph, the narrator sees all "from every point and angle"; he sees the "unimaginable universe" (*BAR* 161). Predictably, necessarily, neither protagonist can give verbal shape to his vision and this establishes, depending upon one's bias, either the "nonlinguisticality" of certain experiences or the sovereignty of solipsism in his life.

Mr. Palomar's empirical investigations also aim at viewing phenomena from every possible angle, at seeing all. In seeing objects and events thus in their entirety, Palomar will achieve a perspective that is limited neither by the context in which the phenomena occur nor by the context of the viewer. He uses different means, but Mr. Palomar's goal is the same as that of Tzinacán and the narrator of "The Aleph"—a kind of pure, total perception—although this apotheosis of perception resembles Husserlianism more than Berkeley's position, perhaps because it is anchored to the "real," the eidetic. In the final section of chapter 1, however, Palomar's confident, zealous brand of empiricism suffers an affront. We find Mr. Palomar (who has the same name as a great American observatory) gazing raptly at the sky, considering, in turn, the moon, the planets, and the stars.

As Palomar views the moon, he comes to realize the transience of any given phase of it, of any lunar image that the light of the sun casts back to earth. Empiricism wishes to isolate a phenomenon, to freeze a moment. The moon resists such treatment. As he peers at the moon he considers what his eyes tell him he is seeing. Is he looking at a palpable object, a new winter moon, set against an azure sky? Or is this "whitish shadow" a great rent in the sky, "a crevice that opens onto the void behind"? Further, does the approach of dusk and the heightening of the moon's blankness indicate a receding sky or an impetuous stepping forth of the moon? Here, the ambiguities of perception prevent Palomar from distinguishing between foreground and background. He has a similar experience when he observes the planets and the stars. Considering Saturn and Jupiter through a fifteen-centimeter telescope, Palomar identifies many features of the planets that are imperceptible to the naked eye. Later, unaided by the telescope, Palomar struggles to relate his newly detailed view of the planets to the firmament. Again, Palomar finds his perception of the world complicated by the availability of different perspectives. Finally, as he contemplates the stars, he questions the accuracy of his observations. As he stares at a dark expanse of the firmament, a faint glimmer rewards his concentration, but he cannot be sure of what he sees. Perhaps the glimmer is illusion; perhaps it is a reflection from his glasses; perhaps it is a star. His observation of the stars avails "an unstable and contradictory knowledge." The celestial charts have failed him; "he distrusts what he knows."[21]

In chapter 2, Palomar attempts to read the text written by social and cultural tradition. He considers the significance of the Roman cityscape, for example, soon realizing that the "surface of things is inexhaustible." He studies the delectable wares of a Parisian charcuterie in an effort to understand the present through these edible legacies of the past, transforming "every food into a document of the history of civilization."[22] A cheese shop becomes a "dictionary" with the mastering of its nomenclature affording Palomar tenuous conceptual entry into an unexpectedly complex semiotic world. Chapter 2 is fascinating. In it, Palomar constantly confronts the tension between desire and scientific method, reiterating the incapacity of either one to overcome the aporia of knowledge.

The cultural-anthropological interests of chapter 2 yield to more speculative, more metaphysical interests in the final chapter, "The Silences of Mr. Palomar," in which Palomar continues to contemplate patiently the conditions of his own existence, paying particular attention to *how* and *why* he understands phenomena. In the opening section, "Mr. Palomar's Journeys," he ventures to three non-Western locales, extrapolating an important lesson from events at each one. Visiting the famous garden of rocks and sand of the Ryoanji of Kyoto, Palomar finds himself incapable of following the Zen Buddhist imperative of shedding one's personality in order to intuit "Absolute Self." For Palomar, personality is an inextricable part of being. In gazing at the configuration of rocks and sand, he identifies two "nonhomogeneous harmonies": the harmony of capricious, unpatterned, natural forces, and the harmony of regular human structures that "aspires to the rationality of a geometrical or musical composition, never definitive."[23] Palomar's response to the garden is decidedly Western. Yet, though operating within the classic subject-object dichotomy, though emphasizing personal sovereignty, Palomar expresses a yearning for a harmonizing of the "nonhomogeneous harmonies" of man and nature.

The two vignettes that follow the meditation in the sand garden bring to light other aspects of Mr. Palomar's strongly Western outlook. His visit to Mexico, to the ruins of Tula, the ancient capital of the Toltecs, confirms his proclivity to postulate significance. Though puzzled by the iconography of Toltec architecture, Palomar cannot resist

21. Ibid., 34, 47.
22. Ibid., 55, 70.
23. Ibid., 94.

interpreting the animal symbolism. Although aware that his interpretations cannot stand alone, that their need of elaboration plunges him into exegetical *mise en abyme*, he persists: "Yet he knows he could never suppress in himself the need to translate, to move from one language to another, from concrete figures to abstract words, to weave and reweave a network of analogies. Not to interpret is impossible, as refraining from thinking is impossible."[24] In the final vignette of the opening section, a trip to an Eastern country allows Palomar to realize a simple, though important, truth. Although we are frequently unable to assign a cause to every effect, causes nonetheless exist. The cumulative philosophical weight of the three vignettes is Cartesian in one respect: we think, therefore we are. In each vignette, thought confers existence upon the thinking subject, thought is indistinguishable from being. In each instance, knowledge follows from the analysis of experience. However, Palomar is not Descartes. *Discourse on Method* projects a supreme confidence in man, in God, in reason. By contrast, Palomar is pessimistic, acutely aware of human limitation in a random, godless universe.

The three subsections of "Mr. Palomar in Society," especially "The model of models," summarize the epistemological inquiries undertaken throughout *Mr. Palomar.* In "The model of models" Palomar contemplates the strengths and weaknesses of inductive and deductive reasoning. Initially, Palomar favors deduction and the construction of a single model through which to understand events. He distrusts induction for he finds his experiences inconclusive and vague. Though fascinated by the "serene harmony of the lines of the pattern," he gradually becomes troubled by the capacity of the "human landscape" to distort and defy "the harmonious geometrical design [he has] drawn in the heaven of ideal models."[25] Palomar finds himself requiring a number of models to understand the variegated events of reality, to contend with the many realities he confronts. He toys with the notion of a model of models, a great umbrella model that will subsume all models, one that will enable him to identify and redress social ills, for example. He balks ultimately at codifying his thoughts within a system, fearing that his remedies may occasion worse abuses than currently exist. Although initially mesmerized by the geometrical beauty of systems conjured up by reason, at the end of "The model of models" Palomar falls back on experience, choosing to check his convictions, not against a priori views, but against values given shape by present circumstance.

24. Ibid., 98.
25. Ibid., 109.

In *Mr. Palomar* and many Borgesian fictions we find teasing allusions to perfect systems and transcendental truths. For both Calvino and Borges, to posit the existence of such truths, let alone their accessibility, indicates profound self-deception. However, the corollary of this latter point is not that there is a better way of achieving knowledge, of "doing" philosophy, but that explanation is as much, or more, a *narrative* response to a desire to know as an incontrovertible, autotelic claim. In short, truth is perspectival and self-deception an inescapable by-product of the pursuit of truth. In an interview, Alberto Coffa takes Borges to task for failing to elucidate the visions of the ineffable that occur in "The God's Script" and "The Aleph," calling these evasions a "trick." Borges, with his characteristic impish candor, admits frankly that elaboration is impossible for him because he simply does not know of what the ineffable consists.[26] For Borges, as for Calvino, it is not the quiddity of truth that is of moment; rather, each author focuses equally on the yearning for knowledge and the quest for knowledge this yearning impels.

Unlike Palomar, in the final analysis, Borges's protagonists are inveterate architects of metaphysical systems. Yet, as the narrator says of the Tlönian metaphysicians, "they know that a system is nothing more than the subordination of all of the aspects of the universe to some one of them" (*F* 25). For Borges, as for Calvino, system-building is strategic myopia; it is an act of epistemological hubris that denies the fundamental contingency of our being. However, wisdom lies not in building a better system but in recognizing the limits of all systems, and indeed of all nonsystems (for Palomar opts finally not for system but for simple, tentative induction). Borges ridicules the human need for pattern while at the same time admitting the necessity for pattern. In the end Palomar turns to a plodding empiricism in an effort to break the hold of system and abstraction on his life. Yet this course seems quite as limiting as the epiphanies and spontaneous fantasies of the Borgesian protagonist. At the conclusion of the novel, Mr. Palomar attempts to blind himself to his own mortality by wedding empiricism to Eleatic paradox: "He decides that he will set himself to describing every instant of this life, and until he has described them all he will no longer think of being dead." Through the infinite subdivision of parts, Palomar will, in his own view, like Zeno's arrow, like Zeno's rabbit, remain enmeshed in process. This seems an unbecoming casuistry for one committed, not to the "ideal," but to the "real." Indeed, the real intervenes at this point, bringing to a close the novel

26. Alberto Coffa, "I Always Stood in Fear of Mirrors" (*BEC* 167).

and Mr. Palomar's hopes of forestalling the inevitable: "At that moment he dies."[27]

Calvino's remarks in an interview suggest his strong empathy for Mr. Palomar. Of the novel, Calvino notes:

> *Palomar* is an album from life. . . . With *Palomar,* I tried to rehabilitate a literary genre which has fallen into disuse, namely, the description. The operation of description is sometimes a frustrating one because when you reach the most minute detail, there is always another detail still more minute. The sense that my book gives is of the inexhaustibility of reality. Every chapter is both a reflection and a description. It's about the process of knowledge.[28]

Over the course of the novel Palomar comes gradually to a qualified self-understanding. The various vignettes are parables of sorts, each with a philosophical, rather than a moral, lesson. In the end, Palomar like his creator accepts the fundamental incommensurability that exists between his world and his descriptions of that world. Neither author nor protagonist is heroic, however. Neither exhibits the confidence and bravado of the classical humanist. In the late twentieth century, we simply do the best we can while maintaining as few illusions as possible. Thus, Palomar and many of his Borgesian counterparts (and Oedipa Maas and the unnamed protagonists in Samuel Beckett's *Company* and Robert Coover's *Spanking the Maid,* for example) conduct a search for knowledge that is on the one hand absurd, mock heroic, and doomed to fail and on the other hand reasonable, necessary, and fundamentally *human.* Or, as Emir Rodríguez Monegal has more succinctly put it, the difference between parody and allegory is not great (*BAR* 355 n. 68).

I began this essay by ascribing a classicism to Calvino and Borges, by emphasizing their inclination to rework established forms, to restate traditional problems, both literary and epistemological. What then is their contribution to contemporary letters? What garners for them such a broad and substantial readership when they seem to have so little "new" to say, when they contest the very notion of the "new"?

The problem of creative limits has troubled a number of contemporary writers. John Barth's essay "The Literature of Exhaustion" is the most celebrated discussion of the topic, if not the most widely understood. The weight of misunderstanding has been sufficiently burdensome to Barth to elicit a clarification. The title of the coda, "The Liter-

27. Both quotations are from Calvino, *Mr. Palomar,* 126. Borges considers Zeno's conundrums in "Avatars of the Tortoise."

28. Alexander Stille, "An Interview with Italo Calvino," *Saturday Review* 11:2 (1985): 37–39 (38).

ature of Replenishment," reflects a change of tone but not of thesis. In the later essay, Barth reflects:

> I agree with Borges that literature can never be exhausted, if only because no single literary text can ever be exhausted—its "meaning" residing as it does in its transactions with individual readers over time, space, and language. . . . The number of splendid sayable things—metaphors for the dawn or the sea, for example—is doubtless finite; it is also doubtless very large, perhaps virtually infinite.[29]

Calvino and Borges (and Barth in his own work) fashion lustrous garments from the threadbare hand-me-downs of their precursors. Their patchworks never succeed, never seek to succeed, in obscuring the largesse of literary and philosophical tradition—neither do they conceal their own technical virtuosity or inventive design, however. Each revitalizes old problems by presenting them in imaginative, contemporary context.

In her recent study of twentieth-century parody, Linda Hutcheon points out that parody can range from ridicule to approbation of its subject, that parody is often not only derisory but respectful as well.[30] In *If on a winter's night a traveler* and *Mr. Palomar* and in much Borgesian fiction, the respective authors present complex parodies of both textual and epistemological conventions. Yet in neither instance does the author suggest that he, himself, is above that which he parodies. These parodies mock and praise, simultaneously. Imitation, here, is both the lowest and highest form of respect. Paradox, it seems, is the one constant in postmodern literature. Postmodern parodists find themselves in a curious position, that of parasites who lend vitality to their host even as they tap its energy. From our consideration of Calvino and Borges, we learn that, just as there is never a "first word," never a truly "original" thought, neither is there a "last" word or definitive opinion. It is, therefore, perhaps appropriate to conclude with an inconclusive remark worthy of that famous Cretan, an early postmodern rhetorician in his own right, but one that I *borrow* here from a contemporary successor of his, the author of *Invisible Cities:* "There is no language without deceit."[31]

---

29. John Barth, "The Literature of Replenishment: Postmodernist Fiction," *Atlantic* 245 (January 1980): 65–71 (71).

30. Linda Hutcheon, *A Theory of Parody: The Teaching of Twentieth Century Art Forms* (New York: Methuen, 1985), 37.

31. Calvino, *Invisible Cities,* 48.

Geoffrey Green _____

Postmodern Precursor

The Borgesian Image in
Innovative American Fiction

I.

    How are we to assess Borges's contribution to contemporary fiction? Any assessment would seem to call for a particular detachment, perhaps elicited by a momentary pause in the ceaseless flow of time. But from what fixed point may we contemplate the essence of Borges and his effect on our literature? Our literature is ongoing, with Borges's presence ingrained within it: only the human Borges is gone; but this, he would have maintained, hardly matters since "nobody really dies, for they all still project their shadow."[1] Fiction today proceeds in the projected shadow of Borges. His work, like Pierre Menard's, is both visible and invisible—a visible body of work and an invisible series of concordances. The anonymous author of Borges's obituary in the *New Yorker* expressed this forcefully: "Once we have read [Borges], we sense his curious presence everywhere—in the past, in chance happenings, in the context of our own lives." How is it possible to appraise this presence that is "sensed" everywhere? It is appropriate that an answer may be found in Borges's writing, since "for Borges it was only in writing that the living moment could be held, saved from oblivion."[2]

    In his well-known essay "Kafka and His Precursors," Borges remarked that he "had considered [Kafka] to be as singular as the phoenix of rhetorical praise; after frequenting his pages a bit, I came to think I could recognize his voice, or his practices, in texts from diverse literatures and periods" (*L* 199). It is not so much what is unique in Kafka, Borges maintained (or in Borges himself, and here we must recall his characteristic modesty), but the way in which his presence (his "voice" and his "practices") makes itself apparent in diverse texts and lives on in writing. Borges presented in the essay several examples of Kafka's

---

    1. Jorge Luis Borges, "Borges on Life and Death," with Amelia Barili, *New York Times Book Review,* July 13, 1986, pp. 1, 27–29 (27).
    2. "Obituary," *New Yorker,* July 7, 1986, pp. 19–20 (19).

"influence" upon writers who were his antecedents: Zeno, Kierkegaard, and Robert Browning all contained the presence of Kafka.

Following Borges's example, it would be no major task to sift through
Borges's literary predecessors and demonstrate the existence of a Borgesian quality. But what is more significant, I believe, is Borges's proposal that, although "the heterogeneous pieces I have enumerated
resemble Kafka; if I am not mistaken, not all of them resemble each
other" (*L* 201). It is Kafka's presence that facilitates the recognition of
similarity; two works that may be said to contain the trace of Kafka may
bear no evident resemblance one to the other—only to Kafka. So it is
with Borges. He is everywhere present in contemporary fiction. But
the writings in which he exists and the authors whose works display his
characteristic sense, "not all of them resemble each other."

Octavio Paz noted perceptively that Borges "turned all traditional
points of view on their heads, and obliged us to regard the things we
see and the books we read differently." In order to perceive the effect of
Borges on literature and the world, we must perceive both from a
different perspective. Borges possessed "a unique vision not so much
for what he sees as for the place from which he sees the world and
himself. A point of view, more than a vision."[3] That perspective, then, *is*
Borges, the place from which he oriented himself.

Returning to Borges on Kafka, he maintained that "in each of these
texts we find Kafka's idiosyncrasy to a greater or lesser degree, but if
Kafka had never written a line, we would not perceive this quality; in
other words, it would not exist" (*L* 201). Thus it is that to consider the
legacy of Borges in fiction is to trace the silhouette of Borges himself. In
order to perceive his influence we must have learned to recognize his
visage. And this is achieved by reading him, and, as a result, by reading
him in others. "Every writer," Borges believed, "*creates* his own precursors. His work modifies our conception of the past, as it will modify the
future" (*L* 201). We create Borges as our precursor by reading him, just
as his reading insinuates itself into our understanding of the literary past
and helps shape the form of our literary future.

The reading of Borges, however, does not allow us to create him
from nothing, to refashion him entirely in our own image. It is a re-
ciprocal process in which Borges is created by his creating us. We
perceive Borges because, as a result of Borges, we perceive ourselves
differently. In his essay "A Note on (toward) Bernard Shaw," Borges
insisted that "a book is more than a verbal structure or series of verbal
structures; it is the dialogue it establishes with its reader and the intonation it imposes upon his voice and the changing and durable images it

3. Octavio Paz, "In Time's Labyrinth," *New Republic,* November 3, 1986, pp. 30–34 (34).

leaves in his memory" (*L* 213). To read Borges, then, is to create him, and in order to create him within ourselves we must first converse with him, speak with him, "hear" his recognizable voice and intonation. Reading Borges is an interaction, a shared activity, an enterprise one *resumes*. The title of the Shaw essay is instructive as well: a note "toward" Bernard Shaw. The quality that is suggested is of an ongoing process, a pursuit, a direction: the dialogue with Borges that is the reading of Borges enables us to orient ourselves toward Borges. But where is Borges? He is never just *there;* he is always and endlessly changing, just as we change. The *New York Times* obituary quoted Borges as saying, "To me, reading has been a way of living."[4] So we proceed *toward* Borges as a way of living; we read him as we read our lives. Writing after Borges's death, Octavio Paz stated that he had "not stopped reading [*Ficciones*] and conversing silently with its author."[5] Borges's influence exists as that vector marking the space between where we think we are and where he seems to be at that moment as a result of the reading-in-progress.

In no other twentieth-century author do we find quite this sense of a personal interaction with all of literature, with the sum of all possible readers. Borges put forth the concept in his Shaw essay that "a book is not an isolated being: it is a relationship, an axis of innumerable relationships" (*L* 214). A reader and an author relate through the text, and the nuances and textual insinuations of writing are equivalent to the interactions of a human association—a friendship, a love affair, a strange and intriguing liaison. "One literature differs from another," Borges claimed, "prior or posterior, less because of the text than because of the way in which it is read" (*L* 214). This assertion opens up many possibilities: not only are there many alternate ways of reading Borges, but the way in which we read literature before Borges is not the same as the way in which we read literature during and since Borges. "All reading," Borges asserted in an interview, "is an elaboration even as experience is an elaboration. Every time I read something, that something is changed. And every time I write something, that something is being changed all the time by every reader. Every new experience enriches the book" (*BEC* 92).

Borges, whose appreciation of the authorial selves of the many writers he loved was fueled by his sense of himself as being less than those he admired, was teaching us how to read (and to read him) when he quoted Shaw as saying: "I understand everything and everyone and I am nothing and no one" (*L* 215). Borges was creating Shaw just as we

---

4. "Obituary," *New York Times,* June 15, 1986, pp. 1, 30 (30).
5. Paz, "In Time's Labyrinth," 30.

are to create Borges—in our own image, but as a collaboration. The "essential theme of the novel of our time [is] man's character and its variations" (*L* 216): the form of Borges's writing *is* Borges, his character and its variations. When asked why he did not use the novel form, Borges's reply was: "The reason is that I *can't* write a novel, though I can write short stories, and that's that" (*BEC* 88). We incorporate literature into the space within ourselves that is empty, that is receptive to the presence of something other than ourselves. Borges argued in his Shaw essay that "each of us" comprises "the interesting interlocutor in a secret and continuous dialogue with nothingness or the divinity" (*L* 216), so all writing is a registry of our existential status, of our position as readers and as things read.

"An interlocutor," Borges proposed, "is not the sum or average of what he says: he may not speak and still reveal that he is intelligent, he may omit intelligent observations and reveal his stupidity" (*L* 214). Thus the participants in the dialogue of reading may create character and its variations not only by enunciation but through silence. Implication and omission—the Borgesian elements of nothingness—are integral components of the ongoing interaction that Borges has conceived between his reader and himself. What is said (by Borges) is an aspect of what has been said (by his precursors): what exists to be said (by post-Borgesian writers) follows from what was.

In the pages that follow I will seek to disclose a sense of the image of Borges in our postmodern fiction. Such an enterprise entails the charting of a readerly collaboration between Borges and the particularly innovative American writer—as perceived by us, Borges's contemporary readers. For Borges is, after all, an enduring perspective, a point of view. We read Borges as we read our lives, as a way of living. Thus, where I discern the Borgesian image depends upon my perspective, my experience of Borges. All writing is a chronicle of our existential status as subjects and objects; we are all, simultaneously, readers and texts to be read. As Borges noted in an interview in 1969, "I don't think about myself, but many people seem to be thinking about me."[6]

II.

Reading Borges provides us with a lesson about the instability of generic expression. He wrote, Octavio Paz noted, in "three genres: the essay, the poem, and the short story. The division is arbitrary. His essays read like stories; his stories are poems; and his poems make us think, as

6. Jorge Luis Borges, "Interview," with L. S. Dembo, in *The Contemporary Writer,* ed. L. S. Dembo and Cyrena Pondrom (Madison: University of Wisconsin Press, 1972), 113–21 (113).

though they were essays. The bridge connecting them is thought."[7]
Forms are not fixed entities that convey ideas; they are endlessly changing, evolving, transforming themselves into still other forms. For Borges
this was true because he lived as much in the world of literature as he
did in the world with which literature was said to be concerned. In the
1969 interview, he "wonder[ed] why a dream or an idea should be less
real than this table for example, or why Macbeth should be less real
than today's newspaper."[8] Writers who were struggling with the intricacies of form, with the appropriate generic vehicle for contemporary
expression, found in Borges the insight that what we read constitutes a
part of life: literature that is about itself as literature is nevertheless
evoking a world, putting into effect not one image but a sequence of
images that utilize language to construct a perspective of the world that
is as real as anything else.

It is a question not so much of fixed literary forms but of the ultimate
volatility of the world's forms—the infinite variety of human experience. "My memory," Borges asserted, "is chiefly of books. In fact, I
hardly remember my own life" (*BEC* 7). Reading is human experience
that leads to the expression of ideas about reading and the writing that
we read. Literary history is a part of history and, thus, a part of life.
Reading is the act of living through (and in) the text one reads. Hence we
encounter, in "Pierre Menard, Author of the *Quixote*," the assertion that
"to be, in some way, Cervantes and reach the *Quixote* seemed less
arduous to him—and consequently, less interesting—than to go on
being Pierre Menard and reach the *Quixote* through the experiences of
Pierre Menard" (*L* 40).

For John Barth (the contemporary American fiction writer who has
most abundantly expressed his appreciation of Borges's example), the
significant realization is how Borges escapes from being preoccupied
with the "used-up-ness" of literary forms. "The important thing to
observe," he mentioned in his 1967 essay on Borges "The Literature of
Exhaustion," "is that Borges *doesn't* attribute the *Quixote* to himself,
much less recompose it like Pierre Menard; instead, he writes a remarkable and original work of literature, the implicit theme of which is the
difficulty, perhaps the unnecessity, of writing original works of literature." Barth maintained that at a time when generic forms were perceived by writers as being exhausted or enervated, Borges's "artistic
victory, if you like, is that he confronts an intellectual dead end and
employs it against itself to accomplish new human work."[9]

7. Paz, "In Time's Labyrinth," 32.
8. Borges, "Interview," 115.
9. John Barth, *The Friday Book: Essays and Other Nonfiction* (New York: Putnam's,
1984), 69, 69–70.

John Barth's dedication in his fiction to the use of form to achieve form may be seen as his way of conversing with Borges. In *The Friday Book,* his collection of rich and suggestive literary essays, Barth developed a metaphor based on the phrase "algebra and fire" from Borges's "Tlön, Uqbar, Orbis Tertius": "Let Algebra stand for technique, or the technical and formal aspects of a work of literature; let Fire stand for the writer's passions, the things he or she is trying to get eloquently said. The simple burden of my sermon is that good literature, for example, involves and requires both the algebra and the fire; in short, passionate virtuosity." Barth's stated goal for his fiction—the integrated unity of form and feeling—proceeds from his ongoing reader's dialogue with Borges. And, in appropriately Borgesian fashion, Barth mentioned in a tribute to Borges that he admires the fiction of Borges "more than my own."[10]

When we take into account the conceptual interaction between Barth and Borges, it is not surprising to encounter passages in Barth that remind us of Borges—even in works that Barth wrote before he was aware of Borges. Thus, we find a passage in *The End of the Road* in which the Doctor informs Jacob Horner that "no two people are ever paralyzed in the same way. The authors of medical textbooks . . . like everyone else, can reach generality only by ignoring enough particularity. They speak of paralysis, and the treatment of paralytics, as though one read the textbook and then followed the rules for getting paralyzed properly. There is no such thing as *paralysis,* Jacob. There is only paralyzed Jacob Horner. . . . I don't treat your paralysis: I treat paralyzed you."[11] How much does this world address Borges? Consider this passage from "Tlön, Uqbar, Orbis Tertius": "There are no nouns in Tlön's conjectural *Ursprache,* from which the 'present' languages and the dialects are derived: there are impersonal verbs, modified by monosyllabic suffixes (or prefixes) with an adverbial value. For example: there is no word corresponding to the word 'moon,' but there is a verb which in English would be 'to moon' or 'to moonate'" (*L* 8). The Doctor's instructions to Jacob emphasize that he must always make active choices, even arbitrary ones, in order to remain in motion, in life. The point here is that Borges emerges—echoing his discussion of the literary presence of Kafka—throughout the writings of those who have read him. And once we have read him, there is no easy dividing line that distinguishes a clear "before" or "after" phase: to read Borges is to recognize him in us and ourselves in him, in a manner that disrupts previously accepted notions of literary influence and evolution. As

10. Ibid., 167, 142.
11. John Barth, *The End of the Road* (New York: Bantam, 1969), 80–81.

Borges insisted, "I'm always rereading rather than reading" (*BEC* 126).

John Barth's novel *Sabbatical* opens with a sense of a story unfolding in time that contradicts our sense of the completed text that is the novel we are reading: "There was a story that began, / Said Fenwick Turner: *Susie and Fenn*— / Oh, tell that story! Tell it again! / Wept Susan Seckler." The narrator alternates between third person and first person because Fenwick and Susan are composing (or have already composed, depending on when one reads the text) the novel that is about them. The effort of being sufficiently objective about one's subjective self in order to perceive oneself as a unity and commit this to writing is something that Borges also addressed, in his parable "Borges and I": "The other one, the one called Borges, is the one things happen to" (*L* 246). To what extent is this "otherness" a function of the process of narration? Accordingly, in *Sabbatical,* we find "Graybeard Fenn would be happy to give it another go; we [Fenn and Susie] have fiddled with our tale through this whole sabbatical voyage."[12] Before events unfold, we are presented with their occurrence as text, as story; and then we are confronted with the criticism by Fenwick and Susan of the literary passage we have read. *Sabbatical* is John Barth's unique way of addressing an idea in which Borges, recalling "Borges and I," would have recognized himself: that literature is experience; the writing of a story is as much an experience as the living of the events narrated in the story.

Would Borges recognize himself in the Barth novel? Or might he suggest that he was "influenced" by Barth's novel when he wrote his "Theme of the Traitor and the Hero"? In that story, we are (again) faced with the contradiction between a finished story and an uncompleted theme. The narrator describes not a story but the outline for a story: "In my idle afternoons I have imagined this story plot which I shall perhaps write someday and which already justifies me somehow" (*L* 72). Are we reading the "idle" development of this story as it unfolds through the narrator's "arbitrary" compositional choices? Or is this text the completed story and is the "now" of our reading the "someday" to which he alludes? There is no set time or place: "Let us say (for narrative convenience) Ireland; let us say in 1824" (*L* 72). Just as in the Barth novel, the sketch of the story is the story and includes, as well, a variety of possible interpretations of itself. Note, in the Borges tale, the parodic vision suggested by "the young, the heroic, the beautiful, the assassinated Fergus Kilpatrick" (*L* 72). Barth's Fenwick and Susan interpret their text as we read it, deciding to "remove" certain passages of ungainly diction—which, of course, we have already read. Borges's nar-

12. John Barth, *Sabbatical: A Romance* (New York: Putnam's, 1982), 9.

rator informs us that Ryan "after a series of tenacious hesitations . . . resolves to keep his discovery silent" (*L* 75): an impossible task since we readers have already read what Ryan will not write. Is it any wonder that Borges concluded in "Borges and I": "I do not know which of us has written this page" (*L* 247)?

III.

Following Borges's example on Kafka, I record here a few additional instances in which we may recognize Borges's voice in diverse texts. In a recent interview with Larry McCaffery, Robert Coover remarked, "Borges said we go on writing the same story all our lives. The trouble is, it's usually a story that can never be told—there's always this distance between the sign and the signified, it's the oldest truth in philosophy—and that's why we tend to get so obsessive about it. The important thing is to accept this unbridgeable distance, and carry on with the crazy bridge-building just the same."[13] Coover's comment highlights the nature of his continuing conversation with Borges: how to "carry on with the crazy bridge-building" of storytelling despite the fact that one may be destined to repeat the same obsessive story repeatedly. One reason that we repeat a story is that we may feel that we did not get it right the first time. The realization that this inability of a text to embody the designated meaning results from the "distance between the sign and the signified . . . the oldest truth in philosophy" and leads to the perception of the exhaustion of narrative forms and to the attempt to somehow bridge the gap and continue to tell stories.

Literary forms are perceived as being exhausted when there is a sense of the inevitability of narrative being sequential. The assassin-narrator of Borges's "The Garden of Forking Paths" struggles with this sense—with events occurring in literary (as well as historical) time. He attempts to resist this notion as follows: "Then I reflected that everything happens to a man precisely, precisely *now*. Centuries of centuries and only in the present do things happen; countless men in the air, on the face of the earth and the sea, and all that really is happening is happening to me" (*L* 20). Since experience, in the narrator's view, occurs in the present tense, a switch to the past tense will enable an actor to live through an undesirable fate as if he were its author: "The author of an atrocious undertaking ought to imagine that he has already accomplished it, ought to impose upon himself a future as irrevocable as the past" (*L* 22). But it is only in the presence of Dr. Stephen Albert, the scholarly sinologist, that the narrator comes to understand an alter-

13. Jackson Cope and Geoffrey Green, ed., *Novel vs. Fiction: The Contemporary Reformation* (Norman, Okla.: Pilgrim Press, 1981), 55.

native to his conceptual dilemma: the literary labyrinth of his ancestor. Albert explains to him that his ancestor had not created a novel and a labyrinth, but a novel that was a labyrinth. There was a "forking in time, not in space. . . . In all fictional works, each time a man is confronted with several alternatives, he chooses one and eliminates the others; in the fiction of [the narrator's ancestor], he chooses—simultaneously— all of them. *He creates,* in this way, diverse futures, diverse times which themselves also proliferate and fork" (*L* 26).

In many of the fictions in Robert Coover's *Pricksongs and Descants,* there is the literary embodiment of this narrative principle. In "The Magic Poker" the narrator announces, "I wander the island, inventing it. . . . But anything can happen." The narrator not only is the creator of the story through the telling but also reacts to the way in which the story's multifarious unfoldings confound his design or expectation: "Wait a minute, this is getting out of hand! What happened to that poker, I was doing much better with the poker, I had something going there, archetypal and even maybe beautiful, a blend of eros and wisdom, sex and sensibility, music and myth."[14] Similarly, "The Gingerbread House" retells the fairy tale so that a labyrinth of narrative possibilities is constructed. And "The Elevator" documents a variety of experiential variables that may and do occur as a man enters an elevator. Since the story must be told through a linear narration, and since the events are simultaneous, there is the effect of the fiction proceeding along the "forking paths" of alternative possibilities that Borges had postulated in his story.

Coover's "The Babysitter" carries forth the forking effect to achieve an altogether extraordinary velocity of interchangeable narrative events: we are in time and in all times—rather than saying either this or that may occur, all things occur, and none of them, since literature contrives the illusion of reality and is ultimately a text of words, itself a forking off from life. Coover, in dialogue with the Borges who described the labyrinth, selects all possible choices about an evening spent by a babysitter and the couple that hires her. Thus, in Borges's words, "diverse futures" and "diverse times" are "themselves [seen to] proliferate and fork." But because of the nature of language, we as readers, are unable to perceive the forking all at once, as it were. We experience the illusion of simultaneity while reading it by way of sequential depictions—and, of course, this "unbridgeable distance" is precisely what Coover sought to evoke in his fiction.

John Updike is another writer who may be observed conducting a

14. Robert Coover, *Pricksongs and Descants* (New York: New American Library, 1969), 20, 30.

correspondence with Borges through writing. In his collection of essays *Hugging the Shore,* Updike, describing Borges, said, "The act of repossession, by a mind that has wandered far, characterizes his literary production ever after [1921], and gives it its air of haunting dislocation, of surreal specificity and abysmal formlessness, of nostalgia for the circumambient." What Updike appreciates in Borges are not qualities that one ordinarily associates with Updike's own work. "Few major writers granted long life," he noted, "have proved so loyal to their initial obsessions and demonstrated so little fear of repeating themselves."[15] Yet, despite the initial response that Updike's concern with form and his need for location, ambience, and character are aspects that suggest an un-Borgesian demeanor, his loyalty to his own recurrent obsessions has been established, in novel after novel, over the course of his career. Indeed, Updike's works display a fondness for changes of a superficial nature that only thinly veil his own sense of appropriate terrain, his Updikean confidence in his own "country," a sense shared with Borges of having "little fear of repeating" oneself. Despite Updike's desire to occupy principally his indigenous landscape of American suburban living, every so often he has a desire to alter the perspective, to proceed from a point of view utterly unlike his own habitual mode. In this, it may be suggested, he is conversing with Borges. Here is Borges's darkly ironic Nazi narrator in "Deutsches Requiem": "There is nothing on earth that does not contain the seed of a possible Hell; a face, a word, a compass, a cigarette advertisement, are capable of driving a person mad if he is unable to forget them. Would not a man who continually imagined the map of Hungary be mad?" (*L* 145). For Updike's Colonel Ellelloû, dictator of the imaginary African nation of Kush in *The Coup,* the map is of the United States. The colonel's mad focus is on the United States as a demonic presence as much as it is on his own country of Kush. He recognizes that "there are two selves: the one who acts, and the 'I' who experiences. This latter is passive even in a whirlwind of the former's making, passive and guiltless and astonished."[16] Ellelloû's Borgesian duality drives him to narrate his story in both the first- and third-person voices. He is himself and also outside himself: sometimes to achieve the illusion of detachment or objectivity; at other times to achieve, through language, an escape from the burden of being the self he hates. One is reminded of Borges's story "The Shape of the Sword," in which the Englishman tells the tale of how he had been betrayed by Vincent Moon, only to reveal at the end that "I have told you the story

15. John Updike, *Hugging the Shore: Essays and Criticism* (New York: Vintage, 1984), 782, 779.

16. John Updike, *The Coup* (New York: Knopf, 1978), 7.

thus so that you would hear me to the end. I denounced the man who protected me: I am Vincent Moon. Now despise me" (*L* 71). Moon, in narrating his story, assumed the perspective of the person he had betrayed—in order to complete the narrative, and because it relieved his burden of guilt if only for the length of the telling.

The quandary of opposing versions of the self is in fact an aspect of contradictory perceptions of reality. Oedipa Maas's realization, in Thomas Pynchon's *The Crying of Lot 49*—that "there either was some Tristero [conspiracy] beyond the appearance of the legacy America, or there was just America and if there was just America then it seemed the only way she could continue, and manage to be at all relevant to it, was as an alien, unfurrowed, assumed full circle into some paranoia"[17]— recalls the conclusion of Borges's "The Lottery in Babylon": "The Company, with divine modesty, avoids all publicity. Its agents, as is natural, are secret. The orders which it issues continually (perhaps incessantly) do not differ with those lavished by impostors. . . . That silent functioning, comparable to God's, gives rise to all sorts of conjectures" (*L* 35). "Various futures" (either within ourselves or in the depicted world) occupy the same moment in time; our sense of reality splits, and we exist in a simultaneous first and third person—a mirror reality.

IV.

In his essay, "Partial Magic in the *Quixote*," Borges mused on the relation between fiction and life: "Why does it disturb us that Don Quixote be a reader of the *Quixote* and Hamlet a spectator of *Hamlet*? I believe I have found the reason: these inversions suggest that if the characters of a fictional work can be readers or spectators, we, its readers or spectators, can be fictitious" (*L* 196). Through our reading about a fictional character reading about a character reading (and so on), the illusory security of reading is transformed into a claustrophobic depiction of "reality" that does not refute the notion that someone, somewhere, is "reading" us. The presumption that we read from privileged ground is contradicted by a new suspicion that all perspectives are equally privileged—or that none are. The world becomes the state of our subjective perceptions. The result is that reality may be viewed as a text and that the text maintains its own reality. This vision is expressed at the end of Borges's "The Circular Ruins": "Not to be a man, to be the projection of another man's dream, what a feeling of humiliation, of vertigo! . . . With relief, with humiliation, with terror, he understood that he too was a mere appearance, dreamt by another" (*L* 50).

The subjectivity of perception—its literariness—is never so apparent

17. Thomas Pynchon, *The Crying of Lot 49* (New York: Bantam, 1967), 137.

as when we read about (or are ourselves in the midst of) sensations of the most severe and extreme nature: for it is precisely when events are the most urgent that we perceive them as being dreamlike and hazy. In Borges's brilliant story "Emma Zunz" there is the assertion that "one attribute of a hellish experience is unreality, an attribute that seems to allay its terrors and which aggravates them perhaps" (*L* 134). In order to achieve revenge against the man who destroyed her father's life, Emma Zunz transforms her body into a work of fiction, a text designed to be read by others. She is author and character simultaneously; her life is used to realize a vengeance that will forever remain concealed. In order to be able to accuse her enemy of violating her, she causes herself to be violated by another. She initiates it, in fact, selecting a "coarse" individual so that "the purity of the horror might not be mitigated" (*L* 134).

When she confronts her enemy, the realms become confused: "more than the urgency of avenging her father, Emma felt the need of inflicting punishment for the outrage she had suffered" (*L* 136), the violation that she had orchestrated in order to succeed in her plan. The central conceit of her plan—that, before he died, she would tell him her scheme to kill him and escape unscathed—must be discarded, since he dies from her bullets before she is able to recite her speech. She phones the police and tells them "something incredible has happened": her employer, the man who betrayed her father, raped her, and she murdered him in self-defense (*L* 137).

The evidence to support Emma's assertion is Emma herself. Her body is a text with multiple meanings; the creative abilities with which she organizes her life enable her to endure the most horrific experiences as a kind of detached authorial presence while the sense of the pain is projected onto the contrived reality. "Actually," the narrator concludes, "the story *was* incredible, but it impressed everyone because substantially it was true. True was Emma Zunz' tone, true was her shame, true was her hate. True also was the outrage she had suffered: only the circumstances were false, the time, and one or two proper names" (*L* 137).

John Hawkes's novel of nightmarish intensity, *The Lime Twig*, situates itself in this terrain of dream-become-reality and life as a dreamy illusion. The dreams of Margaret and Michael Banks are described: "knowing that her own worst dream was one day to find him gone, overdue minute by minute some late afternoon until the inexplicable absence of him became a certainty; knowing that his own worst dream, and best, was of a horse which was itself the flesh of all violent dreams." The novel proceeds to realize these dreams of horror, as if the creative aspects of hallucinatory visualization are the seed of the embodiment. When Margaret Banks experiences a brutal and horrendous beating at the hands of a monstrous thug, she finds herself resisting the reality of what she has suffered: "She hadn't believed [the] beating, really, though it put her out for an hour or more. Later, lying strapped to the bed, she told herself it was what she might have expected: it was something done to abducted girls, that's all. She thought she had read a piece about a beating." When the thug had come to beat her with a truncheon, "it made her think of a bean bag, an amusement for a child."[18] At the novel's end, Michael, as if in acknowledgment that, through his dreams, he bore some responsibility for his wife's fate, launches himself as a projectile to disrupt the horse race his imagination had earlier conceived. Like Emma Zunz, he is both architect and implement. Hawkes's distinctive vision concludes, in fact, with the police "reading" the body of the dead Hencher and misinterpreting it—they see the one accident in this novel of violent intentions as a deliberate homicide and are thus off on a wild goose chase that ignores the very real crimes committed before their eyes.

Don DeLillo is another writer whose distinctive vision is entirely unique and yet evokes Borges. *The Names* explores one man's obsession with a cult that engages in ritual murder. The realization is presented that:

> the world has become self-referring. . . . This thing has seeped into the texture of the world. The world for thousands of years was our escape, was our refuge. Men hid from themselves in the world. We hid from God or death. The world was where we lived, the self was where we went mad and died. But now the world has made a self of its own. . . . What happens to us now that the world has a self? How do we say the simplest thing without falling into a trap? Where do we go, how do we live, who do we believe? This is my vision, a self-referring world, a world in which there is no escape.

We are confronted with the "nightmare of real things, the fallen wonder of the world."[19] *The Names* recalls "Tlön, Uqbar, Orbis Tertius," in which Borges refers to the "intrusion of this fantastic world into the world of reality" (*L* 16): "the world," he concludes, "will be Tlön" (*L* 18).

In "An Autobiographical Essay," Borges wrote, "When I was young, I thought of literature as a game of skillful and surprising variations; now that I have found my own voice, I feel that tinkering and tampering neither greatly improve nor greatly spoil my drafts" (*AOS* 259). Exploring the way in which Borges appears as a presence in our contemporary fiction encompasses a game of conceptualization: we are to realize Borges's voice within other texts just as the "I" in "Borges and I"

18. John Hawkes, *The Lime Twig* (New York: New Directions, 1961), 33, 126, 127.
19. Don DeLillo, *The Names* (New York: Knopf, 1982), 297, 339.

realizes: "I recognize myself less in his [Borges's] books than in many others" (*L* 246). Undoubtedly, other authors might be brought forth, just as there may be perceived Kafka-esque touches in pre-Kafka literature besides Zeno, Kierkegaard, and Browning. In my particular conversation with Borges, I hear his voice in the wonderful trilogy of novels by R. M. Koster—*The Prince* (1973), *The Dissertation* (1975), and *Mandragon* (1981)—in which an imaginary Latin American country is created and chronicled through the textual "evidence" of a doctoral dissertation; I sense his presence in the extraordinary historical minimalism of Edward Whittemore's *Quin's Shanghai Circus* (1974), *Sinai Tapestry* (1977), *Jerusalem Poker* (1978), and *Nile Shadows* (1983); I think of him as I savor the witty philosophical musings of Rebecca Goldstein in *The Mind-Body Problem* (1985); and I am reminded of his embrace of exotic imaginative realms in Celia Gittelson's *Saving Grace* (1981). But "tinkering and tampering" at this point will have no discernible effect. I believe that I have suggested a theme: the naming of specific authors is merely the "game of skillful and surprising variations" that each reader of Borges must continue to play individually in the fiction of our time.

And what is the fiction of our time? Do we call it postmodern, postcontemporary, self-reflexive, late modernist, poststructuralist, deconstructionist? If we mention the qualities to which I alluded earlier— a sense of unreality, self-reflexivity, subjectivity of perception, dissociation of self and object, confusion of generic distinctions, indeterminacy of meaning, the world as a hermeneutic realm of textual meaning, the exhaustion of literary form, intertextual resonances—do we describe the qualities of American postmodern literature? Or are we recognizing, in the fiction of our time, the voice and practices of Borges?

"I live in memory," he remarked in the *Borges at Eighty* interviews; "imagination, I should say, is made of memory and of oblivion" (*BEC* 20). Borges is truly our precursor, and, echoing "Borges and I," we become his alter ego: "everything belongs to oblivion, or to him" (*L* 247).

Malva E. Filer

Salvador Elizondo and Severo Sarduy
Two Borgesian Writers

Since the sixties, critics and scholars have emphasized the impact of Borges's works on the development of our contemporary narrative. In *La nueva novela hispanoamericana* (The new Spanish American novel) Carlos Fuentes states that without Borges's prose there would not be a modern Spanish American novel. The validity of this judgment, generally accepted as evident, should be corroborated, however, by a detailed study of narrative concepts and techniques of distinctive Borgesian quality that can be detected in the most recent works of Spanish American writers. This study is primarily concerned with the process of reelaboration and transcontextualization of the Borgesian legacy as it is continued and transformed in the works of two authors born in the thirties: the Mexican Salvador Elizondo and the Cuban Severo Sarduy.[1]

Borges has communicated his ideas on literature in fragmentary form. In his prologue to *Elogio de la sombra* (In praise of darkness) he declares that he does not have an aesthetic theory of his own and that, in general, he does not believe in aesthetics.[2] However, his essays and works of fiction show evidence of the theoretical foundation on which his narrative practice is based. These texts, permeated by the author's analytic attitude toward language, have attracted critics and theoreticians such as Jean Ricardou, Gérard Genette, and others related with the so-called *nouvelle critique*. Michel Foucault, in his preface to *Les Mots et les choses* (The order of things), points out a central aspect of Borgesian writing that corresponds to his concept of heterotopia.[3] The

---

1. Carlos Fuentes, *La nueva novela hispanoamericana* (Mexico City: Joaquín Mortiz, 1969). I believe that the concept of transcontextualization proposed by Linda Hutcheon is particularly helpful in describing the links connecting the texts analyzed here. Hutcheon conceives of parody as a creative way of approaching tradition, a process that involves revisiting and assimilating the previous literary texts while, at the same time, revising, subverting, and transforming them. The absorbed material is incorporated and replayed within a different context, where textual productivity actualizes and expands its possible meanings (Linda Hutcheon, *A Theory of Parody* [New York: Methuen, 1985]).

2. Jorge Luis Borges, *Elogio de la sombra* (Buenos Aires: Emecé, 1969).

3. One of the first critics to study Borges's impact on *la nouvelle critique* was Emir

passage in "The Analytical Language of John Wilkins" that motivated Foucault's commentary and that he said prompted the writing of his book is representative of a language of rupture where words are fragments of orders so different that it would not be possible to contain them in a common space. This type of language is not accidental in Borges but corresponds to his concept of the literary work as a verbal artifice. It is evident, for example, in his prologue to *A Universal History of Infamy,* where he states, "Scaffolds and pirates populate [this book], and the word 'infamy' in the title is thunderous, but behind the sound and fury there is nothing. The book is no more than appearance, than a surface of images" (*UHI* 12).

As Alazraki has observed, in "The Aleph" Borges confronts the failure of words as signs of things and accepts that they are signs of a new reality, independent of any extratextual reference.[4] The inability of words to fully express reality also emerges in "The Yellow Rose" of *Dreamtigers,* through the revelation experienced by the dying poet Giambattista Marino: "Marino saw the rose as Adam might have seen it in Paradise, and he thought that the rose was to be found in its own eternity and not in his words; and that we may mention or allude to a thing, but not express it" (*Dt* 38). Marino's volumes of poetry could not mirror the world; they were one thing more added to it. While the above-mentioned texts convey, in essence, the nonreferential character of literary language, "Pierre Menard, Author of the *Quixote*" illustrates the idea of reading as a form of writing. Here and elsewhere writing is viewed as a translation that modifies as well as reproduces the previous texts. These are some of the ideas that have most influenced the following generation of Spanish American authors.

Salvador Elizondo became known in 1965 with the publication of *Farabeuf o la crónica de un instante* (Farabeuf or the chronicle of an instant), a book in which "words become the experience that is being described, and reading and experiencing the plot are one and the same."[5] Philosophical, ethical-religious, and aesthetic concerns have converged in the conception of this most complex novel in which we

---

Rodríguez Monegal. He shows how Foucault, Barthes, and Genette, among others, have written on Borges's texts and used them in the elaboration of their own theories, sometimes engaging in what he considers a productive "misreading" (Emir Rodríguez Monegal, "Borges and *La Nouvelle Critique*," *Diacritics* 2:2 [1972]: 27–34). Michel Foucault, *Les Mots et les choses* (Paris: Gallimard, 1966), translated as *The Order of Things: An Archeology of the Human Sciences* (New York: Vintage, 1970).

4. Jaime Alazraki, *La prosa narrativa de Jorge Luis Borges,* 2d ed. (Madrid: Gredos, 1974).

5. I am quoting from the excellent, unsigned description printed on the cover of the book. This and subsequent translations from the Spanish, unless otherwise indicated, are mine.

recognize the model of the *nouveau roman*. Its narration represents a search for the meaning of life and of personal identity in that elusive moment of death that words try to capture. The author acknowledges, however, that "cursive and successive writing can only obtain a reflection of that instantaneity, already mediated": not temporal instantaneity, but rather "the instantaneity of sensation produced by the reading."[6] Thus the Chinese torture to which Dr. Farabeuf subjects his lover and victim is only an ideogram, the writing of an idea. This is why Sarduy correctly affirms that *Farabeuf* is "the book of sadistic literalness." Or, as the author himself declares, what occurs there is totally artificial; its horror is a dramatic effect and its representations "cannot take place," since "it is impossible to represent the mental drama of Farabeuf."[7]

Elizondo has carried to its final consequence the Borgesian concept of writing as "a surface of images" in his pursuit of a pure writing in vacuo, that is to say, a writing that is not representable. His characters thus profess to be a mental product, an image, a text reflected in a mirror or simply "an accumulation of words."[8] It should also be emphasized that in *Farabeuf* the chronological sequence is destroyed and words are signs of diverging, converging, and parallel times much like those Borges made Ts'ui Pên conceive in "The Garden of Forking Paths." The narration unfolds in the confluence of fragments of the past reelaborated through the incessant flow of memory; in the anticipatory images of a future as much desired as it is feared; and in a present that vanishes at the very moment it is mentioned. Here, as in Borges, the destruction of chronological time means a negation of personal identity. Individual identity becomes illusory without the accumulation of recollections of past experiences that serve to support the self. If continuity is illusory, then what we have are "moments of a man," not a man himself. Likewise, Elizondo's feminine character is fragmented in the images of her own memory and in those the mirror arouses in her mind. The flow of anticipatory images of death attributed to this protagonist and the "mental drama" of Dr. Farabeuf also echo Borges's story "The Secret Miracle": Jaromir Hladík, after living through hundreds of deaths before being executed, during one

6. Salvador Elizondo, "Entrevista," interview with Jorge Ruffinelli, *Hispamérica* 16 (1977): 33–47 (34).

7. Severo Sarduy, *Escrito sobre un cuerpo* (Written on a body; Buenos Aires: Sudamericana, 1969), 29; Elizondo, "Entrevista," 40. In studying Sarduy, I also used Roberto González Echevarría, *La ruta de Severo Sarduy* (Hanover, N.H.: Ediciones del Norte, 1987), as a background work.

8. Salvador Elizondo, *Farabeuf o la crónica de un instante* (Mexico City: Joaquín Mortiz, 1965), 94.

year that elapses only within his mind concludes a drama that does not take place except as "the circular delirium" interminably lived and relived by the character Kubin.

In Elizondo's subsequent works, we continue to encounter characters and narrative forms that confirm the link between his writing and that of Borges. "La historia según Pao Cheng" (History according to Pao Cheng) in *Narda o el verano* (Narda or summer; 1966) exhibits a marked similarity to "The Circular Ruins," for example. In Elizondo's story, Pao Cheng was a philosopher who, more than thirty-five hundred years ago, claimed to know the history of the world in advance. Cheng "figured out" the great events that would occur in "every town throughout several millennia" as if they were written on a turtle's shell. In one of the future cities, which he imagined down to the smallest detail, he saw a man who was writing a story entitled "La historia según Pao Cheng." It dealt with Pao Cheng, a philosopher of antiquity who claimed to know the history of the world in advance. Cheng understood that he was only "a memory of that man," and that if that man forgot him, he would die. The man also wrote on the paper, "If that man forgets me I will die"; scarcely had he finished writing these words when he understood that "he had condemned himself, for all eternity, to continue writing the history of Pao Cheng, because if his character was forgotten and died, he, who was no more than a thought in the mind of Pao Cheng, would also disappear."[9] The similarity between this story and Borges's "The Circular Ruins" is so obvious that it requires no commentary. Similarities can also be seen between "Tlön, Uqbar, Orbis Tertius" and "La fundación de Roma" (The foundation of Rome), a story included in *El retrato de Zoe y otras mentiras* (The portrait of Zoe and other lies; 1969), and between "The Dead Man" and "El ángel azul" (The blue angel) from the same collection. "La fundación de Roma" describes a universe where time moves backward and everything, human and otherwise, goes toward its dissolution. This world where living is forgetting is eventually destroyed by a god's introduction of the mirror, which reinstates memory and the yearning for love. Elizondo's story was inspired by a newspaper report on a scientific theory, in much the same manner as Borges's description of the planet Tlön was patterned after the principles of Berkeley's philosophical idealism. "El ángel azul" evokes (as does "The Dead Man") an environment of passion and violence (more criminal in Elizondo's than in Borges's story); in both cases the protagonist is presented as doomed from the very beginning.[10]

9. Salvador Elizondo, *Narda o el verano* (Mexico City: ERA, 1966), 103, 105–6.
10. Salvador Elizondo, *El retrato de Zoe y otras mentiras* (Mexico City: Joaquín Mortiz, 1969).

Of greater importance, however, is the evolution of ideas on the relation between writing and reality in two more ambitious books by Elizondo, *El hipogeo secreto* (The secret cave; 1968) and *El grafógrafo* (The graphographer; 1972). In this context, mention should also be made of *Cuaderno de escritura* (Notebook for writing; 1969), where we find a significant chapter on the poetry of Borges. Elizondo states that Borges's work represents "the highest possibility of a language . . . directed toward invention, which is, also, the most prodigious and difficult of poetic tasks. Borges's work, as that of the encyclopedists of 'Tlön, Uqbar,' is the vast account of a fictitious and mental civilization; his poetry, just as the piece of metal of his story, is the fact that verifies the certainty of its existence."[11]

El hipogeo secreto is primarily a novel about the writing of a novel. Its narrator declares that his book "is conceived on two levels: that of the life of the writer who writes the book, and that of the story he is narrating."[12] The story, which occurs in a city with the suggestive name of Polt and whose complete manuscript is already contained in a "red leather album," exhibits unmistakable signs of unreality. The narrator himself indicates his intention of maintaining "the ambiguity of all identities," including his own. In fact, the level corresponding to the life of the author writing the book unfolds in an atmosphere as unreal as that of the story itself. Elizondo's novelistic technique and fabulations undoubtedly operate within the realm of fantastic literature, as Octavio Paz indicated.[13] In *El hipogeo secreto,* as in Borges, a world of dreaming characters is dreamt, but this world is contained in the eternal present of the stone, as it was conceived by the ancient Chinese. Its language strives to express the fascination with the mystery of the mineral world, the world that never dies. The narrator and his secret society, the Urkreis, propose—quite simply—to solve the enigma of the universe. The answer is found in the inscription on the stone that reveals the nature of time. This brings to mind a significant phrase from "The Library of Babel," "O Time your pyramids," as well as Borges's fantastic solution to the mystery of time in his story on Tlön. In *El hipogeo secreto,* as on the fantastic planet, time is "an eternal present toward which all temporal perspectives flee and these, of necessity, are more than three." The search of Elizondo's narrator is the same as that of Borges's librarian, and there is clear allusion to that in his description of the secret society's attempts to decipher the message: "Throughout

11. Salvador Elizondo, *Cuaderno de escritura* (Guanajato: Universidad de Guanajato, 1969), 58.
12. Salvador Elizondo, *El hipogeo secreto* (Mexico City: Joaquín Mortiz, 1968), 58.
13. Octavio Paz, *El signo y el garabato* (The sign and the scrawl; Mexico City: Joaquín Mortiz, 1973).

the millennia of their search enormous underground archives have been established in which, by means of a binary classification, the destiny of men is registered in an infinite number of guides. . . . These volumes are nothing but coded catalogs of small, private libraries, modest collections of unusual books, in some of whose worn and reread copies we may be inscribed, before and after this time, as a succession of words."[14]

Through different routes, then, Elizondo's novel enters into the universe of the fantastic, which is also Borges's universe. In both, the invention of reality in the "surface of images" of the writing is the poetic solution to the insoluble philosophical enigmas that occupy their minds and their imaginations. Likewise, we recognize in *El hipogeo secreto* other features that are usually associated with the author of *Ficciones,* such as the cultivation of suspense and the inclusion, for the reader's benefit, of clues both real and false. An example of the latter is the repeated reference to *Les 500 millions de la Bégum* (The begum's fortune) by Jules Verne, together with the narrative's self-characterization as an adventure novel.

In *El grafógrafo,* Elizondo has carried his concept of writing in vacuo to the limit. The discourse of the book is not representation of a reality, or subordination of form to meaning, but rather the discourse is itself the meaning. The author's intention is clearly expressed: "Cut the serpentine umbilicus that connects a word with a thing and you will find that it begins to grow autonomously, as does a child; it then flourishes and matures when it acquires a new, common, and transmissible meaning." *El grafógrafo* rejects the possibility that writing is representative of either sensible reality or mental image and admits only the existence of the universe of discourse: "Only one real, concrete form of thinking exists, the writing."[15] In 1977, in order to exit from this blind alley where his experimentation with language had led him, Elizondo declared that in the book he was then writing (*Camera lucida,* 1983) he had to "invent a special scenario in which the impossible writing, set forth as possible within that space, is realized: that space is the desert island . . . the empty room."[16]

14. Elizondo, *El hipogeo,* 20, 152.

15. Salvador Elizondo, *El grafógrafo* (Mexico City: Joaquín Mortiz, 1972), 16, 61. Victorio G. Agüera has analyzed the philosophical background of Elizondo's concern with the discontinuity between mental perception and writing in *El grafógrafo.* He shows that Elizondo's early adherence to Husserl and Wittgenstein's phenomenological concepts has been replaced in this book by a graphocentrism closer to Derrida's views (Victorio G. Agüera, "El discurso grafocéntrico en *El grafógrafo* de Salvador Elizondo," *Hispamérica* 29 [1981]: 15–27).

16. Elizondo, "Entrevista," 39.

In *Camera lucida,* Elizondo's greatest concern is the origin of the images that invade and obsess his own mind as a writer and the alchemy through which those images are retained and transformed into literary texts. On the desert island he cannot differentiate between himself as the author and himself as the character. "Writing . . . is reduced at the same time that it is duplicated in the attempt to write a novel about its author," or about its author's "imagining and writing a text of such nature that it goes on creating itself." The author imagines himself, as does the narrator of "Borges and I," accompanied by that "entity which he has invented." His character was composed of the "fragments of other characters which, in turn, formed yet another character, namely the author." The author-character "has remained *in vitro,*" as a display eternally constructed and torn down by the mind in the mirror of writing. The text expands like a labyrinthine construction in time (in the same manner as the garden of Ts'ui Pên), embracing in one given moment "all possible conjectures," which "advance uncontrollably, accumulating conjectures of new novels, constantly original, about the inhabitant of the desert island."[17] The writing is invisible, as was that of the *Quixote* of Pierre Menard, or that which Hladík wrote prior to his death. Elizondo's author-character rereads, composes, and mentally corrects the rough draft of an imaginary log and after reading the sheets throws them into the fire.

There are numerous coincidences and affinities between Borges and Elizondo. If we confine ourselves to *Camera lucida* we can indicate, for example, the Borgesian fantasy and humor of "Anapoyesis," a tale about the "scientific" project of Professor Aubanel, which consisted of liberating the energy encapsulated in an unpublished poem of Mallarmé. Similarly representative is the story about the invention of the "chronostatoscope," developed through "Los museos de Metaxiphas" (The museums of Metaxiphas) and "La luz que regresa" (The light that returns). The narrator describes the "chronostatoscope" as an instrument invented by Professor Moriarty in 1997, by means of which one can observe historical events at the time and place where they occur, both in the past and in the future. As can be seen here, the Borgesian text grows and expands in Elizondo's text. His rewriting appropriates and modifies the legacy of the master in the inscription of new realities. As I will soon demonstrate, Sarduy also writes within this new Spanish American literary tradition to which Borges has contributed his founding texts.

When considering Severo Sarduy's literary background, it should

17. Salvador Elizondo, *Camera lucida* (Mexico City: Joaquín Mortiz, 1983), 17, 17, 22, 23, 23.

first be noted that the Cuban writer started his literary career in the environment created by José Lezama Lima and his review *Orígenes,* whose influence decisively oriented the development of Sarduy's theory and practice of the neo-baroque. Also important are his subsequent links with structuralists such as Roland Barthes, Julia Kristeva, François Wahl, and Phillippe Sollers and his active participation in the *Tel Quel* group, whose journal he has collaborated on since 1965. The theoretical principles of the *nouvelle critique* and the reading of Lévi-Strauss, Lacan, and Derrida, among others, have been incorporated into his essays as well as into his narrative. At the same time, the links between his fiction and essays and Borges's work (while not as explicit as those that bind him to Lezama Lima) are also traceable, as is demonstrated in a brief but perceptive essay by Suzanne Jill Levine.[18] Concurring with her, I point out the fact that Sarduy has recognized the centrality of the parodical element in Borges's work, an element that is also crucial to his own conception of the neo-baroque. He observes, for example, that in *Six Problems for Don Isidro Parodi* Borges, as Cervantes, "assumes a known corpus, assimilated through common thought . . ., of which the novel is the eulogistic and burlesque reiteration."[19] Expanding on Sarduy, it is permissible to affirm for example that *A Universal History of Infamy,* whose "excessive title," according to Borges, "proclaims its baroque nature" (*UHI* 12), is a parody of both biography and history and their supposed scientific rigor. Such skepticism is evident, also, in his description of Tlön, in its archaeologists capable of "the interrogation and even the modification of the past which . . . is now no less plastic and docile than the future" (*L* 14); and in "Theme of the Traitor and the Hero," where history is drama and fiction, and the official biography of the hero is an invention that time has legitimized as truth.

That Sarduy travels the same paths frequented by Borges is evident in the definitions of writing in the first chapter of *Cobra* (1972), particularly in the statement that "writing is the art of restoring History," which introduces, as Emir Rodríguez Monegal has stated, "the assuredly false biography of the character in question."[20] For Sarduy, as for Borges and Elizondo, the reality of the text is the text itself. Borges creates characters who conquer and then reject immortality, as in "The Immortal," or

18. Suzanne Jill Levine, "Borges a *Cobra* es barroco exégesis," in *Severo Sarduy,* ed. Julián Ríos (Madrid: Fundamentos, 1976), 89–105.

19. Severo Sarduy, "Notas a las Notas a las Notas. . . . A propósito de Manuel Puig," *Revista Iberoamericana* 76–77 (1971): 555–67 (555).

20. Severo Sarduy, *Cobra* (Buenos Aires: Sudamericana, 1972). The quotation is from the translation *Cobra,* trans. Suzanne Jill Levine (New York: Dutton, 1975), 8. Emir Rodríguez Monegal, "Las metamorfosis del texto," in Ríos, *Severo Sarduy,* 35–61 (49).

who live diverse and contradictory existences, as in "The Lottery in Babylon." These characters are clearly conceived as verbal objects, whose transformations operate on the surface of writing, and who correspond to Borges's idea that "one single immortal man is all men" (*L* 115). Sarduy's characters are also made of the same verbal material; they are characters whom the word freely sketches and transforms throughout the text, as occurs with Help and Mercy in *De donde son los cantantes* (From Cuba with a song; 1967). "Help and Mercy are gifted with (and abuse) the power of metamorphosis: chorus girls at the opera, and two bit whores," Sarduy says. He claims that "both want to disappear, to be someone else: therefore the constant transformation, the wealth of cosmetics, artifices."[21] Help and Mercy recapitulate the history of Cuba in a long journey that begins in Moslem Spain and ends in a recent epoch, with a procession that goes from Santiago to Havana, a probable allusion to Castro's march and his triumphal entry into the capital city.

The protagonist of *Cobra* is also transformed through makeup, adornments, various attempts to reduce the size of his masculine feet, and a sex-change operation. Cobra aspires to become a "perfect queen," a "doll." Having failed in his attempts, he returns to his masculine state, from which he seeks to transcend the body and achieve Nirvana. More closely related to our theme, however, is the "dermic silversmith," another character in *Cobra,* in whose biography we perceive a kinship with the multiple Joseph Cartaphilus of Borges's "The Immortal." Among various data, we note the following: "He fought in the court of a maharajah. . . . He had escaped the Kashmir revolution with a suitcase of jewels that he squandered . . . in flowered barges—the lake brothels of the North . . . and in fixed tournaments . . . against the champions from Calcutta; he had revived a wrestling school in Benares, and in Ceylon a tea concession. . . . He was a spice importer in Colombo," and, after crippling six Turkish champions in Smyrna, he went over to the West, as an opium trafficker and ivory smuggler in Copenhagen, Brussels, and Amsterdam. He cultivated "to obsession an Oxford accent" and "an officially oriental beard."[22] This ubiquitous character, whose unusual traits and prodigious itinerary arouse not astonishment but rather ironic commentaries on the part of the narrator, has all the essential characteristics of a typical Borgesian character. The author of *Cobra* may well be adding his own parody to that earlier model.

Suzanne Jill Levine states in the above-mentioned essay that there is a

21. Severo Sarduy, *De donde son los cantantes* (Mexico City: Joaquín Mortiz, 1970). The quotation is from the translation "From Cuba with a Song," trans. Suzanne Jill Levine, in *Triple Cross* (New York: Dutton, 1972), 235–329 (328).

22. Sarduy, *Cobra* (1975), 8–10.

continuity between the apocryphal orientals in *A Universal History of Infamy,* the Chinese in *De donde son los cantantes,* and the Indians and other orientals in *Cobra.* In both cases what is offered is, in effect, a mask—the Orient imagined by Western man as part of his own culture. Likewise, a possible antecedent of the mystical searches, which Sarduy transforms into caricature and parody in *Cobra* and in *Maitreya* (1978), would be Borges's fiction "The Approach to al-Mu'tasim." Roberto González Echevarría sees in the chapter of *Cobra* entitled "Para los pájaros" (For the birds) a probable allusion to the story of the Simurg, the king of birds, which Borges mentions in a footnote to his work.[23] This story conveys the notion of identity between the seeker of the divine presence and that which is sought; or, more philosophically, the idea that the divine principle radiates its presence in varying degrees over all creation, as explained by Plotinus. In Borges's "The Approach to al-Mu'tasim," written as a commentary to a novel by a fictitious Hindu author, it is stated that "in the measure to which the men questioned have known al-Mu'tasim more intimately, in that measure is their divine portion the greater—though it is always clear that they are mere mirrors" (*F* 40). This idea is also implicit in *Maitreya,* but here the search is made through the exacerbation of excessive sensuality. In this respect, Sarduy follows Lezama Lima's *Paradiso,* where the glimmer of the divine principle and the ideal ascent toward it are conceived in purely sensual terms.[24]

In his prologue to *A Universal History of Infamy,* Borges states: "The theologians of the Great Vehicle point out that the essence of the universe is emptiness" (*UHI* 12). Sarduy's work, as well, constantly alludes to emptiness, the concept that gives substance to *Maitreya's* final reflection. The characters of this novel utilize, in caricature, the entire repertoire of magic: amulets, drugs, extraordinary visions, diabolical births, orgiastic feasts, and sadomasochistic rites. Sarduy's text claims with Borgesian irony (and a coincidence of words with the above-quoted prologue): "They twisted . . . the moderating precepts of the Great Vehicle. . . . They lacked . . . metaphorical audacity." *Cobra's* aspiration to achieve Nirvana is resumed in *Maitreya* in an even more debased and burlesque version. The Buddhism for mass consumption, the commercialized, unauthentic Orient presented here is only a mask with nothing behind it. The narration concludes with a radical skepticism parallel to that of Borges: "They mimicked rites to the point of idiocy or tedium. In order to prove the impermanence and vacuity of

23. Roberto González Echevarría, "Memoria de apariencias y ensayo de *Cobra,*" in Ríos, *Severo Sarduy,* 63–86 (75).

24. Lezama Lima, *Paradiso* (Madrid: Alianza, 1983). English translation by Gregory Rabassa (Austin: University of Texas Press, 1988).

everything."[25] At the same time, however, Sarduy's text toys with several philosophical concepts, in the Borgesian manner. I point out, for example, the following coincidence. In "The Analytical Language of John Wilkins," Borges cites a paragraph from Hume (of Gnostic origin), which raises the possibility that the world might be the rudimentary sketch of some infant God, or the work of a subordinate god, or the confused production of a decrepit divinity. We encounter the same idea, translated into the colorful language of Sarduy, in this paragraph from *Maitreya:* "The universe—recited the dwarf as if he were in a white, hexagonal room, caressing a pelican choking on a wriggling salmon—is the work of a hurried and clumsy god."[26] In the chaotic Library of Babel (the universe), which Borges precisely conceives as a number, perhaps infinite, of "hexagonal galleries," the members of a blasphemous sect "weakly imitated the divine disorder" (*L* 51, 56); and in "The Lottery in Babylon" it was established that "accepting errors is not contradicting chance," but "corroborating it" (*L* 33). Similarly in *Maitreya* the reflection of the dwarf—a typical textual creature of the author—concludes with a declaration that his goal is to achieve "total chaos." The "leagues of senseless cacophonies, of verbal jumbles and incoherencies," mentioned by the narrator of "The Library of Babel," are, in Sarduy's text, a "joke in poor taste which includes everything, from the aurora borealis to the Tahitian omelet."[27] Borges plays with the philosophical and theological ideas with which, for centuries, human intelligence has endeavored to understand the principles that rule the universe. While he does not consider them to be instruments of knowledge, he admires the ingenuity and imagination invested in them. As for Sarduy, he plays with a repertoire of magic and esotericism imported from the Orient, whose false and popularized version provides Western man with new, illusory explanations he no longer finds in the theoretical and philosophical systems of his own culture.

The most recent literary production of Severo Sarduy includes his essay collection *La simulación* (Simulation; 1982) and his novel *Colibrí* (Colibri; 1984). These works correspond to a process equivalent to that which produced *El grafógrafo* by Salvador Elizondo. Like the Mexican writer, whose novel *Farabeuf* he studied in *Escrito sobre un cuerpo,* Sarduy in his later books has made his rejection of representative writing even more radical and explicit. Nothing is thinkable, he says, while art and literature seek to establish an impossible relation between model and copy, so that "one of the terms may be an image of the

25. Severo Sarduy, *Maitreya* (Barcelona: Seix Barral, 1978), 34, 187.
26. Ibid., 112.
27. Ibid., 113.

other": this would imply the self-contradictory proposition that what is different may be the same.[28] However, his own writing is not dualistic but is fostered by "an intensity of simulation that constitutes its own end, outside of that which it seeks to imitate." Nevertheless, the referential function of discourse cannot be made to disappear. *Colibrí* is, as Adriana Méndez Rodenas correctly observes, the battleground between the text-simulacrum and the realistic text, between simulation and verisimilitude.[29] This is particularly manifest in the chapter with the title "Guerra de escrituras" (War of writings). On the intratextual level, the work repeatedly declares its condition of verbal artifact, of representation or simulacrum behind which lies nothing, an "empty decoration, with neither depth nor support." On the intertextual level *Colibrí* introduces, although transgressed and adulterated, fragments of traditional Spanish American texts such as *Doña Bárbara* (whose protagonist can be detected under the disguise of la Regenta) and *La vorágine* (The vortex), to which we encounter repeated irreverent allusions.[30] This irreverent writing of canonical texts also has pioneering antecedents in Borges's works. It may be sufficient to recall, for example, the "The Life of Tadeo Isidoro Cruz (1829–1874)," published in 1944, and "The End" (1953), both of which are tales that rework and "complete" the nineteenth-century Argentine poem *Martín Fierro* of José Hernández. Nor should we overlook his earliest study on "La poesía gauchesca" (Gauchesque poetry) in *Obras Completas,* in which he hails José Hernández as an innovator, not a mere follower, of the *gauchesco* tradition.[31] Sarduy's attitude regarding past cultural models is, in general, more closely related to that of Borges than to that of his compatriot Cabrera Infante, who in *Tres tristes tigres* (Three trapped tigers) creates ingenious stylistic pastiches with texts from the generation of writers that preceded him. In *La simulación* we find an explanation of Fernando Botero's painting that is also a definition of Sarduy's point of view and that, at the same time, continues and expands the Borgesian position: "Not to deny the compact and codified continuity of figures, but to consider them as an unfinished sequence," to which a new image is added. This new

28. Severo Sarduy, *La simulación* (Caracas: Monte Avila, 1982), 11.

29. Adriana Méndez Rodenas, review of *Colibrí* in *Revista Iberoamericana* 130–31 (1985): 399–401 (399).

30. Severo Sarduy, *Colibrí* (Barcelona: Argos Vergara, 1984), 111; 48, 150, and 176.

31. Edna Aizenberg shows that Borges's interest in the cabalists centers on the hermeneutic procedures by which they make "new ideas seem to derive naturally from the old biblical text" (Edna Aizenberg, *The Aleph Weaver: Biblical, Kabbalistic and Judaic Elements in Borges* [Potomac, Md.: Scripta Humanistica, 1984], 104). Likewise, Borges conceives of writing as a transformation, modification, and renovation of traditional texts, a concept that he applies to some representative works of Western culture as well as to *Martín Fierro,* the Argentine canonic book.

image indicates "irreverence with regard to the model, disrespect of that which is no longer taken as a paradigm, but as a simple sketch which has yet to be completed, re-created, reversed, or reflected in an impertinent imitation: an 'inflated,' baroque simulacrum." Sarduy seems to be attracted to Botero's work for reasons parallel to those that prompted Elizondo to write about Alberto Gironella's painting. In both cases, pictorial art offers a deeper insight into cultural meaning through the irreverent imitation of consecrated models. Sarduy's writing is closer to this baroque transgression than Elizondo's and closer, in this sense, to Borges's parodical intertextuality. So it is not surprising that in the final paragraph of *La simulación* the author recalls that Borges sees all faces in one face, "since universal combination is limited and its configurations are repeated in a time without *telos*."[32]

The preceding pages have underscored two aspects I consider to be representative of Borges's influence on the work of younger Spanish American writers. They are the postulation of a nonreferential and self-reflexive writing and the concept of writing as the deconstruction of the repertoire of universal philosophy and culture. The analysis of Elizondo's works shows that Borgesian themes, narrative technique, and ironic humor are incorporated and transformed within the texts of the Mexican author. On the other hand, Sarduy's books are parodic, irreverent, and radically skeptical, as are those of the Argentine writer. His textual creatures and apocryphal orientals, as well as his many allusions to Borges's fiction, indicate Sarduy's productive reading and rewriting of Borges's work. Elizondo and Sarduy are writers of marked individuality, whose works exhibit unmistakably distinctive features. When incorporating and modifying the Borgesian legacy, each, with his own imagination, contributes to a written palimpsest that reflects the multiple faces of Spanish American culture.

32. Sarduy, *La simulación*, 87, 87, 134.

IV
The Visual Arts

Richard Peña

Borges and the
New Latin American Cinema

At least since the publication of Edgardo Cozarinsky's *Borges y el cine* (Borges and the cinema; 1974), the relationship between the cinema and the work of Jorge Luis Borges has been the subject of intense speculation and at times heated debate.[1] Yet by far the greatest part of the discussion has centered around the influence of Borges on a number of European, principally French, filmmakers: Alain Resnais, Alain Robbe-Grillet, and especially Jacques Rivette. By and large, the "new Latin American Cinema"—admittedly an unwieldy term, but one that will be used here to encompass the work of filmmakers since the fifties in Brazil, Cuba, Mexico, Argentina, and elsewhere in Latin America—has ignored Borges, seeking inspiration instead from the "magic realism" of Gabriel García Márquez, Alejo Carpentier, Guimarães Rosa or, in the case of some Brazilian filmmakers, from the *modernismo* of Mario and Oswald de Andrade. Partially because of the recurrent, rather narrow criticism of Borges's writing that saw it as the supreme example of art disengaged from the political and social environment, few exam-

1. Edgardo Cozarinsky, *Borges y el cine* (Buenos Aires: Sur, 1974). The following works were also consulted in the preparation of this essay: Gilbert Adair, "The Rubicon and the Rubik Cube," *Sight and Sound* 51 (1981–1982): 40–44; "Après Allende: Entretien avec Raoul Ruiz," *Positif* 164 (1974): 14–18; Robert Brown, review of *The Three Crowns of the Sailor* in *Monthly Film Bulletin* 611 (1984): 366–67; Christine Buci-Glucksman and Fabrice Revault D'Allons, *Raoul Ruiz* (Paris: Dis Voir-Sarl, 1987); Michael Chanan, ed., *Chilean Cinema* (London: British Film Institute, 1976); Ian Christie, "Raúl Ruiz and the House of Culture," *Sight and Sound* 56 (1987): 96–100; Thomas Elsaesser, review of *The Hypothesis of the Stolen Painting* in *Monthly Film Bulletin* 611 (1984): 368–69; "Entretien avec Raoul Ruiz," *Positif* 123 (1971): 45–51; "Entretien avec Raoul Ruiz," *Positif* 274 (1983): 23–31; Paul Hammond, review of *City of Pirates* in *Monthly Film Bulletin* 612 (1985): 6–7; Alain Philippon, "Raoul Ruiz: fantôme de la vidéo," *Nouvelles Littéraires* 2742 (1980): 55–61; Alain Philippon, "Raoul Ruiz: Grenoble-Le Havre," *Cahiers du cinéma* 375 (1985): 1–2; *Raúl Ruiz* (Madrid: Filmoteca Nacional de España, 1978); Jonathan Rosenbaum, review of *Dogs' Dialogue* in *Monthly Film Bulletin* 612 (1985): 390–91. The following articles in *Afterimage* 10 (1981), an issue devoted entirely to Raúl Ruiz, proved particularly useful: "Between Institutions: Interview with Raúl Ruiz," pp. 103–15; Ian Christie, "Exile and Cunning," pp. 70–71; Ian Christie, "Snakes and Ladders: Television Games," pp. 78–86; Malcolm Coad, "Great Events and Ordinary People," pp. 72–77; Raúl Ruiz, "Image, Memory, Death: Imaginary Dialogues," pp. 95–102; Raúl Ruiz, "Object Relations in the Cinema," pp. 87–94.

ples of Borgesian influence in the Latin American cinema can be found,
at least until recent years. Paradoxically, Borges is a rare example of a
major Latin American intellectual figure working before 1960 who
showed any real interest in the cinema at all; from 1931 to 1944, he
contributed frequent film reviews and articles on cinema to the magazine *Sur* and even went so far as to claim the films of Joseph von
Sternberg as a decisive influence upon his work. Among the older
generation of Latin American writers, perhaps only Vicente Huidobro
demonstrated a similar level of interest in the new medium.

Of course, one must logically ask what would in fact constitute
evidence of "Borgesian influence" on the work of a given filmmaker?
Surely mere adaptation to the screen of a writer's work could not
generally be readily seen as influence. The problem is compounded in
the case of Borges due to the fact that he had always worked in short
literary formats that do not lend themselves to the requirements of
feature-length films.

One way to approach this question would be to examine Borges's
own writing on cinema. The reviews and articles published in *Sur* can
hardly be said to add up to a coherent "theory of cinema," yet one can
see certain crucial threads running through many of these pieces. In a
way that finds no parallel in his time, Borges explores the process and
problems of cinematic narration: how stories are told, and especially
the relationship of characters to the narrative process. Borges imagines
an active viewer situated somewhere between the work of the filmmaker and the film world as it exists on screen; the viewer should be
able to move freely between both, losing himself or herself in the
distinction between the film as artistic creation and the film as separate
reality. Thus Borges rails against the Hollywood tendency, in films such
as John Ford's *The Informer,* to overindulge in the rendering of local
color or atmosphere; clearly the film is being shot in a California film
studio, not in Dublin, so that the insistence to authenticate the settings
and costumes does little but call attention to itself as a symbol of the
production's expense. Similarly, he objects to a tendency, certainly on
the rise in the American cinema of the late thirties and early forties, to
weigh down characters with excessive motivation for their actions;
thus his admiration of *Citizen Kane,* a film based upon the premise that
even an infinite number of points of view on a man would be insufficient to fully describe or know him.

These kinds of concerns, about the problems of narration and representation, were approached by Latin American filmmakers such as
Glauber Rocha, Julio Bressane, Fernando Solanas, and Octavio Getino
in the sixties, through a political position that sought to create a Latin
American or Third World film aesthetic which would deny the prem-

ises of the classical (or studio-based) and art (or *auteurist*) cinemas. Narration and representation were not themselves problematic; rather, it was their use by the dominant (Hollywood or European) cinema that must be challenged.

The Latin American filmmakers who would attempt to create a cinema directly aware of Borges's concerns would be that generation of principally Argentine and Chilean filmmakers who, generally due to political reasons, would find themselves living in Paris in the seventies. As a scriptwriter, the Argentine Eduardo De Gregorio would have a crucial influence on the work of Jacques Rivette, a founding member of the French New Wave and one of the filmmakers most open about the influence of Borges on his work. In *Céline and Julie Go Boating* (1974), which was coscripted by De Gregorio, Rivette and the principal actresses, a magician (Céline) and a librarian (Julie), accidentally meet and become friends. Céline tells a wild story about her tenure as a nurse-governess in an old mansion run by a peculiar ménage à trois; throughout the film, the two take turns entering into the house, although each time they emerge from it they are struck with amnesia. Fortunately, they have access to a magic candy that, when sucked, allows them (and us) the chance to see everything that has transpired inside the house: a lurid melodrama of jealousy that alternately stars Céline and Julie as the nurse-governess. The scenes within the house, in which the "characters" of Céline and Julie become aware of themselves as "characters" in another film, perfectly embody the Borgesian paradox of being both within and outside of the space of cinematic narration. Characters in Rivette's work, especially in those films coscripted by De Gregorio, are constantly seeking ways in which they can enter the "plot," a term that is often literalized to mean conspiracy. The search for the plot becomes the ordering principle not only of *Céline and Julie Go Boating* but also of Rivette's other films, *Out One/Spectre, Duelle, Merry-Go-Round,* and *Le Pont du Nord;* the story becomes how a character, often one with little or no connection to anything else, becomes part of the story. One is reminded of detective Lönnrot in "Death and the Compass": his solving of the mystery is but one part of the mystery itself.

Other European-based Latin American exiles, such as Hugo Santiago (*Les Autres* [The others], whose script was in fact written in collaboration with Borges and Bioy Casares) and Edgardo Cozarinsky himself (*Les Apprentis sorciers* [Apprentice sorcerers]), would attempt similar kinds of experimentation with narrative, yet no one would more successfully answer the call for a Borgesian cinema than the Chilean Raúl Ruiz. An exile from his native Chile since 1973, Ruiz is almost universally considered one of the most important filmmakers working anywhere today; his work has been widely discussed, and in 1983 the prestigious film journal *Cahiers du cinema* devoted an entire issue to his work.[2] Yet rarely is Ruiz considered a "Latin American" filmmaker; beyond the fact that his work since 1973 has been produced largely in France and in French, there is the regrettable charge that Ruiz's kind of cinema, and the issues he confronts, are too "European," as if issues of narrative and representation would be of no real interest to Latin Americans. Of course, this kind of easy putdown has consistently plagued the work of Borges as well.

To begin with, we can ask "who is Raúl Ruiz?" Born in Puerto Montt, Chile, in 1941, Ruiz grew up in a middle-class family; for most of his youth his father was employed as a ship captain, a fact that will come as no surprise to those familiar with his films. After studies in theology and law at the University of Santiago, Ruiz left school to devote himself to full-time writing, thanks to a Ford Foundation grant received in 1962. His first literary efforts were in theater, and by his own estimate he had written well over one hundred plays before moving into cinema.

In 1964, Ruiz went to film school in Santa Fe, Argentina, at the program run by Fernando Birri, an Argentine documentarist and one of the most important ideologues of the "new Latin American cinema." Ruiz left after a year, claiming that he "had to forget everything they taught me," and returned to Chile. Shortly after his return, he fell in with a group of intellectuals and cineasts that would form the nucleus of the "new Chilean cinema" of the late sixties: future directors such as Miguel Littín, Pedro Chaskell, Aldo Francia, and others, who were hoping to create a cinema in the spirit of the Brazilian *Cinema Novo* of the same period—a cinema that offers a bitter reflection on social reality while challenging the modes of dominant filmmaking practice. His first feature, *Tres tigres tristes* (Three sad tigers)—no relation to the Cabrera Infante novel of similar name—was completed in 1967; Ruiz recalls that the same camera used for that film was used simultaneously for Littín's *The Jackal of Nahueltero* and Francia's *Valparaíso, Valparaíso*. Politically, Ruiz joined the Socialist party, then allied with Allende's Popular Front. During the Allende years, he worked closely with Chile Films, the national film agency, on a number of films and television programs, although several of his works were attacked at the time for being "divisive" or "obscure."

Following Allende's overthrow, Ruiz fled to Europe, eventually settling in France. The sheer quantity of his output since 1974 is simply staggering; to date, Ruiz has completed well over fifty feature films, shorts, and videos. In 1985, for example, he completed four feature films, three one-hour children's films, two chapters (each an hour long)

2. *Cahiers du cinéma* 345 (1983).

of a serial, plus several shorts. To complicate matters, in August 1985 Ruiz became director of the Maison de Culture in Le Havre, where he hopes to produce films, videos, and stage productions for artists such as Manoel de Oliveira and Sergei Parajanov.

Faced with a filmography as varied and as rich as that of Ruiz, the hunting down of parallels or influence threatens to become somewhat pedantic; there are echoes of everyone and everything from the Cabala to Italo Calvino, from Robert Louis Stevenson to the horror films of the British Hammer Studios, yet this very encyclopedism is, arguably, extremely Borgesian. For Borges the entire weight of all of world literature—plus the presence of quite a few books that have never been written—forms a constant background to his writing; for Ruiz we can add the weight of world cinema, along with the visual traditions associated with the performing arts in general.

The films of Jacques Rivette, Jean-Marie Straub, Chantal Akerman, and other European experimental filmmakers working with screen narrative in the seventies were often preoccupied with the problems of storytelling. The classical Hollywood cinema had been a storytelling cinema par excellence and had of course developed a large number of codes and practices to render meaning or convey facts. For Rivette, Straub, Akerman, and others, who were often linked under the unfortunate rubric of "structuralist" filmmakers, their goal became the breakdown or deconstruction of classic narrative style; their films were often about the difficulty, and the implications, of telling a story.

Ruiz in a sense represents an extension, although the inverse, of their work. Rather than finding storytelling difficult, Ruiz is intoxicated by it—the difficulty often becomes the way in which the infinite number of stories suggested by an image might be limited or defined. In interviews, Ruiz likes to cite the example of the close-up. Today the close-up is universally understood as a rhetorical device meant to heighten emotional involvement, yet for the earliest film audiences the close-up was merely a giant monstrous head; in fact, film pioneer Georges Melies even made a film based on this, *The Man with the Rubber Head*. Ruiz finds stories everywhere, and his films, rather than deconstruct classical narrative, often bear witness to the results of what happens when narration abandons or subverts the rules and practices that make classical narratives intelligible. This can be seen through an examination of three of Ruiz's finest works, *The Hypothesis of the Stolen Painting* (1978), *The Three Crowns of the Sailor* (1982), and *City of Pirates* (1983).

Made for the French television series *Camera Je, Hypothesis* (Figure 1) began as a proposal by Ruiz to make a film on the aesthetic theories of French theorist and novelist Pierre Klossowski; according to Ruiz,

Figure 1. *The Hypothesis of the Stolen Painting.* Directed by Raúl Ruiz. (Photo courtesy of The Film Center, School of the Art Institute of Chicago.)

soon after agreeing to work on the film, Klossowski somewhat myste-riously decided to leave Paris and go on vacation. Left with a crew and a budget, yet no clear script, Ruiz hastily assembled what he would later term, significantly, a "fiction about theory," in which several of Klos-sowski's ideas, especially those relating to the use of *tableaux vivants* in nineteenth-century painting, could be explicated.

As a voice-over narration reads various conflicting commentaries on the work of Tonnerre, an obscure painter, the camera glides silently over a group of six rather unremarkable genre paintings, randomly displayed in a large hall. At points in the narration, a man seen moving between the paintings announces the sources of the quotations cited; he is the Collector, a dapper, sixty-ish-looking gentleman. After hav-ing briefly viewed the works, we are told by the Collector what is most remarkable about them: when first exhibited, they seem to have touched off an enormous scandal that eventually brought in the police and forced Tonnerre to flee France for Italy. How could such works, such seemingly banal, academic paintings, be responsible for these events? The Collector then proceeds to explain how the meaning of the paintings can only be understood through the existence of a seventh painting, once an integral part of the group but now lost. Re-creating the various scenes depicted in the paintings through the use of actual figures in *tableaux vivants,* the Collector attempts to unravel the various mysteries in these works—the bizarre, unnatural lighting patterns, the groupings of figures, the theological references—yet all his explanations hinge on the acceptance of the missing seventh painting, whose existence the Collector cannot prove.

With the casual but supremely well-informed manner of the Collector, and frequent interruptions by the off-screen narrator often disputing the logic of the Collector's theories, *Hypothesis* is an often hilarious parody of the kind of "sophisticated" art documentaries typified on American television by the work of Kenneth Clark or Robert Hughes. Yet Ruiz's account of the mystery of Tonnerre evokes the most basic process of cinematic reception: how images are ordered and their meaning derived. Without a knowledge of the codes present in the paintings, codes apparently well understood by nineteenth-century Parisians who found the works scandalous, the paintings remain simply repositories of dead symbols. After announcing his final conclusion— that the paintings represent various stages of a forbidden pagan ritual— even the Collector admits that his hypothesis is not really convincing. The power of Tonnerre's images lies not in their meaning but in the elusiveness of that meaning.

Ruiz's final sequence has an almost nightmarish quality; as the courteous Collector leads us out of his home, the camera glides past all the figures, still motionless, from the *tableaux vivants,* implying that the Collector will forever be trapped in a world full of symbols whose meaning cannot be deciphered. That realization, especially after the remarkably ingenious, if finally unconvincing, detective work witnessed in the previous hour, gives *Hypothesis* a haunting, poignant quality that allows it to transcend the limits of a mere formal exercise. As an exile, Ruiz has been thrust, like the Collector, into a world full of symbols he cannot fully comprehend, as his knowledge of the codes for these symbols is imperfect or incomplete. "Meaning," as such, becomes a jealously guarded institution, visualized in *Hypothesis* through the military-looking figures who seem to be patrolling the corridors of the house.

The Collector, of course, can be compared to any number of detective or detective-substitutes found in Borges's stories. He announces the solving of an enigma—where one was not previously suspected to exist—and then his failure to do so simply makes reality as we know it that much stranger, that much more unknown. *Hypothesis,* as do many other Ruiz films, points to the existence of some kind of secret society (not unlike the inventors of Tlön) that is in fact responsible for this state of affairs, but again there is little comfort in this knowledge. One can return to the world of street noise at the end of *Hypothesis,* just as one can return to a translation of Browning's *Urn Burial* at the end of "Tlön, Uqbar, Orbis Tertius," yet afterward one cannot help but sense how artificial the normal world can seem after what has just been revealed.

By far Ruiz's best-known work, *The Three Crowns of the Sailor* (Figure 2), although also produced for television, enjoyed moderately successful commercial runs in several European capitals and helped trigger widespread interest in his work. What Ruiz accomplished in two dimensions in *Hypothesis* he set out to render in three in *Three Crowns.* The film begins as a student wanders the fog-covered streets of Warsaw after killing his tutor; he meets a sailor, who offers him a chance to escape aboard a ship ready to set sail if the student will listen to his life story—and pay him three Danish crowns. The pair retires to a brightly lit dance hall, where the sailor begins describing the life he has led—a life that seems to have been a compendium of mariners' lore and sea tales. Years before, the sailor had set out from Valparaíso aboard a ship arranged for him by a blind man, who was subsequently murdered. In Buenaventura he meets a prostitute who lives surrounded by dolls with electric eyes and who affixes a wad of chewing gum on her child's coffin to register every customer she's ever had. In Singapore he meets a Chinese philosopher stricken with a malady that makes him grow progressively younger; in Dakar, he meets a dockworker who claims that his life has been so complicated that it would take at least one hour to explain every minute of it. Meanwhile, the sailor discovers that his fellow shipmates are all dead, and that they can only defecate by emitting maggots from their skin. Finally, the stories end, the sailor is paid, and the student, sensing his mission, kills the sailor and then takes his place on board the ship surrounded by ghosts, including that of the sailor. "You always need a living sailor on a shipful of dead," speaks the student over the film's final image. "That man was me."

Like the paintings of Tonnerre in *Hypothesis,* the sailor's stories in *Three Crowns* are provocative precisely because of their seeming un-connectedness. The stories are those both of the sailor and of every one who's ever set out to see. Stories grow out of other stories, and all the while they are contained within the larger story of the sailor's narrative; the lines between the stories, and between the teller and the listener/ viewer, become increasingly blurred. Patterns linking tales seem to emerge, and then recede. In an important sense the sum total of all the stories taken together can be likened to the effect of reading a volume of Borges's short pieces; one imagines patterns of meaning and connec-tions between characters that are never really explicit and yet feel cor-

Figure 2. *The Three Crowns of the Sailor*. Directed by Raúl Ruiz. (Photo courtesy of The Film Center, School of the Art Institute of Chicago.)

rect. The unity of the stories is perhaps that of their author—the sailor or, by extension, Borges—yet what is the author other than a kind of terminal through which the experience of all sailors (or of all writers) flows?

The problems posed by the narrative structure of *Three Crowns* are further emphasized through cinematic means. Ruiz favors extreme deep focus compositions, which often feature some object or body part blown up way out of proportion in the foreground while characters or events are set in distant backgrounds seemingly an infinity away. The effect of this odd use of perspective can be extremely disorienting, as it becomes impossible to arrive at a fixed audiovisual point of view for most scenes; we are usually as busy trying to discover where we are as we are busy determining what's going on.

In most traditional uses of voice-over narration, the off-screen voice serves as both a narrative guide and a narrative boundary; the viewer is wed, as in a classic mystery or crime film, to the point of view of the narrator, seeing and hearing what the narrator sees and hears. In a sense, the word (the voice) controls the image; in *Three Crowns,* the image continually seeks to usurp the power of word. In one extraordinary sequence, the narrator (that is, the sailor) himself comments that he can no longer be sure if it is he or someone else who actually controls his body and senses; as he speaks, the camera lunges wildly across deck, as if being pulled from all sides. We assume at first that what we are seeing is a rendering of a subjective, first-person point of view from the perspective of the sailor, yet at a crucial moment, the figure of the sailor looms up from the bottom of the screen and then runs off-screen, while the camera continues to gyrate. Like the author in "Borges and I," one is not precisely sure who is the source of the above-described sequence; the sailor is both narrator and subject, viewer and viewed.

Many critics have pointed to the importance of the theme of exile and the exile experience with Ruiz's films, and while this is certainly correct, one should note the ways in which the exile experience is used in his work as a metaphor for the Latin American experience itself. As the sailor travels around the world, he creates an imaginary "family"—a black "father" from Africa, a Chinese "son" from Singapore, two Arab "brothers" from Tangiers—all of whom he collects in a bar back in Valparaíso. The sailor's family is in a sense the "family of humankind" itself, made up of an incredible mixture of races and cultures—in short, Latin America itself. As Borges wrote in "The Argentine Writer and Tradition," the contemporary Latin American is the Jew of the modern world: a figure both within and outside Western culture, yet richly informed by other sources and traditions. In Borges, however, this privileged position enables the Latin American to offer a special kind of

Figure 3. *City of Pirates*. Directed by Raúl Ruiz. (Photo courtesy of The Film Center, School of the Art Institute of Chicago.)

critique of Western culture, based partially on the richness of Latin America's influences. In Ruiz, this richness merely leads to sensory "overload"; the sailor has had so many experiences and has lived through so much that the most he can do with his stories is simply enumerate them. This idea of overload has been much discussed in recent times with regard to the rise of "postmodernism," and indeed Ruiz has often been cited as the first postmodern filmmaker. Yet perhaps the ultimate irony is that the postmodern condition has been Latin American reality for a very long time; the avant-garde can finally attempt to experience or describe what Latin Americans have lived with all along.

In his next major feature, *City of Pirates* (Figure 3), Ruiz returned to the problem of how images come together to form stories, but from a perspective that is decidedly distinct from that of *Hypothesis*. "A free adaptation of Peter Pan," according to Ruiz, *City of Pirates* begins as an exiled family (living, we are told in a title, in the colonies) is forced to change residences. Upon exploring her room, their daughter Isidore discovers a young boy who may or may not be the culprit of a heinous crime: the slaughter of his entire family. After murdering her father, Isidore and the boy escape to an island where, after landing, the boy disappears. No sooner is he gone, though, than a young man, Tobi, appears in his place. Tobi, who is seemingly possessed by the spirits of his entire family, keeps Isidore a prisoner at first but eventually lets her go; the boy returns and forces Isidore to kill Tobi.

In jail for murder, Isidore is visited by two soldiers, who tell her that the boy is actually a child-god (whom they serve) and that she has been chosen to bear his child. The child is born, a crippled hunchback, and lives alone with Isidore until one day they come across Tobi lying wounded in a cave. Her son kills him, and then she asks him to do the same for her. In a final sequence, the rotting corpses of Isidore and her mother stare out a window, while in the distance the figure of a young boy can be seen heading their way.

As I hope the above outline indicates, *City of Pirates* is a film of enormous complexity, both visually and on the narrative level. Added to Ruiz's typical game-playing with perspective and point of view is an exceptionally rapid editing pace; there must be two or three times more individual shots in *City of Pirates* than are usually contained in a film of its length. Yet it is the problem of actually deciphering the images themselves that seems to interest Ruiz here. Throughout *City of Pirates,* there is a sense in which Ruiz seeks to drain images of their meaning, of their very identity. This, of course, was a surrealist strategy in the cinema; one thinks of the array of objects—a bishop, a giraffe, a Christmas tree—that Gaston Modot tosses out of a burning window in *L'Age d'or* (The golden age). Yet in the surrealist cinema, the approach used by Buñuel and others was to "underdetermine" images; their lack of connectedness to each other or to the story was emphasized. In *City of Pirates,* the images are in a very real sense overdetermined; each image seems so loaded, so charged with possible meanings and connections on several levels—contextual, narrational, colorific, literary, and so on—that in a way the images become unmoored, detached, allowed to float freely. They simultaneously seem to refer to everything and to nothing but themselves. This is never a situation of one of these images seeming meaningless; if anything, Ruiz's images are uncontrollably meaningful. As we see in the opening image of the film, the sea appears to be rolling in and rolling out simultaneously.

With the almost impossible multiplicity of meanings and patterns that emerge in *City of Pirates,* the concept of creative articulation— already touched upon in *Hypothesis* and *Three Crowns*—becomes quite problematic. The figure of Ruiz as *auteur,* as the ultimate source of meaning in his work, is obscured by the fact that there is simply too much meaning going on in the text. Perhaps more effectively than those of any other contemporary director, Ruiz's films are essentially created or re-created by each viewer, according to the particular set of meanings that an individual might apply to the work. In a sense, the artist becomes simply a medium through which the premises for reflection on a wide range of topics and issues might be elaborated.

This notion of the disappearance of the artist can actually be seen to run throughout Ruiz's work. In several films, it is evoked through the image of a dismembered, dispersed corpse, as in the short *Dogs' Dialogue,* the serial *The One-Eyed Man,* or his early feature *The Scattered Body and the World Upside Down,* a title that almost sounds like a summary of the whole of Ruiz's filmography. The disappearance or absence of the artist also forms the central theme of his adaptation of Pierre Klossowski's *The Suspended Vocation,* in which a contemporary filmmaker attempts to piece together a film on a clerical order using footage shot by others in two earlier periods, a process that unleashes a barrage of new meanings.

Another evocation of this problem of the creation of meaning in Ruiz's work can be seen in his frequent introduction, just as a story line seems to be slipping into complete incoherence, of the existence of a secret society, such as the one to which the two soldiers in *City of Pirates* belong, that appears to have either caused, planned, or been aware of the logic behind all that has been shown. The existence of these secret societies, often hidden behind the blind alleys and false leads generously provided by the narratives, offers at least partial comfort for those seeking a way to thread together the many loose ends, yet the very suddenness with which these societies appear only underscores the difficulty of finding a coherent story in the films.

Finally, in *City of Pirates* the process through which meaning is lost or gained can be seen in the theme of possession that runs throughout the film. Early in the film, there is an extraordinary shot taken from inside the mouth of Isidore's father, as he asks his wife to examine an aching tooth. It is a wonderfully shocking—and shockingly funny—moment, because of course it parodies the notion of the omniscient and omnipresent camera found in the classical cinema; for example, the ubiquitous fireplace shot, in which the camera peers out from behind the flames at two cozy lovers. Ruiz, however, alerts us to the hidden horror of this standard device; the camera has taken over the space of the human head, radically redefining it, and we can only shudder at the violent, bloody consequences. The idea of the camera's ability to take possession of objects and characters is further addressed in the number of seemingly "possessed" characters who appear in *City of Pirates*—the bounding ball inhabited by Isidore's dead brother, the mother and daughter who switch identities, and of course Tobi, who changes from Tobi to Carmela to Mama to the Colonel to Jeremy and back again, all while Isidore watches him from a doorway. The narrative space of *City of Pirates* is defined by this kind of instability, in which images may lose their identities or, by extension, lose their significance, at any instant.

While nothing in Borges approaches, to my mind, the radicalness of Ruiz's "visual skepticism," there is a sense in which the act of writing itself can be interpreted as having the same magical powers that filming has for Ruiz. By writing about Tlön, the authors of the encyclopedia seemingly have conjured up a world that now will exist alongside ours. Pierre Menard can become the author of *Don Quixote;* Cervantes as ultimate referent for the written words that compose the novel is as easily interchangeable as one of Tobi's identities. In writing a work, an author sends his/her creation into the world of words, of literature, at which point the author becomes simply one level of reference; the words and stories are free to roam about and connect to myths, other stories, or even real lives.

With his remarkable knowledge of world literature, Borges was amazingly cognizant of the enormous responsibility that writing entailed. This responsibility was not merely a kind of "engagement" in the Sartrean sense; instead, the responsibility was an awareness of the enormous power and effect of even the most unconscious choice of words, figures of speech, or metaphors. With the emergence of Raúl Ruiz, Latin American cinema at last has a filmmaker willing to approach his medium in the same spirit.

FILMOGRAPHY

Hypothesis of the Stolen Painting (L'Hypothèse du tableau volé), 1978, France

Director: Raúl Ruiz
Screenwriter: Raúl Ruiz, based on an idea by Pierre Klossowski
Cinematographer: Sacha Vierny
Editor: Patrice Royer
Art Direction: Bruno Beauge
Sound: Xavier Vauthrin
Music: Jorge Arriagada
Cast: Jean Rougeul (the Collector), Gabriel Gascon (voice of Visitor), Chantal Palay, Alix Comte, Jean Narboni, Stéphane Shandor

The Three Crowns of the Sailor (Les Trois Couronnes du matelot), 1982, France/Portugal

Director: Raúl Ruiz
Screenwriters: Raúl Ruiz, Emilio del Solar, François Ede
Cinematographer: Sacha Vierny
Editors: Valéria Sarmiento, Jeanine Verneau

Art Director: Bruno Beauge
Sound: Jean-Claude Brisson
Music: Jorge Arriagada
Cast: Jean-Bernard Guillard (Sailor), Philippe Deplanche (Student), Nadège Clair (María, a prostitute), Jean Badin (First officer)

City of Pirates (La Ville des pirates), 1983, France/Portugal
Director: Raúl Ruiz
Screenwriter: Raúl Ruiz
Cinematographer: Acacio de Almeida
Editor: Valéria Sarmiento
Art Directors: Isabel Branco, María Jose Branco
Sound: Joaquim Pinto, Vasco Pimentel
Music: Jorge Arriagada
Cast: Hugues Ouester (Tobi), Anne Alvaro (Isidore), Melvil Fouqaud (Malo, the boy)

Jules Kirschenbaum

Dream of a Golem

I worked on *Dream of a Golem* for over a year. The possibility of immanent revelation, which is the feeling in many of Borges's stories, was the quality I wanted to catch in the painting. His stories "The Aleph" and "The God's Script" are examples of this, but the quotation I used from "The Circular Ruins" more precisely describes this craving of the artist or golem-maker. "The purpose which guided him was not impossible, though supernatural. He wanted to dream a man; he wanted to dream him in minute entirety and impose him on reality." These few sentences reveal the world of transcendent desire that I tried to suggest in my work. Each of my paintings is vaguely connected to an author. I do not try to illustrate anything. Reading the same pages over and over helps me sustain a mood over a long period of time.

I have an affinity for the world Borges creates. He said, "I am not a thinker. I am merely a man who has tried to explore the literary possibilities of metaphysics and religion." Although that is a very unpopular endeavor in the visual arts, I have in my own way tried to explore those possibilities in painting. I have always loved the early religious art of the quattrocento. Borges's stories are like those paintings, where starkly shaped forms are set against gold leaf and sealed against the natural world. Everything is intensified; nothing is superfluous. Even Borges's vast knowledge is used sparingly, just enough to give substance to his fantasy. James Joyce said that he could justify every word in his books. The same is true of Borges, and his severe exactness has meaning for me in my efforts to arrive at more rigorously designed images. The power he generates without the use of expressionistic gestures is another important lesson. It might seem strange that a painter could learn anything about style from a writer, but Borges's lean, evocative prose has been a significant influence.

Borges is able to bring the past into the contemporary world. The search for the new in so much modern art has led us to cut ourselves off from important knowledge. Borges reintroduces fragments from the archaic mysteries of the Cabala, alchemy, and other esoteric thought in a way that gives depth to his writing. The short essay "The Fearful Sphere of Pascal" evokes this when he writes that "universal history is the history of the different intonations given a handful of metaphors."

244

Dream of a Golem. Tempera and oil on panel. Height 40 inches; width 45 inches. The Metropolitan Museum of Art, Anonymous Gift, 1986 (1986.104).

Other artists have acknowledged the importance of our connections to the past. Interestingly they have been some of the most important innovators of twentieth-century art. The contemporary poet Robert Bly wrote, "If one wants to remain a poet—you cannot depend on your peers, but must find some way back to the nourishment of the ancestors." However, few artists have integrated this into their work as Borges has done.

For me Borges is an exemplary man and artist. He combines the inner and outer worlds in a magical way. His wisdom is surprising and profound. "Forgetting is the only forgiveness and the only revenge." He represents the best of humanity through his sanity and gentleness, his acceptance of all people, all religions. He seems to stand above the mindless strife of the world.

V
Hebraism and
Poetic Influence

Edna Aizenberg ⸻

Borges and the Hebraism of Contemporary Literary Theory

I.

While I was looking at Borges's impact on contemporary letters, at the ways he anticipated, shaped, or shared major trends in current writing, something struck me greatly. His interest in Judaically derived concepts of language and strategies of reading and writing has become the dernier cri of much literary criticism: what Borges began in the thirties and forties is not unrelated to what Jacques Derrida and Geoffrey Hartman and Harold Bloom are doing in the sixties, seventies, and eighties.[1]

In 1931, in his now-classic essay "A Vindication of the Cabala," Borges wrote: "This is not the first time [this] has been attempted, nor will it be the last time it fails, but it is distinguished by two facts. One is my almost complete ignorance of the Hebrew language; another is that I do not wish to vindicate the doctrine, but rather the hermeneutical or cryptographic procedures which lead to it" (*BAR* 22). What Borges was proposing to do in the essay—the vindication of Judaic hermeneutic or cryptographic procedures—is clearly one of the directions today's critical discourse is taking. To use a term of Hartman's, Borges helped create the "text milieu," the Hebraic text milieu in which criticism now operates.

Douglas Atkins, in an article entitled "Dehellenizing Literary Criticism," describes the Hebraism of theorists like Hartman, Derrida, and Bloom as part of a realignment of a still-classicist criticism with an

---

1. The following works were consulted during the preparation of this essay: Robert Alter, "Old Rabbis, New Critics," review of *Midrash and Literature* and *Golden Doves with Silver Dots, New Republic,* January 5 and 12, 1987, pp. 27–33; G. Douglas Atkins, "Partial Stories: Hebraic and Christian Thinking in the Wake of Deconstruction," *Notre Dame English Journal* 15:3 (1983): 7–21; Harold Bloom, "The Masks of the Normative," *Orim: A Jewish Journal at Yale* 1 (1985): 9–24; Jacques Derrida, "Shibboleth," in *Midrash and Literature,* ed. Geoffrey H. Hartman and Sanford Budick (New Haven: Yale University Press, 1986), 307–47; Susan A. Handelman, "Fragments of the Rock: Contemporary Literary Theory and the Study of Rabbinic Texts—A Response to David Stern," *Prooftexts* 5 (1985): 75–95; Geoffrey H. Hartman, *Saving the Text: Literature, Derrida, Philosophy* (Baltimore: Johns Hopkins University Press, 1981); and David Stern, "Literary Criticism or Literary Homilies? Susan Handelman and the Contemporary Study of Midrash," *Prooftexts* 5 (1985): 96–103.

already "dehellenized" literature, a fictional, poetic, and dramatic creativity that "long ago threw over classicism and its valoration of decorum, linearity and centering."[2] What the "Hebraists" propose to do is to effect the same kind of revolution in critical language as has been effected in literary language. (Indeed, the distinction between the two is one of the things they want to revolutionize and—Hebraically— obliterate.) Their project thus aims at dislodging the Greek-Western logos: speech, "reasoned" expression, the word as a shadow or incar- nation of a higher presence or substance, idealization, separation, uni- vocity. Only by so doing, these critical iconoclasts believe, only by freeing hermeneutics from logocentrism and making commentary con- tinuous with the literature it seeks to read, can the interpretive endeav- or work in "this fictional time of Borges."[3]

The phrase "this fictional time of Borges" is Bloom's, and his choice is fully intentional. For it was Borges who, early on, recognized that Judaism had linguistic-textual traditions different from the dominant Greek-inspired models, "alien" and "even shock[ing] to our Western minds," as he put it, but fruitful for his brand of irreverent literature (*SN* 95, 99). Thus, important aspects of the Hebraic tradition became—to quote Bloom again—"the principle . . . that generates Borgesian writ- ing."[4] I would like to comment briefly on three of these aspects, and to note how each appears in the work of one of the three critics—Derrida, Hartman, or Bloom.

II.

The first aspect could be called the deification of the Writ, or perhaps the primacy of writing—Derrida's great theme. In "A Vindication of the Cabala" as well as in other places—the lecture "The Kabbalah," the essay "On the Cult of Books"—Borges discusses the centrality of writ- ing in Judaism, a centrality flowing from the root idea that "the Pen- tateuch, the Torah, is a sacred book. An infinite intelligence has conde- scended to the human task of producing [*redactar*] a book" (*SN* 98). The key word here is *redactar* (literally, "to write"): in the Jewish view, writing is holy (and primary) because it is God's very instrument. It is, Borges says, "an end in itself, not a means to an end" (*OI* 118). The Cabala extended and radicalized this positive attitude toward writing so far as to hold that the elements of all creation were not God's spoken utterances but the letters of the sacred Hebrew alphabet. (This is the notion that Borges says "must shock our Western minds.") "Twenty-two

2. G. Douglas Atkins, "Dehellenizing Literary Criticism," *College English* 41 (1980): 769–79 (770).

3. Harold Bloom et al., *Deconstruction and Criticism* (New York: Seabury, 1979), 21.

4. Harold Bloom, ed., *Jorge Luis Borges* (New York: Chelsea, 1986), vii.

letters," Borges quotes from the *Sepher Yetzirah,* the cabalistic tract that deals with this subject, "God drew them, engraved them, combined them, weighed them, permuted them, and with them produced everything that is and everything that will be" (*OI* 119). The Text, in other words, precedes and forms the world through an alphabetic *ars combinatoria,* which in its infinite divine meaningfulness constitutes a "cryptography . . . worthy of consideration and decipherment" (*SN* 99). Meaning is thus not sought in a nonlinguistic realm external to the Text. Language and the Text are the locus of meaning.[5] But this meaning is not a meaning or the meaning, but rather meaning-as-process: the ongoing search for significance through consideration and decipherment, the process that in the Hebrew tradition is known as midrash or interpretation.

Such Hebraic sanctification of the letter ran entirely counter to the Hellenic disdain for writing that, Borges notes (citing the *Phaedrus* and other Greek sources), was considered "merely a succedaneum of the spoken word," often the word of a god, of a higher presence (*OI* 116–17). Christianity, Borges goes on, inherited these scruples: it absorbed the Judaic concept of a Holy Writ but continued to maintain that "the letter kills and the spirit brings life" (*SN* 97; *OI* 119; *BAR* 24).[6]

There is no need to belabor the point that Borges turned the letter-centered cosmos of Judaism and the Cabala into his metaphor for the universe and his philosophy of literature. Much like the Jews' Torah, his writing is a "totalizing utopia" (to quote Genette), a writing that "attracts fictively into its sphere the totality of existing and non-existing things."[7] It is therefore a writing that refuses to be a succedaneum, a supplement to an outside presence or realm, but rather sees itself as a self-justifying end. At the same time, however, it is a writing that insists on and often self-consciously thematizes its own tentativeness, the fact that it is a process, an interrogation, a commentary, not a stasis, centered and univocal.

5. Susan A. Handelman, "Jacques Derrida and the Heretic Hermeneutic," in *Displacement: Derrida and After,* ed. Mark Krupnick (Bloomington: Indiana University Press, 1983), 98–129 (109).

6. Judaism does have an oral tradition, and Rabbinic Judaism recognized the authority of two Laws: the Written Law (Scripture) and the Oral Law (the interpretations of the Torah originally transmitted by word of mouth from generation to generation by recognized sages). This in no way contradicts the fact that "for the Hebrews meaning, signification, etc., are inseparable from text. Judaism does not recognize an a-textual problem." Writing, in other words, is not external to speech but is the place where meaning is generated (José Faur, *Golden Doves with Silver Dots: Semiotics and Textuality in Rabbinic Tradition* [Bloomington: Indiana University Press, 1986], 100, xxvii).

7. Cited in Emir Rodríguez Monegal, "Borges and *La Nouvelle Critique,*" *Diacritics* 2:2 (1972): 27–34 (30).

In describing Borges's affinities with the Jewish textual tradition, I have already outlined many of the basic motifs of Derrida's attack on Western logocentrism, for Derrida anchors his assault in the juxtaposition of the "Socratic and the Hebraic, the poverty and the wealth of the letter, the pneumatic and the grammatical."[8] Interestingly, Derrida, the deconstructor of Western philosophy, the Algerian Jew who in an autobiographical passage in *Glas* points to the hidden yet revealed Torah as the "origin" of his literature, converts Borges into one of his tutelary deities in "Plato's Pharmacy." Derrida acknowledges that the Argentine master is a kindred spirit by including two epigraphs from Borges in his essay, both of which deal with writing as a universe and with the universe as a cryptography.[9] While writing is the secondary, expelled form of signification in Greco-Western thought, Derrida, like Borges, adopts it as the more appropriate or approximate *imago mundi*, since for him, too, presence is a sham (remember Borges's comments on the impossibility of penetrating the divine scheme of the cosmos in "The Analytical Language of John Wilkins"), and the only thematics possible is the writerly thematics of "active interpretations, which substitutes an incessant deciphering for the disclosure of truth as the presentation of the thing itself."[10]

Derrida and Borges, then, choose as their paradigm what Derrida calls the "expelled other" of Western metaphysics. The term *expelled other* is not incidental, for this "outcast, expatriated, condemned to wandering and blindness" is writing—but it is also the Jew who "elects writing which elects the Jew." Indeed, as Derrida says, quoting Jabès, the "fatherland of the Jews" is a "sacred text surrounded by commentaries."[11] Borges concurs: the Jew, stoned, burned, and asphyxiated, is the man who is the Book; and Israel is, above all, the Sacred Book, the mirror of every face pored over it (*OC* 997, 996). For him as for Derrida, Judaic writing, which is of necessity commentary (call it deferral, difference, fragment, trace, belatedness), is an important way to rewrite the Western tradition, and both he and Derrida make use of it—from a

8. Jacques Derrida, "Edmond Jabès and the Question of the Book," in *Writing and Difference,* trans. and intro. Alan Bass (Chicago: University of Chicago Press, 1978), 64–78 (73).

9. Jacques Derrida, *Glas* (Paris: Editions Galilée, 1974); Jacques Derrida, "Plato's Pharmacy," in *Dissemination,* trans. Barbara Johnson (Chicago: University of Chicago Press, 1981), 61–156. The two epigraphs are from "Pascal's Fearful Sphere" and "Tlön, Uqbar, Orbis Tertius." On Derrida's interest in Borges, see Emir Rodríguez Monegal's piece in this volume and Roberto González Echevarría, "Borges and Derrida," in Bloom, *Jorge Luis Borges,* 227–34.

10. Jacques Derrida, *Of Grammatology,* trans. Gayarti Chakravorty Spivak (Baltimore: Johns Hopkins University Press, 1976), xxiii.

11. Derrida, "Edmond Jabès," 64, 65, 65, 67.

Judaic position of "strategic marginality," I might add—in their icono-
clastic texts.[12]

III.

I have repeatedly mentioned commentary as the essence of Hebraic
textuality. The work of Hartman and Bloom focuses on this essence—
again with Borges as a significant anticipator. In *Criticism in the Wilderness,* and more directly in the anthology *Midrash and Literature,*
Hartman posits midrash as an important path—perhaps the most important path—for criticism today. Borges, who appears in both books,
is presented as a major challenger of the dichotomy between text and
commentary, collapsing the neat, linear, classical separation between
them in favor of a Judaic "contamination": a midrashic dynamic in
which Text (the Torah) and scholia (the exegeses of succeeding generations) interact *trans lineam* and together search for truth.[13]

Hartman advocates this midrashic dynamic as a critical stance for a
number of reasons. First, he believes that a life in literature, like a life in
scripture, is "experienced in the shuttle space between the interpreter
and the text." In the "spacious scene of writing," be it Holy Writ or
secular letters, source text and secondary text enter into a mutually
supportive relation, in which host gives life to guest and guest, through
the "interpreter's broad associative knowledge," gives force and vigor
to host.[14] Second, Hartman is convinced that the separation between
one type of writing and another is artificial and erroneous, since every
writing, be it critical or fictional, displays the characteristics of midrash: it is inevitably intertextual, part of a network of texts, and it is
inevitably a belated commentary on other words. Finally, Hartman
argues, all knowledge is midrashic in the sense that it is always mediated by a text. "There is no absolute knowledge," he notes, "but rather a
textual infinite, an interminable web of texts or interpretations."[15]

In the introduction to *Midrash and Literature,* Hartman calls Borges
"Reb Borges," using the title given to the midrashic sages of old—and
rightly (if jocularly) so, for it was the Argentine master who early on
understood the centrality of midrash in the Jewish concept of textuality. Borges concludes his essay vindicating Jewish mysticism with a
powerful summation of the force behind the ongoing interaction of

12. González Echevarría, "Borges and Derrida," 232.
13. Geoffrey H. Hartman, *Criticism in the Wilderness: The Study of Literature Today*
(New Haven: Yale University Press, 1980), 206.
14. Hartman and Budick, *Midrash,* xi; Hartman, *Criticism,* 206; J. Hillis Miller, "The
Critic as Host," in Bloom et al., *Deconstruction,* 217–53.
15. Hartman and Budick, *Midrash,* xi; Hartman, *Criticism,* 202.

Torah and commentary: "A book impenetrable by contingency, a mechanism of infinite purpose, of infallible variations, of revelations lying in wait, of superimposed light. . . . How could one not question it to absurdity, to numerical excess, as did the Cabala?" (*BAR* 24). Borges captured the significance of the midrashic impulse in such comments. As he indicates, the Cabala was an extreme and innovative expression of the midrashic impulse.[16] Its seminal writings, including the Zohar or Book of Splendor, were commentaries on Scripture and provided him with an invaluable textual model.[17]

If Hartman sees intertextuality and belatedness as the quintessence of the midrashic dynamic, Borges does so no less. His works vindicate a literature lived in the shuttle space between prooftext and gloss as they assume the posture of "parasites"—but parasites that vivify the host, by questioning the prooftext, releasing its lurking revelations, and actualizing its superimposed lights. (Think in this regard of Borges's biblical stories or his rewritings of Greek myths; of Pierre Menard, of the glosses on *Martín Fierro,* or of "Kafka and His Precursors.") If Hartman sees understanding as possible only "through the detour of the writing/ reading experience," through a "hermeneutic 'infinitizing' that makes all rules of closure appear arbitrary," Borges, again using the Cabala (specifically the cabalist Luria), asserts: "Isaac Luria declares that the eternal Writ / Has as many meanings as readers. / Every version is a true one." In her analysis, included in *Midrash and Literature,* Myrna Solotorevsky points to the similarities between this idea and Borges's texts, "which diegetically consist of a variety of versions of a certain discourse," as in "Three Versions of Judas"; or incidentally pit different interpretations against each other, as in "The Dream of Coleridge"; or "evoke a variety of interpretations on the part of the reader," as in "The South." These, and other midrashic strategies in Borges, are linked to his conviction that a fragmentary metatextuality is the only state possi-

16. On the innovativeness of the Cabala, consult Gershom Scholem, *Major Trends in Jewish Mysticism* (New York: Schocken, 1941); Gershom Scholem, *On the Kabbalah and Its Symbolism* (New York: Schocken, 1969); and Moshe Idel, "Infinities of Torah in Kabbalah," in Hartman and Budick, *Midrash,* 141–57. Joseph Dan makes the point, underlined by Borges in "A Vindication" and in "The Kabbalah," that in Judaism the "totality of the text" had significance—not only the "meaning of terms and words but also their sound, the shape of the letters, the vocalization points and their shapes and sounds," and so on. There were "countless ways other than ideonic content and meaning by which the scriptures transmit a semiotic message" (Joseph Dan, "Midrash and the Dawn of Kabbalah," in Hartman and Budick, *Midrash,* 128).

17. I have discussed aspects of this in *The Aleph Weaver: Biblical, Kabbalistic and Judaic Elements in Borges* (Potomac, Md.: Scripta Humanistica, 1984), and Myrna Solotorevsky looks at it as well in "The Model of Midrash and Borges's Interpretive Essays and Tales," in Hartman and Budick, *Midrash,* 253–64.

ble, with absolute truths enclosed in absolute texts beyond our understanding or grasp.[18]

IV.

Harold Bloom, in his own recent midrash on Borges, which is a recompilation of "receptions" of Borges published between 1963 and 1983, concentrates on his South American precursor as "a great theorist of poetic influence." Bloom includes Alazraki's study on "Kabbalistic Traits in Borges' Narration," noting, "Ultimate hermeticism, the Jewish Kabbalah, is charted by Jaime Alazraki, who finds in Kabbalah the principle of reading old texts afresh that generates Borgesian writing." Alazraki does more than observe this particular cabalistic trait in Borges's narration, but Bloom isolates it as the facet that interests him most, indicating through his misprision that Borges and Jewish hermeticism are not absent from such volumes as *The Anxiety of Influence, A Map of Misreading,* or, less circumspectly, *Kabbalah and Criticism.*[19]

What Bloom developed in these texts was a theory of poetic influence that came to see in the Cabala, in the mystical hermeneutics of the expatriated wanderers (Bloom also uses the image), the paradigm for much of Western literature. The notion is startling to say the least (from the point of view of traditional, classicist criticism, a criticism that frequently also had Christian overtones) but Bloom insists, remarking that writers from the "Renaissance through today have sought occult authority in the Kabbalah" although he suspects that "this seeking concealed a more professional concern." (Borges's name immediately comes to mind here.) "However 'unconsciously,'" Bloom continues, "poets seem to have known that their . . . work followed the Kabbalistic model. Not their content nor their form derived from the Kabbalistic example, but rather the more crucial matter of their *stance,* their stance towards tradition and towards their precursors."[20]

18. Hartman, *Criticism,* 244; "A Manuel Mujica Láinez," in Jorge Luis Borges, *La moneda de hierro* (Buenos Aires: Emecé, 1976), 49 (my translation); Solotorevsky, "The Model of Midrash," 254, 263.

19. Bloom, *Jorge Luis Borges,* 2; Jaime Alazraki, "Kabbalistic Traits in Borges' Narration," *Studies in Short Fiction* 8:1 (1971): 78–92, reprinted in Bloom, *Jorge Luis Borges,* 79–91; Bloom, *Jorge Luis Borges,* vii; Harold Bloom, *The Anxiety of Influence: A Theory of Poetry* (New York: Oxford University Press, 1973); Harold Bloom, *A Map of Misreading* (New York: Oxford University Press, 1975); Harold Bloom, *Kabbalah and Criticism* (New York: Seabury, 1975).

20. Bloom, *Kabbalah,* 82; on the Christian underpinnings of T. S. Eliot and the New Critics, for example, see Harold Bloom, *Yeats* (London: Oxford University Press, 1970), 23–24; Bloom, *Map,* 30; Bloom, *Kabbalah,* 87; and Susan A. Handelman, *The Slayers of Moses: The Emergence of Rabbinic Interpretation in Modern Literary Theory* (Albany: State

The stance Bloom refers to is articulated by Borges when he mentions Luria's teaching that the Writ has as many meanings as readers; when he talks about the Cabalists' questioning the Scripture to absurdity through such devices as the vertical reading of the sacred text or the sum of the numerical value of the letters (*BAR* 22); and when he observes that this sometimes excessive, revolutionary modus operandi was designed to incorporate heterodox (primarily Gnostic) thought into Judaism, "to justify it with Scripture" (*SN* 97). The stance is, in other words, a dialectical relationship with a venerable canon, or, as Bloom describes it, an interplay of the apparently opposed principles of "repetition and discontinuity."[21]

According to Bloom, post-Enlightenment writers were, like the Cabalists, confronted with an "over-determined" textual tradition: a "massive and completed Scripture" already surrounded by a structure of commentaries in the case of the esotericists; previous, strong works of literature in the case of the secular authors. Such venerable canons could not be wished or washed away. Their burden, their influence, had to be coped with consciously or unconsciously. How, then, could fresh and vital impulses be accommodated into the tradition? Through misreading and rewriting, says Bloom, through a revisionism that, in the manner of the Cabala, proclaims its fidelity to tradition and insists that it is as old as the hills, yet that in reality "swerves so far from its canonical texts as to make the ancestral voices into even their own opposites."[22]

The Cabalists' hermeneutical and cryptographic techniques and their audacious freedom of interpretation (embodied in such bold statements as the one by Isaac Luria cited above) were, as Borges and Bloom indicate, the instruments used to open up the Writ to their own needs— primarily an updating of Judaic teaching to meet the requirements of new generations buffeted by skepticism and exile. Secular writers, likewise faced with the challenge of renewing literary tradition so as to express *their* doubts and displacements, have similarly adopted the hermeticists' approach. Employing the example of post-Enlightenment English-language poetry, Bloom proposes that every poet engages in a cabalistic process of misreading and rewriting his precursors. With even greater audacity he further proposes that the specific paradigm for this misprision has been another of Luria's revisionary doctrines: his triadic dialectics of creation through *zimzum* (concentration), *shevirat*

University of New York Press, 1982), 179–80. Bloom, *Kabbalah*, 90–91 (emphasis in the original).

    21. Bloom, *Map*, 30; Bloom, *Kabbalah*, 39.

    22. Bloom, *Kabbalah*, 83, 33, 34. The word *Cabala* means "reception" or "tradition."

ha-kelim (destruction or substitution), and *tikkun* (correction). In literary terms this means "creation through the contraction of an internalized precursor text."[23] An earlier text, says Bloom, is condensed, made to vacate part of itself in order to make room for the successor. But this is an anxious process, this need to engage the forebear, this realization that one has failed to create oneself. It sets up defensive reactions in the ephebe—self-saving caricature, for instance. The ephebe not only has to defend himself from the ancestor's overbearing influence; he also has to surrender a portion of himself in order to internalize the ancestor. Thus, his correction or rewriting of the ancestor can never be complete. It will always be a partial gesture, forever caught in the divide between surrender and self-realization, forever trying to wrestle the precursor to a truce.[24]

Borges, whose texts Bloom likewise considers to be generated by the cabalistic principle of misreading and rewriting, has enunciated this principle in such essays as "La aventura y el orden" (Adventure and order) and "The Argentine Writer and Tradition." In the second essay he unequivocally accepts the Western tradition and its canon as the stuff of which his literature is made, but at the same time he indicates that the way to deal with this tradition is "without superstition, with an irreverence which can have, and already does have, fortunate consequences" (*L* 184). In his stories, Borges puts the dialectical cabalistic posture into practice, producing fictions that inevitably derive from time-honored writings (the Bible, the *Iliad,* Dante, Shakespeare, Cervantes, Kafka, and others) yet which inevitably, in his words, falsify and distort these forerunners.[25] One of Borges's favorite revisionary operations, Rodríguez Monegal reminds us, is the "parodic miniaturization of a vast work of art"; for example, the *Divine Comedy* in "The Aleph," the *Quixote* in "Pierre Menard, Author of the *Quixote*," and More's *Utopia* in "Tlön, Uqbar, Orbis Tertius." This is strikingly reminiscent of Bloom's observation regarding the applicability of the Lurianic theory of creation to literature, and I think it helps clarify why Bloom believes that "Borges . . . has given us the first principle for the investigation of poetic influence": " 'every writer *creates* his own precursors.' "[26] Borges, Bloom's

23. Ibid., 80.

24. Ibid., 39–43, 71–86; Bloom, *Map,* 95–97. For these ideas, see also Harold Bloom, *Agon: Towards a Theory of Revisionism* (New York: Oxford University Press, 1982), 82–85; Bloom, *Anxiety,* 5, 30.

25. See the introduction to *A Universal History of Infamy* and compare it with Bloom's "Creative correction . . . [is] the particular mark of modern revisionism" (*Anxiety,* 29).

26. Emir Rodríguez Monegal, *Jorge Luis Borges: A Literary Biography* (New York: Dutton, 1978), 416; Bloom, *Yeats,* 4 (emphasis in the original).

precursor in the adoption of a cabalistic aesthetic, provided him with the same model as did Luria, as did the Cabala in general—the model of a literature in which successors produce the new by realizing, transgressing, and transforming the old.

V.

"This is not the first time it has been attempted, nor will it be the last time it fails, but it is distinguished by two facts. One is my almost complete ignorance of the Hebrew language; another is that I do not wish to vindicate the doctrine, but rather the hermeneutical or cryptographic procedures which lead to it" (*BAR* 22). In the preceding pages I have traced some of the significant points of contact between Borges's Hebraism and the Hebraic text milieu of certain influential critics. But it is important to observe that Borges's statement of espousal of a Hebraic poetics contains what has been seen as the invalidation of that poetics. While Borges's writings and the writings of his critical ephebes have enthusiastically embraced the textual heritage of the House of Galilee, questions have been raised about what Susan Handelman termed "the emergence of rabbinic interpretation in modern literary theory." (The doubts are about the ephebes, not about Borges; but just as he anticipated the Hebraism, so he appears to have been prescient of the objections to it.)

"My almost complete ignorance of Hebrew." One question is the nature of the hermeneutical Hebraists' relation to the Hebraic tradition—their expertise in that tradition, and whether Judaism really shaped their ideas or was an ex post facto garb for a body of thought developed elsewhere, with at best "self-referential associativeness" to Judaism.[27] Another misgiving, of greater consequence in my opinion, can be connected to Borges's disavowal of Cabalism as creed, his non-vindication of the Cabala as doctrine.

Like Borges, none of the critical Hebraists is a Cabalist, a talmudic sage, or even a professor of Jewish studies. This has made their work suspect in the eyes of some devoted to Jewish scholarship, who have asked—implicitly or explicitly—how those without training in the hermeneutical methods of the rabbis, for example, can be applying Judaism to literature.[28] The corollary to such skepticism is the matter of the *secondariness* of Judaism in the thinking of, say, Derrida, who (despite his allusions to the Torah and to the Jew as the autochthon of the Book) is seen as developing his views from a critique of Saussurian linguistics

27. David Stern, "Moses-cide: Midrash and Contemporary Literary Criticism," *Prooftexts* 4 (1984): 193–204 (199).
28. Ibid., 199.

and from a post-Nietzschean revolt against metaphysics, rather than from Rabbi Akiva or Isaac Luria.[29] Borges, it is interesting to note, repeatedly underlined his lack of erudition in Judaism—"I have almost no right to be discussing this," he said in a lecture on the Cabala (*SN* 97)—and his successors do not claim specialized knowledge either.[30] Yet lack of erudition is not automatically complete ignorance, particularly given the *purpose* motivating Borges and the Hebraist critics. All of them, Borges (the non-Jew) and Derrida, Hartman, and Bloom (the Jews), have Judaic knowledge, and their considerable intellectual gifts have permitted them to expand that knowledge in the directions that interest them—witness as illustration Hartman's *Midrash and Literature,* a volume that brings together Judaica scholars and literary theorists. Further, what animates these Hebraists is not what impels the mystic, or the midrashist, or the academician of Judaica; their concern is not centrally with Jewish life and learning but with philosophy—in the case of Derrida—and literature. (Though in Bloom and Hartman one increasingly sees such a concern.) Because of this they use Judaism according to Borges's prescription: "without superstition, with an irreverence which can have, and already does have fortunate consequences." Scholem captures the posture well, contrasting it with his own as a historian:

> Borges is a writer of considerable power of imagination and does not claim to represent a historical reality, but rather an insight into what the kabbalists would have stood for in his own imagination. What I did was to try to describe the world of the kabbalists by analyzing their own works and ideas without overstepping, essentially, these limits. It is only here and now, that, very rarely, I have made what I called 'ahistorical' assumptions about . . . the kabbalists.[31]

It seems to me that a similar response could be made to the matter of what came first, Judaism or something else. Borges was exposed to Judaism in adolescence, at about the time he was introduced to modern literature—much of which (for instance, Kafka and German Expressionism) he identified with the Hebraic. Derrida reveals an easy familiarity with Jewish practice from his childhood days and is far from unfamiliar with traditional and untraditional Jewish thought. Bloom

29. See, for instance, Shira Wolosky, "Derrida, Jabès, Levinas: Sign-Theory as Ethical Discourse," *Prooftexts* 2 (1982): 283–302.

30. Bloom, to cite one case, admits his almost total dependence on the cabalistic scholarship of Gershom Scholem, one of Borges's primary informants as well (Bloom, *Kabbalah,* 24).

31. Gershom Scholem, letter to the author, June 22, 1980. On Scholem's historical and "ahistorical" uses of Cabalism, see David Biale, *Gershom Scholem: Kabbalah and Counter-History* (Cambridge: Harvard University Press, 1979).

freely admits that he did not set out on his "enterprise" with a cabalistic schema consciously in view, "but it was there nevertheless."[32] But where does such information take us? The important thing is that aspects of the Hebrew heritage have played a not-insignificant role in the philosophical-literary practice of Borges and his ephebes; that there is no concealment of this fact; indeed, that there is an openness, even a pride, in being able to incorporate and highlight the Judaic. As Borges said, intellectuals create their precursors, and these have wanted to create at least some of their weightiest precursors as Jews.

The "doctrinal" question, on the other hand, will not go away so easily, and, in the manner of Borges, every one of the critics (and their critics) alludes to it. For in the final analysis a gulf separates the contemporary cult of the Text—"a book, any book is a sacred object for us," Borges remarks—from the traditional Judaic belief that "the Pentateuch, the Torah, is a sacred book" (*OI* 116; *SN* 98). The gulf is belief, and although current criticism has been called "sacral" partly because of its vindication of the Hebraic, it can be argued that its "Judaic" textuality exemplifies the kind of self-saving caricature that, in Bloom's view, characterizes post-Enlightenment writing.[33]

Judaism deified the Writ as an instrument of creation and as the place of interminable significance calling for continuous decipherment, but the maligned Transcendental Signified was the Author of the Writ—that is what made it polysemous and totalizing. Borges was well aware of this when he emphasized, "An infinite intelligence has condescended to the human task of producing a book. . . . In that book, nothing can be accidental" (*SN* 98). Interpretation was thus an ongoing necessity, a deferred, multivoiced process of grasping truth in fragments or versions, yet a process with an aim: "Study aggadah [midrash]," the rabbis taught, "for by doing this you will come to know Him who by His word created the world and you will cling to His ways."[34] Derrida sees this goal of rabbinic interpretation in a negative light, as the "unfortunately necessary road back to an original truth," and he contrasts it with poetic interpretation, which "does not seek any truth or origin, but affirms the play of interpretation." Hartman likewise recognizes that Jewish writing, "*liberated* by the broad encyclopedic form of biblical literature and a commentary process," is "also *hemmed in* by an exemplary tradition which attributes everything to a divine source." Divinity as *Auctor* (author/authority) is what ultimately shaped Jewish textuality; even Cabalists like Luria who, as Bloom argues, "read and

---

32. Aizenberg, *The Aleph Weaver*, 11–17, 126–29; Bloom, *Kabbalah*, 87–88.

33. Howard I. Needler, "Sacred Books and Sacral Criticism," *New Literary History* 13:3 (1982): 393–409.

34. Cited in Stern, "Moses-cide," 198.

interpreted [Scripture] with excessive audacity and extravagance," were, in the words of Scholem, his mentor, "decidedly conservative." They "fully accepted the established religious authority," which indeed they "undertook to reinforce by enhancing its stature and giving it deeper meaning." There was no parodic miniaturization of the precursor Text; the Torah, though viewed as an *opera aperta* with infinite potentialities of meaning, was treated with reverence, not irreverence, because in it, according to the Cabala, "the divine character of man finds its perfect expression even as it discovers God's infinity reflected in the amorphous text."[35]

This is a long way from what Borges writes in "The Analytical Language of John Wilkins." Describing the words of Wilkins's language, he observes, "Every letter is meaningful, as the letters of the Holy Scripture were meaningful for the Cabalists." But the analogy breaks down, and the break is precisely the burden of contemporary Hebraism and contemporary writing. "The impossibility of penetrating the divine scheme of the universe," Borges goes on, "cannot dissuade us from outlining human schemes, even though we are aware that they are provisional. Wilkins's analytical language is not the least admirable of those schemes" (*BAR* 143). Language, writing, texts are no longer links between heaven and earth; they are certifications of rupture, of impenetrability. Yet their power—if now provisional—endures, since they still retain the mystique of the Writ as "God's secret dictionary," His divine scheme (*BAR* 143). Hence *imitation* of sacred textuality becomes a path for post-Enlightenment writing, which in a double gesture undoes the old certainties of Scripture even as it tries to appropriate its residual authority, its strength. That helps explain Borges's interest in the Cabalists' Torah, for as he makes clear in "On the Cult of Books," their veneration of the Bible as an Absolute Book facilitated the vindication of the making of books, of literature, as a self-justifying, primary activity. It also helps explain why Bloom sees the Cabala as the paradigm not only for poetic writing but also for critical writing: like the Jewish mystics who shaped the Text in their image, so the critic shapes texts in his. "The true poem is the critic's mind," Bloom says. "Involuntarily we always read as superior beings." Hartman sounds a similar note: "Pleasure may return to the critic if he imitates older, more sacred modes of commentary." Or even more boldly, he states: the fact "that criticism is a contemporary form of theology will seem sadly obvious to those who object to its inflation."[36]

35. Derrida, *Writing and Difference,* 311; Geoffrey H. Hartman, "On the Jewish Imagination," *Prooftexts* 5 (1985): 201–20 (209; emphasis in the original); Scholem, *On the Kabbalah,* 21; Idel, "Infinities," 152.

36. Bloom, *Kabbalah,* 91; Hartman, *Criticism,* 176, 54.

But this attempt to relate secular writing to the theological and to inlate criticism by wrapping it in the mantle of the sacred, however heterodox, has met objections, as Hartman himself admits. These range from Jonathan Culler's remonstrances about the dangerous promotion of religion by Hartman and the like to the critiques of Howard Needler and others about the will to unquestioned power in Bloom's theories, for instance. Perhaps Borges, Hebraist pathbreaker for postmodernism's appropriation of the desacralized sacral, still preserves the modesty of a poet of loss, of a nonusurper (which Bloom criticizes in him), a modesty that is absent in at least some of the thinking and pronouncements of his ephebes.[37] Perhaps, though Borges makes imaginative use of the religious, he understands that hubris is not the way profane writers should approach sacred writing. Rather, it is to recognize the loss, the pain, and the anxiety of the impenetrability that is the price of the Enlightenment, and recognizing it, to create from the fragments of the sacred provisional schemes that, like Borges's literature, are admirable achievements of the human mind.

---

37. Jonathan Culler, "Comparative Literature and the Pieties," *Profession 86* (1986): 30–32 (31); Needler, "Sacred Books," 406–9; Stern, "Moses-cide," 202; Bloom, *Jorge Luis Borges,* 2.

Edna Aizenberg

Introduction to Two Lectures by Borges

I.

I owe the discovery of these two lectures by Borges to the conjunction of a friendship and a book. The long-standing friendship was with Jacobo Kovadloff, a distant prototype of Santiago Fischbein or Eduardo Zimmermann; the book was an obscure but pregnant copy of the modestly entitled *Conferencias*.[1] The event took place some seven years ago. Kovadloff, who knew I was at work on a study of the Bible and the Cabala in Borges, called me one day to say he had found some material I might find of interest. Did I know that Borges had lectured more than once at the Argentine-Israeli Institute for Cultural and Scientific Exchange on Paraguay Street, and was I aware that his lectures— one on Job, the other on Spinoza—were included in a collection issued by the Institute? Intrigued and excited, I told Kovadloff I had absolutely no idea of what he had just told me; further, I could safely conjecture that probably neither did anyone else: the provenance of the volume, the circumstances of its publication, and the fact that most Borges scholars were occupied elsewhere had all but made *Conferencias* into one of those shadows of a book about which Borges was so fond of writing.

Kovadloff promised to send me a copy of the lectures as soon as he could. A few days later an envelope arrived. It contained a section of the mysterious anthology (pages 93 to 102) bearing the heading, "El libro de Job. Baruj Spinoza. Conferencias de Jorge Luis Borges." Underneath were these words: "Eminente escritor, poeta y erudito. Gran conocedor de la literatura inglesa y del inglés antiguo. Su vasta obra, hermosa síntesis de honda espiritualidad y fino lirismo, ha alcanzado repercusión mundial" (Eminent writer, poet, and scholar. A great connoisseur of English literature and Old English. His extensive work, a beautiful synthesis of deep spirituality and fine lyricism, has attained universal stature). The description, succinct but far from imprecise, gave way to yet another title, "El libro de Job," followed by Borges's lecture on the suffering Uzzite. "Baruch Spinoza," on the other hand, was nowhere to be found. Despite the promise of the heading, there

1. *Conferencias* (Buenos Aires: Instituto Cultural y Científico Argentino-Israelí, 1967).

was no text of a presentation—*more geometrico* or otherwise—on the philosopher from Amsterdam.

For reasons I forget now, I never received a second envelope from my friend. So the next step in my journey toward the elusive discourse—indeed toward the elusive volume—would have to take place in Buenos Aires. The visit I had planned to the city by the estuary would now inevitably include a visit to the old mansion at 1535 Paraguay Street.

The librarian at the Institute advised me that not many copies of *Conferencias* remained; but, given my purpose, he would make me a gift of one. He handed me a book, weathered yet serviceable. Inside, amid the multifarious homages, roundtables, and lectures organized by the Institute in 1966, were the objects of my search. ("Spinoza" scarcely exhausted pages 103 to 112.) With relief, I accepted the gift. My heart was gladdened by this auspicious find.

II.

That Borges accepted an invitation to speak at the Instituto Cultural Argentino Israelí, and that he chose Job and Spinoza as his subjects, is no surprise. Since his Genevan days, the author of *The Aleph* had been interested in Jewish culture, viewing it "as an integral part of our so-called Western civilization" (*AOS* 257). Israel was for him one of the essential peoples of the West (see the beginning of the lecture on Job), its heritage a fountainhead for both the conceptual framework and the imagistic resources of the Occident. Judaism, parting from the Bible, was not only the origin of much of Western thought; it was at the same time the origin of a mytho-poetics used to convey that thought: the foundational writings of Scripture and their metaphoric, parabolic language.

Borges could thus find in the Hebraic tradition elements basic to his literature, a literature that presents abstract speculations in the form of imaginative narrations and that considers the storyteller's craft to be less the invention of the new than the iteration of the old. If, as Borges said, "the myths of Israel . . . touch us like music, like our own intimate voice," then retelling them becomes a creative act, a means of expressing personal perplexities through the voices of the past.[2]

The Book of Job is perhaps the biblical text that best exemplifies the union of speculations and symbols that Borges seeks to re-create in his work. The book not merely embodies this union but is also centered in a meditation and a metaphor particularly dear to Borges: the notion of

2. "Banquete del 25 aniversario," *S.H.A.* (Sociedad Hebraica Argentina, Buenos Aires) 20:338 (1951): 6–7.

an incomprehensible cosmos presided over by an impenetrable divinity, and the image of two mythologized beasts, Behemoth and Leviathan, exemplars of those imaginary beings whose uncanniness incarnates the uncanniness of the universe. In his lecture, Borges makes it clear that his fascination with the Book of Job is above all due to these characteristics, as he artfully recalls the tale of the righteous man from Uz. He examines (only to reject) various interpretations and leads his audience to what he thinks is the true explanation—"God declares by means of these descriptions [of the monsters] that he is inscrutable, that His nature does not have to be understood by man." What Borges encounters in the Book of Job is, in effect, his central postulate and poetics, a theory of fantastic literature that holds the essence of the genre to be its capacity for inventing impossible figures, figures that convey the sense—or nonsense—of an impossible world.[3]

"In the Book of Job the poet is reasoning but happily for us he is also poeticizing." Reason and poetry: the combination that is primordial in the ancient biblical text is also basic to Spinoza. This may seem strange in a philosopher devoted to pure reason, who distrusted the imagination as a means of knowledge. But to Borges it is precisely the ingenuity of Spinoza's system, the "powerful imagination" at work behind "the deliberate aridity of the philosopher," as he puts it, that is most attractive. Like the writer of the Book of Job, the Dutch thinker—a heretic progeny of the book's creators—set out to explain the mystery of God or Nature; and he did so, in large measure, by fashioning what Borges considers an imaginary being—an infinite substance called God whose endless modes are beyond human comprehension (except for two, space and time). According to Spinoza this "inconceivably rich" substance, God, underlies and gives coherence to all existence, much in the way geometric laws sustain all triangles or govern all circles; according to Borges, however, it is a marvelous trope. Its very audacity and its very prodigiousness make it certify not the rationality of the universe but (again) its fundamental absurdity.

In Borges's reading, then, Spinoza is indeed a successor of the mythmakers of biblical Israel. And Spinoza's myth, re-created, is another example of Borges's aesthetic put into practice. As in the case of the Book of Job, Spinoza is a "substance" that helps shape Borges's entire oeuvre; he is likewise an archetype to be reinscribed in specific works, in "Death and the Compass," for example, a fiction constructed out of Spinoza's geometry of the divine, and in "Tigres azules," where a profes-

---

3. Specific references to the book can be found in many Borges texts, among them the narrations "Everything and Nothing" and "Tigres azules" (Blue tigers) in *Rosa y azul* (Buenos Aires: Sedmay, 1977).

sor of Spinozist logic discovers the dizzyingly multiplying stones that defy the laws of mathematics—that is, the presumed laws of God and the universe. It is these very stones that Borges described in his lecture, and in fact much of the story can be directly related to Borges's presentation.

"The stones . . . were also Behemoth and Leviathan, the animals which in Scripture signify that the Lord is irrational."[4] This statement is a fitting summary of the relationship between Job and Spinoza; of their importance for Borges; and of the significance of these lectures, themselves rewritings of the precursor texts.

III.

A translation is also always a rewriting. This one has attempted to retain the meandering, free-associative character of Borges's oral words, with their incongruities and idiosyncrasies. (For example: Borges "regularizes" and modifies the statistics of Job's wealth, given in the Bible as seven thousand sheep, three thousand camels, five hundred yoke of oxen; his citations from Scripture, in the context of his retelling of the Job narrative, are often eccentric, half quotation, half paraphrase.) There are only two types of emendations. Titles of works and direct quotations from the writings of others misquoted by Borges have been corrected; and sentence and paragraph divisions have been altered to achieve greater readability.

Borges's texts have always been a compound of "substantial truth and accidental errors" ("Forms of a Legend"). These are one more illustration of that felicitous fact.

---

4. Borges, "Tigres azules," n.p. (my translation).

Jorge Luis Borges ————————————

The Book of Job

Despite your hospitality I consider myself somewhat of a stranger here. But two reasons mitigate that impression. The first is that I was brought up as a Christian, within Western culture; Christianity—beyond our personal beliefs or doubts—is an amalgam of two nations that have been essential for the Western world: Israel (Christianity is an offshoot of Judaism) and Greece. I believe that we are all Hebrews and Greeks, by the mere fact of belonging to Western culture—Rome, after all, was a kind of extension of Hellenism—beyond any vicissitudes of our blood, our multiple blood. (I say multiple since we each have two parents, four grandparents, and so on, in a geometric progression.)

So I feel I have some right to speak about the Book of Job today, even though I don't know Hebrew and have not been able to read the text in the original, along with the rabbinic commentaries.

The second reason I want to mention is that Job himself, as we read in the opening lines of the book that bears his name, was not an Israelite; he came from the land of Uz, a land of idol worshipers.

A great Argentine poet once composed a short poem entitled "Job, Dios y Satanás" (Job, God, and Satan), whose six lines I will now try to recall:

> Entre este mísero judío
> triste y ansioso de la muerte
> y un Dios feroz que se divierte
> en la enternidad y el hastío,
> Satanás, el Ángel Sombrío,
> se hace divinamente fuerte.

> Between this wretched Jew
> Sad and desirous of death
> And a fierce God distracted
> By eternity and by weariness,
> Satan, the Dark Angel,
> Grows divinely strong.

"The Book of Job" was originally published as "El libro de Job" in *Conferencias* (Buenos Aires: Instituto de Intercambio Cultural Argentino-Israelí, 1967), 93–102. © 1967 by Instituto de Intercambio Cultural Argentino Israelí. Translated and published with permission. English translation published in this volume for the first time.

The poem is beautiful, so it would be pedantry to tell Martínez Estrada—or rather the shade of Martínez Estrada, since he himself is dead—that Job was not a Jew, that he was born among idol worshipers (though he is still presumed to be a descendant of Abraham).

Now, with regard to the epithet "fierce," which the poem applies to God: the ultimate objective of my lecture will be to demonstrate that we cannot apply any human epithet to God; we cannot measure Him by our standards. As for Satan, the Dark Angel, he is not that at all in the first two chapters of the Book of Job; he is rather a kind of heavenly inspector, an angel who roams the earth examining people's actions, and who is on friendly terms with the Divinity, since he engages in conversation with Him. It seems to me that Martínez Estrada allowed himself to be carried away by the evil connotation of the name "Satan," by the tradition surrounding the word. As I have said, Satan only appears in the first two chapters of the book, then disappears without further mention. He is not a Dark Angel, he is not divinely strong; he is simply one of a number of participants in the assembly that God holds with His angels.

I've spoken of my ignorance of Hebrew, an ignorance I hope to remedy some day—though at age sixty-six it's unwise for me to make long-term promises, since the long is really quite short. Still, this ignorance of mine has led me to reread the Book of Job in an admirable seventeenth-century English version. I have likewise read—at least partially—the very curious and almost forgotten translation of the Book of Job by the great Spanish poet Fray Luis de León, who, if I am not mistaken, was of Jewish stock, as well as a work by another great Spanish poet, Don Francisco de Quevedo y Villegas, *La constancia y paciencia del santo Job* (The constancy and patience of Saint Job). Nor have I overlooked the study and translation into French by the great Orientalist Renan, in addition to a number of other articles that have come my way.

When I was a child I also read the Book of Job. I didn't read it in its entirety, of course—I was then incapable of following the arguments put forth by Bildad, Eliphaz, and the other two friends. But what I did read with a fascination tinged with horror were the descriptions of Behemoth and Leviathan who—this shows how much the descriptions impressed me—began to haunt my nocturnal fantasies, my night fears.

I would now like to recall the Book of Job for you—though you could surely enlarge on my summary; but first I'll say a few words about its author, its uncertain, anonymous, and immortal author.

Froude, in a study based on two literal German versions of the Book of Job (one by the Orientalist Erwald), says that it is the greatest literary masterpiece of all time, greater than Shakespeare, Dante, the *Iliad*, the

Odyssey, and the *Aeneid.* With regard to the date of authorship, very little is known. Some place it back in the age of the patriarchs. Quevedo thought that it was written before the time of Moses, who translated it into Hebrew from some Semitic dialect and rendered the first two chapters into verse thanks to a special revelation. According to Quevedo the book was written by Job himself. He cites as proof certain passages in the text where Job says, "Would that this work were engraved in bronze or lead," and claims that only Job could have given these words an authoritative ring. (Today, of course, no one can accept this theory—even Quevedo presents it as conjecture.) I think now—the Orientalists can correct me on this—the tendency is to date the book some three or four centuries before the Christian era, rather than twelve or fifteen centuries.

H. G. Wells, who was not a scholar but certainly a man of genius, believed the Book of Job was later than Plato's *Dialogues.* He thought that its Hebrew author knew the *Dialogues* and had set out to compose a Hebrew philosophical dialogue in the Platonic tradition. Wells knew his Bible very well (he was a Protestant) and in his *Experiment in Autobiography* he says that of all his works—these include the admirable volumes *The Time Machine, The Island of Dr. Moreau, The Invisible Man,* and *The First Men in the Moon*—one of the most important is *The Undying Fire.* The book, as the author indicates and as a reading confirms, is a modern adaptation of the Book of Job. In place of a righteous, God-fearing man from the land of Uz living in the days of the patriarchs, we have a doctor living in the year 1916 who has lost his son in the war; who will undergo an operation; who dialogues with his friends about his misfortunes; and who, under the effects of anesthesia, speaks face to face with God, a god seen here in the guise of a wise old man who is working in his laboratory, trying to create an acceptable world out of debased matter. What Wells did was to write a modern Book of Job, a book in which he quite deliberately retained the names of the protagonists of the biblical text.

Let us now look at the text of the Book of Job, however briefly. It begins in a very straightforward manner, which contrasts with the poetic diction of the debates. In Quevedo's treatise on the work we read that Aristotle's doctrine of the three tragic unities (time, place, and action) was inspired by the Book of Job, presumably transmitted to Greece by the Phoenicians. Quevedo believed—his chronology is quite implausible, I think—that the tragedians Aeschylus, Sophocles, and Euripides were inspired by the Book of Job, and he finds parallels between Greek drama and the biblical work.

We could cite the testimony of another illustrious figure: the testimony of Milton. In his *Paradise Regained* he invents a verbal contest between Christ and the Devil. Satan, after having failed repeatedly to tempt Christ, resorts to temptations more subtle than those of the flesh or of earthly power: he resorts to the temptations of art and philosophy, showing Christ the city of Athens, the Academy, and the Greek tragedians. But Christ rebuts the Devil; he says that in the older Hebrew literature there were tragedies far superior to those of Aeschylus and Sophocles, and he cites the Book of Job in support, since the work is conceived in dramatic form and is made up of speeches.

But let us return to the story of Job. Job is a man from the land of Uz, from Edom. He is a righteous, God-fearing man; we are told about his virtues and then about his wealth: seven thousand camels, seven thousand asses, seven thousand sheep. We are also told about his children, about the regard everyone quite rightly had for him, and then, all of a sudden, we shift to a prologue in heaven—the "Prolog in Himmel," as it is called in Goethe's *Faust*. We see God speaking with his angels and asking one of them: "Satan, what have you been doing?" (The presumption is, of course, that God knows the reply.) Satan answers that he has been roaming the earth and walking on it to and fro. God asks him if he has noticed anyone on earth like His servant Job, serving God. Satan tells Him that, after all, it isn't so strange for Job to love and respect God so much, since God has blessed him with all manner of moral and material fortune; but let Him just withdraw His hand from Job, and Job might not be so righteous or love God so much. God then permits Satan to touch Job's possessions; the children are among these possessions.

After that we see Job with his wife, when four messengers arrive, one, I suppose, from each of the cardinal points. The first tells him that the Chaldeans have attacked his land, have killed his slaves, have killed his children, and that he alone has survived to bear the news. A second comes from the south, a third from the east, a fourth from the west, all with analogous news. Job's wife then reproaches him for holding fast to his faith and tells him, "Curse God and die." But the scribe did not dare to set down those words; all the commentators are agreed on that. What she says in the text is, "Bless God and die," which can be understood in one of two ways: either as an ironic comment, or as a polite form of saying "Curse God." Job answers her with the words later recalled by Quevedo in the epitaph he composed for Job's supposed pyramid-tomb: "The Lord has given and the Lord has taken away; His will be done."

After that there is another assembly in heaven and God uses the same words. He asks Satan, "What have you been doing?" Satan answers that he has been roaming the earth. God asks him if he has noticed His servant Job, and if he has seen Job's fortitude and patience. The Devil replies that until now God has only touched Job's possessions, but were He to touch Job himself, who knows if Job would continue to be so patient. God then grants Satan power over Job but not over his life; Satan may wound Job but not kill him. Satan then inflicts him with a disease, which is variously diagnosed as mange, leprosy, or elephantiasis. And Job appears, in the way he will be seen for centuries thereafter: seated on a dungheap, his head covered with ashes as a sign of mourning, scraping himself with a potsherd. After that, three of Job's friends arrive, as well as a fourth friend, Elihu, all of whom love him.

To us these friends seem like quasi-diabolical figures. But Froude notes that in those days there was a belief in the moral government of the world. Despite the impression conveyed by some deliberately mistranslated passages, there was no belief in the immortality of the soul. So that if we posit a just, all-powerful God, then the misfortunes that afflict man are punishment for his public and private sins, just as his prosperity is a reward.

Job's friends arrive from different regions; they see him seated on the ground, they rend their robes, they scatter ashes on their heads—all this already forms part of the metaphoric style of tragedy—and they spend seven days and seven nights commiserating with him in silence. (Froude says that we shouldn't see any evil intent in this conduct; Job himself must have felt as his friends did.) Finally, Job breaks the silence and curses the day on which he came forth from his mother's womb, saying, "May that day perish among days; may it be utter darkness. Why was I born? Was it to fall into this deepest abyss of misery and strife?"

The friends then begin to debate with Job. At first their arguments are abstract, though they all insinuate—and by the end, in the face of Job's stubborn denials, they no longer insinuate but openly declare— that he must have sinned in some way, since such calamities could only be punishment from God. Job says in reply that he might have sinned in his youth, as everyone does, but that he has repented accordingly and is a just man.

One of the friends then says that Job's very remark is a sin; he tells Job that man cannot presume to be just, that it is blasphemous for him to continue believing in his innocence in the face of the sudden, systematic, multiple, and overwhelming punishment he has received. He tells Job that God has undoubtedly punished him for something, that things cannot happen in any other way.

Job, despite everything, continues proclaiming his innocence; he says that he would like to appear before God to proclaim this innocence—not only before the three friends, and a fourth friend who will arrive later, but before the divinity Himself.

God then speaks to Job from a whirlwind, from a cloud that we can assume—as did Quevedo—was above Job's head. He begins His speech full of irony, telling the unfortunate Job: "Gird your loins like a man, clothe yourself with glory and splendor; refute Me, show Me that I am in the wrong." (God, of course, says nothing about the two earlier dialogues with the angels.) He expatiates on His power and asks Job who he is; if he knows the home of snow, the dwelling place of hail; if he knows the confines of the universe. He refutes Job through his ignorance.

After that God enumerates His works. He begins by describing the war horse, in a passage that has been compared to an analogous one in Virgil. He then talks about two monsters, first about Behemoth, whose name is plural. (It means "animals," according to Fray Luis de León.) This animal is so big that it is equivalent to many. God describes how man's weapons are shattered by Behemoth's hardness, and He then talks about another animal, Leviathan, a sea monster. These animals have traditionally been identified as the elephant and the whale, but if I am not mistaken, Orientalists now identify them as the hippopotamus and the crocodile. What seems certain is that the author was very familiar with Egypt.

Another curious feature of the dialogue between God and Job is that nothing is said about a chosen people, about God's covenant with Israel; on the other hand, there are abundant references to astronomy, or rather to Babylonian astrology, to the Pleiades, to the stars. There is also what for me constitutes a very significant moment (to which I will return) when Jehovah, speaking from the whirlwind (God is invisible), passes from the theme of Behemoth and Leviathan to Himself; He passes from these monstrous creatures to Himself, their Maker.

After that Job no longer protests his integrity. He declares that he is unworthy to contend with God; and God rebukes Job's friends—the very friends who had wanted to justify the calamities He had heaped upon Job—and orders them to offer a sacrifice. The friends carry out the sacrifice. God restores to Job all that he has lost. He restores his health, and Job again fathers seven daughters and seven sons and dies vindicated and satisfied with days.

Such is the story of Job, which I have summarized quite imperfectly, of course.

Let us now look at three possible interpretations of the text. The first was prevalent until the nineteenth century. These lines from Quevedo exemplify it well:

> Y trabajos ansiosos y mortales
> cargan, mas no derriban, nobles cuellos . . .
>
> Dios . . . está solo fuera de los males,
> y el varón que los sufre, encima dellos.

And vexatious and mortal cares
Burden, but do not fell, noble necks . . .

God . . . alone is beyond all sorrows,
And the suffering man is above them.

The Book of Job is thus understood as a kind of fable of stoicism: man must suffer and still retain his faith. As Job himself says: "Though He slay me, yet will I trust in Him." Furthermore, in the treatise *La constancia y paciencia del santo Job,* Quevedo sees Job as a prefiguration of Christ and of the still-to-come martyrs of future days.

When we get to the nineteenth century another interpretation of the work is suggested. Now its central theme is no longer considered to be the constancy of Job in the midst of his travails, but the problem of evil: if God is just, if God is all-powerful, why does evil exist in the world? During the eighteenth century Leibniz searched for answers to this problem. He imagined a library composed of a thousand volumes; these volumes were a thousand copies of the *Aeneid*—Leibniz regarded the *Aeneid* as the perfect book. He says: the library composed of a thousand copies of the *Aeneid* would be inferior to a library that contained not only the *Aeneid* but also works much inferior to it; this second library would be superior in its variety to the first one. But what this argument doesn't take into account is that as long as they remain unread, books are merely dead things, objects. On the other hand, for a person to be wicked, to be stupid, or perhaps to be condemned to hell is a misfortune; so that the argument from variety doesn't seem very convincing.

An argument borrowed from the world of painting has also been used; it's been said that in a picture there are always small dark zones, areas of opacity necessary to the harmony of the composition as a whole. Similarly it's been said that in music there can be dissonance— but the argument is worthless if we are talking about human beings, if we keep in mind that none of us would like to be the worst volume in a library or a dissonance or a dark spot.

If we reject the interpretation that the author set out to justify evil (besides, in the text God doesn't justify what He has done; He simply confounds poor Job with His dread and His glory without giving him any explanation at all), there remains the explanation given by Max Brod in his book *Heidentum, Christentum, Judentum* (Paganism, Christianity, Judaism). This is that the two passages about Behemoth and Leviathan, considered by some to be just interpolations, are not interpolations at all but contain the essence of the argument. Because God, when He describes Leviathan, asks, "Who can force open the doors of his face?"; that is, Who will dare open the mouth of the whale?

He then talks not only about how strange Leviathan is but also about its beauty, and He compares the eyes of that half-zoological, half-fantastic monster to the eyelids of the dawn.

According to this interpretation these monsters, which are not indispensable to the argument, are not there as proof of the grandeur of God—God who can create the elephant with its might, yet have it eat grass like an ox and, if need be, destroy it; God who can create the whale and kill it. Rather, they appear there precisely because they are powerful, monstrous, and, above all, incomprehensible (since there is no apparent reason for them to exist in the universe, and no apparent purpose for them in the divine economy) as symbols of God. According to this third interpretation, which I believe to be the true one, God declares by means of these descriptions that He is inscrutable, that His nature does not have to be understood by man.

To talk about God's justice or goodness is in itself a kind of audacity: it is to measure the divine with a human yardstick. I believe it was Aldous Huxley who said that there is no good reason for an intelligent twentieth-century man to understand God; and I believe that the true, though possibly unconscious, purpose of the Book of Job is to underline this inexplicability and inscrutability of God. God doesn't justify himself: He declares His power; He invokes the examples of Behemoth and Leviathan; He says nothing about the motives for the trials to which He has subjected Job after His dialogues with the Devil.

The Book of Job is thus a skeptical book: not in the sense that the existence of God is denied, but in the sense that we cannot understand or measure God; the universe exists, our misfortunes and on occasion—perhaps on rare occasions—our good fortune also exists, and we don't know why, except that there is a moral sense that tells us to act in one way and not in another. That is, by being righteous Job was right. I think this last explanation is the true one.

Before concluding, however, I would like to recall that there are two ways of thinking, which one of James Joyce's commentators called "day thinking" and "night thinking."

The Romantic poet Samuel Taylor Coleridge thought that we are always reasoning, even while we dream. He says: if someone is sleeping and feels any sort of pressure on his chest—the pressure of his arm or a blanket or anything whatsoever—then without even waking up he conjectures, "I feel pressure on my chest because a lion has lain down on top of me." But rather than proposing this explanation as an hypothesis, he gives it visual form; he dreams there is a lion on top of him, and he has a nightmare. This constitutes a type of reasoning, albeit a false and undoubtedly weak type of reasoning, since the man is asleep and his level of intelligence is very low.

Well then, according to Carl Jung, human thought is very much like dreams; that is, mythology precedes philosophy. In a certain Greek text we read, "the sea is the father of all the gods." This is an example of mythic thought. Then, in the pre-Socratic period, we read that Thales of Miletus said, "Water is the origin or root of all things." Here we already have abstract thought, but the Hebrew imagination, precisely because it was so vivid, was accustomed to thinking by means of metaphors; this is what makes reading the Book of Job difficult. At times we can't follow the arguments easily: Job and his friends don't debate with each other directly, they employ abstract images, words such as those I have cited about the "home of snow," the "eyelids of the dawn," or the "monster that can drink the Jordan in one swallow."

What we have in the Book of Job is an attempt, an ancient attempt, to think in abstract form; but the author is, above all, a poet, a great poet. He tends to think by means of metaphors. Even Plato, in that admirable dialogue that narrates the final day in the life of Socrates, proceeds from logical arguments in favor of the immortality of the soul to myths about the River Lethe or about Tartarus. (The Greeks could think on both levels: on the level of images and on the level of abstract reasoning.) In the Book of Job the poet is reasoning, but happily for us he is also poeticizing. I believe if there is one book that deserves to be called sublime, that book is the Book of Job.

It is an enigmatic book—though not in the style of Góngora or Joyce, who are professionally enigmatic, who set out to be so. It is an enigmatic book because it deals with the enigma that is the universe, that we are, and because the author thinks by means of symbols, of metaphors. I believe—and I've read a number of literatures—that there is no book stranger and more inexhaustible than the Book of Job.

I have cited three interpretations of the work: the stoic; the one regarding the origin of evil; and still another that posits the inscrutability of God and the universe as the essence of the book. If this lecture serves as a stimulus for you to reread that infinite book in the original or in translation, then I have not spoken in vain today.

Translated by Edna Aizenberg

Jorge Luis Borges

Baruch Spinoza

Bertrand Russell, in his *History of Western Philosophy,* states that of all the great philosophers the most lovable is Baruch Spinoza. I fully agree with that statement, as I am sure would have been the case with Renan, Froude, and others who have left us pages on him.

My lecture today will be an extremely cursory and deficient exposition of Spinoza's system; it won't be a justification—I'm not sure I subscribe to that doctrine—but even less a refutation. Still, as that philosophy has something inhuman about it, something inaccessibly inhuman, almost divine about it, I'd like my lecture to be preceded by a few words about the man Spinoza, since there is, it seems to me, a kind of discord between the saintliness, or near saintliness, of his life, and his doctrine—or rather the strange form in which he chose to expound his philosophic system.

The facts can be limited, simplified. We have, first of all, the contrast between Spinoza's tolerance and serenity and the temper of his century, the seventeenth century, an age of religious wars, of persecutions, of intolerance, of the first great upheavals of modern times.

Let us now examine these facts. Spinoza was born in Amsterdam in 1634. He is considered a Portuguese Jew, even though it is believed his mother tongue was Spanish. His ancestors may have been Marranos, Jews who were forced to profess Catholicism but who retained their faith in Judaism. The fact is that Spinoza's family emigrated from Lisbon and settled in Amsterdam, and it is there that he received his education. He knew Spanish, Portuguese, Dutch (naturally, Holland was his homeland and he was a fervent Dutch patriot), Latin (the language in which he wrote his works and corresponded with thinkers from Germany, England, and France), Hebrew, and—somehow—French and Greek.

Spinoza seems to have understood early on that his vocation was philosophy. He was excommunicated for holding that God has a body and that this body is the universe. According to Spinoza each of us is physically part of the body of God, along with the plants, the animals,

"Baruch Spinoza" was originally published as "Baruj Spinoza" in *Conferencias,* 103–12. © 1967 by Instituto de Intercambio Cultural Argentino Israeli. Translated and published with permission. English translation published in this volume for the first time.

and the minerals. Spinoza was excommunicated. There was an apparent assassination attempt. There was an unhappy affair of the heart, but in its wake he realized that his destiny was thought, what he would call intellectual love—because, in Spinoza, love, sober, laconic, modest love is never far away. This is evident from the theorems, definitions, axioms, postulates, and corollaries of his *Ethics,* as well as from his correspondence and his *Theological-Political Treatise*—Spinoza was interested in many things.

Politically he seems to have followed Hobbes. He believed in the primacy of the State over the Church, but we must recall—as Bertrand Russell reminds us—that he was writing in Holland, then the most tolerant state in Europe. Besides, tolerance has never been a hallmark of the Church, except when it is in decline; when the Church is powerful it isn't tolerant, and it tends to use fire as an argument.

Spinoza was undoubtedly influenced by Descartes. He was also influenced, despite some hostile and disdainful pressure, by the Cabala. There is an excellent Jewish tradition that teaches that the man of letters should not earn his living from his profession, and so Spinoza became a grinder of optical lenses. I believe that this tradition of a handicraft—of manual labor, if you will—coupled with an intellectual pursuit is far superior to what is customary today. Today the writer is usually a journalist; he can be a journalist with impunity: take the case of G. K. Chesterton or George Bernard Shaw. But since both professions, journalism and literature, make use of the same instrument—language—one of them often predominates, much to the detriment of the other. In contrast, the Hebrew tradition of an occupation totally removed from language, from the work, from the vocation, from the mission of thinking and writing, seems to me far superior. That's why the idea of a writers' union—an idea I at one time professed—is fundamentally wrong. A carpenter, for example, has to compete with other carpenters—he can belong to a union. But how can we writers compete with the author of the Book of Job, with Dante, with Shakespeare, or with Heine? An artisan works with his contemporaries, while literature is eternal.

Spinoza led a frugal life, even though he engaged in lively intellectual commerce with his contemporaries. The most famous of these was Leibniz, who at times concealed his debt to Spinoza and tried to downplay his friendship with him. Spinoza was offered the chair of philosophy at the renowned University of Heidelberg but declined the post; he likewise declined an offer from the king of France because he believed that any of these obligations would compromise his freedom. He preferred to live modestly in Amsterdam, dying of tuberculosis at the age of forty-three. (Tuberculosis was then incurable in The Hague.)

His friends loved him, even his merely epistolary friends: this is very important. We can't say that he forsook personal happiness; rather, we should envy his bliss, for there is no greater joy, I believe, than the exercise of one's intelligence, particularly when that intelligence belongs to a Baruch or Benedict Spinoza. I have no doubt that this modest, frugal man was a happy man, so there is no need for us to pity him.

Spinoza gave a great deal of thought to his book before writing it; I am not referring here to those treatises in which he anticipated what has been called higher biblical criticism because he denied the antiquity of certain biblical books—the Pentateuch, for example—but rather to his major work, the *Ethics.*

I have seen an English version of Spinoza's work, *Short Treatise on God, Man and His Well-Being,* in which the editor tried to delete as much as he could of the philosopher's geometric apparatus (Spinoza took Euclidean geometry as his model), since this book makes for easier and perhaps more convincing reading than the *Ethics.* But the editor did little more than to transpose the order of the pages and to delete the references to one or another axiom, postulate, or definition, along with such phrases as, "This is proven by the corollary to theorem A," and the letters "Q.E.D." (*Quod erat demonstrandum* [Which was to be proved]).

By the way, I want to deplore the fact that the world has lost—irreparably, I think—an international language like Latin; those that have been devised since, Volapük, Esperanto, and so on, are mere games. Their own inventors call them auxiliary languages, and studying them is like securing—not without difficulty—the key to an empty chest. If we know Latin we possess not only a vast literature but also the very roots of our language. To know Latin is to have access to Virgil, Tacitus, Seneca, and Lucan; to the medieval philosophers; and to Spinoza. In contrast, the invented auxiliary languages are merely philological curiosities.

I think we can now explain Spinoza's geometric method. First, we should keep in mind that the exact sciences are based on mathematics; they are not empirical. To the Romans the symbol of the impossible, the metaphor for the impossible, was a black swan; the image appears in one of Horace's verses, if I am not mistaken. But then, when the continent of Australia was discovered, it was proved that black swans really exist: we can see them on Australian stamps. Furthermore, even before the discovery of Australia, the idea of a black swan did not represent an impossibility for the imagination; a Roman could imagine a black swan, even though he might have thought that black swans didn't really exist.

If an astronaut says that he has arrived on some planet, and on this planet there are stones that think, or stones that fly, or stones that are capable of engendering other stones before they die, I can believe him without finding any logical contradiction in his words. But if I'm told that on some planet, no matter how far away, stones of a certain type have been discovered, and if you take three of these stones and add one more, the result is nine, I know in advance the whole thing is a lie. Because we intuitively understand that one plus three equals four; we have no need to resort to personal experiments with chess pieces, apples, clocks, drinking glasses, or people. According to Bertrand Russell this is due to the fact that mathematics is a vast tautology; to say one plus three is to say four in a slightly more complex manner.

Be that as it may, mathematical truths are intuited; they don't depend on experience, which cannot contradict them. Spinoza—like all of his century, like Plato, of course—understood that there was something vulnerable about empirical truths. That is why he chose Euclidean geometry as the model for his book. Geometric definitions are not empirical. If we say that a dot has no dimensions, we are referring to an ideal dot, since any dot, even one drawn with the point of a very fine pen, occupies some space, some extension. (We can verify this with a magnifying glass or a microscope.) To talk about a line that is merely long is to talk about an intellectual concept, not about reality: every line has thickness, and if it has been drawn in ink on a piece of paper, it undoubtedly also has somewhat greater height than the paper itself.

The example of a shadow is frequently given. It is said that the shadow we cast is merely flat—but this is false, since to talk about a shadow is to talk about part of a nonilluminated surface. The shadow as such doesn't really exist, be it with one, two, or three dimensions. Though in fact there are three: every object is solid.

Nevertheless, parting from these concepts: from the dot; from the line composed of an infinite number of dots; from the surface composed of an infinite number of surfaces, each stacked on top of the other as in an infinitely thin deck of cards—from all these definitions we arrive at a consummate geometry. (Of course, a perfect circle, a circle in which all of the points are equidistant from the center, doesn't really exist.) That is one of the reasons Spinoza chose to write his book in this manner, even though the procedure was undoubtedly not his personal invention but was conceived under the influence of Descartes, and possibly under the influence of the Cabala. Spinoza conceived his system, and then used the geometric method to expound it.

There is another reason as well: mathematics is associated with logic. For Spinoza, the universe was fundamentally logical and therefore subject to logical explanation—much in the same way one teaches geometry or explains arithmetic and algebra.

Here, then, we have two reasons to explain—I don't know if to justify—the very curious fact of a philosophical work composed as if it were a manual of Euclidean geometry.

Froude says that Spinoza's system—like all philosophies—is primarily directed to our imagination, not to our rational faculty. It does seem to me that through the deliberate aridity of the philosopher we can sense a very powerful imagination at work. In England, after his death, there appeared the word *pantheism,* which means that everything is God. Novalis, in the now-famous lines, wrote: "Spinoza ist ein gott-trunkener Mensch" (Spinoza is a God-intoxicated man). But the word *intoxication* suggests something that doesn't comport with Spinoza's serenity; it is the beautiful expression of a great Romantic poet but it doesn't suit Spinoza.

Spinoza says that in order to make any tool whatsoever, other tools are needed. Thus we might think that it is impossible to make a hammer, say—not to mention more modern, more complex tools—since in order to make a hammer other tools are needed, and these, in turn, call for still others, and so we run the risk of continuing this way on to infinity. But, adds Spinoza, there are certain essential notions from which all others can be derived. Philosophers have erred in not starting out from these essential notions, from the primary tools that can be used to make other tools, which make still more—a hammer can be used to make swords, for example—and so on.

That is why Spinoza starts out with definitions—and let us start with the most arduous definition of all: the idea of God as a substance, an infinite substance. (The word *substance* should be understood here in its etymological sense: it is what underlies other things.) Spinoza defines an infinite substance as one that is a cause of itself or, to quote his own words, "whose essence involves existence." This is what is called the ontological argument in theology. I think Saint Anselm uses it in the following way: he asks his interlocutor to imagine a perfect being, an all-knowing, all-powerful being who recalls everything in the past, who foresees the future, who is, in essence, the God of the theologians. He then asks the interlocutor if this perfect being exists; the interlocutor answers that he doesn't know for sure, to which the saint replies: you have undertaken to imagine a perfect being, a being who is the very one you have imagined but who in fact exists. This is how the existence of God is supposedly proved.

Hegel carries this argument to absurd extremes. He asks his imaginary interlocutor to imagine the most fragile of creatures, an ant, a creature we can annihilate by merely stamping our foot. He then says: if an ant, a fragile little ant, is able to exist, how can an all-powerful, all-knowing God not be able to exist? At first sight the whole thing seems like some kind of joke, because to say that the ant is able to exist is to presuppose an ant prior to the will to exist. But Spinoza believes in precisely this argument. He states that by definition, by virtue of a mere verbal structure, there is a substance which is *causa sui* (cause of itself) and that infinite substance is God.

Since God is infinite, he has infinite attributes—just as in a circle we have an infinite number of points. Spinoza says that we have knowledge of two of these infinite modes of the divinity: thought and extension. Instead of thought and extension we could also say time and space. I think for the purposes of a lecture this is rigorous enough. We live in time and in space.

There is something called psychological parallelism. For example, it is generally believed that when we are very sad we cry, but William James held that we could just as easily maintain that we are very sad because we are crying; the two processes can be strictly contemporaneous: we feel sadness and we feel a teardrop fall. The first evidently corresponds to thought and the second to space; these are the two attributes of God.

What we are experiencing at this very moment, your listening to me, my attempting to expound Spinoza's doctrine—all of this is part of the mind of God, who is the only being in existence. Everything else—the vast universe, the possibly infinite flow of time—all of these are attributes of God, *parts* of God.

Here begins what is marvelous, what is strictly new about Spinoza's philosophy. The idea that everything is God is an ancient one; there is a verse in Virgil which reads, "Omnia sunt plena Iovis" (All things are full of God). Spinoza goes even further, however. He says that all things are, in their own way, parts of God: material things and we as well. But we live not only in space, in our bodies, which are a portion of space; we also live in our consciousness, which, because it is one, in some inconceivable way endures throughout time. I can think about my childhood, and it's like thinking about a stranger. Yet I know I was that child, and I know that the memories I have of that child are personal memories. This identification of God with the universe doesn't exhaust Spinoza's philosophy, of course; we find it among the Greeks, among the Hindus, among other, earlier thinkers.

What is new in Spinoza is the idea that in addition to being, God possesses all of time, all of the vicissitudes of time, all of the events, dreams, and reveries of time; in addition to being, God possesses space and the most minimal circumstances of space—what a microscope can reveal in a drop of water, and the galaxies and planets as well.

Spinoza further believes that God exists in an infinite number of other ways, ways that surpass the limits of the human imagination. I will illustrate this marvel with an example: I decide to raise my arm; I am raising it at this very moment, and I am aware that it is raised. This occurs in time—in thought, as Spinoza would say. It also occurs in space, since my arm was here before, and now it's here, higher, straight up. But at the same time, according to Spinoza, an infinite number of other things are occurring in God. Whenever I move, whenever I feel or act, infinite things are occurring in God. These things are inconceivable, since the infinite modes or attributes of God are adjectives if we compare them with the only divine noun: God. Infinite things are occurring, but we cannot imagine them; we can only imagine everything under the species of time and space.

Let us think of God, then, as an infinite circumference; in this circumference there are, as I have said, an infinite number of radii, but only two are known to us: space and time. There remain an infinite number, infinity minus two—the infinity of facts unknown to us. We live and we die, and we are an infinitesimal part of the infinite divinity. This is, without a doubt, an invention or discovery of Baruch Spinoza.

It was believed that the medieval theologians had carried the idea of God to its maximum plenitude by holding Him to be all-powerful, all-knowing, and so on. But for Spinoza all this is minimal: God is inconceivable, He is inconceivably rich and inconceivably infinite. (In saying infinite I don't mean very numerous, I mean strictly infinite.)

In George Cantor's mathematics a transfinite number is one in which the parts are not less than the whole; Cantor illustrates this with three infinite series. The first consists of all the whole numbers; we begin with one, we continue with two, three, and four, and we, and all the generations of the future, will die before reaching the end of the series. We then have a second infinite series. This second series—I am explaining it in the simplest way possible—consists of uneven numbers: one, three, five, seven, nine, eleven, and so on. But this series, which is only one half of the previous one—it excludes the even numbers—is also infinite. There is yet a third series. If we take the series of whole numbers minus hundreds of millions, let's say, what remains is still infinite. This is the way Spinoza saw his God: as strictly infinite.

Let us now consider other aspects of Spinoza's *Ethics*. What does he think about man? He believes that man must love God, but God for him is coextensive with nature. That is why he uses the two words as synonyms: "Deus sive Natura" (God or Nature). They are both the same thing, except that nature is one of the attributes of God as well.

Man must love God with intellectual love; that is, he must love the order of the universe. This has been called *amor fati,* (the love of destiny). Every person must love his own destiny, even if it is an unhappy one; it's all part of the universe, of God's perfect universe. We must love: if we can't love as much as we want, we must love as much as we can.

Spinoza says that we must love God without any hope of being loved by Him in return. Goethe saw this as an example of abnegation, but it is nothing of the sort. It is, rather, a consequence of Spinoza's concept of the divinity. Our individual destiny is of no importance to God. This is the direct opposite of, let's say, Miguel de Unamuno, who said that God is, above all, the producer of immortality. Spinoza didn't believe in personal immortality; man was unimportant to him. Yet Baruch Spinoza, who lived for forty-three years in Holland, where he would die, wrote: we feel that we are immortal, but not as individuals—as individuals we are mere adjectives of God. We are immortal as part of the divine immortality.

He then talks about the emotions: he believes that God is capable of emotion, and so is man. Spinoza doesn't condemn us; he condemns what he calls the passions, since passions can dominate us. What Spinoza condemns is very strange. He begins by condemning fear and hope. The argument he puts forth is that time is unreal; only eternity is real; the rest is adjectival—for example, fear and hope, which refer to the future. Besides, they are anxieties, trepidations, and Spinoza—like the Stoics—desires serenity above all.

This reminds me of a kind of joke of Bernard Shaw. On the gate to Dante's Inferno there is an inscription that reads: "Lasciate ogne speranza voi ch'intrate" (Abandon all hope, ye who enter here). It has generally been interpreted as a divine threat, since it is preceded by the lines: "Per me si va ne la città dolente, / per me si va ne l'etterno dolore, / per me si va tra la perduta gente" (Through me ye go unto the city of woe; / through me ye go to everlasting pain; / through me ye go to dwell among the lost). But Bernard Shaw says that this was written to console the reprobates. When they read, "Abandon all hope, ye who enter here," what they are reading are God's words of consolation. From the moment they are in hell, nothing worse can occur to them. "What is hope?" asks Shaw: a form of moral responsibility. I don't think Spinoza would have understood it this way, but he agrees with Shaw in condemning hope. The great Spanish poet of Jewish stock, Fray Luis de León, likewise condemns it when he says, "vivir quiero conmigo" (with myself I want to live), and then adds that he wants to live "libre de amor, de celo, / de odio, de esperanzas, de recelo" (free of love, envy, hatred, hope, or fear).

Free of hope, because hope is a form of intranquillity. Spinoza condemns—and this is without a doubt his own invention or discovery—any repentance, any remorse. He says that a man may do evil, but to repent after having done it is to add another sadness. There would then be two states in him worthy of condemnation: first, the guilty act itself, and second, the ensuing shame, the sorrow for an act committed in the past, in time, which is unreal. All this leads us to Spinoza's optimism, much more profound than that of Leibniz, who spoke about the best of all possible worlds.

Philosophers have said that philosophy is a meditation on death. This is what the existentialists, from Kierkegaard on, claim. But Spinoza, with his grave, serene joy, says that philosophy is a meditation on life. He condemns hate, he also condemns love when it isn't an emotion but a passion that dominates us.

As for free will, Spinoza doesn't deny its existence; he believes that we are free when we act according to our inclinations; but he at the same time believes that everything in the world is predestined. One of his friends, the secretary of the Royal Society of London, saw a contradiction in that, so Spinoza explained this very difficult problem to him in a letter. In the first place, he said, evil doesn't exist because it is negative. Then, he said, everything wants to persist in its being: the stone always wants to be a stone, the tiger, a tiger. Spinoza adds the example of a stone that falls from a high promontory and says that if the stone could think at that moment, it would think: I am falling because I want to. Our acts are fated. I don't know, for example, if I will now leave my hand up in the air, or put it on the table. But when I put it down, I was convinced that I had free will—and there is none other, according to Spinoza.

What I've said is far from concluded: I simply hope to have provided an outline and, above all, a stimulus for a study of Spinoza, which will surely be much deeper than my own.

Translated by Edna Aizenberg

About the Contributors

Edna Aizenberg is Associate Professor of Spanish and Coordinator of Foreign Languages at Marymount Manhattan College. She is the author of *The Aleph Weaver: Biblical, Kabbalistic and Judaic Elements in Borges* (1984) and has published studies on contemporary Latin American literature and Jewish-Hispanic literary relations.

Jaime Alazraki is the author of *La prosa narrativa de Borges* (1968); *Jorge Luis Borges* (1971); *Versiones. Inversiones. Reversiones. El espejo como modelo estructural del relato en los cuentos de Borges* (1977); *Critical Essays on Jorge Luis Borges* (1987); and *Borges and the Kabbalah* (1988). He is Professor of Latin American Literature and Chairman of the Department of Spanish and Portuguese at Columbia University.

Ana María Barrenechea is Professor Emeritus at the University of Buenos Aires where she directs the Instituto Dr. Amado Alonso and edits the journal *Filología*. Professor Barrenechea is the author of *La expresión de la irrealidad en la obra de Jorge Luis Borges* (1957; 1967; expanded ed. 1984; English ed. *Borges the Labyrinthmaker* [1965]) and of articles on Borges collected in her *Textos hispanoamericanos: De Sarmiento a Sarduy* (1978).

Françoise Collin teaches at the Collège International de Philosophie in Paris, which is headed by Jacques Derrida. She is the founder of the feminist journal *Les Cahiers du Grif* and author of *Maurice Blanchot et la question de l'écriture* (1971; 1986).

Christine de Lailhacar teaches European languages and literatures, and sociology, at the State University of New York, Maritime College, where she is Assistant Professor of Humanities. One of her advisors for her degree in comparative literature/semiotics was Umberto Eco. She has published articles in comparative poetics.

Malva E. Filer is Professor of Spanish American Literature at Brooklyn College, City University of New York. Her critical works include *Los mundos de Julio Cortázar* (1970); *La novela y el diálogo de los textos: Zama de A. Di Benedetto* (1982); and articles on major contemporary Latin American writers.

Geoffrey Green, Associate Professor of English at San Francisco State University, is the executive editor of the journal *Critique* and coeditor of *Novel vs. Fiction: The Contemporary Reformation*. In addition to *Literary Criticism and the Structures of History: Erich Auerbach and Leo Spitzer* (1983), he is author of *Freud-Nabokov/Nabokov-Freud: Literature, Psychoanalysis, Interpretation* (1988).

Rafael Gutiérrez Girardot is Professor of Hispanic Studies at the University of Bonn. His publications on Borges include *Jorge Luis Borges: Ensayo de interpretación* (1959) and articles in *L'Herne, Merkur,* and other journals.

Jules Kirschenbaum is Professor of Art at Drake University. His work is exhibited at major museums, among them the Metropolitan Museum of Art; the Museum of Modern Art, New York; the Whitney Museum, New York; and the Chicago Art Institute.

Suzanne Jill Levine, Associate Professor of Romance and Comparative Literatures at the University of Washington, has translated Borges and other contemporary authors. Her most recent translation is *Maitreya* by Severo Sarduy (1987). Her critical studies include *El espejo hablado* (1975), on García Márquez; *Guía de Bioy Casares* (1982); and articles on Borges.

Julie Méndez Ezcurra studied art, literature, and photography in Argentina and Europe. She has headed the Department of Photography at the Museum of the City of Buenos Aires and has worked as a photographer for Argentina's major newspaper, *La Nación.* Ms. Méndez Ezcurra currently specializes in architectural photography.

Marta Morello-Frosch has published extensively on recent Argentine fiction and has written on Argentine elements in Borges's work. She is Professor of Hispanic Literature at the University of California, Santa Cruz.

Gerry O'Sullivan is in the Comparative Literature and Literary Theory Program at the University of Pennsylvania. He has published articles in critical theory and poetics.

Richard Peña, Program Director of the Film Society of Lincoln Center, holds a degree in Latin American history and literature from Harvard University. He is at work assembling a collection of writings on Third World cinema.

Herman Rapaport is Associate Professor of English and Comparative Literature at the University of Iowa and specializes in critical theory. He is the author of *Milton and the Postmodern* (1983) and has recently completed a book-length manuscript entitled *Heidegger, Derrida, and the Temporal Clue.*

Emir Rodríguez Monegal was, until his death in 1985, Professor of Contemporary Latin American Literature at Yale University. His books on Borges include: *Borges par lui-même* (1970); *Borges: hacia una interpretación poética* (1976); *Jorge Luis Borges: A Literary Biography* (1978); and *Borges: A Reader* (1981), coedited with Alastair Reid.

Robert Ross is Publications and Research Director of the Edward A. Clark Center for Australian Studies at the University of Texas at Austin. He is the author of *Australian Literary Criticism, 1945–88: An Annotated Bibliography* (1988) and editor of *Antipodes: A North American Journal of Australian Literature.*

Jerry A. Varsava is Assistant Professor of English at Memorial University of Newfoundland. He has authored articles devoted to twentieth-century fiction and is completing a study of the mimetic function of postmodernist fiction.

Index

Index to Works by Borges Cited in Text